IBN KHALDÛN'S PHILOSOPHY OF HISTORY

IBN KHALDÛN'S

PHILOSOPHY OF HISTORY

A Study in the Philosophic Foundation of the Science of Culture

by Muhsin Mahdi

The University of Chicago Press

International Standard Book Number: 0-226-50183-3

THE UNIVERSITY OF CHICAGO PRESS, CHICAGO 60637

The University of Chicago Press, Ltd., London

First published in 1957 by George Allen and Unwin Ltd.
London, W.C. 1
First Phoenix Edition 1964
Second Impression 1971
Printed in the United States of America

INTRODUCTION TO THE PHOENIX EDITION

Ibn Khaldûn has been called the father, or one of the fathers, of modern social science and cultural history. When the writer embarked on the present study, he had no reason to doubt this assertion and certainly no intention of refuting it. He meant merely to find out what it means and to ascertain whether the evident similarities between many of the conclusions of Ibn Khaldûn's investigation of history and society and those of modern social science and cultural history reflect a deeper similarity of view concerning the nature and function of science or philosophy—that is, whether Ibn Khaldûn had accomplished the break with the Socratic tradition that is visible in European thought during the sixteenth and seventeenth centuries.

First, he considered the suggestions that were being made by some Islamists to the effect that one could explain Ibn Khaldûn's thought by investigating its background in the history of certain specifically Islamic—that is, nonphilosophic—disciplines, e.g., Islamic jurisprudence. These suggestions proved helpful, especially after they were recast in terms of Ibn Khaldûn's own discussions of these disciplines. From the analysis of these discussions emerged the statement of Ibn Khaldûn's view of what he calls the Islamic legal or positive sciences, and the clarification of the distinction between these sciences and the rational or philosophic sciences under which he includes his study of history and, especially, his new science of culture.

Next, he proceeded to investigate Ibn Khaldûn's view of science or philosophy. Most of the modern students of Ibn Khaldûn had propounded the thesis, or else assumed, that his view is largely identical with the view underlying the political and social thought of the more recent fathers of modern political and social science, e.g., Machiavelli. To begin with, the writer looked for a possible historical explanation of this thesis. He formulated the following hypothesis. If Ibn Khaldûn preceded Machiavelli in developing a truly modern science of politics and society, and if the major link between Machiavelli and Islamic thought is so-called Latin Averroism, then the answer may lie in the relation between Ibn Khaldûn and Averroes. Ibn Khaldûn had, in fact, studied Averroes in his youth, and one could not exclude the possibility that he had received or developed a version of Averroism similar to that which formed the background of Machiavelli. But when no trace of the radicalism or literalism of so-called Latin Averroism could be found in Ibn Khaldûn's view of the relation between philosophy and the religious law, this hypothesis had to be abandoned. Furthermore, when the comparison of the basic tenets of Ibn Khaldûn's philosophic thought —both in themselves and in their bearing on his views of history, politics, and society—with those of the moderns revealed that in every decisive respect Ibn Khaldûn sided with Averroes and Averroes' Muslim and Greek masters against the moderns, the original thesis that in his view of science or philosophy Ibn Khaldûn was the precursor of Machiavelli and the moderns had to be abandoned as well.

But the attempt proved useful. For in the process the writer began to doubt many of the received notions about Islamic philosophy—that it was essentially syncretistic, Neo-Platonic, idealistic, unmindful of religious and political realities, and so forth. Slowly, he came to realize that Islamic philosophy—quite independently of the decisive change of perspective that took place in European thought in the sixteenth and seventeenth centuries —was capable of being much more secular, political, and realistic, than he had assumed. And he had to ask the question whether this change of perspective is a necessary condition for an adequate study of history and of society as it actually exists. Hence, without seeking in any way to minimize Ibn Khaldûn's contribution, he turned to investigate the possibility that the principles upon which Ibn Khaldûn built his new science of culture were those of Islamic philosophy in general and Islamic political philosophy in particular. The present study embodies the results of this investigation.

The writer was under no illusion that the publication of this study would put an end to a long-standing and widespread interpretation of Ibn Khaldûn's thought. He was therefore particularly grateful for the generous and warm reviews it received.

He had not suspected that there was such a wide realization that the traditional view of Ibn Khaldûn's fatherhood of modern social science and cultural history is not completely satisfactory, that the time has perhaps come for a re-examination of the philosophic foundation of modern social science and cultural history, and that a fresh look at the history of social thought based on a more critical view of modern social science and cultural history may contribute to this re-examination. Since the publication of this study, it has become more fashionable to say that the philosophic basis of Ibn Khaldûn's thought is embedded in Greek and Islamic philosophy. While by no means sufficient, this is a step in the right direction.

The chief difficulty faced by the student of Ibn Khaldûn who has been able to free himself from the presumption that he already knows what Ibn Khaldûn means to convey and who permits Ibn Khaldûn to guide him through the background of his thought, is that he is forced, first by Ibn Khaldûn, and then by the authors to whom Ibn Khaldûn refers, to abandon a large number of received opinions, both Islamic and modern, about certain crucial aspects of Islamic thought. This process was begun in the present study, but the writer is now aware that it did not, and at the time could not, go far enough; and this state of affairs was complicated by the fact that many of the texts that have direct bearing on Ibn Khaldûn's thought had not yet been edited. By concentrating on the works of Fârâbî and Averroes, the writer tended to overemphasize the contrast between the more Platonic character of Islamic political philosophy and the more Aristotelian approach of Ibn Khaldûn (below, pp. 275, 291). This did not take into account the explicit efforts of Avicenna and Ghazâlî (basing themselves on Aristotle's *Nicomachean Ethics*) to draw an apparently sharp line between the theoretical and the practical sciences, and to supply the practical sciences with a relatively independent framework. The writer was misled by the fact that both Avicenna and Ghazâlî used this framework primarily to study the Islamic law and the moral virtues. He did not draw the further conclusion that this framework could be made the basis of other practical sciences as well, including the study of history and the science of culture that was developed by Ibn Khaldûn (who paid close attention to the works of these two authors). The Arabic translation of Aristotle's *Rhetoric*, and the commentaries on it by

Avicenna and Averroes, which have been edited in recent years, form another body of literature that deserves close study for its bearing on Ibn Khaldûn's thought. It is not an exaggeration to say that it supplied Ibn Khaldûn with a number of his key concepts and tools, e.g., rhetorical ' induction ' (*i'tibâr*, cf. *'ibra*, below, pp. 65 ff.) or ' example ' (*burhân*, *mithâl*) and the elaborate analysis of the passions (below, pp. 177 ff.). Had these works been available to the writer, they could also have enabled him to see through the textbook fashion in which Ibn Khaldûn presents Aristotelian logic and natural science, which the writer innocently reproduced despite his own misgivings. However, these and similar questions must first be clarified within the broader context of the history of Islamic philosophy. Ibn Khaldûn is an excellent guide who can introduce a modern student to Islamic civilization in a comprehensive and critical manner. But because he deliberately narrows his theoretical horizon so as to enhance its practical application, the principles and method of his new science of culture are not comprehensive enough to serve as a basis for understanding the entire range of issues that engaged the attention of Islamic philosophy.

The present study was completed in 1954 and published in 1957. The opportunity of this edition has been used to correct a few mistakes and make a few stylistic changes, and to add a few items to the bibliography (p. 297 n. 2). Some of the issues raised in this study have been subsequently developed by the writer in the following articles: ' Ibn Khaldûn,' *Approaches to the Oriental Classics*, ed. Wm. Theodore de Bary (New York: Columbia University Press, 1959), pp. 68–83; ' Die Kritik der islamischen politischen Philosophie bei Ibn Khaldûn,' *Wissenschaftliche Politik, Eine Einführung in Grundfragen ihrer Tradition und Theorie*, ed. Dieter Oberndörfer (Freiburg im Breisgau: Verlag Rombach, 1961), pp. 117–51; an English version of the latter article forms the second of two chapters on Ibn Khaldûn contributed to *A History of Muslim Philosophy*, ed. M.M. Sharif (2 vols; Wiesbaden: Otto Harrassowitz, 1963——), chaps. XLVI, XLIX; ' Ibn Khaldûn,' *International Encyclopedia of the Social Sciences*.

CHICAGO, ILLINOIS, 1964

PREFACE

> It is a curious fate that history should for a long time have been considered and treated as the most humble form of knowledge, while philosophy was considered as the highest, and that now it not only is superior to philosophy but annihilates it.
>
> BENEDETTO CROCE[1]

1. In no other field has the revolt of modern Western thought against traditional philosophy been so far-reaching in its consequences as in the field of history. The case between the ancients and their modern critics in its extreme form can be formulated as follows: For the ancients, 'historical knowledge is impossible';[2] while for their modern critics all knowledge is historical. For the ancients, history means the description and explanation of actual events which are useful both as examples for men of action, and as material for the practical and theoretical sciences. Since the end of philosophy or science is the demonstration of necessary and explanatory conclusions which claim universal validity, history is, at best, the most humble of sciences because its conclusions are necessarily relative to particular events. For their modern critics, philosophy par excellence is the philosophy of history or the 'complete philosophy conceived from an historical point of view'.[3] The modern critics of traditional philosophy assert, not only that all *facts* are historical, but also that all *reality* is historical.

Thus the issue between the ancients and the moderns seems to raise the deeper issue of the nature of scientific knowledge and of Being. The ancients assert that behind the facts of history and experience there are universal and objective essences, natures, and causes, to which the concepts and judgments of the mind should correspond. These essences, natures, and causes are intrinsically and logically prior to the mutable facts of history and experience despite the fact that, in the order in which they are known, they are posterior to these: for they are the principles that underlie them and give them their intelligibility. The

[1] *History as the Story of Liberty*, trans. Sylvia Sprigge (George Allen & Unwin 1941) 35.
[2] R. G. Collingwood *The Idea of History* (Oxford 1946) 6.
[3] *Ibid.* 7.

moderns start with the denial of objective essences, natures, and causes. Thus the horizon of the real is reduced to the facts of history and experience. Science and philosophy, insofar as they venture beyond the facts of history and experience, are hypothetical constructions which have no objective counterparts.

To those for whom the revolt of the moderns against the ancients is not merely an event of the past which has been settled in favour of one party or another, but a disturbing present reality raising the deepest and most significant problems of human life and thought, and demanding humble and conscientious enquiry, there is one question among others which requires serious consideration: What did the ancients think of the possibility of a science of history and what would be the precise character of such a science when developed according to their general conception of the nature of science or philosophy? Or to reformulate this question in terms of the history of thought: Is it true that such a science has never been attempted, and, therefore, we have no factual grounds upon which to answer the preceding question?

The fact that Ibn Khaldûn (a Muslim disciple of the ancients [*qudamâ'*] and their Muslim followers, especially Averroes) not only attempted to consider the problem of history, but also developed a science of history, or a 'science of culture' (*'ilm al-'umrân*) as he called it for important reasons, must, therefore, have more than antiquarian interest. Ibn Khaldûn realized that history is more immediately related to action than political philosophy because it studies the actual state of man and society. He found that the ancients had not made history the object of an independent science, and thought that it was important to fill this gap. But he did not think that the construction of the new science required considerable changes in the established principles of scientific investigation, or questioning the validity of the norms established by political philosophy. On the contrary, he found that only by admitting the validity of these principles and norms as developed by the ancients could the new science be constructed. This is clearly shown by the fact that he applied these same principles and norms in constructing the new science of history. Further, he was aware that the projected science could not be the noblest of sciences: for in order to explain historical events, it must remain close to them, and, consequently, be satisfied with a humble share of theoretical completeness and universality.

2. The object of the following study is to examine the philosophic foundation and principles of Ibn Khaldûn's new science of culture, to show that an adequate understanding of his contribution to the study of the various aspects of human society requires an understanding of his all-comprehensive approach to the study of man and society which is based on philosophic principles, and to explain the precise nature of these principles and how they are applied in the field of history. This cannot be achieved by summarizing and paraphrasing Ibn Khaldûn's conclusions; or through the method of explaining them as the product of certain historical conditions; or by interpreting them as the product of an unconscious desire to create a 'positive', 'historical', or 'truly scientific' science of society; or by studying Ibn Khaldûn as a 'precursor' of modern social science, and considering his concern with philosophic and religious matters as residues of the prejudices and dogmatism of the Middle Ages from which a Muslim thinker in the fourteenth century could not liberate himself.

The basic methodological approach of the following study adopts certain aspects of the traditional method of philosophic commentary. The object of this method is to ascertain the *deliberate intention* of the author instead of seeking to explain his meaning as the product of his psychological or social conditions. It concentrates on the text of the author and preserves its integrity. And its exclusive aim is the elucidation of what the author says and the way he says it. It does not challenge the possibility that a reader may have a deeper knowledge of the subject matter than the author he is reading. But it assumes that the reader can never know what the author deliberately meant to say better than the author himself, and that the full understanding of what the author intended to say must precede interpretations and judgments based on principles other than those accepted by the author.

3. The study is divided into five chapters each of which considers the totality of Ibn Khaldûn's thought from a different perspective. Since for Ibn Khaldûn, the aim of the study of

history is prudent action, his reflections on history cannot be studied apart from the conditions of his time, the alternative possibilities of action presented to him under these conditions, and the significance of the conclusions of his reflections on history for the course of action he chose from among these alternatives. This is the object of Chapter I, which attempts to show the interrelation of Ibn Khaldûn's experiences, reflections, and decisions. It will be shown that Ibn Khaldûn's practical career and scientific thought can be understood more fully when studied together.

But a factual acquaintance with the conclusions of Ibn Khaldûn's reflections on history is not the same as the full comprehension of their theoretical significance. This latter requires the comprehension of the principles from which, and the complete method of argumentation through which, his conclusions were actually reached. The proper introduction to these principles and that method should determine Ibn Khaldûn's philosophic position with respect to the nature and principles of scientific knowledge and of the social order, or his conception of the nature and principles of theoretical and practical philosophy. This is the object of Chapter II, which begins by showing Ibn Khaldûn's philosophic intention in writing his major work, the 'History', and attempts to analyse his attitude toward the various schools that posed alternative answers to the fundamental problems of philosophy, to examine his conception of the nature of philosophy and its relation to the religious and revealed Law, and to explain his conception of the social role of philosophy and the philosopher in the Islamic community.

When these fundamental questions are answered, it becomes possible to pose the specific question of the relation of Ibn Khaldûn's philosophy of history, or his new science of culture, to other practical sciences and, particularly, to the art of history. After an exposition of the major trends of Islamic historiography, Chapter III attempts to answer this question through the analysis of the method and intention of the introductory sections of the 'History' where Ibn Khaldûn himself examines the works of major Muslim historians, shows the necessity of the new science of culture, and distinguishes it from other practical sciences.

This is followed by an exposition of the subject matter and problems of the new science in Chapter IV, with the intention of revealing its general structure and the relationship among its parts, and preparing for the examination of its principles, method, and end in Chapter V. Chapter V attempts to disengage and explain the nature and causes of culture according to Ibn Khaldûn. It starts with the re-examination of the relation between the science of culture and history in order to define further the principles of the science of culture in relation to its immediate end as a useful tool for historical scholarship. It then proceeds to examine Ibn Khaldûn's conception of the four principles or causes which constitute the nature of culture, namely, the various parts like economic activity and urban institutions, which are its matter; the state, which is its form; solidarity, which is its efficient cause; and the common good, which is its end.

ACKNOWLEDGMENTS

It is a happy privilege to express here my gratitude for the serious and pleasant atmosphere for study and research made possible by the Committee on Social Thought at the University of Chicago under whose auspices this study was begun and carried to completion. I am particularly indebted to Professor John U. Nef, its chairman, for his interest and encouragement, to Professor Otto von Simson for reading the entire manuscript and making valuable suggestions, and to Professor Yves R. Simon for reading Chapter V and recommending some improvements.

Those who are acquainted with the present state of scholarship in Islamic philosophy will no doubt recognize my indebtedness to Professor Leo Strauss of the Department of Political Science. He followed closely the progress of this study, and gave generously of his time to discuss many of the problems as they arose in the course of my research and to suggest improvements upon the text.

Finally, this study owes most to Professor Nabia Abbott of the Oriental Institute. I am profoundly indebted to her for her painstaking help, valuable advice, and constructive criticism during all the stages of my research.

The many shortcomings of this study are, of course, my own.

CONTENTS

CHAPTER I

Historical Background and Fragments of a Biography

I

Historical Background

1. Ibn Khaldûn's life span covered the last two-thirds of the fourteenth century and most of the first decade of the fifteenth. He participated actively in the political life of western North Africa, and to a lesser degree of Muslim Spain and Egypt. He was intimately acquainted with the contemporary history of these regions; and he knew of the important events taking place in the rest of the Islamic Middle and Far East, of the desperate, yet continued, resistance of Byzantium against the Ottoman Turks, and of the renaissance of western Europe. These events, whether personally experienced or gathered from the contemporary historical literature, accounts of ambassadors, travellers, and pilgrims, had a deep and lasting impact upon his thought. He saw the importance of these events in the rapid pace of the movement and in the radical character of the change which produced them. Unlike the movements and changes of the preceding four centuries which had left intact the essential structure of the Islamic community, those heralded by the plague of the mid-fourteenth/eighth century created totally new conditions.[1] These conditions needed to be recorded for the

[1] *Q* I 51–52.

For the explanation of title abbreviations used in the footnotes, cf. Bibliography (below pp. 297–310).

Where two dates are given, the first is *anno Domini* and the second is *anno hegirae* (the year of Mohammed's flight [*hijra*] from Mecca to Medina, A.D. 622). This order has been reversed in the Bibliography. Where only one date is given, it is *anno Domini*, except where followed by A.H. which indicates that it is *anno hegirae*.

The Arabic alphabet is transliterated as follows: ' (except at the beginning of a word), *b*, *t*, *th*, *j*, *ḥ*, *kh*, *d*, *dh*, *r*, *z*, *s*, *sh*, *ṣ*, *ḍ*, *ṭ*, *ẓ*, ', *gh*, *f*, *q*, *k*, *l*, *m*, *n*, *h* (except for feminine ending where it either becomes *t* or is omitted), *w*, *y*; short vowels: *a*, *i*, *u*; long vowels: *â*, *î*, *û*.

benefit of future historians, to be studied with the aim of understanding what they reveal concerning the nature of history, and to be used as an aid for intelligent practical action. A brief account of these contemporary events, drawn largely from Ibn Khaldûn's own works, may, therefore, prove useful for understanding the genesis and nature of his thought.[1]

The domains of Islam were far more extensive in the fourteenth century than they had been in the eighth under the glorious reign of Hârûn al-Rashîd (ruled 786–809). The Crusaders had been repelled from the shores of Syria, and the successful counter-offensive in Asia Minor and in the Balkans had reduced the dominions of Byzantium to an insignificant area. Muslim possessions in Spain and the islands of the Mediterranean were steadily shrinking, but the gains of the Ottoman Turks, and the recent converts in the Sudan, Russia, India, Indonesia, and central Asia, were so extensive that they dwarfed the losses in the West.[2]

Internally, however, conditions were less uniform and hardly as impressive. For centuries, conquerors from all directions had successively inflicted deep and frequent wounds upon that vast body: The Saljûq Turks, the Crusading Christians, the Berbers and the Hilâli Arab nomads, and, finally, the Mongols, undertook the mission of destruction, burning, and pillage. They intensified and hastened the inner forces of disintegration. Major cities fell to ruins. Irrigation systems were destroyed with the consequent decline in agriculture. The disruption and dislocation of the administrative machinery led to the breakdown of means of communication, and the curtailment of international and local trade. The oppressive taxes, needed to wage the incessant wars, and the practice of farming out lands to feudal generals who promised money and soldiers in return (frequently too little and too late), added to the decline and confusion.[3] In many regions, such as western North Africa, the Syrian coast, Iraq,

[1] For an attempt to explain Ibn Khaldûn's thought as the product of the contemporary history of North Africa, cf. G. Bouthoul *Ibn Khaldoun—sa philosophie sociale* (Paris 1930) 2 ff., esp. 14, 16.

[2] *Bq* III 217 ff., V *passim.* The two most convenient general treatments of the subject in English are: P. K. Hitti *History of the Arabs* (5th ed.; New York 1951) 297 ff., 537 ff., 671 ff.; C. Brockelmann *History of the Islamic Peoples*, trans. J. Carmichael and M. Perlmann (New York 1947) 107 ff., 163–255.

[3] Yet in certain regions like Egypt military feudalism was instrumental in restoring economic order and relative political stability. Cf. below pp. 20–21.

and northern Persia, an urban population was thus left easy prey to the inroads of desert tribes, pirates, famines, and plagues. But the Islamic world was not evenly inflicted with these disasters. Diversity and inequality in the various aspects of cultural life were characteristic of the fourteenth century; and it is necessary to examine more closely the several regions for a better comprehension of the whole.

2. The Mongols divided and ruled eastern Islam from India to the banks of the Euphrates. Muslim India suffered from its ambitious, cruel, and violent rulers as well as from the lack of a respected tradition in intellectual life, administrative machinery, or public morality. The attempt of the Tughluq dynasty (1320–1413) to keep India unified under its suzerainty failed when it lost Bengal and southern India in 1339. A little more than a decade later, the breakdown of Muslim India started to proceed at an accelerating pace. Independent Muslim kingdoms flourished during this century in Delhi, Deccan, Bengal, and Kashmir. But because of this decentralization, they could not stand the raids of their powerful neighbours to the north. Thus, when Tamerlane led his ravaging armies through northern India in 1398–99, that region was left in complete anarchy.[1] Transoxania and northern Persia, whose cities had been the rivals of Baghdad and Damascus in prosperity, were among the territories that suffered most from the Saljûq and Mongol invasions. In the rest of Persia, only the isolated south-western province of Fârs was able to preserve some of its economic and cultural prosperity.[2] Iraq too had suffered from the successive invasions and had lost its position as seat of the caliphate. But during this period it was able to recover some of its past prosperity. Like northern Persia, most of its cities were now but ruins; and those that still pulsed with life, like Baghdad, were in continuous danger of occupation from outside, and of periodic internal revolts by the dispossessed and unemployed mobs that were ever ready to loot whatever the conquerors had left behind.[3]

[1] *Bq* V 515 ff., *T* 352 ff., 365, 382; cf. *Cambridge History of India* III (Cambridge 1928) 127 ff., 198 ff.

[2] *Q* II 380, III 92–93, 274, *T* 359, 364, 381.

[3] *Q* II 117, 192, 263, 345, 380, *Bq* IV 473, 490 ff., V 28, 46, 54, 63, 68, 551 ff.; cf. 'Abbâs 'Azzâwî *Ta'rîkh al-'irâq bayn iḥtilâlayn* ('Histoire de l'Iraq entre deux occupations') I (Baghdad 1935) 387 ff.

In Anatolia, the Ottomans, who had a strong and well-organized army that was constantly replenished from the east, continued to look westward.[1] They almost completed the conquest of Asia Minor and, in addition, conquered and settled in the Balkans. Byzantium, on the defensive and for centuries without an effective fleet, was further weakened by internal dissension and the influx of invaders from all directions. Its boundaries now hardly extended beyond the walls of Constantinople.

The struggle between the Ottomans and Byzantium was a real blessing for Egypt, which was spared the terrible scourge of the Mongols who reached as close as Damascus in the east, and the disruptive influence of the Arab and Berber nomadic tribes that bordered its western frontiers. Its Turkish Mamlûk rulers (1250–1517)—who started their reign by clearing their domains of the remaining Crusaders and by successfully resisting the Mongol invaders—inherited the cultural and political institutions of their predecessors, including an exceedingly efficient administration. These were preserved by a succession of farsighted and extremely able rulers throughout the thirteenth and the first four decades of the fourteenth century.[2] Under the last of these, Nâṣir (d. 1341), Mamlûk Egypt reached its economic and cultural height; yet, his extravagance was partly responsible for the four decades of anarchy that followed his reign and led to the downfall of his dynasty. During that period of anarchy, economic hardship and civil war prevailed. Then, in 1382 a new Mamlûk dynasty came into power (1382–1517). It was able to restore order; and in some measure, the economic and cultural prosperity of the country was revived for more than a century to come.

Under the Mamlûks, except for short periods of intrigue and disorder, Egypt was perhaps the most prosperous and civilized kingdom in the whole Islamic world, or at least this is how it seemed to Ibn Khaldûn and his compatriots in western North Africa.[3] It ruled western Syria (including Palestine and its holy places) and the province of Ḥijâz with its sacred cities of Mecca and Medina. It had partial control of the political destiny of Yemen; the princes of eastern Syria turned to it for protection;

[1] *Bq* V 561–63; cf. *CMH* IV 653 ff.

[2] *Q* I 297, *Bq* V 380 ff., *T* 315 ff.

[3] *T* 246, 251, 256, 281–84, *Q* I 297, 325–26, II 252, 308–9, 338–39; cf. Hitti *op. cit.* 683 ff.

and the distressed rulers of Baghdad sought its help. In the economic field, Egypt possessed a virtual monopoly of the most remunerative trade route of the time, the route to India. Because of this route, it was able to support its administration, its army, and a luxurious—if extravagant—ruling class whose taste for, and interest in, building mosques, schools, and hospitals, resulted in extensive domestic economic activity. Under the patronage of a refined and generous aristocracy, the minor arts and the sciences, both religious and mundane, flourished. Egypt became the artistic and intellectual centre of Islam.[1] Compared to the chaotic conditions then prevalent in the rest of the Islamic world, Egypt's prosperity seemed dazzling to the eyes of the merchants, travellers, and pilgrims who passed through it; and they told of its glamour and fascination in the remote outposts. When Ibn Khaldûn asked one of his friends who had just returned from pilgrimage about Cairo, he was answered: 'He who has not seen it, has not known the glory of Islam.'[2]

3. The regions extending from Tripoli to Granada (for which the Arabs used the general appellation: 'the West' [al-Maghrib])[3] shared little of the relative stability and prosperity of Egypt. Since the middle of the eleventh century, North Africa had been liberated from Arab domination through the successive rise and spread of two Berber dynasties, the Murâbiṭs and the Muwaḥḥids.[4] But the liberation had hardly begun when the region suffered heavily under the invasion of Banû Hilâl, a new wave of Arab nomads let loose by the Fâṭimids who were then ruling Egypt. The Hilâlis, in collaboration with Berber nomads, destroyed the agriculture and agricultural industries for which the region, especially Tunisia and Tripolitania, had been famous since Roman times.[5] By the middle of the thirteenth century, the authority of the second Berber dynasty was challenged, and North Africa was divided into three contending kingdoms for the rest of the thirteenth and all of the fourteenth century: the Marînids ruled in Morocco, the Ziyânids in western Algeria, and

[1] *T* 251, 256, 279, 285, 290, 296, 312–13. Cf. *Q* II 380–84, III 274, 282–83.
[2] *T* 247–48.
[3] *B* I 123–25.
[4] *B* I 303 ff., II 9 ff.
[5] *B* I 16 ff.; G. Marçais *Les Arabes en Berbérie du XIe au XIVe siècle* (Constantine-Paris 1913) 62–64, 70–72.

the Ḥafṣids in eastern Algeria, in Tunisia, and in Tripolitania.[1] The three ruling dynasties were internally weak: different branches of each dynasty, as well as cousins and brothers within each branch, fought to dislodge the others. Whatever strength these dynasties had left, they spent in fighting each other. Consequently, they were all but powerless before the destructive raids of the nomadic tribes that forced them out of the interior and restricted their rule to the narrow coastal strip which was continuously threatened by the nomads as well as by the fleets of the maritime Christian states to the north.

The Ḥafṣid state of Tunisia and eastern Algeria enjoyed some prosperity in the second half of the thirteenth century and the first decade of the fourteenth, mainly because of the advantageous location of Tunis, its capital, which was the most important seaport on the North African coast west of Alexandria. Under the Ḥafṣids, Tunis boasted of sumptuous new palaces, mosques, schools, public baths, and efficient water systems. It was here that Ibn Khaldûn was born; his family was one of the many Muslim Spanish families that took refuge in Tunis and transformed its northern part into an Andalusian garden reflecting their sophisticated charm and cultured elegance.[2] In spite of the fact that epidemics and invasions took a heavy toll of its population toward the middle of the fourteenth century, the city continued to impress visitors with its intense activity and vitality.[3] Its guilds, marketplaces, and naval arsenal were bustling with local and international maritime trade; its waterfront and its custom houses were crowded with foreign ships, sailors, merchants, and brokers, who came from all over Europe and the East. Politically and militarily, however, the Ḥafṣids were on the

[1] Eastern Tripolitania, or Cyrenaica, remained nominally under the Mamlûks while actually held by the Arab nomads who, together with the nomads of southern Algeria, succeeded in disrupting the inland trade route with the East.

[2] *Q* II 311, III 261–62, *B* I 447. Cf. R. Brunschvig *La Berbérie orientale sous les Ḥafṣides des origines à la fin du XVe siècle* (Paris 1940–47) I 338 ff.

[3] *B* II 187, *passim*, *T* 27, *passim*. For the population of Tunis at this time cf. Brunschvig *op. cit.* I 356–57. De Boer's contention (cf. *Geschichte der Philosophie im Islam* [Stuttgart 1901] 182 n. 1) that Ibn Khaldûn grew up in a small city and hence did not possess a real knowledge of life in the big city has no foundation, and all the evidence we have about Tunis points in the opposite direction. More than 100,000 survived the black death in Tunis. Thus, Tunis was probably as populous as Paris during that period. Only Milan and Venice (with a population close to 200,000 each) surpassed it in that respect (cf. Brunschvig *loc. cit.*; R. Lopez *CEH* II 303).

defensive. They could not drive out the Sicilians, who occupied the island of Jerba, until 1334, and then only with the help of the Neopolitan and Genoese navies. Around the middle of the fourteenth century, their power ebbed noticeably, and they were twice conquered by the Marînids of Morocco. The Ḥafṣids did not recover their former prestige until the fifteenth century.[1]

To the west of the Ḥafṣids ruled the Ziyânids (or 'Abd al-Wâdids) with their seat in Tlemcen. They were continually harassed and invaded by their neighbours to the east as well as by their more powerful neighbours to the west.[2] Tlemcen was beautified in the thirteenth century with the help of Spanish architects and artisans, and it enjoyed a favourable trade position and prosperous local industries. But in the fourteenth century, it suffered heavily from frequent sieges and destructive battles.[3]

The energies of the Marînid dynasty of Morocco were consumed in internal strife until the advent of two rulers, Abû al-Ḥasan (1331–48), who extended his kingdom eastward with the capture of Tlemcen and Tunis, and his son Abû 'Inân (1348–58), who brought Muslim Spanish architects and artisans to rebuild his capital Fez. Under him, Fez replaced Tunis as the centre of cultural activity in North Africa.[4] During Abû 'Inân's reign, North Africa enjoyed a short period of peace in relative prosperity which, viewed in the context of the prevalent anarchy of the time, was a great achievement. The peace did not last, mainly because of the delicate power structure of the area. The Marînid hegemony over North Africa was real, but this control did not necessarily mean political stability in the region. Whenever a neighbouring ruler feared them, he had always the possibility of restraining their power by realigning political and military relations with other states, Muslim or Christian. Thus, the two other Berber states of North Africa and the Muslim Spanish state of Banû al-Aḥmar, although weak and continually threatened and in many instances actually occupied by the Marînids, always managed to keep their autonomy or to regain it once it had been lost.

[1] Brunschvig *op. cit.* I 144 ff.
[2] *B* I 454 ff., II 100 ff.; *EI* IV 1220*b*–21*a*.
[3] *B* II 211–12, *passim*; cf. *EI* IV 802*b*.
[4] *B* II 158, *T* 55 ff.; Ibn al-Aḥmar *Rawḍa* 20–22.

Muslim Spain was reduced in the fourteenth century to the small southern strip which constituted the kingdom of Granada. The ruling dynasty, Banû al-Aḥmar ([or the Naṣrids] 1232–1492),[1] came to power through an alliance between its founder, Muḥammad Ibn Yûsuf (d. 1273) and the Castilians; and Banû al-Aḥmar continued to pay tribute to the Castilians and to attend their parliament as vassals, except when in alliance with the Berber rulers of North Africa they felt strong enough to stand against them in battle. Keeping the precarious balance between the Christians to the north and the Berbers to the south, was a complicated and difficult task. Consequently, whenever an inept ruler reigned and whenever internal dissension prevailed, the rich and prosperous lands of the kingdom would invariably be laid waste by the Christians and the Berbers as they fought their destructive wars, which were never decisive because the contestants were usually forced to return back to their kingdoms by locally unstable conditions.[2] An astute ruler like Muḥammad V (ruled 1354–59 and 1362–91), well aware of the problems of the balance of power he had to keep, could secure relatively long periods of peace during which he could attend to the artistic and cultural life of his kingdom which, in spite of its political tribulations, was looked at with envy by all of North Africa.[3] For since the decline of the Eastern influence and the degeneration of the indigenous Berber culture in North Africa, Muslim Spain had become the main artistic and intellectual centre of western Islam.[4] As the Christian reconquest advanced, the highly cultured élite either moved south to what later became the kingdom of Granada or, like Ibn Khaldûn's family, crossed over to North Africa where it was attracted by commercial possibilities and court patronage in Tunis, and later, in Tlemcen and Fez. In the fourteenth century, Muslim Spain could still produce a great man of letters like Ibn al-Khaṭîb (d. 1374/776)[5] whose literary craftsmanship and wide learning made him the pride of

[1] *Bq* IV 170 ff., *B* II 273 ff., 367 ff.; Ibn al-Khaṭîb *Iḥâṭa* I 39–40; Ibn al-Aḥmar *Rawḍa* 23–25.

[2] *B* II 126 f., 314, 541 ff.; Ibn al-Khaṭîb *Lamḥa* 31, 44–45, 62–63.

[3] *Bq* IV 176–78; Ibn al-Khaṭîb *Lamḥa* 119. Cf. G. Marçais *La Berbérie musulmane et l'Orient au Moyen Age* (Paris 1946) 295–304.

[4] É. Lévi-Provençal *La civilisation arabe en Espagne: Vue générale* (Paris 1949) 35 ff.

[5] *GAL* II 260 ff.

Granada. His panegyrics were coveted by the Marînid court in Fez and his works were read by the learned men of Egypt.[1] Nevertheless, the cultural life of Granada during this period was only a pale reflection of a brilliant past whose vigour and buoyancy had vanished.

4. The general decline of the Islamic states of the West can be further exemplified by studying them in relation to the Christian North and, particularly, in relation to those countries with which they had direct contact. Politically, the Islamic states were passive and on the defensive, except for the inconsequential raids of the Marînids into Christian Spain. Even these raids were not always successful. In 1340, the Marînids were defeated at Ṭarafa, and two years later the Spanish Christians occupied Algeçiras, the important seaport opposite the Moroccan coast, which was not recovered until 1369.[2] In 1390 Louis de Bourbon, with Genoese help, attacked Mahdiyya, south of Tunis, seeking booty, and he did not leave until he was given ransom and some commercial concessions.[3] In 1399 the Spanish Christians even gained a foothold in Morocco itself and sacked Tetuan.

This political and military picture was closely connected with the economies of both sides. It is true that Christian Europe witnessed a collapse in its economic prosperity and the destructive Hundred Years' War in the fourteenth century. But in contrast to the general and prolonged process of decline in the Islamic world, the decline of economic activity in Christian Europe was a temporary affair. It was preceded by two centuries of exceptional increase in local and foreign trade, and industrial production; and it was followed in the mid-fifteenth century by the new progress of the Renaissance period.[4] Consequently, in spite of the adverse conditions prevalent in the North during the fourteenth century, the maritime trade of the Mediterranean was virtually monopolized by the city-states of Genoa, Pisa, Florence, and Venice. Christians and Jews, with the expansion of banking and credit institutions, had become the sole middlemen in international trade. With the development of mining and

[1] *T* 121; Sakhâwî *I'lân* 127–28; Maqqarî *Nafḥ* IV 248 ff.

[2] *B* II 386 ff., 484–85; A. Gonzalez Palencia *Historia de la España musulmana* (Barcelona 1945) 112–13.

[3] *B* I 618 ff.

[4] Cf. *CMH* VII 340 ff.; John U. Nef *CEH* II 456–58, 469 ff.

metallurgy, and the textile industry, as a result of the Early Industrial Renaissance, Europe had also become a source of expanding export trade. In contrast, not only were there no new developments in agricultural and industrial techniques in North Africa for the last two centuries, but there was actually continuous decay and destruction of the existing economy. This left the region that had been the traditional granary of southern Europe with no surplus for export.[1] In the artistic and intellectual fields, similarly, there was nothing in the Islamic states to compare with the Early European Renaissance, the rediscovery of classical antiquity, or the rise of national literatures.[2]

To conclude: The picture of the Islamic world during the fourteenth century as depicted by Ibn Khaldûn, and for the most part substantiated by other sources, is one of general decline and disintegration. A few isolated areas, notably southwest Persia, Egypt, and Muslim Spain, were able to preserve some vestiges of what was once a dynamic, expansive civilization. But in contrast with the youthful growth of that civilization in the eighth-ninth centuries and with the conditions prevailing in contemporary Christian Europe, even these areas were relatively stagnant. Western North Africa, where Ibn Khaldûn grew up and spent fifty years of his life before going to Egypt, was the worst part of the Islamic world in this respect. It presented him with a spectacle of chaos and desolation. If Muslim civilization in other parts had declined, in North Africa it had virtually ceased to exist.[3] The desire to understand the nature and causes of the conditions prevailing in the Islamic world, and particularly in North Africa, during his lifetime, and to learn the lessons they could teach him on the nature of human history, were among the main motivations in Ibn Khaldûn's reflections on history.

[1] Cf. *CEH* II 209, 289 ff., 304–15.

[2] Ibn Khaldûn was acquainted in a general way with the economic and intellectual activity of western Europe (cf. *Q* III 93, where he mentions the advance of the philosophic sciences in that region). His main source seems to have been the Christian merchants he met. Cf. *Q* II 244–45; below pp. 40–41.

[3] Cf. *Q* II 246–47, 268–69, 352, 380 ff.; Ibn al-Khaṭîb *Lamḥa* 9.

II

Early Life and Training

1. Ibn Khaldûn was born in Tunis in May 1332/Ramaḍân 732. His family claimed descent from a Yemenite tribe originating in Ḥaḍramawt, the central part of the southern coast of Arabia. In the early history of Islam, that tribe was known for its pro-Ummayad leanings. It entered Spain during the Muslim conquest of that country as part of the Yemenite army. Toward the end of the tenth/fourth century (during the disintegration of the central government in Spain) Ibn Khaldûn's family became well known for its leadership in the revolutionary activities in Seville. Its members were prominent in the administration of the city and one of them, 'Umar Ibn Khaldûn (d. 1057–58/449), distinguished himself as a scientist and philosopher.[1] Around the middle of the thirteenth/seventh century, when Seville was threatened by the Christians, the family left for North Africa; it was welcomed in Tunis, received at court, and granted land holdings in the kingdom. Some of its members held administrative posts under the Ḥafṣids and were beset by the misfortune that befell the dynasty in the latter part of the century. Ibn Khaldûn's grandfather, Muḥammad, retired to lead a quiet religious life and encouraged his son to do the same. Mystic orders were becoming increasingly popular, and the father and son joined Abû 'Abd Allâh al-Zubaydî's circle, one of the most respected in the city of Tunis.[2]

Of Ibn Khaldûn's childhood and early youth in Tunis, we know little apart from the details of his studies, and the background and character of his masters. We can assume that he shared his family's active participation in the intellectual life of the city and, to a lesser degree, in its political life. Economically

[1] For the history of Ibn Khaldûn's family, cf. *T* 1 ff., *C* I 16–17, *Bq* IV 135–36; Ibn al-Khaṭîb in Maqqarî *Nafḥ* IV 6. 'Umar was the student of the philosopher and astronomer Majrîṭî, cf. Ibn Ḥazm *Jamhara* 420: 10; Ṣâ'id *Ṭabaqât* 71; Qifṭî *Ta'rîkh* 243; Ibn Abî Uṣaybi'a *'Uyûn* II 41.

[2] *T* 9–11. For the fall of Seville and its subsequent history, cf. *B* I 350, 399, 447, II 284, 301–2. Ibn Khaldûn's family had connections with the founders of the Ḥafṣid dynasty of Tunis when the latter were governors of Seville. Cf. *B* I 454, 459, 461–62, 518. Further details on the mystic orders of Tunis are given by Brunschvig *op. cit.* II 335–40.

well-to-do and patronized by the rulers, the household in which he grew up was frequented by the political and intellectual leaders of western Islam, many of whom took refuge there and were protected against angry rulers who sought to imprison them for their undesirable political activities and affiliations.[1] Ibn Khaldûn's education began under these favourable conditions and was enriched by personal contact with the best Muslim Spanish and North African masters residing in the city of his birth. In addition, he was able to study with some of the great scholars of Morocco who were brought to Tunis in 1347/748 by the Marînid ruler Abû al-Ḥasan.[2]

Ibn Khaldûn's elementary education included the reading of the Koran and the study of the collections of Traditions approved by the Mâlikite school of Law to which he belonged, the fundamentals of Islamic theology, the rudiments of the religious Law, and the elements of mysticism. His advanced studies included detailed work on these disciplines with the aid of commentaries and other major works written about them. Also included, were the rational or philosophic sciences (*'ulûm 'aqliyya*), viz., logic, mathematics, natural philosophy (perhaps including astronomy and medicine), and metaphysics. The relevant linguistic, biographical, and historical sciences, and the art of writing scholarly works, were added as necessary tools for the study of these sciences. Finally, since Ibn Khaldûn was also interested in the practical affairs of government, he followed an apprenticeship that included specialized training in the art of writing official court correspondence and of handling practical administrative matters.[3]

[1] *T* 27, 37, 40.

[2] *T* 15 ff., 44 ff. Ibn Khaldûn followed these masters upon their return back to Fez.

[3] *T* 15 ff., *Q* III 278 ff., 296, 348 ff., 358–59; Ibn al-Khaṭîb in Maqqarî *Nafḥ* IV 6–7; cf. Brunschvig *op. cit.* II 255–66. The literary style of Ibn Khaldûn's court correspondence (cf. *T* 22, 41 ff., *Q* II 21 ff.) was highly praised by his friend and great literary figure of Muslim Spain, Ibn al-Khaṭîb (cf. Maqqarî *Nafḥ* IV 11 : 6–7). Neither Ibn Khaldûn nor his biographers inform us about the place of history in his early education. Ibn Khaldûn's silence concerning this subject may have been the result of the ambivalent position of history among the sciences (cf. F. Rosenthal *A History of Muslim Historiography* [Leiden 1952] 38–39, *passim*). We know, however, that the study of history was part of the programme of Muslim elementary and higher education, it has always formed part of the general education of a cultivated Muslim, and it was occasionally taught formally in schools and more frequently studied through private readings (*ibid.* 40 ff.). We also know that history was one of the main subjects studied by scholars like Ibn Khaldûn who were planning for a career in government.

Ibn Khaldûn's early training in, and writings about, the religious and philosophic sciences provide the background for his future career and his mature thought as expressed in the ' History '. His reticence about his early training and writings, especially on philosophic matters, must not prevent us from seeking to explore this subject; for he gives us enough hints to make us suspect that this reticence is intentional and that the problem is of major significance.[1] The most fundamental question that must be asked in this connection is: What was the approach of the sciences he studied during this period to the all-important problem of the relation between revelation and reason in the study of society?

2. From the beginning, Islamic religious thought concentrated on the problem of the practical social order, the order of doing (*af'âl*), as it existed in the Islamic community. Given the Koran and Tradition (the sayings and deeds of the Prophet: *ḥadîth*), the problem was how to apply the principles and precepts contained in them, and the historically conditioned and limited practices of the early community of Medina (the city of the Prophet), to the new and changing situations met by the community as it expanded and developed.[2]

During the eighth/second century, the oldest of the four orthodox schools of Law was founded in Medina by Mâlik Ibn Anas (d. 794/179).[3] Mâlikism emphasized the ' living tradition ' (*sunna*) of Medina, i.e., the ideas and practices of the community of the Prophet and the early generations of Muslims in that city. It was essentially a conservative and provincial school that tried to preserve the tradition and attitudes prevailing in the primitive and relatively isolated community in Arabia; it used prudential judgment (*ra'y, opinio prudentium*) and reasoning to defend the beliefs and practices of that community.[4] The provincialism of Medina and its school found acceptance in North Africa where similar social and cultural conditions prevailed; and western

[1] Cf. below p. 35 n. 2.

[2] *Q* III 1 ff., 8–9, 25, 38; cf. I. Goldziher *Muhammedanische Studien* (Halle 1888–90) II 51 ff., 86–87; G. Bergsträsser *Grundzüge des islamischen Rechts* (Berlin 1935) 15, *passim*; J. Schacht *The Origins of Muhammadan Jurisprudence* (Oxford 1950) 22 ff.

[3] *GAL* I 175 ff.

[4] Goldziher *op. cit.* II 28, 78–80, 213–17.

Islam was won to Mâlikism in the first decades of the ninth/third century.[1]

In contrast to Mâlikism, the schools of Iraq had to cope with the new social situations resulting from the establishment and expansion of a world empire. This could not have been done had they continued to follow a provincial and inflexible tradition like that of Medina. Instead, they used prudential judgment, personal elaboration (*ijtihâd*), reasoning by analogy (*qiyâs*), and consensus (*ijmâ'*, *communis consensus*), to defend the *spirit* of the Koran and Tradition, and to develop a body of religious Law that could cope with the new conditions.[2]

In the tenth/fourth century, Mâlikism was challenged in the West by the extremist Khârijites, and officially disestablished by the heterodox Shî'ites and later by the strict unitarian Muwaḥḥids. By the end of the thirteenth/seventh century, when Mâlikism was again officially recognized and encouraged by the Ḥafṣid rulers of Tunis, and the doctors of the school occupied most of the legal and administrative posts in the kingdom, Mâlikism had undergone significant changes in its approach to many religious and legal problems. These changes were primarily due to contacts with the schools of Iraq and the adoption of the more recent development in religious thought in the East, represented mainly by the students of Fakhr al-Dîn al-Râzî (d. 1209/606)[3] who effected a new rapprochement between rational philosophic knowledge and religious studies.

Under the impact of the Iraqi school, western Mâlikism in general, and that branch of it that was under the direct impact of Râzî's ideas in particular, allowed a wider latitude for personal elaboration. Furthermore, the important economic and social changes that took place in western Islam since the tenth/fourth century had created a new 'living tradition' consisting of usages and practices that could neither be ignored nor explained

[1] *Q* III 8–9, *T* 300, 304. Shaṭbûn (d. 819–20/204 [cf. *T* 309 n. 1]) is reputed to have been the first to introduce the school of Mâlik into the West.

[2] These fundamentals of the religious Law were first systematized by Shâfi'î (d. 820/204 [*GAL* I 178 ff.]) in his famous *Epistle* (*Risâla*). Cf. Schacht *op. cit.* 120 ff., *passim.*

[3] *GAL* I 506 ff. *Q* III 8 ff., 41–43, *passim.* The three important leaders of the new school, Ibn Zaytûn, Ḥaskûnî, and Mishaddâlî, all travelled to the East and studied under masters who had adopted the ideas of the Iraqi schools and who had been under the renovating influence of Râzî. Cf. *Q* II 378 ff., *T* 21 n. 3, 28; Ibn Ḥajar *Durar* IV 181–83.

by the primitive ' living tradition ' of Medina as set down by Mâlik. The new school, therefore, naturally found itself concerned with the problems of custom (*'urf*) and habit (*'âda*), and their place within the Law. Such concern meant interest in concrete social conditions, an interest which led to the consideration of the problems of common interest or the common good (*maṣâliḥ 'âmma*), of social necessity (*ḍarûra*), and of how the commands of the religious Law (*sharî'a*) could be interpreted *propter utilitatem publicam* to meet the demands of concrete social life and yet preserve their validity and universality.[1] The consideration of these problems opened the way for the elaboration of the concept of ' God's [universal way or] tradition ' (*sunnat allâh*) in contrast to the more limited and once ' living ' tradition of Medina.[2] The more conservative branch of western Mâlikism considered such legal accommodation of concrete social conditions as a concession, though a necessary one, which did not alter the ideal character of the older tradition. Another possibility remained open, and it was Ibn Khaldûn who elaborated it: The particular traditions, including that of Medina, could be studied as expressions of an underlying universal order of things, an order that could be ascertained by observation and valid reasoning. With the proper *interpretation* of the Koran and Tradition, it could be found that the demands of the religious Law do not on the whole differ from the demands of the natural order. In short, there is only one order, but it is revealed to man in two ways: through divine revelation and through natural reason. As divine revelation could be misinterpreted, and as human reason could err, these two ways may differ, but the difference remains accidental.[3]

3. In addition to its concern with the relation of the Law to concrete social problems, the new school of Mâlikism in the West followed the tradition of Râzî in its attitude toward the rational sciences. The leaders of the school are, therefore, to be classed with the dialectical theologians (*mutakallimûn*) whom

[1] I. Goldziher ' Das Prinzip des *istiṣḥâb* in der muhammedanischen Gesetzwissenschaft ' *WZKM* I (1887) 229–30; T. W. Joynboll ' *Istiḥsân* ' *EI* II 561*a*; Brunschvig *op. cit.* II 295–97. Brunschvig does not sufficiently emphasize the apparent fact that in studying these problems western Mâlikism was following the schools of Iraq, Syria, and Egypt, which had been in existence for centuries.

[2] Cf., e.g., *Q* I 155, *passim*.

[3] *Q* I 355; cf. below pp. 93–95, 179 ff., 257 n. 7.

Ibn Khaldûn called the 'moderns' (*muta'akhkhirûn*) as distinguished from the 'ancients' (*aqdamûn*). Both schools accepted the use of reason in religious argumentation. The difference lay in the specific principles accepted and used by each, and the effect of these principles upon their conceptions of the relation of rational knowledge to revelation. This difference can be best illustrated, following Ibn Khaldûn, by stating their respective positions regarding the relation of logic and being. According to the 'ancients', represented by Bâqillânî (d. 1013/403),[1] 'a false proof entails the falseness of the object to be proved'.[2] In other words, they held that if it is shown, e.g., that the proof of God's omniscience is false, it follows that God is not omniscient. Starting from what they considered as religious dogmas, they formulated a rational system based upon principles and methods of proof which led to conclusions identical with these dogmas. Then, they demanded that their principles and methods of proof be accepted as valid; for to reject them or to prove their falseness, they argued, will be the same as rejecting and proving the falseness of the dogmas themselves. The 'moderns', on the other hand, followed the philosophers in differentiating between the nature of (1) logical entities which they conceived as beings of reason or second intentions (*ma'qûlât thawânî, intentio rationalis*) and (2) the beings of nature or first intentions, holding that these two should correspond to each other, but could accidentally differ. Consequently, they affirmed the reality of both (against the denial of the 'ancients' of any outside reality corresponding to logical entities) as well as the possibility of the falseness of the beings of reason without the corresponding falseness of the beings of nature. We shall explore at a later stage the various consequences of this change for the subsequent development of Islamic religious thought and particularly in relation to Ibn Khaldûn.[3] Its general significance, however, can be indicated here. It signalled a victory for the Islamic philosophic tradition of Fârâbî (d. 950/339),[4] Avicenna (d. 1037/428),[5] and Averroes (d. 1198/595),[6] not only because of the decisive role of their thought in

[1] *GAL* I 197.
[2] *Q* III 40 ff., 113 ff.
[3] Cf. below pp. 102 ff.
[4] *GAL* I 210 ff.
[5] *GAL* I 452 ff.
[6] *GAL* I 461 ff.

bringing that change about, but also because the change meant that religious thought became more tolerant of, and more receptive to, their approach.[1] Furthermore, because the new logic adopted by dialectical theology (*kalâm*) was to a large extent the same Aristotelian logic studied and defended by these philosophers, there was now an apparent common ground for discussion between philosophy and dialectical theology, and for the acceptance by dialectical theology of the physical and metaphysical ideas of the philosophers. To be sure, the change did not mean the complete absorption of dialectical theology by philosophy or *vice versa*. They remained two separate disciplines. But that was largely due to the insistence of the philosophers that such absorption would lead to a confusion of the ends of the two disciplines which would be injurious both to philosophy and to dialectical theology.[2]

Ibn Khaldûn studied both traditions of dialectical theology, especially the tradition of Râzî, but considered dialectical theology as a whole to be merely a useful weapon in combating heresies and preserving the faith of the common Muslim against the encroachment of philosophical doubts. Apart from that purely social function, he rejected the dialectical use of philosophy by theology; and since he thought that philosophy was no longer confusing the public, he added that ' dialectical theology is no longer necessary '.[3] This meant that as a student of philosophy, Ibn Khaldûn sided with the purely philosophic tradition in Islamic thought, the tradition of Fârâbî, Avicenna, and Averroes.[4]

[1] Cf. Ibn Khaldûn's description of Râzî's *Maḥṣûl* in *Q* III 22.

[2] The views of the ' moderns ', as imported to Tunis by Ibn Zaytûn and others, were still taught during Ibn Khaldûn's youth. There are numerous commentaries on Râzî's works by North African and Spanish scholars of that period that have been preserved (*GAL* I 506–7). Cf. Ibn Ḥajar *Durar* IV 181–84. The works of Avicenna together with the commentaries of Râzî and Ṭûsî, continued to dominate the philosophic thought of the East down to Ibn Khaldûn's time (cf. *Q* III 117). In North Africa, 'Abd al-Raḥmân Ibn al-Imâm, and his brother 'Îsâ, were the most distinguished among those trained by Ibn Zaytûn's students (cf. *T* 21, 28–31, *Q* II 378 ff.). It was under the latter in Tlemcen that Ibn Khaldûn's master, Âbilyy, studied logic (*T* 21, 33–34).

[3] *Q* III 43.

[4] Cf. his glowing eulogy of metaphysics (*'ilm ilâhî*), *L* fols. 3v–4r: ' It is the noblest [of the sciences]. He who knows it is superior in happiness, and many rewards are made ready for him. The [other] sciences need it and it does not need them, their principles depend upon it and it does not depend upon them.' Below pp. 73 ff.

Ibn Khaldûn was initiated into that tradition by his favourite master Âbilyy (d. 1356/757).[1] Born in 1282–83/681, Âbilyy showed interest and competence in mathematics early in his life. He was forced to become the general of the Andalusian regiment, a post which he deserted to head East for pilgrimage, hiding in the company of beggars. Near Tlemcen, he met a disappointed Shî'ite leader who had come from the East as a propagandist for the heterodox cause. He joined him on his way back to Mecca, and later to Karbalâ', a Shî'ite centre in Iraq. According to Ibn Khaldûn's story—our only source—Âbilyy was sick during that journey and, consequently, could not benefit from the great Egyptian teachers of the time or (and we suspect that this is the intention of the story) from the teachings of the heterodox Shî'ite leaders who championed the cause of philosophy in the East during that period.[2] Back in the West, Âbilyy continued to study philosophy and tried to avoid being inducted into government service as chief treasurer, where his knowledge of mathematics could be put to use. He fled to Fez, hiding in the house of the Jewish mathematician Khallûf al-Maghîlî, where he continued to study mathematics. Later he went to Marrâkush to study mysticism, mathematics, and philosophy, with the 'master of the West' Abû al-'Abbâs Aḥmad Ibn al-Bannâ' (d. 1321/721).[3] Soon, he became the most celebrated teacher and 'the most proficient of his contemporaries in the philosophic sciences'.[4]

Âbilyy was among the scholars accompanying the Marînid ruler Abû al-Ḥasan to Tunis in 1347/748. There he met Ibn Khaldûn's father and lodged in his household. Through his father, Ibn Khaldûn, though still a young man of sixteen, was able to attend Âbilyy's circle. In the following year the black death swept through Tunis, and Ibn Khaldûn's parents and most of his other teachers were among its victims. For the following three years, he studied with Âbilyy until the latter left to join the Marînid ruler Abû 'Inân.[5]

[1] Ibn Ḥajar *Durar* III 288–89.

[2] *T* 34–35. Cf. *Q* II 173–74.

[3] *GAL* II 255; Ibn Ḥajar *Durar* III 289; *T* 21, 21 n. 4, 22, 306, *Q* III 96–97.

[4] *L* fol. 4v; Ibn Ḥajar *Durar* III 289; cf. *T*. 21, 33–34; Ibn al-Qâḍî *Durra* 283 (No. 784). Âbilyy's students included many of Ibn Khaldûn's friends. Cf. *T* 22, 45, 47, 62.

[5] *T* 21–22, 55, 371. Ibn al-Qâḍî (*Durra* 283, 291) reports that Âbilyy was (during that time!) the Judge of Tunis and calls him 'the Jurisconsult' (*faqîh*).

Ibn Khaldûn's studies with Âbilyy started with mathematics and logic, and then branched out to include the various philosophic sciences.[1] Âbilyy's own approach to philosophy cannot be ascertained from the meagre and vague references made to him by Ibn Khaldûn and other biographers. From what he taught his students, it is apparent that he did not follow a particular philosophic tradition, but read with them the major works of Avicenna, Râzî, and Averroes.[2] It was probably he who first introduced the works of the leading Shî'ite philosopher Naṣîr al-Dîn al-Ṭûsî (d. 1274/672) into the West,[3] and we know that Ibn Khaldûn studied one of Ṭûsî's works with him.[4]

Ibn Khaldûn's preference for philosophy as against the dialectical theology of the 'moderns' is apparent from the titles of the works he wrote during that period and from the contents of the one that has survived. These works included treatises on logic and mathematics, and 'many' epitomes of Averroes' works.[5] The surviving work is a summary of a work by Râzî in

[1] Ibn Khaldûn's studies under Âbilyy started with mathematics, followed by logic and 'those [disciplines] that *come after logic*: the fundamentals of religion and of the religious Law (*aṣlân*), and the philosophic sciences (*'ulûm al-ḥikma*).' *T* 37, cf. 22, where the sequence is not as clear. Cf. Ibn Khaldûn's eulogy of his master as the one who had revived metaphysics in the West after its long decline (*L* fols. 3v–4r).

[2] Ibn Khaldûn does not mention the specific works he read with Âbilyy while studying the rational sciences. He does, however, give us an indirect hint concerning the works Âbilyy read with his advanced students in philosophy. Speaking of his friend Muḥammad Ibn Aḥmad al-Sharîf al-Ḥasanî who studied with their mutual master Muḥammad Ibn 'Abd al-Salâm (d. 1348–49/749 [cf. *T* 19 n. 3, *Q* III 14; *GAL* I 306]), Ibn Khaldûn says: 'It was even *claimed* that he [Ḥasanî] used to meet him [Ibn 'Abd al-Salâm] *alone* in his house and read to him the chapter on mysticism from Avicenna's *Book of Directives* (*Kitâb al-ishârât*), *since he had mastered this book with our teacher Âbilyy*. He also read to him a large portion of the *Book of Healing* (*Kitâb al-shifâ'*) [of Avicenna] and the epitomes of Aristotle ['s works] by Averroes.' *T* 62–63. Thus, in his peculiar style, Ibn Khaldûn tells us the reason why he could not mention what he studied with Âbilyy directly: even the powerful and highly respected Judge of Tunis had to go to his home and be alone with his student when reading such works.

[3] *GAL* I 508 ff.

[4] Cf. *L* fol. 4v.

[5] Ibn Khaldûn's complete silence in the 'History' and the *Autobiography* about his early works is certainly curious and deserves comment. Cf. below p. 61. Hitherto, we only knew that Ibn Khaldûn did write numerous treatises in this period and the titles of some of them from a single passage by Ibn al-Khaṭîb in his short biography of Ibn Khaldûn (in his *Iḥâṭa*, quoted in Maqqarî *Nafḥ* IV 11, *Azhâr* I 190). Since the *Iḥâṭa* was completed in 1361–62/763, we can assume that all the works mentioned there, except the last, were completed before that date. Ibn al-Khaṭîb mentions the following titles: (1) a commentary on a poem eulogizing the Prophet called *al-Burda* by Muḥammad Ibn Sa'îd

which the latter presents a ' Compendium of the Sciences of the Ancients and of the Moderns '. As a dialectical theologian, Râzî criticizes many of the philosophic schools in this work and, particularly, some of the doctrines of Avicenna. The Shî'ite philosopher Ṭûsî had already written extensive notes on the work in which he doubted Râzî's understanding of the position of the philosophers in general and of Avicenna in particular. Ibn Khaldûn studied Ṭûsî's criticisms together with Râzî's work with Âbilyy.[1] In his summary of Râzî's work, called the *Gist of the Compendium*,[2] he adopts almost all of Ṭûsî's criticisms.[3] Ibn Khaldûn's attraction to philosophy was not limited to the early stage of his studies. Throughout his later career in North Africa, Spain, and Egypt, he continued to study, and enquire about the new developments taking place in the philosophic sciences and the activities of the students of Râzî and Ṭûsî—especially in the East.[4]

The character of Ibn Khaldûn's early religious and philosophic studies meant that he had to face the basic problem of Islamic thought, the tension and opposition between the approaches of orthodoxy and the philosophers to the study of man and society. For orthodoxy, the ultimate truth about man and society had been revealed in the Koran, and through the Tradition of the Prophet and the consensus of the Muslim community. Whatever concessions orthodoxy may have made to the philosophic

---

al-Bûṣîrî (d. 1294/694 [*GAL* I 264]), (2) many epitomes of Averroes' works (cf. the complete inventory of Averroes' works in P. Manuel Alonso *Teología de Averroes* [*Estudios y documentos*] [Madrid 1947] 54-95), (3) a treatise on logic written for Muḥammad V, king of Granada, (4) an epitome of Râzî's *Muḥaṣṣal* (see below), (5) a book on arithmetic, and (6) a commentary on a work on the fundamentals of jurisprudence by Ibn al-Khaṭîb himself (reported as being in progress, cf. also Maqqarî *Nafḥ* IV 244).

Of these writings, the epitome of Râzî's ' Compendium ' (*Muḥaṣṣal*) is extant. The Escurial MS of the *Lubâb* (referred to in this study as *L*) was finished in April 1351/Ṣafar 752 (thus Ibn Khaldûn composed it when he was only twenty years of age). Cf. *L* fol. 65r.

[1] *L* fol. 4v. Ṭûsî's ' Summary ' (*Talkhîṣ*) is printed as notes to the Cairine edition of the *Muḥaṣṣal* used in this study.

[2] *Lubâb al-muḥaṣṣal*. *L*. fol. 3r.

[3] *L passim*. Ibn Khaldûn's own comments and those of Ṭûsî are preceded with the phrase: ' and one may say ' (*wa-li-qâ'ilin an yaqûl*). This phrase follows practically all of Râzî's arguments.

[4] Cf. *Q* III 92–93, 117 274, *Bq* V 532; Ibn al-Khaṭîb in Maqqarî *Nafḥ* IV 11; below pp. 54, 57. There is even some evidence (Sakhâwî *Ḍaw'* IV 148: 25) that Ibn Khaldûn followed Râzî's method while teaching in Egypt.

approach, it never ceased to hold to the primacy of the religious Law over reason. For the philosophers, on the other hand, the order was the reverse: they upheld the primacy of rational enquiry in both the theoretical and the practical sciences. We shall soon meet the tension and struggle between orthodoxy and philosophy in Ibn Khaldûn's life, and later in his major work, the ' History '.

III

Political and Scholarly Career in Western Islam

1. In the year 1352/753 Ibn Khaldûn's master, Âbilyy, was called to Fez by the Marînid ruler Abû 'Inân. The black death had already taken Ibn Khaldûn's parents and many of his Tunisian masters. The scholars brought to the city by the Marînid ruler Abû al-Ḥasan had all left. Ibn Khaldûn was now lonely and eager to follow Âbilyy to Fez, the city which had become the centre of political power and cultural life in North Africa. He was not, therefore, very pleased when the Tunisian monarch called upon him to accept the insignificant post of a secretary in the chancery (*kâtib al-'alâma*), and took the opportunity of the monarch's defeat in battle soon afterwards to move west.[1] He spent the next two years travelling and following the political activities of the Marînid ruler while the latter was consolidating his power. When Abû 'Inân finally returned to Fez, Ibn Khaldûn was mentioned to him in his study councils, and he was sent for to be made a secretary in charge of writing the royal proclamations (*tawqî'*):[2] a comparatively unimportant post in itself, but it gave him the opportunity to continue his studies in Fez with his former masters, to meet the ambassadors to the court, and to be in close touch with the political life of North Africa and Muslim Spain.[3]

While following the subsequent political career of Ibn Khaldûn, we must keep in mind that since their conquest by

[1] *T* 55–56; Ibn al-Khaṭîb in Maqqarî *Nafḥ* IV 7: 3–4. For the origin and functions of this office, cf. Brunschvig *op. cit.* II 61 ff.

[2] *T* 59, 62; Ibn al-Khaṭîb in Maqqarî *Nafḥ* IV 7: 4–6. For the functions of this office, cf. *Q* II 23 ff.; Brunschvig *op. cit.* II 36; Dozy *Supplément aux dictionnaires arabes* (Leiden 1881) II 831*b*. Ibn Khaldûn met Abû 'Inân toward the end of the year 755 A.H. (*T* 58, 95) and not 756 A.H. as in *T* 66.

[3] *T* 58–66.

Islam in the seventh-eighth/first-second centuries, western North Africa and Muslim Spain were border-countries where political adventurers and sectarian visionaries sought their fortune. Constant struggle with the Berber tribes to the south and the Christians to the north, and frequent changes of ruling dynasties, moulded the political character of the region and prevented the establishment of a deep-rooted political tradition. During Ibn Khaldûn's time, the region was ruled by petty tyrants whose personal qualities were decisive in determining the character of the communities they ruled. To be active in politics under such conditions meant establishing some kind of relation with one of these tyrants, and one's political role depended largely upon how this relation stood.

In the court of Abû 'Inân, Ibn Khaldûn met two men who were destined to play important roles in the political life of North Africa: the Ḥafṣid prince Abû 'Abd Allâh,[1] whom Abû 'Inân was using in his attempt to divide and control the Ḥafṣid dynasty of Tunis,[2] and 'Amar.[3] Through them, Ibn Khaldûn, still in his early twenties, was initiated into active political life. Abû 'Inân suspected that Ibn Khaldûn was plotting against him with the Ḥafṣid prince, and both were imprisoned in 1357/758. The prince was freed shortly afterwards, but Ibn Khaldûn remained in prison for more than twenty-two months, and was not freed to resume his office until the murder of Abû 'Inân by his vizir and the accession of his son.[4] Shortly after the murder of Abû 'Inân, we find Ibn Khaldûn active in a plan to overthrow his son and support his exiled brother, Abû Sâlim, who succeeded his minor nephew to the Marînid throne at the age of twenty-six.[5] Under Abû Sâlim, Ibn Khaldûn became the chief of the chancery (*kâtib al-sirr wa-l-tawqî' wa-l-inshâ'*), and was

[1] Muḥammad Ibn Yaḥyâ, Abû Zakariyyâ. *T* 66; Ibn al-Khaṭîb in Maqqarî *Nafḥ* IV 7: 6 ff.

[2] Ibn Khaldûn's account of his relation with Abû 'Abd Allâh is not very consistent and tries intentionally to suppress important facts. He denies the charge of conspiring with the Ḥafṣid prince against Abû 'Inân, yet he confesses that the prince promised him a high position. He did subsequently receive the highest office under him in Bijâya. Cf. *T* 66–67, 91, 94–99; below pp. 44–45.

[3] 'Amar Ibn 'Abd Allâh. *T* 77, *B* II 463–70; Ibn al-Aḥmar *Rawḍa* 25, 28–30.

[4] From Ṣafar 18, 758 A.H. to Dhû al-Ḥijja 24, 759 A.H.; cf. *T* 66–68, 95–96; Ibn al-Aḥmar *Rawḍa* 23: 6–7. Neither Ibn Khaldûn nor Ibn al-Khaṭîb (cf. Maqqarî *Nafḥ* IV 7: 6 ff.) mentions the real reason behind that imprisonment. Ibn al-Khaṭîb adds that it was partly due to Ibn Khaldûn's lack of caution!

[5] Ibn al-Aḥmar *Rawḍa* 27; Ibn al-Khaṭîb *Lamḥa* 105.

later put in charge of the high court of justice (*khuṭṭat al-maẓâlim*).[1] Nevertheless, Ibn Khaldûn's hopes ended in complete disillusionment. Abû Sâlim did not become the wise and strong sovereign he had expected him to become, but a weak, shortsighted, and illiberal tyrant who had no other interest beyond preserving his power.[2] Ibn Khaldûn's position in the court declined; and the offices he occupied were signs of gratitude for past political support and not of an effective role in deciding state policy. Instead, the ill-devised machinations of Ibn Marzûq, the adviser and long-time friend of the sovereign, prevailed and resulted in the downfall of both through a revolution led by Ibn Khaldûn's friend, 'Amar.[3] But 'Amar, too, failed Ibn Khaldûn and refused to let him play an important role in the new regime. In the meantime, the Ziyânid ruler Abû Ḥammû had succeeded in regaining his dynasty's power. Ibn Khaldûn decided to leave the Marînid court and seek his fortune in Tlemcen. 'Amar, fearing Ibn Khaldûn's designs, prevented him from joining the Ziyânids, but allowed him to choose any other part of the West. Ibn Khaldûn chose Muslim Spain and in 1362/764 left for Granada.[4]

Thus ended the first phase of his political experience: Young and over-ambitious, he sought positions of influence in the only state in North Africa which had the power to unify the region, establish political stability in it, and perhaps rejuvenate its cultural life. He failed completely. Muslim Spain, however, presented him with new conditions, opportunities, and hopes.

2. Compared to North Africa, Muslim Spain was decidedly more prosperous, civilized, stable, and leisurely. In a work written during this period, Ibn al-Khaṭîb describes the grandeur of the cultural life of Granada, the opulence of its agricultural produce, the luxury and taste of its inhabitants, and the beauty and charm of its women. The population was docile, obedient, and paid taxes promptly. They were free of religious heterodoxy

[1] *T* 43, 70, 77; Ibn al-Khaṭîb in Maqqarî *Nafḥ* IV 7: 11–12. For the functions of the office, cf. *Q* I 399 ff., II 21–23; E. Tyan *Histoire de l'organizasion judiciare en pays d'Islam* II (Paris 1943) 141 ff.

[2] Cf. Ibn al-Khaṭîb *Iḥâṭa* I 164–69.

[3] *T* 49 ff., *B* II 462–65.

[4] *T* 77–79; Ibn al-Khaṭîb in Maqqarî *Nafḥ* IV 7: 14–16.

and strife.[1] All that Muslim Spain needed was the right ruler who, with understanding and foresight, could save it from the designs of the Christians to the north and the Marînids to the south, and encourage and enhance the material and cultural prosperity which was already there.

Ibn Khaldûn had failed in North Africa, but he had not lost his hope and ambition. Muslim Spain presented ample opportunity for new adventure, and he was ready to try his fortune again. To the same Ibn al-Khaṭîb, we owe the highly revealing characterization of Ibn Khaldûn as he entered the Spanish scene: 'He commands respect, is able, . . . unruly, strong-willed, and full of ambitions for climbing to the highest position of leadership.'[2]

Ibn Khaldûn's acquaintance with Muḥammad V (reigned 1354/755–1391/793), the ruler of Granada, dated back to 1359/760–1361/762 when the latter was driven out of his kingdom as a result of a revolution that enthroned his brother, and came to Abû Sâlim's court in Fez seeking help to regain his power.[3] Before the expulsion of Muḥammad V, the affairs of Muslim Spain were actually conducted by two men: the wise, able, and elder statesman and general, Riḍwân,[4] and the brilliant writer and secretary, Ibn al-Khaṭîb. During that revolution, Riḍwân was murdered and Ibn al-Khaṭîb was imprisoned. Abû Sâlim demanded the release of Ibn al-Khaṭîb, and he joined Muḥammad V in Fez. There he met and became a close friend of Ibn Khaldûn who seems to have helped him and his sovereign's cause in the Marînid court. When Muḥammad V finally left for Spain to regain his throne with the help of the Castilians,[5] Ibn Khaldûn looked after his family which he left in Fez. Ibn Khaldûn's friendship with Ibn al-Khaṭîb, and the services he rendered to Muḥammad V, assured him of a warm welcome from the ruler as well as the vizir who was now the real administrator of the kingdom.[6] He was lavishly entertained at court and

[1] Ibn al-Khaṭîb *Iḥâṭa* I 24 ff., 34–38, cf. *Lamḥa* 12 ff., 27 ff.; *Q* I 278 ff., 298 ff., II 309–10; Miguel Lafuente *Historia de Granada* III (Granada 1844) 288 ff.

[2] Quoted by Maqqarî *Nafḥ* IV 6: 27–28.

[3] *B* II 453–57; Ibn al-Khaṭîb *Iḥâṭa* I 237 ff., *Raqm* 97, 108 ff., *Lamḥa* 100 ff.

[4] Ibn al-Khaṭîb *Iḥâṭa* I 238–39, 329 ff., 342.

[5] Ibn al-Khaṭîb *Lamḥa* 101–2, 114, 117; cf. Lafuente *op. cit.* 400 ff.

[6] *T* 79 ff.; Ibn al-Khaṭîb in Maqqarî *Nafḥ* IV 7; *EI* III 879*b*–80*a*; Ibn al-Khaṭîb *Lamḥa* 103.

enjoyed the company of the learned Ibn al-Khaṭîb and other Muslim Spanish scholars. He soon sent for his family to join him, indicating his intention of settling in Granada.

In 1364/765 he was sent on an embassy to Pedro I, the Cruel, king of Castile and Leon (reigned 1350–69),[1] to conclude a peace treaty between him and the ruler of Muslim Spain. They met in Seville, the home of Ibn Khaldûn's Spanish ancestors. Pedro, learning from his Jewish doctor Ibrâhîm Ibn Zarzar[2] about Ibn Khaldûn's activities in North Africa and the position of his ancestors in Seville, was very pleased to meet him, asked him to stay in Seville, and offered to return to him his ancestors' holdings in the city (an ambitious man like Ibn Khaldûn could be of great use in Pedro's designs to neutralize the Muslim kingdoms by setting them against each other). Ibn Khaldûn politely declined the offer and, having ended his mission successfully, returned with gifts to Granada.[3] This was Ibn Khaldûn's only direct and personal contact with Christian Europe and its culture.[4] In Spain, a country to which he felt deep attachment, Ibn Khaldûn saw the ruins left by centuries of Muslim-Christian warfare, and could foresee the misfortune awaiting the shrinking part held by the Muslims. The mission he had just accomplished was itself an indication of the Muslims' position: It was not a peace concluded between equals, but between a threatening Christian monarch and a frightened Muslim ruler eager for a tributary position.[5]

Yet, Muslim Spain had advantages lacking in all other Muslim states in the West. It was materially and culturally prosperous. The fighting caste, levied from the Berbers of North Africa and

[1] For the reign of Pedro the Cruel during that year, cf. the Christian Spanish contemporary historian Pedro López de Ayala (1332–1407) *Cronica del Rey Don Pedro* ['Cronicas de los reyes de Castilla' Vol. I] (Madrid 1779) 380 ff. López de Ayala does not mention Ibn Khaldûn's mission.

[2] *T* 85, 371. Ibn Zarzar had known Ibn Khaldûn in Abû 'Inân's court (cf. *B* II 450).

[3] *T* 84–85; Ibn al-Khaṭîb in Maqqarî *Nafḥ* IV 17: 8–9.

[4] For the cultural life of Christian Spain and its literature during that period, cf. J. Hurtado, J. de la Serna, and Á. Gonzalez Palencia *Historia de la literatura española* (Madrid 1949) 33–34, 113–35.

[5] As one of his obligations as the vassal of the king of Castile, Muḥammad V had to supply him with a regiment of knights that fought as a regular force in his army. López de Ayala *Cronica del Rey Don Pedro* 368: 'Otrosi llegó estonce un Caballero del Rey de Granada, que decian Don Farax Rodoan [Faraj Riḍwân!], con seiscientos ginetes, que el Rey Mahomad enviaba en ayuda del Rey de Castilla.' Cf. also 383, *passim.*

Christian slaves, had superior ability and equipment, and was completely controlled by the ruler. In order to preserve itself, Ibn Khaldûn seems to have concluded, Muslim Spain needed, above all, a wise ruler. Muḥammad V seemed amenable to instruction. He was not only approachable, but obligingly responsive to Ibn Khaldûn and delighted with his ideas.[1] Ibn Khaldûn wasted no time in taking the first steps to educate the young ruler in philosophy. His experience in North Africa had taught him that he could not succeed politically merely as an adviser to an ignorant ruler; for such a ruler, like Abû Sâlim, could always be prevailed upon by others to follow the road of political expediency and opportunism. Here, however, was a young ruler in his mid-twenties who was already in power and who gave the impression of being intelligent, virtuous, and prudent.[2] If he could be trained and guided to become a wise man, the state of Ibn Khaldûn's hopes might at last be realized. Since Ibn al-Khaṭîb was conducting the practical affairs of the state, the ruler had the leisure to be instructed by Ibn Khaldûn. Ibn Khaldûn and Muḥammad V sat alone in long sessions during which Ibn Khaldûn explained his ' purpose '[3] to the ruler and instructed him with the help of his early works on philosophy, mathematics, and the fundamentals of religion and Law. These works included a treatise on logic (a subject indispensable for the education of the statesman according to Averroes' paraphrase of Plato's *Republic*),[4] which Ibn Khaldûn wrote specifically *for the ruler* (*'allaqa li-l-sulṭân*).[5]

Ibn al-Khaṭîb was at first suspicious of the long private meetings between Muḥammad V and Ibn Khaldûn, and when he learned what Ibn Khaldûn was trying to do, probably from Muḥammad V himself, he was extremely angry and ' the

[1] *T* 91.
[2] Cf. Ibn al-Khaṭîb *Lamḥa* 100.
[3] Cf. *T* 277: 3.
[4] ' Averroes discusses the indispensable value of logic for the education of the future statesman and insists on beginning with logic, possible since Aristotle has created logical science, and not with mathematics, with which Plato naturally begins the course of study. For Averroes mathematics, thanks to Aristotle's Logic, now takes second place.' E. Rosenthal ' Notes on Some Arabic Manuscripts in the John Rylands Library ' *Bulletin of the John Rylands Library* XXI (1937) 482–83.
[5] Ibn al-Khaṭîb in Maqqarî *Nafḥ* IV 11: 3: ' And he wrote a work on logic for the sultan in the days when he [the sultan!] was *studying the rational sciences*.'

atmosphere was darkened ' between him and Ibn Khaldûn.[1] Ibn Khaldûn was virtually forced to leave Granada. The cause of Ibn al-Khaṭîb's hostile reaction to Ibn Khaldûn's intentions was not blind ignorance or rigid conservatism, but practical political wisdom. He was now in his early fifties, while Ibn Khaldûn was still young and in his early thirties. He had lived all his life in Muslim Spain, and knew the conditions of the country and the character of his ruler much more intimately than Ibn Khaldûn. He had the advantage of having learned the practical art of politics under Riḍwân, a wise and able statesman and general. Finally, he had studied philosophy and was well acquainted with the ' purpose ' of Ibn Khaldûn's educational programme for his ruler.[2] He respected Ibn Khaldûn's learning,[3] but he thought that his intentions were unwise and dangerous to the peace of the state which it was his duty to preserve.[4] He did not believe that Muḥammad V had the necessary qualifications for understanding, controlling, and using the knowledge Ibn Khaldûn was imparting to him.[5] Ibn Khaldûn was a dangerous man, and he had to leave Granada. But he will leave invested with an official proclamation (*marsûm*) citing the great services he had rendered to the ruler, the grief of the ruler for his ' voluntary ' departure, and the welcome that would await him if he ever decided to come back.[6] Once Ibn Khaldûn was at a safe distance in North Africa, Ibn al-Khaṭîb started a long and exceedingly friendly correspondence with him, inquiring anxiously about his future plans, informing him of the political and literary events in Muslim Spain, and describing his latest works on history, literature, and mysticism.[7]

As for Ibn Khaldûn himself, he tried to forget the episode as soon as he left Muslim Spain. The subsequent career of Muḥammad V proved that Ibn al-Khaṭîb's fears were completely justified. The prospective ' philosopher-king ' turned out to be what Ibn al-Khaṭîb had suspected: a cruel tyrant.[8] Ibn al-Khaṭîb

[1] *T* 91, 97.
[2] *B* II 491 ff., 497.
[3] Cf., e.g., *Q* III 348–49, *T* 109: 3; Maqqarî *Nafḥ* IV 6–7.
[4] Cf. Ibn al-Khaṭîb *Lamḥa* 101, 107, 110; *T* 117–19, 123–24
[5] Cf., e.g., his letter to Muḥammad V in *T* 150–51.
[6] *T* 91–93.
[7] *T* 103 ff.
[8] Maqqarî *Nafḥ* IV 286–87, 289.

had to flee to North Africa and Muḥammad V did not rest until he was imprisoned, publicly condemned for holding unorthodox philosophic and mystical views, and finally brutally murdered. Ibn Khaldûn, who did not cease praising Ibn al-Khaṭîb, and spoke and wrote about him with affection,[1] tried in vain to save his life when he was imprisoned in North Africa. By the time he wrote his *Autobiography*, it is apparent that he considered his attempt to convert Muḥammad V a complete failure in judgment. Although Muḥammad V continued to praise Ibn Khaldûn's learning and intentions, Ibn Khaldûn himself tried his best to suppress all explicit information relating to this episode in his life.[2]

3. In August 1364/Ramaḍân 765, Ibn Khaldûn's friend, the Ḥafṣid prince Abû 'Abd Allâh, realized his long-cherished hope of gaining control of Bijâya. He had already promised Ibn Khaldûn in Fez the important office of prime minister or chamberlain (*ḥâjib*),[3] and as soon as he was in power, he sent for him and offered him the post. At that time, Ibn Khaldûn was still hoping that his designs for the ruler of Granada would materialize, but nine months later, when Ibn al-Khaṭîb made it clear that he was not going to tolerate his activities, he left for Bijâya where he was received with pomp and ceremony, and

[1] Maqqarî *Nafḥ* IV 17, 195–201; *Q* III 320–21, 399, 409, *T* 140–41, 155.

[2] Ibn Khaldûn's treatment of this episode is consistently and intentionally vague. All details bearing on it are omitted from the letters between him, Ibn al-Khaṭîb, and Ibn Zamrak. In *T* 140, he pretends to have 'forgotten' Ibn al-Khaṭîb's letter dealing with Ibn Khaldûn's life in Spain (cf. Ibn Khaldûn's answer in *T*, esp. 142). In *T* 274, he omits passages from Ibn Zamarak's letter with the remark that 'they dealt with questions that need not be mentioned here'. Ibn Khaldûn's friendship with Ibn Zamrak, which continued after Ibn Khaldûn's journey to Egypt (cf. *T* 226–27, 262–74), is another piece of circumstantial evidence for the interpretation of the character of Ibn Khaldûn's activity in Spain. It is well known that it was Ibn Zamrak who was responsible for Ibn al-Khaṭîb's death (cf. Ibn al-Khaṭîb's son's marginal note on the copy of his father's *Iḥâṭa* which was in Cairo: 'He was the cause of my father's murder.' [Maqqarî *Nafḥ* IV 285, cf. 274 ff., 286, 290–91]). Finally, there are the remarks of Muḥammad V concerning Ibn Khaldûn's 'purposes', 'loyalty', and 'beliefs', that need explanation (*T* 277). Had it not been for the fact that most of our information about the contemporary history of Muslim Spain comes from Ibn Khaldûn and Ibn al-Khaṭîb, we might have been in a better position to arrive at fuller and more reliable knowledge of the relation between Ibn Khaldûn, Ibn al-Khaṭîb, Muḥammad V, and Ibn Zamrak.

[3] *T* 97. For the function of this office under the Ḥafṣids, cf. *Q* II 12–13; Brunschvig *op. cit.* II 54 ff. The functions of the chamberlain in the West usually included being the representative of the ruler, chief of his vizirs, and his war and finance minister. Cf. *EI* II 206*b*–7*a*.

immediately put in charge of the city's affairs, thus beginning his third venture in practical politics.[1]

Abû 'Abd Allâh lacked most of the virtues of an efficient ruler, especially those most needed in the confused political life of North Africa at the time. As a young man he had been rash and given to his pleasures. When he finally regained Bijâya, he lost the allegiance of its inhabitants by his severity and insolence. They soon started to look in all directions for help against him, and actually invited both his cousin Abû al-'Abbâs, the ruler of the neighbouring city of Constantine, and the Ziyânid Abû Ḥammû, the ruler of Tlemcen, to their rescue, promising to help them with an internal revolution. Instead of joining hands with his older and more able cousin Abû al-'Abbâs against the Ziyânids of Tlemcen, Abû 'Abd Allâh bought the neutrality of the latter with shameful territorial concessions and revived old feuds with his cousin, wasting his energies on fruitless wars against him.[2] Ibn Khaldûn tried in vain to consolidate Abû 'Abd Allâh's rule in the neighbourhood of Bijâya, and collected the money needed for these wars. But the dissension among the inhabitants of the city and the political impotence of its ruler soon led to the latter's ruin. He was defeated by his cousin and lost his life in battle. Abû al-'Abbâs entered Bijâya (1366/767) little more than a year after Ibn Khaldûn had assumed his office. He sought Ibn Khaldûn's help in consolidating his control of the city, and Ibn Khaldûn served him willingly; but when his enemies started warning the conqueror against him, he left Bijâya where all his hopes for fruitful political action were buried forever.[3]

Ibn Khaldûn's experience in Bijâya was as important for his future political and scientific career as his failure in Granada. In the absence of a reformed ruler, there was still the second-best possibility which he had not yet really tried: to be an adviser to a tyrant and create an efficient state based on moderation.[4] In Bijâya he tried that possibility, and the sad outcome of his

[1] Abû 'Abd Allâh came to power in Ramaḍân 765 A.H., and Ibn Khaldûn left for Bijâya in the middle of 766 A.H.

[2] *T* 98–99, 100, *B* I 584–85, 586.

[3] *T* 99–100, *B* I 585.

[4] For an example of the successful philosopher-adviser and tyrant relationship, cf. the account of Aristotle's relation to Alexander the Great in pseudo-Aristotle *Siyâsa* fols. 1v–2v.

efforts proved to him that the knowledge and judgment of a single man, who did not have an absolute control of power, were not sufficient for the realization of his hopes. Deep in the character of the tyrant, and in the character and history of the people he ruled, there were forces which he had not understood and was unable to control. His failure in Bijâya, in a sense, reinforced his belief in the assumption underlying his attempt to educate the ruler of Granada: the ruler is the soul of the community and a wise man must be in complete control in the state. But it taught him something more. It brought to the surface the inadequacy of his own understanding of the concrete social forces in the community which he had been trying to reform. He began to suspect that, behind the ever-changing political scene, there might be an inner necessity, and that the rise and decline of states might not be the product of deliberate human action or contingent upon human knowledge or ignorance.[1] He began to reflect upon the ambitions and hopes that had led to his successive failures. Were they 'blind' desires leading him to self-destruction? Were they an 'incurable disease'?

> *Is it of use, while my fortune [is leading me] down,*
> *To keep climbing after hopes?*[2]

Writing to Ibn al-Khaṭîb, he told him of all this and more. He spoke of his uncertainty and bewilderment, of his regret that he did not content himself with the restful life he could have enjoyed in Spain had he not followed his uncontrollable passions, and of 'the perplexity that is about to take away the soul'.[3] 'And may in your useful admonition,' he concluded, 'be the cure of this incurable disease, if God wills. . . . For God [alone] is the saviour from the bondage of hopes and the guide to casting off these beguiling fortunes.'[4] These searching reflections led him to seek the knowledge he lacked. The outcome was a new attitude to political action and to the role of knowledge in society.

4. After he left Bijâya, Ibn Khaldûn refused the office of

[1] Cf. Ibn Khaldûn's letter to Ibn al-Khaṭîb (*T* 126) and Ibn al-Khaṭîb's letter to Muḥammad V (*T* 148: 2–5).

[2] *T* 125: 3.

[3] *T* 124.

[4] *T* 125: 4 and 14–15.

chamberlain offered to him by the Ziyânid Abû Ḥammû.[1] Whenever circumstances forced him to engage in political activity, he performed what he was asked to do with complete lack of personal interest and with indifference to the outcome. The following decade was mostly dedicated to research and teaching in Baskara, in the shrine of the mystic Abû Madyan, and in Fez.[2] His most important political activity during this period was in connection with the services he rendered Abû Ḥammû, and later his rival, the Marînid ruler 'Abd al-'Azîz: He obtained for them the allegiance and help of the Hilâli tribes of Banû Riyâḥ, especially the tribe of Banû Dâwûd.[3] These services did not save him from their anger; and he had to leave Baskara, where he had planned to settle, because his activities brought him the envy of its governor, his friend Aḥmad Ibn Maznâ, who was in charge of controlling the tribes Ibn Khaldûn was dealing with.[4] He tried unsuccessfully to keep away from the political confusion that reigned in North Africa. But he continuously received requests for help from the warring rivals who ruled the region, and was frequently involved in their wars and rivalries.[5] Only Granada offered some hope for rest and seclusion. Ibn Khaldûn finally succeeded in crossing over once more to Muslim Spain in the spring of 1375/776, not with the ambitious designs of his youth, but as a tired and embittered man with no purpose save escaping the turmoil of North Africa.[6] The kingdom of Granada had, however, changed since his first visit. Its ruler was no longer the receptive and single-minded man he used to be. He had become a cruel monster, opportunistic and vacillating in his policy. He had turned against Ibn al-Khaṭîb and, when the latter escaped to the Marînid court, he did not cease plotting against the Marînids until Ibn al-Khaṭîb was murdered and his

[1] *T* 102–3.

[2] *T* 103, 134, 135, 139, 226, 227. For the life of Abû Madyan, cf. Maqqarî *Nafḥ* IV 269 ff. From the contemporary accounts, it seems that life was quite difficult for scholars under the Marînids. Ibn al-Khaṭîb (*Iḥâṭa* I 71–72) relates that a certain Ibn al-Qabqâb, whom he had met and admired in Fez, had to withdraw from public life ' like many other learned men '.

[3] *T* 103, 130, 131–34, 135–39, 154–55, 216–18, *B* II 139, 179, 195–96, 201, 204, 487–88. For the importance of the political role of these tribes and of Ibn Khaldûn's relation with them, cf. the detailed accounts in *B* I, II; Marçais *Les Arabes* 309–10, 312, 337–38, 351, 362, 411–20, 429, 481–82, 504–7.

[4] *T* 135, 216.

[5] *T* 100, 103, 131, 133–34, 137, 217–18, 225.

[6] *T* 133–34, 225–26.

property destroyed.[1] When he heard that Ibn Khaldûn had tried to save Ibn al-Khaṭîb, he expelled him from Granada.[2]

Back in North Africa, Ibn Khaldûn was now so determined to avoid any form of political activity that when Abû Ḥammû asked him again to go to the tribe of Banû Dâwûd to win them over to his side, he left him intent on desertion. When he reached the territory of Awlâd 'Ârif, he arranged for excuses to be sent to Abû Ḥammû and, joined by his family, he settled in a secluded pavilion in the castle of Ibu Salâma. There he spent four years completely oblivious to the outside world. He was now in his early forties. The previous twenty years had been spent in active participation in the political affairs of western Islam, and in study and the search for answers to the problems arising from his political activity. He had personally experienced many of the important contemporary events of the region, and he had had access to official documents relating to them. His official duties had brought him in contact with many important persons: ambassadors, officials, rulers, tribal chiefs, and scholars, from whom he had acquired information concerning events in which they had taken part and about others which they had known by virtue of their official or social positions. He had been trying to retire to think about the problems which the contemporary history of western Islam had posed for him. In the castle of Ibn Salâma this opportunity presented itself.

5. His early training in the philosophic sciences had taught him that the understanding of a subject requires an investigation that progresses from the external data, transmitted from the past or acquired through personal experience, to the explanatory and demonstrable knowledge of their cause (*sabab*, *aitía*) and nature (*ṭabî'a*, *physis*). This means that there is behind the external (*ẓâhir*) data an internal (*bâṭin*) rational structure which, if understood, could explain the whys and the wherefores, and render the external data intelligible.[3] Therefore, if history is to be truly understood, it must be subjected to the same enquiry as any

[1] *B* II 491–97, 504–5.

[2] *T* 227.

[3] *Q* I 2. Ibn Khaldûn's student, Maqrîzî (*Khiṭaṭ* I 8–9) says that history should be studied *after* the mastery of the *traditional and rational* sciences. Cf. below pp. 147–48, 153–57. For the distinction between *ẓâhir* and *bâṭin*, cf. *T* 192: 1–2, *Q* I 347–48, 355–56, II 166; pseudo-Aristotle *Siyâsa* fol. 4v.

other rational field of knowledge. The external data pertaining to it should be collected and classified; and then their causes and nature ascertained.

Ibn Khaldûn first considered writing a work on the history of contemporary western Islam, and started, perhaps shortly after his arrival at the castle of Ibn Salâma, to write a general ' introduction ' (*muqaddima*) to such a regional history in which he presented the considerations concerning the external and internal aspects of history just mentioned. During that time, he seems to have had no intention of writing a universal history or studying the internal aspect of history as a special discipline.[1] But while writing this Introduction, new problems came to the fore, making the early plan of the regional history unfeasible. He found that the two aspects of history are intimately related: To understand the causes and nature of historical events, one must start from correct information; but in order to be able to rectify information about events and distinguish the correct from the false, one must know their nature and causes. In order to write an accurate history of contemporary western Islam, it was, therefore, necessary for Ibn Khaldûn to know the internal aspect of history. He studied previous Muslim historians and found that they did not possess such knowledge, but had for the most part merely transmitted information reaching them from their informants.[2] He then asked the question as to whether the nature and causes of historical events had been treated in any discipline other than historiography. He surveyed the disciplines where he thought such problems might have been considered, especially politics, rhetoric, and the fundamentals of the religious Law. He found that they had all treated this problem in an accidental fashion.[3]

As a result, he felt that it was imperative that he himself create a new science to deal specifically with this problem, and to define its principles, method, subject matter, and end. The new

[1] ' History,' wrote Ibn Khaldûn in this Introduction, ' is an account of *an* epoch or *a* generation of men.' He added that the new conditions in western Islam presented him a new spectacle, ' as if it is a new creation and a second beginning '. These new conditions had not been recorded by a major historian. Ibn Khaldûn planned to fill this gap and indicated this intention specifically: ' I am telling in this book of mine all I can about this western region . . . because it is my special purpose to write about the West . . . to the exclusion of other regions, since I am not [personally] acquainted with the . . . East.' *Q* I 51–52.

[2] Cf. below pp. 155–59, 166–69.

[3] Cf. below pp. 156–59.

science had to precede the factual history of contemporary western Islam because it is only after mastering it that he could understand, and write a correct account of, that history. The reader, too, had to know this science if he were to grasp the significance and check the veracity of the history Ibn Khaldûn was planning to write.

The 'early draft' of the Introduction was, therefore, abandoned for the time being. Ibn Khaldûn spent the following two years[1] thinking about the problems of the new science which he later called the 'science of culture'. It was probably during this period that he decided that the limited scope of his planned history was inadequate. In order to be comprehensive, the new science had to be based on data furnished by the history of the world as a whole from its intelligible beginning to his own time, and not merely on the data furnished by the contemporary history of western Islam.[2] For that reason, the plan of the work expanded to include the new science, followed by a universal history. The early draft of the Introduction, with little or no change, was simply prefixed to the new plan to serve as a general introduction to the whole work.[3] In its final form, the work was divided into a Preface, an Introduction, and three Books: the Introduction dealt with the problem of history in general; Book One contained the new science; Book Two, a universal history down to his own time; and Book Three, the originally planned history of western Islam.[4]

6. The first draft of Book One was written from memory and completed in November 1377/mid 779.[5] Ibn Khaldûn was now ready to leave the castle of Ibn Salâma for an urban centre where he could find the necessary books and archives (*dawâwîn*) for

[1] Book One, which contained the new science, was written during the five months ending in November 1377/mid 779, cf. below n. 5.

[2] Ibn Khaldûn frequently seeks to base his theories in Book One upon both Muslim and non-Muslim history, cf., e.g., *Q* I 415, 417, 422. While writing Book One, he seems also to have had the new plan of the history clearly in mind. Cf. his cross-references to Books Two and Three, e.g., *Q* I 361.

[3] It is only through such an explanation of the sequence of Ibn Khaldûn's thought, and the development of the plan of the 'History', that the glaring contradiction between Ibn Khaldûn's explicit statement about his intention to write a regional history of western Islam alone and the more comprehensive plan of the work as contained in the table of contents inserted by Ibn Khaldûn himself in the Preface (*Q* I 6) can be reconciled.

[4] *Q* I 6.

[5] *Q* III 434, cf. *T* 229, 230.

correcting and completing what he had written, and for writing the historical part that was to follow. But he was attacked by a severe illness that lasted for almost a year, after which he left for Tunis whose ruler, Abû al-'Abbâs, had granted him amnesty and invited him back to the city of his birth.

The new Ḥafṣid ruler of Tunis had been gaining power since he had conquered Bijâya in 1366/767 and consolidated his rule in the western part of his kingdom. In 1369/770, his rival Abû Isḥâq, who then ruled Tunis, died; and by conquering the capital, Abû al-'Abbâs became the sole ruler of the Ḥafṣid kingdom.[1] Besides his wide experience in the political life of North Africa, the new ruler of Tunis, now at the mature age of forty-three, had developed a deep understanding of the complex political situation in which he was involved. He restored the power and prestige of a kingdom weakened by strife within the ruling family, and wars against the ambitious Marînids and the Arab tribes of the interior. When Ibn Khaldûn met him in 1379/780, he was on his way to reaffirm his rule in the southern and south-western parts of his kingdom.[2] By then, Ibn Khaldûn had completely changed his attitude toward politics, and did not wish to be involved in any form of political activity whatsoever.

In Tunis, after an absence of three decades, Ibn Khaldûn was intent on carrying out his plans for completing the work he had conceived, and a part of which he had written, during his retreat.[3] Abû al-'Abbâs offered him his patronage and showed a keen interest in the work—aware of the political and military uses to which he could put Ibn Khaldûn's vast knowledge of the history of contemporary North Africa.[4] His patronage, however, was not without its disadvantages. Ibn Khaldûn became the envy of other courtiers and especially of his rival Ibn 'Arafa (d. 1400/803),[5] many of whose students deserted him to join Ibn Khaldûn.[6] They finally succeeded in arousing Abû al-'Abbâs'

[1] *B* I 588–89, 590–92.

[2] *T* 231–32; Brunschvig *op. cit.* I 185 ff.

[3] His ideas about history and the work he was writing influenced even his poetry in that period. Cf. *T* 239–41.

[4] *T* 232–33.

[5] *GAL* II 247.

[6] If we are to believe Ibn Khaldûn's account, the reason for this animosity was Ibn 'Arafa's jealousy, which dated back to his student days, of Ibn Khaldûn's superior intelligence, in spite of his being sixteen years younger than Ibn 'Arafa. Cf. *T* 232, 233, 244.

suspicions against Ibn Khaldûn. He was represented to him as a dangerous man whose intrigues should be feared. They suggested that Abû al-'Abbâs should not leave Ibn Khaldûn alone in Tunis when he went away on his military expeditions. The fate of Ibn al-Khaṭîb and of Ibn Khaldûn's older brother, Yaḥyâ (murdered in Tlemcen in January 1379/Ramaḍân 780)[1], loomed before Ibn Khaldûn's eyes. When Abû al-'Abbâs requested that Ibn Khaldûn accompany him on his expeditions, the latter, knowing of a ship that was about to sail for Alexandria, implored the ruler to allow him to leave for a pilgrimage to Mecca. When Abû al-'Abbâs granted him permission, he hurriedly left Tunis intent on settling in Egypt to resume his studies and scholarly work.[2]

During the four years he spent in Tunis, Ibn Khaldûn rewrote and completed the first version of Book One of his 'History'; wrote a complete version of Book Three, which dealt with the contemporary history of western Islam, the sources for which were available in Tunis; and an incomplete version of Book Two, which dealt mostly with the East.[3] He had unsuccessfully tried to avoid political activity. When he found himself forced away from what he now considered his main work, he left Tunis for Egypt. Behind him, he left the dark and confused West, and his own vain efforts and ruined hopes. To the restful light of the East he looked for the tranquillity and quiescence in which he hoped to spend the rest of his life.

[1] *GAL* II 241. (The correct date is given in *GAL*(*S*) II 340. It is not 1387/788 as in *GAL*(*S*²) II 312.) Cf. *B* II 208.

[2] *T* 232–33, 244–45.

[3] William MacGuckin baron de Slane's assertion that Ibn Khaldûn wrote the Introduction and Book One 'after he had completed the history of the West and of the Berbers' (*Les Prolégomènes d'Ibn Khaldoun* [Paris 1934–38] I 67 n. 1) has no evidence to support it and runs contrary to the explicit statement of Ibn Khaldûn who says (*T* 230) that he started the work during his retirement and 'completed Book One up to the history of the Arabs, Berbers, and Zanâta'. Ibn Khaldûn's statement is also borne out by references in the history of the Berbers to the general argument of, and to specific passages in, Book One. Cf., e.g., *B* II 5. Toward the end of his stay in Tunis, Ibn Khaldûn prepared a copy of the complete work which he presented to Abû al-'Abbâs for his royal library (*T* 233). This seems to be the earliest or 'mother' version of the 'History'.

IV

Ibn Khaldûn in Egypt

1. After a sea journey of about forty days, Ibn Khaldûn landed in Alexandria on December 8, 1382/Shawwâl 1, 784. He was unable to proceed with his plans for pilgrimage, and a month later he went to Cairo. The big metropolis dazzled him. The crowded streets, the towering mosques and palaces, the numerous schools and hostels, the marketplaces abundant with goods, and the Nile, all brought back to his memory the fabulous accounts of the ambassadors, travellers, merchants, and pilgrims, he had met in the West.[1] Here was the archtype of a mature civilization: its roots went deep into the past, its social manners were extremely sophisticated, and its economic prosperity made North Africa look semi-barbarous.[2] However, Ibn Khaldûn soon found that moral corruption was rife along with the blessings of the civilized life of Egypt.[3]

Ibn Khaldûn's fame had preceded him to Cairo. As soon as he arrived, he was asked to teach in the famous University of Azhar; and a little later he was introduced to Barqûq (reigned 1382/784–1399/801), whose recent assumption of power had brought to Egypt an able ruler and to Ibn Khaldûn a steadfast patron. In Egypt, Ibn Khaldûn could finally realize his long-hoped-for dream of a leisurely life devoted to study and teaching. It is true that he was six times burdened with the difficult office of the Mâlikite Grand Judge, that he remained active in the court, and that at least in one case he was involved in a perplexing political incident and in another had to meet and accommodate the passions and curiosity of Tamerlane in Damascus. But all this did not consume more than a few years of the quarter of the century he spent in Egypt.[4]

Ibn Khaldûn's career as a scholar in Egypt is extremely important for his theories of history. It is true that the basic

[1] *T* 246–48.
[2] *T* 251–56, 281–84, *Q* II 338–39, 376 ff., 383.
[3] *T* 255–56, *passim*. Cf. *Q* II 256–61.
[4] Ibn Khaldûn spent nearly two decades out of office absorbed in his scholarly pursuit.

ideas of the 'History' were conceived during his retreat in the castle of Ibn Salâma a few years before his arrival in Egypt. But before the final version of the work could be completed, an enormous amount of research had to be done. The four years he had spent in Tunis were not sufficient for that task. The opportunity of being in the East was utilized to consult books not available to him in North Africa, and to travel and observe the topography of the land, meet learned men, and revise and complete the portion of the 'History', especially Book Two, which dealt with the East. Furthermore, the observation and understanding of the civilization of Egypt, its urban life, and its economic prosperity, provided him with an intimate knowledge of the cultural type represented by Egypt which he could not have acquired from mere hearsay. Finally, Ibn Khaldûn's activity in Egypt expresses his new attitude to political life and his own role in society, which is of the utmost importance for understanding the social ideas embodied in the 'History'.

Writing and teaching went hand in hand in Ibn Khaldûn's scholarly career. The prosperity of Egypt had made teaching a lucrative trade, especially when a scholar held a chair in one of the many schools which enjoyed revenue from agricultural lands and real estate donated to them by the wealthy Mamlûks who sought to preserve a good name and sometimes to provide for their descendents.[1] Ibn Khaldûn held a number of such positions and his income from them must have been considerable.[2] What he taught his students is not always clear. Officially he was charged with teaching the religious sciences, but some of his students report that they also studied Book One, or the theoretical part, of the 'History' with him.[3]

2. As a Mâlikite Grand Judge, Ibn Khaldûn came in close personal contact with the legal and administrative institutions of Egypt, and the relatively widespread moral laxity and corrupt practices among the Egyptians. His original idea that civilization

[1] *Q* II 384; Maqrîzî *Khiṭaṭ* II 295 ff.; Heffening '*Waḳf*' *EI* IV 1096 ff.

[2] *T* 253; Ibn al-Furât *Ta'rîkh* IX 436: 3–8.

[3] Sakhâwî *Ḍaw'* IV 148: 11, VIII 233: 5; cf. F. Rosenthal *op. cit.* 52; W. J. Fischel 'Ibn Khaldûn's Activities in Mamlûk Egypt (1382–1406)' *Semitic and Oriental Studies* ['University of California Publications in Semitic Philology' XI] (Berkeley 1951) 109–10. The general historical sketches in the inaugural lectures (*T* 280–85, 286–93) do not, however, bear any relation to, or imply the actual contents of, the courses taught by Ibn Khaldûn.

and economic prosperity create the germs of social dissolution was thus reinforced. Ibn Khaldûn had no great experience as a Judge in North Africa. Knowing the conditions prevailing in Egypt, he was aware of the difficulties he would meet in discharging his duties, the constant temptations the office would present to him, and the enemies it would inevitably create for him. He tried at first to refuse the office.[1] But Barqûq's insistence left him no choice in the matter. Fortunately, the ruler's constant support helped him in discharging his duties as he deemed proper. He acted with the severity, puritanism, and—one might add—rudeness of a North African who had not undergone the 'civilizing' influences of the Egyptian cultural climate. He tried to apply the Law strictly and impartially.[2] Under the settled social conditions of Egypt, and a capable ruler like Barqûq,[3] Ibn Khaldûn recognized that what had to be combated was, above all, excess and moral corruption.

Ibn Khaldûn's political failures in North Africa and Spain, and his contact with the new cultural conditions in Egypt, had resulted in a decisive change in his attitude toward political action. He had abandoned the attempt of reforming society through personal exercise of power or instructing a prince to become a wise ruler. The understanding of the nature and causes of social events, achieved in his retreat, pointed to a new conception of the role of the learned in social affairs. This attitude was crystallized in Egypt, taking the form of a return to the more philosophically and religiously orthodox view of the duality in the leadership of society: that of the political ruler, on the one hand, and the learned (*'ulamâ'*), and particularly the learned who are in a position to apply the Law (i.e., the Judges), on the other.[4] It emphasized the necessity of close co-operation between the two under the aegis of the Law:[5] the ruler should provide the necessary political stability, protect his subjects, and encourage the learned. The learned should understand, interpret, and apply the Law; and thus save the community from the

[1] *T* 254, 285, 311.
[2] *T* 244 ff., 311, 347, 383. Cf. H. A. R. Gibb 'The Islamic Background of Ibn Khaldûn's Political Theory' *BSOS* VII (1933–35) 27, 31.
[3] *Bq* V 473, 477.
[4] *T* 281, 282. Cf. *Q* II 94–95, 135–36.
[5] *T* 288 ff.; Ikhwân al-Ṣafâ' *Rasâ'il* I 252, 254, IV 33.

internal weakness and moral dissolution that would result if animal passions should reign unchecked.

The office of a Judge was, therefore, of the utmost importance for fighting these evils and protecting the community. The Law is the saviour of the community from degeneration. This was the function of the Law as Ibn Khaldûn understood it, and this function opposed the ' convention ' (*muṣṭalaḥ*) of Egypt which he rejected and fought with a strong and determined faith.[1] This did not please the Egyptians,[2] who argued that he was ignorant of their convention. But in studying the charges and countercharges exchanged between Ibn Khaldûn and Egyptian writers concerning his career as a Judge, we should not let personal rivalries and differences of opinion concerning individual incidents obscure the basic issue. The Law, as Ibn Khaldûn conceived it in Egypt, is not the product of social convention, but rather the judge of the community.[3] This substitution of the Law for the wise ruler is the most important landmark in Ibn Khaldûn's life experience; and the relationship among the wise man, the Law, and the community, is the most important problem in his social thought.[4]

3. In his conception of the nature and function of the Law, Ibn Khaldûn remained a stranger in Egypt. His life would have been immeasurably more difficult had it not been for the understanding and appreciation of his protector Barqûq, to whom he remained devoted and grateful until the latter's death in 1399/801. Ibn Khaldûn had frequented his court since his arrival in Cairo, and was always ready to serve him with his knowledge and advice.[5] Barqûq was quick to recognize Ibn

[1] Cf. the relationship between the functions of the ruler, the Law, and the learned, as expounded in *Q* I 233, 260–62, 341. ' Moderation ' and ' justice ' rather than attempting to force men to realize what is beyond their normal powers is now conceived as the ' natural ' order of things. Cf. *Q* I 341, 349–51.

[2] Ibn Khaldûn's political career in North Africa led the Egyptians to suspect his knowledge of the Law and his integrity. A man that had spent most of his adult life in active political struggle, they reasoned, could not have had the time to study and understand the Law. Cf. Rakrâkî's statement in Sakhâwî (*Ḍaw'* IV 147) and the disparaging remarks of Ibn 'Arafa (*ibid.* IV 146). Some modern traditionists continue to consider Ibn Khaldûn an inferior scholar because of his past political activities. Cf. Aḥmad Muḥammad Shâkir's note on the margin of his edition of Ibn Ḥanbal *Musnad* V 197.

[3] Cf., e.g., *Q* I 64: 2.

[4] Cf. below pp. 73 ff.

[5] *T* 249 ff.

Khaldûn's worth: a statesman and scholar of Ibn Khaldûn's calibre, well acquainted with the inner dynamics of political events in the West, with its rulers, and with its geography, was a great asset.[1] A little more than a year after Ibn Khaldûn's arrival, Barqûq started corresponding with Abû al-'Abbâs, the ruler of Tunis, asking him to send over Ibn Khaldûn's family which Abû al-'Abbâs had kept to insure Ibn Khaldûn's return. The request was complied with, but the vessel that brought Ibn Khaldûn's family and all his worldly belongings was shipwrecked near Alexandria. Grief-stricken, Ibn Khaldûn took the occasion to ask Barqûq to accept his resignation from the post of the Mâlikite Grand Judge, and prepared for pilgrimage to Mecca.[2] There he met students and scholars from the West and from Persia, acquainted himself with the new intellectual movements of these areas (especially in philosophy and Law), studied the topography of the region, and consulted new materials concerning the history of the East. Back in Cairo, he continued to receive news and letters from the West through his compatriots who passed through the city and visited him. He regularly briefed Barqûq about conditions in the West, and sometimes introduced some of the western scholars and political leaders to him.[3] Barqûq was especially interested in the strong horses of the West; and he sent frequent requests for them to North African rulers and awaited their safe arrival with anxiety.[4] In all these exchanges, Ibn Khaldûn enjoyed the honour of being the intermediary, and was happy to render his services to Barqûq.[5]

In 1389/791, a revolt against Barqûq, led by a member of a rival Mamlûk dynasty who was the governor of Aleppo, succeeded in deposing him and disturbing the tranquillity of Egypt for

[1] *T* 251–52. For the political relations between North Africa and Egypt cf. *Bq* V 420–21, 440–41, 479–80, 501, *B* I 506, 528, 561, 659, II 33 ff., 373–74, 392, 540–41, *T* 271–72, 277, 335 ff.

[2] *T* 249–53, 259–60, 285; Ibn al-Furât *Ta'rîkh* IX 16, 31.

[3] *T* 262, 263–67. Ibn Khaldûn's own letters to the West, except for the letter in which he tells of his encounter with Tamerlane (*T* 380–83), are not recorded in *T*; but it is clear that he wrote numerous letters to his compatriots, cf. *T* 270, 276, 339. Ibn Khaldûn was also a source of information about current events in the West for contemporary Egyptian historians. Cf., e.g., Ibn al-Furât *Ta'rîkh* IX 365.

[4] *T* 339, *Bq* V 420, 440–41.

[5] *T* 346.

about a year.[1] When Barqûq regained his throne, he was angry with Ibn Khaldûn for signing, under duress, a legal opinion condemning him. This event disheartened Ibn Khaldûn as none of the important events of his past life had done. In the poem he presented Barqûq explaining his position, the doleful meter and tone aroused the ruler's pity for the stranger whom he had befriended, the guest he had welcomed, and the lonely man he had protected.[2] Barqûq's anger did not last for long, and Ibn Khaldûn was soon back in his privileged position in the court. Before his death in 1399/801, Barqûq asked Ibn Khaldûn to hold the office of the Mâlikite Grand Judge again.

After the death of Barqûq and the ascension of his son Faraj, internal dissensions and a new wave of Mongol invasions kept Egypt in commotion.[3] In 1400/802, Ibn Khaldûn took the opportunity of the ruler's expedition to put down a revolt in Syria to visit Damascus and Jerusalem, where he combined his travels with his scholarly interest, meeting informants and studying in the libraries of Syria.[4] A second opportunity to visit Syria came a year later when the Egyptian ruler left to repel the Mongol invader Tamerlane. Ibn Khaldûn was reluctant to accept the offer to accompany the ruler,[5] and it is not hard to surmise his reasons: Faraj was young and inexperienced, the ruling Mamlûks were suspicious of each other, and desertion and treachery among their ranks was very probable. Finally, the fear of Tamerlane's power and cruelty was more than justified by his past record.[6]

4. Ibn Khaldûn's premonitions were soon realized, and he was left besieged by Tamerlane in Damascus while Faraj, hearing rumours of an uprising at home, deserted his army and fled, after which the rest of the army followed him in small groups to Egypt.

Tamerlane had heard, probably through his numerous spies in the city, that Ibn Khaldûn was with Faraj's army, and he

[1] *T* 326–30.
[2] *T* 331–35. Cf. Ibn al-Furât *Ta'rîkh* IX 160.
[3] Ibn Taghrîbirdî *Nujûm* VI 41–49.
[4] *Bq* V 436, 444, *T* 439–50.
[5] *T* 366.
[6] Ibn Taghrîbirdî *Nujûm* VI 45–46, 47, 49, 50, 51 ff., 57, 59; *T* 351 ff. Ibn Taghrîbirdî describes the Egyptians as 'an army without a general and a general without an army'.

enquired about him from the delegation that came to negotiate the surrender of Damascus. Ibn Khaldûn was among those who favoured the surrender. He was afraid of some rash action by those who opposed his stand and asked to be allowed to leave the city. He was lowered down from the walls and reached Tamerlane's tent where he was presented to the invader.[1] Ibn Khaldûn stayed in Tamerlane's camp for thirty-five days, and the conversation between the great conqueror and the great scholar remains one of the most interesting interviews recorded in history.[2] Tamerlane was extremely interested in meeting an important personality from the western parts of the Islamic world, and there was a great deal of information he wanted to know about these regions. His questions and arguments were sharp, direct, and penetrating.[3] Ibn Khaldûn, on his part, drew upon the experience of his long career to meet the challenge. He had had many encounters in which he had had to pretend, deceive, and mislead rulers, but had never discussed so many things in such a short time and with such a sharp-witted man, and never had he succeeded with such mastery, never had he shown greater wit. As we observe the way he conducted himself in this conversation, we have the distinct feeling that his past failures in North Africa and Spain had not been in vain. Through them, he had gained the wisdom he was searching for, a wisdom that could stand the testing fire of Tamerlane and emerge triumphant.

As Tamerlane started to question him, Ibn Khaldûn instantly surmised that the conqueror had a single purpose which he followed persistently and with determination: he wanted to find the weaknesses of Egypt and the West, which could be of use if the possibility of conquering them offered itself. Ibn Khaldûn answered in a composed spirit, but pursued *his* objective with equal determination and persistency: to paint a simple, consistent, and convincing picture of these regions, a picture that did not betray even one of their many weaknesses which he probably

[1] *T* 368, 381.

[2] The section of *T* dealing with Ibn Khaldûn's encounter with Tamerlane has been translated with copious and informative notes by W. J. Fischel: *Ibn Khaldûn and Tamerlane* (Berkeley 1952) 29–48. I agree with Professor Fischel (*ibid.* 1–3) in doubting most of the information concerning this encounter reported by Ibn 'Arabshâh (*'Ajâ'ib* 211–14, 439–43) and Ḥajji Khalîfa (*Kashf* II 101 [No. 2085]).

[3] *T* 369 ff., 382.

knew better than any other living person. Ibn Khaldûn was finally asked to write a detailed description of the West in such a manner that when the conqueror read it, it would be as if he were seeing the region. This was done in a few days.[1] We do not, and may never, know what this little book contained. But if our interpretation of the meeting between the two is correct, it did not contain much about the political situation of North Africa, or any other subject that might have encouraged Tamerlane to conquer this region.[2] In the next meeting the same pattern was repeated, except that Ibn Khaldûn, having had time to think about the situation, assumed the offensive which he executed with a mastery comparable to that which he had demonstrated in their first meeting. He praised the conqueror, complimented him on all he said, and told him about the greatness and virtues of his people. He had asked his aides about what pleased the conqueror most, and came back with gifts to him. Then he started to circle slowly around his final purpose: to ask, and succeed in having Tamerlane allow him to leave in peace for Egypt. Finally, he succeeded in freeing himself and many of his Egyptian friends who then accompanied him to Cairo.[3]

During the last seven years of his life in Egypt, Ibn Khaldûn continued to be active as a scholar and a Judge. He wrote the last chapters of his *Autobiography* and made new marginal additions to his 'History'. He was four times reappointed as the Mâlikite Grand Judge, the last reappointment coming about one month before his sudden death on March 17, 1406/Ramaḍân 15, 808.[4]

[1] *T* 270, 274.

[2] This purpose was also behind Ibn Khaldûn's concurrence with Tamerlane's aide, 'Abd al-Jabbâr Ibn al-Nu'mân, on the illegality of the claims of the 'Abbâsid pretender who presented himself to Tamerlane as the legitimate Caliph (*T* 374–75). A Caliph-designate could be a useful asset in the event of Tamerlane's invasion of Egypt.

[3] Ibn Khaldûn did not tell Tamerlane about the loss of his family. That would have led to many embarrassing questions, as to why they were detained in Tunis, etc. He left him with the impression that his family was in Egypt (*T* 277, 279). Ibn 'Arabshâh, who knew Tamerlane's character intimately, uses his meeting with Ibn Khaldûn as a dramatic example of the conqueror's shrewdness in evaluating men. In concentrating on Tamerlane, however, he misses the significance of the meeting so far as Ibn Khaldûn was concerned, and underestimates the possible use of his knowledge of the West for the conqueror (*'Ajâ'ib* 439–43).

[4] Ibn Taghrîbirdî *Nujûm* VI 76.

5. During the quarter of the century that Ibn Khaldûn spent in Egypt, he remained spiritually a complete stranger. Outwardly, he kept his Western attire and his manners were not softened by the civilized life of Egypt. But these were the external expressions of a deeper problem. Egypt had welcomed him, offered him protection, security, and leisure to follow his scholarly interests. It satisfied his curiosity to learn about the cultural pattern it represented. It was his second home, but he never considered himself fully at home in it. It appears that the more he learned about the character of its people, the more he preferred the rugged simplicity of North Africa to the decadence of the civilized ways of Egypt.[1] He was in the paradoxical situation of a guest who was not in full accord with his host, yet was forced to remain his guest. Ibn Khaldûn resigned himself to playing his new role, enjoying its privileges and performing its duties.[2] As a result his conduct became more passive and more subtle than before.

The uncontrollable urge to political activity and adventure, which characterized Ibn Khaldûn's life in the West, was now but a disquieting memory. His early political ventures and his early writings seemed now to have been unwise expressions of immature wisdom. In his old age, his thought went deeper and deeper, but with the courage, steadiness, and balance, of one who had seen his goal and is walking in full daylight. The more he learned about different peoples, the more he was convinced of the unchanging pattern according to which they all live and die. He was no longer haunted by the shadows or tempted by the dark caves on the edges of his pathway.[3] He had searched his soul, conjured out the secrets of the world, and done his deeds.

But despite his aloofness, the mellow and eternity-bound skies of Egypt had penetrated the recesses of his soul. He acquired an inner poise and a spiritual calm. As he reclined in his palace overlooking the Nile, fortune seemed less hostile and the world more friendly. He had reached the stage where he could feel

[1] In a letter to Ibn Khaldûn (*T* 119), Ibn al-Khaṭîb says: 'In spite of its defects, no other [region] is preferable to the West.' Cf. *Q* I 225–26, 228–29, 230 ff.

[2] When in Tamerlane's camp, Ibn Khaldûn told him that now he was estranged twice: '*anâ gharîbun . . . ghurbatayn*.' Cf. *T* 377.

[3] Cf. Avicenna *Ishârât* 205–7: 'The Qualities of the Initiate.'

the harmony permeating the universe, and see and enjoy it in the simple things of life: the wit and wisdom of vernacular poetry, the rhythm and movement of a dancing girl, and the beauty of a smiling face.[1]

The simple and direct expression of thought and emotion of his early youth had disappeared along with the bewilderment and questioning, and the piercing intuition of his middle age.[2] Age had taught him many things, but above all how to protect the deeps of his soul from the inroads of others and keep the purity of his hopes and thought away from the imperfect world of realization and expression. He developed and mastered an enigmatic style that concealed more than it revealed.

[1] Cf. *Q* II 308–9, 352 ff., III 359 ff.; Ibn al-Khaṭîb *Rawḍa* as quoted by Maqqarî *Nafḥ* IV 66 ff.; Sakhâwî *Ḍaw'* IV 146–47.

[2] The changing mood of his poetry shows a similar development. Cf. *T* 70 ff., 77 ff., 85 ff., 233 ff., 331 ff.

CHAPTER II

Philosophy and the Law

I

History and Wisdom

1. As an introduction to the method and purpose of Ibn Khaldûn's 'History',[1] we shall discuss the key word of the relatively long and carefully worded title which was apparently intended to be complete in its description of the contents of the book. Ibn Khaldûn introduces and cites the title in the text as follows: '. . . following the method of condensation and abridgment, avoiding abstruse quests by [following] the clear path, and entering through the door of general causes to particular events. Thus, it [the book] encompasses the events of all human history, facilitates [the understanding of] scattered and unwieldy knowledge, and offers the proximate and distant causes[2] of political events. It has become a depository for wisdom and a receptacle for history. Since it comprises the histories of the Arabs and Berbers, both tent-dwellers and urban, treats with less emphasis the great empires contemporary with them, and explains the reminders and *'ibar* contained in the origins of the modes[3] [of culture] and the events subsequent to them, I called it: "The Book of the *'Ibar*, the Record of the Origins and Events[4] of the Days[5] of the Arabs, Persians and Berbers, and of those of their Contemporaries who were Possessors of Great Power." '[6]

[1] This is a descriptive title by which the work has been known since Ibn Khaldûn's time (cf. Sakhâwî *Ḍaw'* IV 147–49; Qalqashandî *Ṣubḥ* VI 356).

[2] Cf. *Q* II 365: 10. The terms *'illa* and *sabab* are frequently used synonymously to mean 'cause', except that in some cases *sabab* is used in a less precise sense referring to motives and apparent causes. Cf. Avicenna *Najât* 386.

[3] *aḥwâl*. Cf. below p. 172 n. 1.

[4] This seems to be the meaning of the phrase *al-mubtada' wa-l-khabar* in the context (*Q* I 7: 13). More literally, it means 'the subject and the predicate' and is a grammatical expression. Cf. M. Plessner in *OLZ* XXXVI (1933) 109–10.

[5] *ayyâm al-'arab* alludes to the '"battle-days" of the Arabs,' the oldest form of Arabic historical literature.

[6] *Q* I 7: 6–14. The complete title in Arabic reads: *Kitâb al-'ibar wa-dîwân al-mubtada' wa-l-khabar fî ayyâm al-'arab wa-l-'ajam wa-l-barbar wa-man*

The key word in the title of Ibn Khaldûn's work which seems to contain some hints and allusions is not 'history' (*ta'rîkh* or *khabar*),[1] but the word '*ibar*; for the work is first and foremost called 'The Book of the '*Ibar*'. We might pass over this word and leave it unexplored, or we might simply choose a less significant aspect of its meaning and translate it as 'instructive examples'.[2] We would then be mocked by the word itself; for,

'*âṣarahum min dhawî al-sulṭân al-akbar* (*Q* I 7: 13–14). This is the precise title as included in the text itself, a fact that minimizes the possibility of copyists' corruptions to which the title-page could be subjected. The title of a MS in the Ibrâhîm Pâsha library in Constantinople as reported by Schulz ('Note sur le grand ouvrage historique d'Ibn Khaldoun, conservé dans la bibliothèque d'Ibrahim pacha à Constantinople' *JA* II i [1828] 139) and the title inserted in the concluding passage of the Ẓâhirî MS (cf. *T*, facs. opposite p. *yd*) run as follows: *al-'Ibar bi-akhbâr al-'arab wa-l-'ajam wa-l-barbar*. Ibn Khaldûn's title has been subjected to misquotation ever since the fifteenth/ninth century. Sakhâwî reports it as follows: *al-'Ibar fî ta'rîkh al-mulûk wa-l-umam wa-l-barbar* ('The '*Ibar* of the History of the Kings, Nations, and Berbers!') (*I'lân* 151). It is interesting to note that Sakhâwî's corruption of the title of Ibn Khaldûn's work went hand in hand with his utter lack of comprehension of its nature, method, and purpose. What he says about Ibn Khaldûn is little more than gossip collected from his friends and masters who were Ibn Khaldûn's students (*I'lân* 71, 93–95, 151). It can hardly be assumed that he even read the '*Ibar* carefully. When writing his *I'lân* in Mecca, he could not remember what he apparently considered an important passage in the '*Ibar* on the usefulness of history (cf. the blank left for later insertion in *I'lân* 32 [= Leiden and Berlin MSS]). In more recent times, misquotation and mistranslations of the general title as well as the titles of the various parts of the work have been frequent (cf. M. Plessner in *OLZ* XXXVI [1933] 109, 113–14; below pp. 146 n. 1, 148 n. 6). The most reasonable translation of Ibn Khaldûn's original title into a west-European language is that of M. Plessner (*OLZ* XXXVI [1933] 109): 'Das Buch der mahnenden Beispiele ['*ibar*]—und das Archiv des Urzustandes und der (späteren) Ereignisse—über die "Tage" der Araber, Nichtaraber und Berbern—und mit ihnen gleichzeitigen Inhaber grosser Herrschaft.' Cf. G. Levi Della Vida in *Oriente Moderno* XXXIII (1953) 160 n. 2. Our translation differs from that of Plessner on two points: (1) We do not emphasize the strict sense of the 'days', but consider the word a literary allusion to the 'Battle-Days' literature (cf. above p. 63 n. 5) serving as a casual transition to the subject matter of the '*Ibar* which is wider than the 'Battle-Days' literature in the method with which it treats historical events as well as in its scope which covers the history of the Arabs and non-Arabs down to Ibn Khaldûn's time. (2) We translate '*ajam* as 'Persians' rather than 'non-Arabs' because Ibn Khaldûn mentions another non-Arab people (Berbers) and thus does not seem to be using '*ajam* as a collective noun for all non-Arabs.

[1] *Ta'rîkh* evolved from designating simple dating to become the most commonly used word for describing historical works and historical activity. On the origin and uses of *ta'rîkh*, cf. Ibn Durustawayh *Kuttâb* 79–80; Khwârizmî *Mafâtîḥ* 79; Ṣûlî *Adab* 184, 187; Ḥajji Khalîfa *Kashf* II 95 ff.; Akfânî *Irshâd* 56; E. W. Lane *Madd al-qâmûs; an Arabic-English Lexicon* (Bk. I, part 1–8; London 1863–93) 46; below pp. 157 ff. *Khabar*, which was used by Arab translators to render Greek *historía* (cf. Aristotle *Prior Analytics* i. 30. 46a24/*Manṭiq* I 200), is used in the title of the '*Ibar* to mean 'event[s]' rather than 'history' as designating a work on history.

[2] Cf. De Slane *Prolégomènes* I 11.

ironically enough, it means, among other things, to pass over and to pass by. It is true that a word, pregnant as it may be with various implications, could become specific when used in a particular context. But the word *'ibar* here stands as a prominent and key word in the title. It is not limited by a specific context, except insofar as it is related to the word ' wisdom ' in the preceding sentence and the phrases indicating the relative emphasis on the various aspects of universal history in the rest of the title. Could *'ibar*, then, be the link between ' wisdom ' and ' history '?

'Ibar is the plural of *'ibra*, a noun derived from the verb-root[1] *'-b-r* whose basic meanings are practically identical in all Semitic languages, especially in Hebrew, Syriac, and Arabic.[2] It means passing on, over, through, by, or beyond; and these acts are usually related to the banks or borders of a river, valley, chasm, or a rock hole. The various concrete and conceptual meanings are derived from this basic act of connecting two points. Thus, it means to travel, to cross, to go beyond the borders of a city or a land, as well as to invade, to go beyond, and to violate a border. It also means to pass from the outside to the inside of a thing. Thus, it is used in connection with the Law to signify the act of transgressing it by disregarding it, and also of penetrating its inner meaning. Another group of related meanings includes to emigrate, translate, convert, and to depose or remove from power; and further, to pass away, vanish, perish, and die. The idea of death takes a more prominent place among the various derivations from the Arabic root of the word: dying or dead—as though one had travelled the road of life and crossed over the bridge of the present world; to destroy and cause death; and the impact of death upon the living. Arabic dictionaries also elaborate extensively on the idea of expressing, explaining, and interpreting the meaning of something; and of wondering about, enquiring into, contemplating, and penetrating to the innermost significance of an object.[3] Since these activities imply examination

[1] The root has more importance in Arabic than in Western languages.

[2] Cf. Lane *Lexicon* 1936*c*–39*a*; W. Gesenius *A Hebrew and English Lexicon of the Old Testament*, trans. E. Robinson, ed. F. Brown *et al.* (Oxford 1952) 716–20; G. Cardahi *Al-Lobab; seu Dictionarium Syro-Arabicum* (Beriti 1887–91) II 240–42.

[3] Thus we have the expressions ' to interpret dreams ' (*'abbara al-ru'yâ*) and ' a dream interpreter ' (*'abbâr*), cf. Koran 12: 43, and Bayḍâwî's commentary in *Anwâr* I 461–62; *Q* I 185 ff.

and comparison, these meanings naturally followed upon the former. Thus we have: to examine or weigh, to meditate upon a book, read it silently, and examine and compare its parts. As a speech or an expression (*'ibâra*) is a bridge through which a person explains himself to another, this word also came to mean any written or spoken phrase that performs that function.

From this brief survey we can see how pregnant with meaning and ambivalent the verb and its derivatives are. It connotes the existence of a barrier, but also the bridging or crossing of that barrier. It means vanishing and death, but also the duration in which the consideration of death enhances life. It indicates the examination of the immediate world of sensible things, but also the penetration of the mystery that lies behind them, and the relation between the two. Finally, it points to the chasm that may exist between two persons, and also the possibility of communication between them.

2. This ambivalence, inherent in the manifest meanings of the word *'ibra* rendered it of great use for writers of popular-wisdom-literature, philosophy, mysticism, and especially history. Popular-wisdom-literature, being essentially cryptic and depending on hints rather than elaborate explanations, found the word's ability to compress diverse meanings and its tolerance of contradictions of great advantage. *'Ibra* was usually used in connection with examples, allegories, and significant proverbs. It intimated that behind these expressions there was a moral to be understood and practised.[1]

Muslim philosophers found the word, with its many conventional usages and its suggestion of what is beyond convention, of particular use when writing for the initiates. They employed it as a rhetorical tool to attract the potential philosopher to their 'way': to lead him toward reflecting upon the external events of the universe of nature and the acts of man, and upon the equivocal expressions of the Koran, and to guide him to the knowledge of the rational principles beyond them.[2]

[1] Cf. Mas'ûdî *Murûj* II 251–52, 253: 2–4; Ibn al-Khaṭîb in Maqqarî *Nafḥ* IV 148.

[2] Cf. Fârâbî (*Milla* fol. 52r–52v) for a discussion of the political use of history. Avicenna, discussing the meaning of 'mysteries' (*Ishârât* 207, cf. 204–6), differentiates between the 'stupid' and the 'true seeker', and says that for the former, mysteries are a laughing matter, while for the latter they are *'ibra*. Ibn Ṭufayl (d. 1185/581 [*GAL* I 460]) in his philosophical novel, *The*

Mystics made a similar use of the word. *'Ibra*, like the rest of their technical terms, was gradually transformed from its traditional meanings to become a tool in their inner journey. In fact, they used *'ibra* to describe the spiritual function of all other mystical terms, i.e., to awaken and lead the disciple through the conventional and external world of 'words' to the world beyond. All significant writings and deeds, the Koran and Tradition included, are *'ibar* or compressed allusions. The mystic does not, like the legist, stop at their apparent, conventional, and rational meanings, but penetrates beyond them.[1] Without this, these writings and deeds remain mere expressions severed from the veiled truth behind them. In adopting *'ibra* as a technical term, mystics concentrated on deepening and exploring the already subtle associations of the word in relation to the ineffable world which they sought in their practice and meditations, and relating it to another technical term, internality or inwardness (*bâṭin*), which they contrasted with outwardness (*ẓâhir*).[2]

It was in relation to history, however, that *'ibra* was most commonly used in the Koran and in the Tradition of the Prophet. Man was urged to 'consider' the past as the evidence,

---

Self-Taught Philosopher (*Ḥayy* 20) uses *'ibra* in its koranic context (quoting Koran 12: 111: 'And in their stories there is *'ibra* for those who understand') to intimate that behind his story, too, there is *'ibra* for those who understand. His friend and disciple, Averroes, states that the use of the imperative form of *'-b-r* in the Koran is a clear command to the philosophers to investigate things through rational demonstration: 'That the Law invites the [rational] consideration (*i'tibâr*) of beings and demands the knowledge of them through it [reason], is clear from many verses of the Divine Book [the Koran] such as: "And learn (*i'tabirû*), O ye who have intelligence." [Koran 59: 2] This is a formal enunciation (*naṣṣ*) [to the effect] that the use of rational demonstration is obligatory.' (*Faṣl* 1, cf. 2, 3, 17–18.)

[1] L. Massignon *Essai sur les origines du lexique technique de la mystique musulmane* (Paris 1922) 98–99, 117 ff., 224.

[2] When Ḥallâj (d. 922/309 [*GAL* I 199]) was asked about the mystical practice of ecstatic audition (*samâ'*) he answered: 'Externally, ecstatic audition is sedition, but internally, it is *'ibra*. Therefore, only he who understands the *allusion* is allowed to hear the *'ibra*.' ('Textes Ḥallagiens' in Massignon *op. cit.* 95 [No. 2]; cf. *ibid.* 32 [No. 42]. The mystic Abû Bakr al-Shiblî (d. 946/334 [*GAL* I 200]) made the distinction between the many (*'âmma*) who busy themselves with the simple recitation of stories, and the few (*khâṣṣa*) who are interested in stories for the sake of *i'tibâr* (cf. text in Sakhâwî *I'lân* 17: 3–4). Ibn al-Khaṭîb uses *'ibra* in a similar fashion contrasting it with its synonym, *wa'ẓ* (admonition or warning): admonition is an external tool for turning the soul from its 'amusements and pleasantry to the atmosphere of sorrow and anxiety'. But once the soul is set on its way to truth, 'then the cover of forbiddance and admonition is folded, unfolding the expanse of *i'tibâr* and Love'. (*Rawḍat al-ta'rîf bi-l-ḥubb al-sharîf*, reproduced by Maqqarî *Nafḥ* IV 93 ff., cf. 74–75, 84, 85.)

allusions, and examples, through which he could pass from the appearance of things to the knowledge of the unseen.[1] The Islamic community was urged to view past events, both reported and experienced, as ' indications ' that should awaken its moral sense and enhance its ability to act according to the demands of God: to penetrate behind the apparently meaningless succession of events and discern the ever-present design of the Creator. *'Ibra* meant both negative admonition, and positive guidance and direction for future action. It warned the community against certain patterns of action, and urged it to learn from the good deeds of the past and to imitate them.[2] The use of *'ibra* in connection with history indicated essentially the activity of looking for the unity of the plan underlying the multiplicity of events, of grasping the permanence pervading their ever-changing and destructible character, and of using the results of such reflections in the management of practical affairs.

The seeds of this conception of the use of history can be discerned in the attitude of the pre-Islamic Arabs to their version of history, the ' battle-days ' (*ayyâm*) literature.[3] The coming of Islam added new dimensions to the meaning of history by deepening its moral aspect and emphasizing the religious element. It presented the believer with the whole compass of universal history, from Creation to the coming of Islam, and predicted the future as culminating in the Day of Judgment. Consequently, for a Muslim to understand history and learn its true *'ibra* meant a spiritual training, obedience to God, and the preparation for the final accounting. The concrete culmination of the two opposite meanings of *'ibra* in relation to history is illustrated by a Tradition attributed to the Prophet: ' *Learn* from the world and do not [merely] *pass* through it.'[4] This attitude toward history, impressed upon the Muslim by the Koran and Tradition, was the true spiritual incentive that led to the intense interest in the past shown by the early generations of Islam.

The prominence of the word *'ibra* in connection with history

[1] Koran 24: 44, and Bayḍâwî's commentary in *Anwâr* II 27; cf. also Koran 3: 13, 4: 43, 12: 43 and 111, 16: 66, 23: 21, 59: 2, 79: 26.

[2] When the Prophet was asked about the Laws of Moses (*ṣuḥuf mûsâ*), he answered: ' They all were *'ibra*.' Cf. Mas'ûdî *Murûj* I 95.

[3] Cf. W. Caskel ' *Aijâm al-'arab*: Studien zur altarabischen Epik ' *Islamica* III[5] (1930) 12 ff.

[4] *U'burû al-dunyâ wa-lâ ta'burûhâ*. Cf. Ikhwân al-Ṣafâ' *Rasâ'il* I 117–18.

in the Koran and Tradition was utilized by traditional-religious Muslim historians[1] who felt the necessity of defending their profession against the attack of theologians who contended that histories, like stories, were amusements that may be tolerated, but should not be allowed to divert the attention of believers from their religious, moral, and practical tasks.[2] Traditional-religious historians responded by quoting one or more of the numerous passages of the Koran in which the serious uses of history are emphasized. Invariably, the word *'ibra*, whose meaning in this context was specified by the Koran and Tradition, is either quoted or used independently with definite allusion to its koranic meaning, or implied by the use of its various interpretive synonyms such as learning, admonition, exhortation, reminder, and example. Since it was the expressed purpose of these historians to defend history on the basis of the Koran and Tradition, they did not attempt to elaborate and expand the word beyond its traditional meaning, but to preserve it and use it as a weapon against the theologians who criticized history. Consequently, we find it often used by these historians in their brief introductions without any real attempt to explore its significance or to apply this latter to the actual historical information they collected. This is true of the traditional-religious historians, most of whom wrote prior to, and during the thirteenth and fourteenth/seventh and eighth centuries (when the word became much more current in historical literature than it had ever been before),[3] as well as of the authors of works on historiography written during that period.[4]

In contrast to theologically inspired historians, those who came under the influence of Greek and Islamic political philosophy, and Persian popular-political-wisdom-literature, elaborated and added new dimensions to the theoretical and practical significance of the word *'ibra*. They related it to experience (*tajriba*), and emphasized that the study of history should lead to reliving it and being educated by it. They wrote history for the explicit purpose of widening their readers'

[1] Cf. below pp. 134 ff.
[2] Ghazâlî *Iḥyâ'* I 58–60.
[3] Cf. Sakhâwî *I'lân* 16–17, 19–23, 28–30.
[4] Ṣafadî *Fawât* 5; Kâfîjî *Mukhtaṣar* 474, 477, 480, 494 ff.; Sakhâwî *I'lân passim*; below pp. 144–45.

experience, particularly their political experience, and of imparting to them the prudence necessary for future political action.[1] They contended that there was some kind of repetition in history, and that the causes of action, and the reasons for the policies upon which action is based, remained constant or did not vary significantly from one age to another or from one people to another. It was in this connection that the word *'ibra* was used by these historians.[2] They attempted to elaborate and apply in their works one of the deeper connotations of the word, i.e., penetrating behind the changing particulars, and learning about the nature and causes of historical events.[3]

3. It is only when considered in relation to the totality of the usages of *'ibra*, its history, and its application in the various fields, that Ibn Khaldûn's choice of it as the key word for his title becomes intelligible, and the content and purpose of the book explicit. In calling his work ' The Book of the *'Ibar* ', he deliberately chose a word with a variety of meanings to describe its subject matter and the manifold aspects of the method he employed. To begin with, he intended to cover the whole compass of universal history, to travel through the events of the past starting with their intelligible beginnings down to his own time. In particular, he intended to narrate the history which he had personally experienced, i.e., the decline of the Islamic world in general and that of the Islamic West in particular. But had this been the only theme, the word ' history ' would have been more appropriate for the title of the work.

Ibn Khaldûn's main objective was not, however, merely to relate history, but also to pass beyond history. He intended to learn from history and not merely to pass through it. He did not confine himself to admonishing his readers by rhetorical use of language,[4] but intended also to interpret history and reveal its secrets[5] through comparison, theoretical comprehension, and the

[1] Sakhâwî *I'lân* 27–28, 39, 45 (45: 14, for *murdiya* [causing death], read *radiyya* [bad] with the Berlin MS); Ibn al-Khaṭîb *Lamḥa* 10: 14–15, *Iḥâṭa* I 82.

[2] Sakhâwî *I'lân* 22, esp. the phrase: *al-siyâsât al-fâḍila* (virtuous regimes).

[3] For the contribution of these historians to Islamic historiography, cf. below pp. 142–44.

[4] *Q* I 66. 'Admonition ' and ' warning ' are related to the rhetorical style used by some of Ibn Khaldûn's predecessors, a style which he criticizes and rejects. Cf. *Q* I 65: 17.

[5] *Q* I 65: 12, 235, 243, 245, 247, II 76, 108, 203, 239.

analysis of the nature and causes of historical events. In approaching history in this fashion, the external events were no longer the main aim or end of his research. They merely supplied the 'matter' from which the general laws that lay behind them were to be derived.[1] These laws in turn explained the events by showing their nature and causes.[2] '*Ibra* was the bridge over which his mind crossed from historical events to their nature and causes, and back to the events. Hence Ibn Khaldûn's use of '*ibra* becomes almost synonymous with reasoning (*naẓar*)[3] and understanding (*fahm*),[4] and with the explanation of historical events through the understanding already achieved by reasoning.[5]

The prominent position of '*ibra* in the title and in the text point in the same direction: a movement from the externals of history to its internal nature. Ibn Khaldûn specifically identifies this effort with scientific or philosophic investigation, and calls it a part of wisdom (*ḥikma*, *sophía*).[6] '*Ibra*, therefore, is not only the link between history and wisdom, but also the process through which history is contemplated with the aim of understanding its nature and of utilizing the knowledge thus gained in action.

In attempting to study history for a philosophic purpose, Ibn Khaldûn was faced with the problem of expressing his ideas concerning important philosophic issues. Consequently, '*ibra* was not only the bridge between the external and internal aspects of history, but also the bridge between commonly accepted opinions about, and the true nature of, divine and natural beings. And it is important to appreciate, at the start, the peculiar difficulties Ibn Khaldûn encountered in the course he chose for himself in transgressing the generally accepted limits of his field, in attempting to pass beyond the common knowledge of external events, and in expressing his ideas concerning important religious and philosophic doctrines. Religiously, socially, and personally, he had chosen a dangerous path that could lead to either salvation or damnation. Philosophers, like dream interpreters and augurers, may end in heaven, but

[1] Cf., e.g., *Q* I 333, 339.
[2] *Q* I 159, 163–64, 331, 332, II 110, 116, 117.
[3] *Q* I 263, 265, 269, 275, 327; cf. Ikhwân al-Ṣafâ' *Rasâ'il* I 254; Jâḥiẓ *Dalâ'il* 2, 3.
[4] *Q* I 313, 344, 374, II 203, 214, 238.
[5] *Q* II 236, 237, 244–45, 246, 251; cf. below Chaps. III, V.
[6] *Q* I 2: 18–19, 7: 9–10.

usually they end in hell. The knowledge they seek can be useful to themselves and to society, but it can also be destructive to both. This is the reason for the grave moral responsibility Ibn Khaldûn felt as a thinker and as a writer. It is a mistake to think that the peculiarly difficult, subtle, and tentative style he adopted was primarily designed to mislead the reader, to protect himself against social persecution, or to make a show of religiosity. Thinking is a precarious adventure, and Ibn Khaldûn's primary concern was how to control and direct his thought, and avoid the hazards to which all thought is exposed: How to pursue philosophic investigation and yet avoid social ostracism, how to interpret the genuine meaning of revelation and yet preserve its verbal integrity, how to explore new fields of knowledge and yet preserve the knowledge already in existence, how to express the results of his research without jeopardizing the social order, and how to communicate with others without leading them to wrong conclusions or unwise actions—these were the problems with which Ibn Khaldûn struggled, and it was to solve some of them that he developed his peculiar style.[1]

Ibn Khaldûn thought that the attempt to study history in this manner was new and that he had originated it.[2] But that did not hold true for science or philosophy in general, whose principles and method of investigation he succeeded in applying to the study of history. Philosophy had come to the Muslims from the Greeks, and its last great representative in the Islamic world prior to Ibn Khaldûn was Averroes. This philosophy, the only one deserving the name, had been on the decline since the time of Averroes, especially in western Islam, ' except for the little you find among few men and subject to the censorship (*raqba*) of orthodox leaders '.[3] The problem of a philosophic investigation of history, therefore, meant first the study and revival of philosophy which had been on the decline. But like other students of philosophy in the Islamic community, Ibn Khaldûn had to work under the censorship of religious orthodoxy. He had

[1] Ibn Khaldûn did not always succeed in solving these problems. Consequently, his style is sometimes not even or sure when compared to other masters of exoteric-esoteric writing like Fârâbî and Averroes. This was also due to his subject matter and to the composite structure of the audience which he coveted.

[2] Cf. below pp. 147, 156 ff.

[3] *Q* III 92.

to lead the life of an investigator in a community that was intolerant and antagonistic to philosophy.[1]

As a result, every truly philosophic endeavour in the Islamic community had to encounter and answer three separate yet related questions: (1) What is philosophy? (2) What is the relation of philosophy to the religious and revealed Law? (3) How is the philosopher to conduct his investigation and communicate its results in a community based on such a Law? The most comprehensive and detailed consideration of these problems by Ibn Khaldûn is to be found in his discussion of the various sciences in the sixth section of Book One of the *'Ibar*,[2] a discussion which on the surface appears as if it were exclusively a neutral ' historical ' account of the sciences. To this discussion we shall now turn to elucidate Ibn Khaldûn's philosophic position as expressed in his answers to these basic questions of Islamic philosophy.

II

Philosophy and the Law

1. The most important distinction made by Ibn Khaldûn in his study of the sciences ' existing in the [Islamic] culture in this [his] era '[3] is the distinction between the natural (*ṭabî'iyya*) sciences and the transmitted (*naqliyya*) sciences.[4] The natural sciences are also called philosophic (*falsafiyya*) and are defined as ' those that man can know by the nature of his thought, and

[1] *B* I 330, 366–67; cf. Fârâbî *Aflâṭun* 22–23 (sec. 32); Maqqarî *Nafḥ* II 125; L. Gauthier *La théorie d'Ibn Rochd (Averroès) sur les rapports de la religion et de la philosophie* (Paris 1909) 162–66, *Ibn Thofaïl, sa vie, ses oeuvres* (Paris 1909) 59 ff., ' Scolastique musulmane et scholastique chrétienne ' *Revue d'Histoire de la Philosophie* II (1928) 234–35, 249–52; L. Strauss *Philosophie und Gesetz* (Berlin 1935) 68 ff., *Persecution and the Art of Writing* (Glencoe, Illinois 1952) 9–10, 18–19.

[2] *Q* II 363 ff., III 1 ff.

[3] *Q* II 385: 1. This qualification is important, since it limits the ' matter ' on which he is reflecting, and the favourable or unfavourable judgments he passes on certain sciences. Thus, while every science as a science is valid and praiseworthy, sciences existing at a certain time may be false and blameworthy. Such judgments have naturally to be based on what a true science is and on the true social role of the sciences. Therefore our interest in trying to understand the theoretical and practical considerations upon which Ibn Khaldûn based his study of the sciences as they were during his time. The discussion of the sciences by Ibn Khaldûn justifies De Slane's parenthetical addition of ' Muslim ' to the title (*Prolégomènes* II 450).

[4] *Q* II 385: 3–4.

through his human perception can arrive at their subject matter, problems, ways of demonstration, and the manner of teaching them—until his reflection and investigation lead him to [distinguish] truth from falsehood in them '.[1] In contrast, the transmitted sciences, which Ibn Khaldûn also calls the positive (*waḍ'iyya*) sciences, ' are all based on the traditions communicated from the divine Legislator [God through the Prophet]. Reason has no role to play in them except in relating their subsidiary problems and the fundamental ',[2] i.e., the ' application ' of the fundamental commands revealed in the Koran and Tradition to particular instances. The positive sciences (and we shall henceforth designate them by that name) are, therefore, primarily legal sciences (*'ulûm shar'iyya*) or sciences based on a divinely inspired Law. Thus, the essential difference between the philosophic and positive sciences is their ultimate source which is human reason and the prophet-legislator respectively. The first group is concerned with what can be known by reason, and to the extent and in the way it is known to it; the second is concerned with what is taught or commanded by a divine legislator (*shâri'*), insofar as it is taught or commanded, and in the way it is taught or commanded by him.

The two groups of sciences differ in another respect, namely, in their unity and multiplicity. Because the positive sciences deal primarily with actions and because these actions have to be based on the Koran and Tradition, they have to be many.[3] They can be divided in accordance with the sources of the commands, the classes of their transmitters, and the ways of relating particular instances to fundamentals.[4] A further division may be based on the various categories of action which these sciences are designed to further. Multiplicity is most evident, however, in the method employed by these sciences; for included in this group are sciences as different in their methods as those ascertaining the variant readings of the Koran, the character of Tradition-transmitters, and the attributes of God. This

[1] *Q* II 385: 3–9.

[2] *Q* II 385: 10–12. In *Q* II 385: 10, *waḍ'* (established or instituted), must read *wâḍi'* (he who establishes, or institutes) with MSS C and D of *Q*, *Bq*, *TT* (cf. De Slane *Prolégomènes* II 451 n. 1).

[3] *Q* II 386: 1.

[4] *Q* II 386.

multiplicity would increase even further if we add the relevant linguistic sciences.[1] The philosophic sciences, on the other hand, cannot be divided according to such theoretically accidental events as the coming of a prophet or the prevalence of a certain language. Their division into mathematics, logic, physics, and metaphysics,[2] essential as it is, is made within an overall unity of basic principles, and especially an overall unity of method—that of rational demonstration.

Closely related to the multiplicity of the positive sciences *within* a certain nation or community (*milla*),[3] is the fact that various groups of positive sciences exist in different communities:

'All these transmitted sciences belong exclusively to the Islamic community and its people, although in general there have to exist in *every* community similar sciences which are homonymous with these in the distant genus (*jins ba'îd*) in so far as they are [all] legal sciences revealed by God to the legislator who communicates them. But in their specificity, [the Islamic positive sciences] are distinctly different from [those of] other communities, for they have annulled them. . . . The [Islamic] Law has forbidden the study of revealed Books other than the Koran. The Prophet said: "Do not believe or belie the People of the Book. Say: 'We believe in what has been revealed to us and revealed to you, and our God and yours is one'."'[4]

Every community, thus, has its own legal sciences as it has its own language. The positive sciences of each community belong to that community exclusively, and are based on its character

[1] *Q* II 386–87, III 278 ff.

[2] *Q* III 87 ff.

[3] For the various meanings of 'nation' or 'community' in Islam, cf. L. Massignon 'L'*Umma* et ses synonymes: notion de "communauté sociale" en Islam' *REI* 1941–46 (cahier unique) 151–57.

[4] *Q* II 387, cf. III 243: 9–13. For other texts in which Ibn Khaldûn uses the term 'Laws' in the plural, cf., e.g., *Q* I 364: 9, III 90: 17–18. The problem of the diversity of Laws, and the positive sciences based upon them, among different communities is a constant theme of Islamic political philosophy, cf., e.g., Ikhwân al-Ṣafâ' *Rasâ'il* IV 22, 25; Fârâbî *Taḥṣîl* 35, *Iḥṣâ'* 45: 3, 107: 9 ff.; Avicenna *Aqsâm* 108: 9; Averroes *Tahâfut* 581–82. Practical philosophy was distinguished from the various groups of practical sciences peculiar to each community by the fact that it treated the general principles of laws and acts in all communities. It specified the manner in which the general principles could be applied in particular communities and situations, leaving for the faculty of prudence the actual decisions in particular acts (Fârâbî *Iḥṣâ'* 104: 10–15). Cf. L. Strauss 'Farabi's Plato' *Louis Ginzberg Jubilee Volume* [English Section; The American Academy for Jewish Research] (New York 1945) 373–74.

and needs.[1] Since the primary end of the positive sciences is action, we can expect each community to act differently in the same sense in which each speaks a different language. What the positive sciences of all communities have in common would also be similar to what all languages have in common, i.e., in their own way they all help the people of each community to communicate among themselves. The philosophic sciences are in this respect at the extreme opposite pole. They are natural to man as a rational being. Therefore, ' they are not the exclusive speciality of any community; the peoples of all communities study them and are equal in [understanding] their principles and problems '.[2]

2. The philosophic sciences are divided into four branches by Ibn Khaldûn: logic, mathematics, physics, and metaphysics. Following a well-established Islamic philosophic tradition, he excludes logic and mathematics from the philosophic sciences properly so-called, considering them propaedeutical.[3] That leaves physics and metaphysics to occupy the centre of philosophic investigation, and philosophy becomes the science investigating natural and divine beings.

This investigation is essentially theoretical; its aim is the theoretical knowledge of things as they are. It is a ' knowledge that does not entail action ',[4] and is not a necessary requisite for everyday action. Its goal, if and when reached, is the identity, or some degree of correspondence, between the mental images, and the things investigated and their causes:

' [It is that] thought which produces the knowledge or opinion about the thing investigated beyond the senses. This is theoretical reason. It consists of conceptions and judgments organized in a special way and according to special rules to produce further knowledge of the same genus [as the first] conception and judgment. Then [the newly produced knowledge] is organized

[1] ' The nature of men varies, their manners are heterogeneous, and their wills are diverse. Various diseases attack [various] souls according to time, place, nature, humour, and habit. Since the legislators are the physicians and astrologers of the souls . . . their prescriptions vary and their Laws differ in accordance with what is appropriate to each community and each group of peoples and nations. . . . For, their purpose is to keep existing health and to bring back the health lost.' Ikhwân al-Ṣafâ' *Rasâ'il* IV 22–23; cf. Fârâbî *Iḥṣâ'* 104–5.

[2] *Q* III 87: 1–2.

[3] *Q* III 94–95, 108 ff. Cf. L. Gauthier *Ibn Rochd* (*Averroès*) (Paris 1948) 49–50, 66–67.

[4] *Q* II 365: 6.

with others to again produce further knowledge. The ultimate end [of theoretical reason] is the conception of existence as it is in its general and specific differences, and its distant and proximate causes. Through this [procedure theoretical] reason[1] becomes perfect in its essence. It becomes pure reason and an apprehending soul. This is the meaning of the essence of man.'[2] Philosophy is essentially a search; it implies initial ignorance, postulates the possibility of knowledge, and moves from ignorance to knowledge. In the actual form in which it exists at any time or place, it may not be complete and its answers may not be final. This is especially true in the more difficult questions of metaphysics or the science of divine beings, where reason is least certain of its ground and often has to be satisfied with probable or most likely opinions.[3] This neither disqualifies reason nor disproves the possibility of attaining its ultimate end which is the demonstrative knowledge of things as they are, since ' reason is a valid criterion of things, and its judgments [when based on actual demonstrations] are certain and admit of no falsity '.[4] It only points to the actual limits of human reasoning and leaves the door open for the possibility of things not known to reason.[5] The Law, on the other hand, supplies the believers with final

[1] *Q* II 365: 11. For *bi-l-fikr* (through the agency of reason) read *al-fikr* (reason).

[2] *Q* II 365. The progress of theoretical reason from potency to act is described in *Q* II 362: ' The rational soul of man exists in him in potency. It emerges out of potency into actuality, first, through the intensive acquisition of knowledge and apprehensions furnished by sense objects, then, through what is acquired with the theoretical faculty, until it becomes apprehension in act (*bi-l-fi'l*) and pure reason. Thus, it becomes a spiritual essence, and perfects its existence.' Cf. *Q* I 175–76, 186–89, 192 ff., II 368, and the intentional contradiction of these texts in *Q* II 370–72, where he attacks the ' metaphysicians ' and recommends prayer and fasting as substitutes for philosophy! The true significance of Ibn Khaldûn's definition of theoretical reason, however, becomes clear when compared to similar definitions by previous Muslim philosophers from whom it is derived. When studied in this context, Ibn Khaldûn's conception of the nature of theoretical reason is the same as the purer Aristotelianism of Fârâbî (*Jam'* 20–21, *Madîna* 62–65) and Averroes (*t. Nafs* 72 ff., 87, 95, *j. Mâ ba'd al-ṭabî'a* 10: 19–20 [sec. 15]), in opposition to the relatively more Neo-Platonic views of Avicenna (*Ishârât* 202 ff., *Sa'âda* 13; cf. L. Gardet *La pensée religieuse d'Avicenna* [*Ibn Sînâ*] [' Études de philosophie médiévale ' XLI] [Paris 1951] 175 ff.) and Ghazâlî *Maḍnûn ṣaghîr* 90 ff.; cf. A. J. Wensinck *La pensée de Ghazzâlî* [Paris 1940] 60 ff.). Avicenna and Ghazâlî are accused by Averroes of having substituted in certain respects the faculty of imagination for that of thought (*Tahâfut* 546). For Ibn Khaldûn's criticism of the Neo-Platonic tradition in Islamic philosophy, cf. below pp. 108–12.

[3] *Q* III 215: 12–13.

[4] *Q* III 30: 15, 210–11.

[5] *Q* III 31, 213, 216, 218; cf. Averroes *Tahâfut* 193, 492.

and definitive dogmas (*'aqâ'id*) about natural and divine beings, especially about the most remote things, like the attributes of God, the creation of the world, and the world to come. It prescribes which acts are obligatory, recommended, permitted, blamable, or forbidden, and describes the rewards or punishment such acts entail.[1] The divine legislator is not bound by the limits of theoretical reason. What he announces must be accepted and never doubted, even when surpassing, or apparently contradicting, what has been known by human reason.[2] Reason must assent to authority. The positive sciences are, thus, ultimately based on the acceptance of the authority of the legislator; the end of their search is to ascertain what the legislator had said or commanded, after which their search ends and reason must rest.[3]

Philosophy proceeds to the penetration of the secrets of existence from the perception of sensible things. It arrives at the unknown through what is known; it knows causes through their effects, and the more remote these causes, the more the intermediaries through which it has to pass and the longer the chain of reasoning it has to employ. Theoretical reason cannot know hidden things, the world of spirits or the nature of God, as they are in themselves; it can only know them ' from behind a veil ' and then only as causes.[4] In contrast, the revealed dogmas of the Law entail no such movement, no progressive chain of reasoning, and none of the limitations of theoretical reason. The legislator informs the believers about the nature of God and His attributes, the world to come, the angels, providence, and the soul,[5] directly. He saves them from the arduous task of searching for the nature of such dogmas ' whose real meaning is hidden ' and not clear.[6] ' He [the Prophet] has ordered us to abstain from investigating them [the causes], to do away with them altogether, and to turn to the Cause of all causes, their Maker and Creator, so that the mood [literally, tincture, *ṣibgha*] of professing the unity [of God] would be firmly established in the soul in accordance with the way we were taught by the

[1] *Q* III 1, 14, 16, 17, 44.
[2] *Q* III 27 ff., 123.
[3] Cf. below pp. 100–3.
[4] *Q* I 192–94, II 362–63, 370–71, 372; cf. Averroes *Tahâfut* 210 ff.
[5] *Q* II 386, III 35, 54.
[6] *Q* III 47: 7–8.

Legislator who knows best our religious interest and the means to our happiness due to his acquaintance with what is beyond the senses.'[1] According to the Law, what is 'heard' from the Prophet should have priority over rational knowledge. The 'believers' should be urged not to waste their efforts exploring the rational truth behind the dogmas taught by the Prophet, since this 'is a gorge in which the mind wanders to no avail'.[2]

Philosophy is both a certain knowledge and a certain *way* through which rational knowledge should be gained. Those who merely learn the conclusions of the theoretical search and accept them without travelling the proper way to them, do not really know these conclusions, but only imagine that they know them.[3] One of the main problems of philosophy, accordingly, is the enquiry into various ways (*ṭuruq*) of knowledge to distinguish the true way from the false ways.[4] The greatest of all philosophers, Aristotle,[5] was the first to clarify and organize the problems of the ways of knowledge. In the eight books of the *Organon* he discussed the ways of achieving certainty and opinions both in regard to the form and the matter of syllogistic reasoning. It was he who distinguished between the true way of knowledge, i.e., demonstration, and dialectical, sophistical, rhetorical, and poetic reasoning.[6] Demonstrative reasoning, as expounded by Aristotle and by Muslim philosophers in their commentaries on Aristotle's logical works, is the proper way to philosophic knowledge because it is the most perfect formal method devised by human reason and because it corresponds to, and abstracts the true nature of things. It leads to certainty because it aims at the 'identity between the definition and the thing defined'.[7] This is the reason why the *Posterior Analytics* (or the *Book of Demonstration*)[8] is the central treatise among the logical works of Aristotle; it is the work that deals with the syllogisms which produce certain and necessary knowledge. The proper method of philosophic investigation for Ibn Khaldûn is, consequently, the *material* logic of Aristotle, the logic in which the nature of the mind meets the nature of the things investigated.[9] Starting from

[1] *Q* III 29, cf. 30.
[2] *Q* III 28: 14–15, 29–31.
[3] Cf. Averroes *Tahâfut* 207, 209, 409.
[4] *Q* III 109: 8–110: 2.
[5] *Q* III 90–91, *C* I 283.
[6] *Q* III 110–12.
[7] *Q* III 111: 6–7.
[8] *Kitâb al-burhân.*
[9] *Q* III 111, 114–15, 255.

the sensible data of experience, it aims at the progressive abstraction of universals until it rests with the simple apprehension of essences. This ascending movement of thought to the supreme genera, or the most general properties of things, is then followed by a descending movement starting from universals and ending in affirmations about the essential attributes of things subsumed under these universals.[1]

Hand in hand with the adoption of this logic went Ibn Khaldûn's criticism of the two major schools of logic in Islamic dialectical theology.[2] The first was the attempt of the 'ancients' to reject *en masse* the basic metaphysical foundation of logical demonstration (i.e., their denial of the objective existence of essences and essential attributes) and to substitute for it an atomistic-occasionalistic universe in which all effects are the direct creation of God rather than the result of causes inherent in the nature of things. This led them to the rejection of the objective existence of universals (genus, species, differentiae, properties, and common accidents) and to view universals and essences as purely mental constructions with no counterparts outside the mind.[3] The second was the attempt of the 'moderns' (e.g., Râzî and Khûnajî [d. 1249/646][4]) to follow the Stoics in their logical nominalism. These writers did not study logic as a tool of knowledge, but 'as an art in itself'.[5] They deserted Aristotle's logical works that treated the content of reasoning and dealt exclusively with its form. 'The works of the Ancients [Aristotle] and their ways,' Ibn Khaldûn says, 'have been deserted as if they did not exist, while they are full of the fruits of logic and its uses, as we have said.'[6]

In contrast to the 'way of demonstration' which leads to the true knowledge of essences, the positive sciences employ a variety of methods. These methods were first and most effectively employed by the Prophet himself, whose wisdom as a legislator

[1] *Q* III 109, 111, 210–11.
[2] Cf. below pp. 104 ff.
[3] *Q* III 114–15, cf. 112.
[4] *GAL* I 463. Afḍal al-Dîn, Abû 'Alî Muḥammad. *Q* III 113, 349.
[5] *Q* III 113.
[6] *Q* III 113: 11–12; cf. 'Alî Sâmî al-Nashshâr *Manâhij al-baḥth 'ind mufakkirî al-islâm wa-naqd al-muslimîn li-l-manṭiq al-arisṭuṭâlîsî* ('Les méthodes chez les penseurs musulmans; et leur critique de la logique aristotelicienne') (Cairo 1947/1367) 21.

and whose miraculous power (*i'jâz*) as a prophet were most clearly demonstrated by his ability to use the easiest and most efficient ways to convince his followers of the truth of his message and the necessity of following it.[1] He started by performing miracles through the succession of which ' the mood of obedience and submission ' was created in his followers, for they ' were dumbfounded and surprised '.[2] Then he instructed them in what is good for them in this world and in the world to come, enticing them by the promise of rewards (*targhîb*) and frightening them with threats (*tarhîb*) if they did not obey him.[3] Through such methods, he succeeded in creating in them the attitude of dogmatic belief.[4]

Ibn Khaldûn, thus, intimates that between philosophy and the Law, and between philosophers and communities based on the various Laws, there is an essential distinction, if not incompatibility, contradiction, and conflict. How, then, can philosophy exist in a community based on the Law? How can the philosopher lead a philosophic life in a community whose principles differ from the principles upon which his life as an investigator is based? In short, what is the proper relation of philosophy to society? This is the most important single practical question that Islamic philosophy, and Greek philosophy before it, faced. The manner in which Islamic philosophy answered this question determined its character and destiny in the Islamic world.

That Ibn Khaldûn, like other Muslim philosophers before him, is seriously concerned with this problem is evident from the way he characterizes philosophy and the Islamic community. For only a philosopher, and a philosopher deeply rooted in, and committed to, the way of the *falâsifa* (Arabic for the Greek *philosophoi* and reserved by Ibn Khaldûn for Plato, Aristotle, Fârâbî, Avicenna, Ibn Bâjja, Ibn Ṭufayl, and Averroes),[5] would characterize philosophy and the Islamic community the way Ibn Khaldûn has characterized them. Contrasting the Islamic community to philosophy in this manner could not be done from

[1] *Q* III 171.
[2] *Q* I 383, 384, 390, 418, III 134–35.
[3] *Q* I 231–32.
[4] *Q* I 231–32, 273, 275, 279, 283.
[5] *Q* III 90 ff., 105, 106, 112, 116–17, 118, 121, 211, 234. Ibn Bâjja (d. 1138/533), cf. *GAL* I 460.

within the sphere of the Law.[1] Without fully appreciating this crucial problem and its far-reaching consequences, Ibn Khaldûn's thought, including the most elementary and basic principles of his method and purpose, will remain a closed book to the investigator. This is particularly true because the main object of the *'Ibar* is the study of society in general and the Islamic society in particular.

3. We shall continue our enquiry into Ibn Khaldûn's conception of the relation between philosophy and society by pursuing our discussion of the relation between the philosophic sciences and the positive sciences; for it is in the relation of these two groups of sciences that we are apt to find the answer to the question of the relation between philosophy and society.

As we study Ibn Khaldûn's enumeration of the philosophic sciences and his separate treatment of each, we are immediately struck by the complete absence of one of the two major branches into which philosophy was divided by Muslim philosophers, namely, the practical sciences (*'ulûm 'amaliyya*)[2] or politics, considered in a wide sense as including ethics, economics, and, to some extent, rhetoric. It is certainly not reasonable to assume that Ibn Khaldûn did not know of that well-established division of philosophy or of the various practical sciences, since a close study of his classification of the philosophic sciences reveals a careful examination and intelligent understanding of the works of the philosophers on the classification of the sciences.[3] Further, Ibn Khaldûn explicitly mentions politics and rhetoric in his attempt to prove the independence of the new science of culture which is the subject matter of Book One of the *'Ibar*. His conclusion, though affirming the distinction between the new science and these practical sciences, indicates nonetheless a close relationship between them because they all attempt a

[1] For the explanation of the nature of prophecy and the relation of the Law to philosophy from the standpoint of the Law, cf. the views of Ibn Taymiyya (*Ma'ârij* 2 ff.).

[2] Fârâbî *Iḥṣâ'* 102 ff.; Avicenna *Aqsâm* 105, 107–8; Averroes *j. Mâ ba'd al-ṭabî'a* 1.

[3] Cf., e.g., the various sciences included under the natural sciences (*ṭabî'iyyât*) (*Q* III 116) with Averroes (*Tahâfut* 509); the criticism of the 'false' natural sciences (*Q* III 124 ff.) with Averroes (*Tahâfut* 509–11); Ibn Khaldûn's conception of the philosophic sciences as universal and the positive sciences as the property of a single community (*Q* II 387, III 87) with Fârâbî (*Taḥṣîl* 35); and Ibn Khaldûn's attitude to philosophy as a certain knowledge and a certain method (*Q* III 109 ff.) with Fârâbî (*Aflâṭun* 4 [sec. 2], 5–6 [sec. 5]).

rational investigation of the nature of society.[1] Yet he deliberately failed to mention them in his classification of the philosophic sciences. In addition, he made certain statements which on the surface give the impression that these sciences were not important or necessary.[2] On the other hand, he expounded and adopted the ' conclusions ' of the central discipline of practical philosophy, or of political philosophy as understood by Muslim philosophers, concerning the distinction between philosophy and the Islamic community.

Another important omission in Ibn Khaldûn's discussions of the various sciences is his failure to state explicitly the proper relation of philosophy to the Law. Is there any relation between these two omissions? The answer would not be far from us if we realize that in Islamic philosophy, practical philosophy, and more specifically political philosophy, was the link and the only link which related the Muslim philosopher to the Islamic community, and philosophy in general to all communities.[3] The tentative conclusion that forces itself upon the enquirer regarding the relation between Ibn Khaldûn's two omissions is, therefore, that they are not only related, but identical in purpose. Ibn Khaldûn did not mention the practical philosophic sciences because he did not want to commit himself publicly concerning the proper relation of philosophy to society which was formulated by Fârâbî, who said unequivocally that ' both parts [i.e., the opinions and the actions] out of which the community is made come *under* philosophy. . . . Therefore, it is philosophy that gives the proofs for what is contained in the virtuous community.'[4] Rather, he tried to give the impression that he was substituting the positive sciences for practical philosophy, or, that for him practical philosophy was nothing but the disciplines derived from the Law.[5]

These omissions are important so far as the non-philosopher, whose opinions and actions are circumscribed by the Law, is concerned. For he will understand, and perhaps accept, Ibn

[1] Cf. below pp. 156–57, 167–68.
[2] *Q* II 126–27.
[3] Cf. Fârâbî *Taḥṣîl* 26 ff., *Iḥṣâ'* 102 ff., *Milla* fols. 51v, 53r, 54v, 57v ff.
[4] Fârâbî *Milla* fol. 53r: 11–12 and 19–20, cf. fols 54v, 58r.
[5] That many orthodox Muslims thought of practical philosophy in such terms is evident from what an orthodox historian of Islamic philosophy, Qifṭî, says: ' As to political matters, their [the philosophers'] doctrines . . . are derived from the Divine Books revealed to the prophets' (*Akhbâr* 53).

Khaldûn's statements about the Law (which from the point of view of the Law are couched in permissible terms). He will not understand the consequences of his statements concerning philosophy, will not miss the absence of the practical sciences (which from the point of view of the Law have been dispensed with), and will have no reason to condemn the author. All this is crucial because the purpose of practical philosophy is not only to define the relation of philosophy to the Law, but, being practical, also to define the role of the philosopher in relation to those who are not philosophers or the community at large. If mentioning practical philosophy could in any way impede or disqualify the philosopher in his relation to the community, it would be practically wise for him not to mention them and commit himself to the opinions of other philosophers in such matters. Simultaneously, he can pursue his investigation as a philosopher by implicitly accepting the principles of practical philosophy and applying them in his analysis of the most important issues which practical philosophy had to explore in the Islamic community. Essentially, these issues were three in number. The first dealt with the source of all communities, including the Islamic, based on divinely inspired Laws. This meant an enquiry into the nature of prophecy and prophetic knowledge. The second dealt with the nature of the social order. The main philosophic problem here was the distinction between the 'few' and the 'many', a distinction which in turn showed the necessity of the Law and the manner in which it should be communicated. The third dealt with the role of knowledge in society and the critique of existing sciences with a view to protect the Law and philosophy, and the many and the few, against possible confusion between their functions and ends. To these three issues we shall now direct our attention.

III

Philosophy in the Islamic Community

1. Since the Islamic community owed its origin, its Law, and its character to a revelation and a prophet, it is natural that the central problem of practical philosophy or political philosophy

in Islam would be that of understanding the phenomenon of prophecy,[1] i.e., the rational explanation of the nature and source of the prophet's knowledge, and the nature and source of the powers through which he performs miracles, convinces the multitude, and induces them to carry out his commands.[2] To Ibn Khaldûn, the phenomenon of prophecy was especially important because it was the source of important social values, institutions, and attitudes, which he had to explain. As a philosopher, however, he was concerned, not only with prophecy as a source of a social order, but also with its *meaning* and with 'explaining the essence of prophecy'.[3]

According to Ibn Khaldûn, prophecy is a *human* phenomenon: The prophet is a human being, his traits are human traits, his knowledge is human knowledge, his powers are human powers, his acts are human acts, and his purpose is a human purpose.[4] This does not mean that every human being is a prophet or can become a prophet through learning and practising a certain art. Nor does it exclude what the Muslims called 'divine selection'. On the contrary, Ibn Khaldûn believes that prophecy is, in a sense, the highest form of human existence. The prophet is an extremely rare individual who must possess special, and rarely attainable, natural powers from birth, and lead a correct life prior to, and during, his mission as a prophet.[5] Consequently, to explain the phenomenon of prophecy, Ibn Khaldûn enquires into the nature of man and attempts to show how a human being becomes a prophet.

The knowledge of the prophet is attained through a movement of the human intellect to the sphere of angelic knowledge or pure

[1] Political philosophy was even defined as the science which dealt with the properties of prophecy. Cf. Avicenna *Aqsâm* 108, *Nubuwwât* 120 ff., 124–25; Akfânî *Irshâd* 58 ff.

[2] Fârâbî *Tanbîh* 16 ff., *Zaynûn* 8–9; Avicenna *Aqsâm* 108, 115, *Nubuwwât* 121–32; Averroes *Tahâfut* 497 ff., 516.

[3] *Q* I 173, III 125–26. Notice how he gives the explanation of the nature of prophecy by the various schools (dialectical theology, mysticism, philosophy, etc. [*Q* I 170 ff.]), and how he finally emerges with his own explanation which is identical with that of the philosophers (*Q* I 173 ff.).

[4] *Q* I 170, 173, 174, 181, II 374.

[5] *Q* I 176 ff., 181, 216, III 54: 18–19, 55: 6–7, 57: 5–7. Cf. Averroes *Tahâfut* 515, 583: 14. Statements by the philosophers concerning the distinct character of prophecy and the superiority of the prophet *in matters pertaining to his office* (i.e., knowledge of the hidden things, legislation of good laws, and leading men to their happiness [cf. Averroes *Tahâfut* 516]) should not be suspected or confused with other statements in which they 'repeat' commonly accepted opinions about prophecy.

intellection and back to the representation of that knowledge in adequate images through which he communicates it to his fellow men. But the prophet does not ascend to pure intellection through the art of reasoning employed by the philosopher. He simply possesses an innate ability (*fiṭra, jabilla*)[1] and an aptitude (*isti'dâd*)[2] that enable him to see beyond the veil of sense objects and attain the knowledge of the spiritual world directly. His powerful intelligence, further, enables him to persist in this practice until it becomes a habit.

Ibn Khaldûn does not specify precisely which of the intellectual faculties attains this knowledge. His description of the way it functions, however, makes it clear that it is the faculty which the philosophers called the intellect *habitus* (*'aql bi-l-malaka*).[3] This faculty is common to all men, but in its highest form it is special to the few who possess powerful intuition (*ḥads*). This superior form of the intellect *habitus* was called the saintly intellect (*'aql qudsî, intellectus sanctus*).[4] According to Avicenna, the intellect *habitus* is situated between the intellect in potency and the intellect in act. It is beyond the potential intellect because it grasps first and necessary principles, but it is still in potency, since it has not yet completely, i.e., theoretically and demonstratively, known them and their consequences.[5] However, in its most perfect form, as in the case of the saintly intellect of the prophet, it does arrive with perfect ease and clarity at the *summary* knowledge of the highest intelligible beings.[6] The faculty through which the prophet attains the truth is thus identified by the philosophers with the primary *habitus* of the intellect which Aristotle had called *intuitive reason* and considered one of 'the states of mind [the other three being scientific knowledge, practical wisdom, and philosophic wisdom] by which we have truth and are never deceived about things invariable or even variable. . . .'[7]

The various degrees of knowledge attainable by this intellectual

[1] *Q* I 176: 13–14, 178: 2–3, II 374: 8.

[2] *Q* I 174: 16, 177: 10, II 374: 3. Cf. A.-M. Goichon *Lexique de la langue philosophique d'Ibn Sînâ* (*Avicenna*) (Paris 1938) 211–12 (Nos. 409, 410).

[3] *Q* II 374: 14.

[4] Avicenna *Najât* 272–74, *Nubuwwât* 122–24, *Qiwâ* 64–66. Cf. Goichon *Lexique* 230–31 (No. 439, sec. 7), 336 (No. 610, sec. 23); Tahânawî *Kashshâf* 1030.

[5] Avicenna *Ḥudûd* 80, *Najât* 270–71.

[6] Avicenna *Nubuwwât* 122; cf. Goichon *Lexique* 230–31 (No. 439, sec. 7); Tahânawî *Kashshâf* 1030: 11–12.

[7] Aristotle *Nicomachean Ethics* vi. 6. 1141^{a}2–4 (Ross).

faculty depend, according to Ibn Khaldûn, on the degree to which man remains chained to his bodily existence. Thus, the first and lowest degree is the knowledge attainable within the bounds of the sensible world (*'âlam jismânî*); in it man is still in possession of his external senses, and has the *habitus* of the sciences and the knowledge through which he gains his living, and learns his duties toward God and the necessity of obeying the prophets. In this stage, man is still bound by his bodily existence and cannot go beyond it.[1]

Next comes the knowledge attainable in the world of sleep (*'âlam al-nawm*). Here, imagination (*khayâl*) roams in the inner (*bâṭin*) realm and, using the same external senses, sees things stripped of time, space, and bodily limitations. This is a common human experience which is nearest to that of the prophets. In fact, part of prophetic knowledge is gained in such a state. The forms or ' images ' (*ṣuwar*) gained in the state of sleep are ' driven by imagination to common sense ', and represented by sensible images which are in turn remembered when the state of sleep is over. To understand the true significance of these sensible images, one must interpret them. It is in such a state also that some are given foreknowledge of what will happen to them in the world to come. The limitation of this state, however, is that it is not always pure and is never guaranteed to have the angelic world of pure intellects as its source. For it is possible that one may be only ' imagining ' that the forms which he has previously gained through the senses, and kept in memory, are coming to him from the angelic world and, thus, have false dreams.[2]

Thirdly, there is the state of death (*'âlam al-mawt*) in which men are totally divested of their bodies and in which they see the same things seen by the prophet. In this state, men preserve their powers of apprehension and are happy or miserable according to their previous deeds. This is the state that completes and gives meaning to our worldly existence; for without it, this existence ' would be a futile sport '.[3]

[1] *Q* I 175–76, II 364–70, 375–76, III 54: 10–11, 55–56.
[2] *Q* I 176, 177: 8–14, 185 ff.
[3] *Q* III 55: 13–15, cf. I 177, III 57–58. We prefer placing this state before that of the prophet (as in *Q* I 177: 14–15). This seems to be its right position in a discussion of the intellect *habitus*.

The prophetic state (*ṭawr al-nubuwwa*) is the highest. It is free from the confusion of the state of sleep, and does not have to wait until the soul leaves the body as in the state of death. It is a state of intense and direct apprehension in which the prophet does in fact become part of the angelic world:

'The prophet sees God and the angels, hears the word of God from Him or from the angels, and sees Heaven and Hell and the Throne and the Chair. Riding the Pegasus, he pierces through the seven spheres in his heavenly journey, and there he meets the [other] prophets and leads them in prayer. He apprehends the various sensible perceptions, as he apprehends [them] in the bodily state and the state of sleep, but [apprehends them] through the necessary knowledge created in him by God and not through the normal perception of men through the senses.'[1] The main distinction between this state and the state of sleep is, therefore, that the vision of the prophet is more certain and direct, and what he sees admits of no error. But like the knowledge gained in the state of sleep, the knowledge thus gained by the prophet has to be preserved by him and communicated through the intervention of imagination and common sense, the faculty which supplies the sensible forms and the commonly understandable language used by the prophet in communicating his visions to others.[2]

This ascension through the intellect *habitus* to the angelic world, or this direct vision (*shuhûd*) of the world of pure intellects which pierces the limitation of physical things and of time and space, is the true meaning of the knowledge of the prophet, of revelation, of the angels' address to the prophet, and of the other conventional terms with which the phenomenon of prophecy is described.[3] It is this knowledge which guarantees the

[1] *Q* III 56–57.

[2] *Q* I 174–75, 177: 15 ff., II 372–74, III 57. Ibn Khaldûn's criticism of Avicenna on the problem of the relation between the state of sleep and that of prophecy (*Q* III 57) is not as important as it appears, since he only objects to equating them. Ibn Khaldûn himself, though differentiating between them, thinks that they are closely related.

[3] *Q* I 166, 168, 178–80, II 372–77. There is probably no more decisive indication of Ibn Khaldûn's *philosophic* interpretation of the phenomena of prophecy than his identification of the 'angels' with the 'pure intellects'. Cf. Averroes *Tahâfut* 495, 516: 8–10; Tahânawî *Kashshâf* 1027: 21 ff.: 'To say that the pure intellects are the same as the angels *is to use Islam as a cover* (*tasatturun bi-l-islâm*) because in Islam angels are subtle and illuminated [bodies] that can perform difficult tasks, can assume different forms, and have wings and senses, while the intellects among them [the philosophers] are separate from matter.'

truth (*ṣidq*) of what the prophet teaches.[1] The aptitude of the prophet for arriving at such knowledge and the actual knowledge gained through his vision of the angelic world are the sources of his special power. These are apparent in the performing of miracles, in legislating for the community, and in leading it to act in a manner conducive to the happiness of men in this world and the world to come.

Miracles are acts emanating from the particular powers that the prophet possesses by virtue of his knowledge and office. They are beyond the normal powers of men and, as the Arabic word (*mu'jiz*) indicates, they prove the deficiency or ' incapacity of men '; they are things which men cannot usually do. But like other Muslim philosophers, Ibn Khaldûn does not say that they are (rationally) impossible in themselves.[2] The proof of this is the existence of similar powers among magicians and others who perform unusual acts, though miracles differ from such acts in that they are always directed, like all that is done by prophets, toward a salutary end.[3]

Performing miracles is an important sign of prophecy because miracles stand as witnesses to the truth of a prophet's claim to his office and because they are an instrument which forces men to believe in what he informs them concerning the world beyond the senses and the world to come. But performing miracles is only one of the signs, and by no means the essential sign, of prophecy. The essential sign of prophecy is the possession of the capacity most directly related to the realization of its end. The end of prophecy is ' guiding the nation to which they [the prophets] were sent to the right path ',[4] and ' to improve men's life '.[5] The prophet must, therefore, possess the ability to decide what is good for men to do, how they should do it, and how they can be made to do it. Ibn Khaldûn and other Muslim philosophers are in agreement in emphasizing the practical or political function of prophecy, and that the true prophet must possess that virtue which deliberates about human actions, decides what

[1] *Q* I 165: 14, II 374.
[2] Cf. Averroes *Tahâfut* 515: 8–10. A miracle is ' impossible for man, possible in itself. It is not necessary in this [respect] to posit that rationally impossible things are possible for the prophets.'
[3] *Q* I 166–68, 170, 172, 191 ff., II 107, III 134.
[4] *Q* II 374, cf. I 165.
[5] *Q* III 54: 20.

is good or bad, legislates the most effective laws for all to follow, and communicates them to his followers in a manner most conducive to their acceptance of, and obedience to, his directives. The most essential requirement of the prophet, therefore, is that he must possess practical wisdom and, most of all, practical political wisdom and legislative wisdom.[1]

An important aspect of the prophet's political and legislative wisdom is creating in the community for which he legislates the attitude of dogmatic belief (*'aqîda îmâniyya*) concerning the divine source of the Law, the truth of his teachings about hidden things, the necessity of obeying his practical prescriptions, and the certainty of rewards and punishments in the world to come. The best condition for the perfect obedience of the Law and the performance of what it commands is to have a *habitus* or a ' state of possession '[2] which is the product of ' acts repeated an infinite number of times so that the *habitus* becomes deep rooted '.[3] Religious belief is such a state moulding the soul so that men will perform the directives of the Law out of inner compulsion and established habit from which it is hard to deviate.[4]

As the basic elements of Ibn Khaldûn's theory of prophecy are thus reconstructed, there remains little doubt concerning his

[1] *Q* I 165–68, II 368, 370, 373: 6–7, 374, III 44. For the relationship between practical wisdom, political wisdom, and legislative wisdom, cf. Aristotle *Nicomachean Ethics* vi. 8. 1141^{b}23–27: ' Political wisdom and practical wisdom are the same state of mind, but their essence is not the same. Of the wisdom concerned with the city, the practical wisdom which plays a controlling part is legislative wisdom, while that which is related to this as particulars to their universal is known by the general name " political wisdom "; this has to do with action and deliberation, for a decree is a thing to be carried out in the form of an individual act.' (Ross) While Ibn Khaldûn continuously links practical reason and practical matters with the functions of prophecy (*Q* II 368–74), he never mentions theoretical reason (*'aql naẓarî*) in this connection. Cf. Averroes *Tahâfut* 426: 7, 516, 580 ff. For the distinction between practical reason and theoretical reason, and their respective functions, cf. Aristotle *Nicomachean Ethics* vi. 3 ff. (the source of subsequent classifications among Muslim philosophers); Fârâbî *'Uyûn* 63 ff., *Aflâṭun* 12 (sec. 16); Avicenna *Najât* 64 ff., 272–74, *Ishârât* 80 ff., *Aqsâm* 104–8; Averroes *Tahâfut* 545–46; Tahânawî *Kashshâf* 1030–31. In *Tahâfut* 476: 6–7 and *Manâhij* 78: 12, 90: 5, Averroes specifies the practical wisdom of the prophet by calling it ' legal-prophetic wisdom ' (*ḥikma shar'iyya-nabawiyya*) in contradistinction to ' rational-philosophic wisdom ' (*ḥikma 'aqliyya-falsafiyya*). But since practical wisdom is a part of rational wisdom, we can suppose that the ' legal-prophetic wisdom ' is different from the ' rational-practical wisdom '.

[2] For this, most adequate, English rendering of *habitus*, cf. Jacques Maritain *Creative Intuition in Art and Poetry* (New York 1953) 49 n. 3.

[3] *Q* III 32: 15–16.

[4] *Q* III 31, 33–34. Cf. Averroes *Tahâfut* 581.

position within the Islamic tradition of political philosophy. When we penetrate beyond the stock of traditional formulas which he repeats in place and out of place to confirm the pious in his orthodox position, his *explanation* of the nature and functions of prophecy becomes unmistakably clear and consistent: The prophet is a unique human being who possesses the aptitude, character, and the intellectual *habitus*, which prepare him to ascend to the knowledge of things hidden from his fellow men. Because of his aptitude and knowledge, he has the power of performing miracles, of communicating his visions in a form most conducive to creating true beliefs in his fellow men, of persuading them to follow a certain course of action, and of legislating the Law (which embodies his communications about hidden things and his directive to specific acts based on such beliefs) in a permanent form. The true prophet, therefore, is not merely an inspired man or a man who has the unusual power of performing miracles. He is primarily a statesman and a legislator, and should have the necessary qualifications for these offices. He needs the power of persuasion through which he can induce his fellow men to believe his assertions about what he had seen and what he considers the best principles of action. He needs the power of laying down summary or detailed directives or commands, and the ability to persuade his fellow men to profess them not only in words but also in repeated ritualistic action, performed out of a deep-rooted ' state of possession '.[1]

2. The second major problem of practical philosophy which Ibn Khaldûn does not explicitly discuss but whose conclusions he adopts concerns the nature of the community for which the prophet legislates the Law. The most decisive of these conclusions is the distinction between the few (*khâṣṣa*) and the many (*'âmma*).[2] The characteristics which Ibn Khaldûn attributes to each of these classes of people leave no doubt as to the philosophic origin and significance of this distinction. The ' ways of the many ' to knowledge are based on the appearance (externals, *ẓawâhir*) of things, while ' the knowledge of the few ' penetrates

[1] For the essentially political character of the regime initiated by a prophet, cf. below pp. 281–84.

[2] E.g., *Q* I 66: 18, 176–77, 208, II 259. Cf. Fârâbî *Taḥṣîl* 36–37; Avicenna *Ishârât* 205; Averroes *t. Nafs* 89–90, where he accepts the distinction as a demonstrated proposition.

into the hidden (*bâṭin*) secrets beyond.[1] The many 'claim', 'presume', 'fancy', 'imagine', 'opine', and 'believe'.[2] The few 'verify' and 'demonstrate'; and they 'know' the 'truth', i.e., the 'cause', the 'meaning', and the 'purpose' of things.[3] This distinction between the mass or the many (who live by imagination and belief, and who cannot achieve knowledge through demonstration) and the intimate circle or the few (who, having the aptitude, leisure, patience, persistence, and proper training, can acquire the art of demonstration) is of crucial importance in Islamic political philosophy.[4] In order to understand its full implications for Ibn Khaldûn's social thought, theory of knowledge, and, consequently, his study of the sciences in the Islamic community, we shall briefly explore the nature of the problem as expounded by Averroes who was the last philosopher to treat it before Ibn Khaldûn, and whose works were studied and commented on by our author.[5]

By subdividing the many into those who by nature believe through rhetorical persuasion and those who are by nature dialecticians (i.e., not satisfied with rhetoric, yet cannot achieve true demonstration), Averroes reintroduced the Aristotelian theory of the three basic methods of demonstration: scientific demonstration or demonstration properly so-called, rhetorical demonstration, and dialectical demonstration.[6] He related these three ways of demonstration to the three classes of people and emphasized their political significance; thus integrating it with the Platonic idea of the few and the many as explained in the *Republic*, a dialogue on which he wrote a commentary.[7] Averroes

[1] *Q* I 43: 10: *manâḥî al-'âmma*, II 211: 8: *madhâhib al-'âmma*, 254.

[2] *za'ama, ḥasaba, tawahhama, takhayyala, ẓanna, i'taqada. Q* II 205, 207, 238, 242, 245, 323, 380, 382, 383.

[3] *ḥaqqaqa, barhana, 'alima* or *'arafa, ḥaqq, sabab, ma'nâ, qaṣd. Q.* I 66, II 211, 238, 242, *passim.*

[4] *Q* III 220; cf. Avicenna *Ajrâm* 54; Averroes *Faṣl* 6, *Manâhij* 61–62, *Tahâfut* 107–8, 361; Plato *Republic* vi. 484A-87A, 502C ff.; Aristotle *Rhetoric* i. 1–2.

[5] Above p. 35 n. 5.

[6] Aristotle *Posterior Analytics* i. 1. 71ᵃ1–10, *Rhetoric* i. 2. 1356ᵃ32 ff.; cf. Gauthier *La théorie* 34, 43–45, *Revue d'Histoire de la Philosophie* II (1928) 233–35.

[7] Cf. Averroes *Faṣl* 8, 25, 26, *Manâhij* 57. 'The many (*jumhûr*),' he explains, 'believe that that which exists is what is perceived by imagination and by the senses, and that what is not perceived by imagination or the senses does not exist.' (*Manâhij* 61–62, cf. 64.) Thus, for the many, reason is inseparable from imagination. They understand best when they are given an image, a semblance, or an analogy which they can perceive by their senses and know through immediate experience. *Ibid.* 77, 89, 121; cf. Fârâbî *Taḥṣîl* 30, 36–37.

also applied the theory of the three ways of demonstration and three classes of people to the Islamic community and attempted to identify explicitly the various sciences in the Islamic community on that basis. In the three works (the *Decisive Treatise*, the *Disclosure of the Method* and the *Incoherence of the Incoherence*),[1] occasioned mainly by Ghazâlî's (d. 1111/505)[2] attack on philosophy, he identified the few or the men of demonstration as the followers of the tradition of Plato and Aristotle, the dialecticians as all the innovators in religion including dialectical theologians, mystics, and those who combined both like Ghazâlî, and the rest of the many as the majority or the devout Muslims who steadfastly accepted the apparent meaning, and carried out the commands of the Law.[3]

The many are by far the overwhelming majority for whom the Law has been revealed, and rhetorical persuasion is the common denominator through which the prophet can address the many and the few. The Law, therefore, has for the most part employed rhetoric and the simple ways of demonstration, i.e., arguments whose premises are few and self-evident, and whose conclusions can be easily deduced from these premises. Further, such simple ways are mostly concerned with knowledge that is practically useful for the many. As to things that are not of immediate practical use, such as the nature of the soul, the many are told that they should not be concerned with them.[4] But in practical matters, the Law is definite and applies to all; the few and the many must enquire into them, understand them, and carry them out.[5]

The simple rhetorical expressions of the Law are, however, only the apparent or external aspect of revelation, necessary because the majority of mankind cannot be expected to be convinced in any other way. There is also a hidden aspect of revelation and the Law designed for the few. This hidden aspect is not communicated through demonstration properly so-called.

[1] *Faṣl*, *Manâhij*, *Tahâfut*.
[2] *GAL* I 419 ff.
[3] Cf. *Faṣl* 6, 8, 10, 18, 19, 25–26, *Manâhij* 67–68. Since these three classes of people exist in every community, and since the function of the prophet is to guide the community as a whole to the right path, it becomes necessary for him to employ all three methods in order to convince the many and the few alike. *Faṣl* 8, 17–18, 23–24, 30–31.
[4] *Faṣl* 26: 1–3, *Manâhij* 79.
[5] *Faṣl* 10, 11–21, *Tahâfut* 429.

It is embodied in the meanings behind the external examples, analogies, hints, and contradictory statements or variants, all of which indicate to the few the need for employing the rational demonstrative method if they are to achieve the complete knowledge of what is behind the externals of revelation and the Law.[1]

Concerning the problem of the relation between philosophy (i.e., its rational and demonstratively proved conclusions) and the Law, or between philosophy and the positive sciences, Averroes says: ' We Muslims know categorically that demonstrative reasoning does not lead to disagreement with what the Divine Law has brought forth. For truth does not contradict truth, but agrees with, and is a witness to it.'[2] When rational demonstration leads to the knowledge of a certain thing, there are three possibilities so far as its relation to the Law is concerned: the Law has not spoken of it and, therefore, no conflict arises; the Law has spoken of it and is in agreement with the results of rational demonstration, and again there is no problem; or the Law is not in agreement with these results and, therefore, ' it needs interpretation. Interpretation (*ta'wîl*) means transferring the signification of the expression from the real to the figurative sense. . . . And we affirm categorically concerning *all* that has been reached by demonstration and is in disagreement with the external [expression] of the Law, that the external [expression of the Law in question] admits of interpretation.'[3]

Having thus decided upon the essential agreement between all philosophically demonstrated conclusions and the Law, Averroes makes it clear that the attempt to reconcile the two should be limited to the few and never divulged to the many. Here he is explicitly following in the footsteps of the ' ancient (Greek) philosophers '[4] who had taught that miracles and the principles of the Laws are things that should never be doubted or discussed, and that ' he who does so . . . needs severe chastisement '. ' What should be said concerning such things is that their origins are divine matters which surpass human reason, and, thus, it is necessary to acknowledge them though ignorant of

[1] *Faṣl* 8, 10, 11, 12, 18, 33. Cf. Avicenna *Nubuwwât* 124, 125.
[2] *Faṣl* 8, 12–13; cf. Avicenna *Ajrâm* 50: 13–14.
[3] *Faṣl* 8–9, cf. *Manâhij* 72, *Tahâfut* 503.
[4] *Tahâfut* 514, 527–28.

their causes.'[1] The reason for such an attitude is explicitly stated by Averroes to be practical. The Law is the source of the virtuous life of the many. The disclosure of rationally demonstrated conclusions to the many and the attempt to reconcile rational knowledge and the Law can only result in confusion and in leading them astray.[2] Interpreting the Law for the many invariably leads to tearing the Law apart and rendering worthless its intended wisdom.[3] This wisdom is the practical wisdom of the prophet, who, like a sagacious physician, has given *all* a miraculously effective common way to live by, while all those who break its spell on men's minds and hearts fail to replace it.[4] A philosopher, therefore, should protect the many by supporting and praising the Law, and by refuting and silencing all who attempt to mislead them through questioning the Law or raising doubts about it. Above all, he should never disclose the conclusions of his rational enquiries and his interpretations of the Law to the many, for by so doing he would be acting unwisely and, consequently, revealing his ignorance of the nature of practical social life.[5]

Such a theory of the three classes of people and three classes of argument supplied the basis for Averroes' concept of the function of the philosopher vis-à-vis other philosophers, the dialecticians, and the many, in the Islamic community. Having decided that neither for the true philosopher nor for the many, serious doubts can arise concerning the interpretation of the Law (for the true philosopher knows its real interpretation and the many are satisfied with its external expression), he held that the two classes can exist in perfect harmony with each other if the philosopher restricts his interpretation of the Law to the ' books of demonstration ' which only his fellow-philosophers would have access to and could understand. In what he writes for the many, on the other hand, he should employ every possible means in his power to confirm the external expression of the Law.[6] Thus, the two healthy classes would coexist without conflict.

This ideal relation had been disrupted ever since the early generations of Islam by the sick class of people who were not

[1] *Tahâfut* 527.
[2] *Ibid.* 428–29, 454, 527, *Faṣl* 10, 12, *Manâhij* 56–57, 63.
[3] *Manâhij* 61–62, 71–72, *Faṣl* 30–32.
[4] *Faṣl* 27–29.
[5] *Manâhij* 71.
[6] *Ibid.* 68, 71.

content with the external expression of the Law and yet could not learn its true meaning through rational demonstration. These were the various groups of dissenting sectarians, dialecticians, and mystics, who, being ignorant of the true purpose of the Law and the true nature of philosophy, have attempted in vain to reconcile them. They have confused the pious many by disclosing to them their doubts about the external expression of the Law and the possibility of rationally justifying it.[1] Being sick, they attempted to change the Law, which had been designed for healthy minds, according to their own sick humour. They planted in the minds of the many doubts about the efficacy of the Law and left the community an easy prey to charlatans and supposed physicians.[2] Such vulgar interpretations have, further, given rise to pretentions of feigned conflicts between reason and revelation, and have led some to reject the Law and others to reject and persecute philosophy.[3] The many have been misled to consider philosophers as their enemies and the enemies of the Law, while in fact it is the sick and confused dialecticians who are their real enemies and the enemies of the Law, and the philosophers are their friends, the upholders of the Law, and the true successors of the prophet.

The true Muslim philosopher was confronting a practical situation in which both the Law and philosophy were in danger. Consequently, he could not continue to hold his tongue, but had to come to the rescue of the Law and to the defence of true philosophy. This is an extremely delicate task, since he is not free to use the method of true demonstration. Like the prophet, of whom he is the true representative in society, he has to employ a common or simple method which is for the most part that of rhetoric and dialectic.[4] Through this method, he must explain the errors of the sick class and the discrepancies of their methods and conclusions. He must teach the pious many, who have come

[1] *Manâhij* 65, 68, 70–71, *Faṣl* 20–21, 25, 26, 29, 32.

[2] *Manâhij* 68–70, 113 ff., *Faṣl* 27–29.

[3] *Manâhij* 70–72.

[4] *Faṣl* 17, 18, 32, *Tahâfut* 209 ff., 356–58, 588. Cf. Fârâbî *Milla* fol. 53v. Averroes' use of the simple method for convincing the many is most clearly shown in the *Manâhij*. There, he tries to refute the interpretations of the Koran by dialectical theologians by using a method similar to theirs, but simpler and nearer to the external expressions of the Koran. This method avoids their major pitfalls, i.e., over-involved and unnecessary interpretations, contradictory statements, and incomplete arguments (*Manâhij* 43–47, 49, 50: 4–5, 51: 19, 53: 5–6).

to think that the Law conflicts with rational demonstration, that it does not do so. Finally, he must investigate the works of those who have attempted to reconcile the Law and philosophy and have ended in producing pseudo-sciences that are neither positive nor philosophic, but a bewildering confusion of both. He has to distinguish the various methods employed in these sciences, and detect the degree and type of certainty achieved by each.[1]

Thus, the distinction between the few and the many, when explored on a philosophic level, becomes the foundation for the theory of prophecy and the distinction between the sciences of the Law and the philosophic sciences. By blurring the distinction between the few and the many, the dialecticians have blurred the distinction between the positive sciences based on the Law and the philosophic sciences based on demonstrative reasoning. Averroes attempted to unravel the confusion of the sciences in his time by exposing the fallacies of Ghazâlî. By Ibn Khaldûn's time, however, the situation had become worse. By reintroducing the distinction between the few and the many, and between the positive and philosophic sciences, Ibn Khaldûn had signalled his intention of reviving philosophy in the Islamic community. To be effective in this effort, he had to study the relation between the sciences of the Law and philosophy, and point out the specific sources of confusion between them, and thus save both and redirect them to their true ends.

3. The third major problem of practical philosophy in a community based on the Law and composed of the few and the many is, then, the elucidation of the proper function of knowledge in the community, the definition of the ends of the two groups of sciences under discussion, and a critique of the various sciences existing in the community at a certain time. This is precisely the object of Ibn Khaldûn in his discussion of the various sciences existing in the Islamic community of his time: to disentangle and expose the various mixtures of positive and philosophic sciences. As to his method, Averroes had already indicated its salient feature.[2] Ibn Khaldûn applies that same method throughout, using rhetoric, dialectic, and simple

[1] *Faṣl* 1 (title), *passim*, *Manâhij* 27 (title), *Tahâfut* 3 (title), *passim*. (Esp. his references to Ghazâlî's use of rhetorical, dialectical, and sophistical arguments.)

[2] Above pp. 93 ff.

demonstrations. The practical purpose of his discussion is clearly indicated by his exposition of the social dangers of the mixed sciences and by his repeated advice to the many to forego their study and obey the Law.[1]

Starting with the positive sciences, Ibn Khaldûn explains and justifies their multiplicity by the fact that the sources from which, and the methods through which, the commands of God concerning specific acts are derived are numerous. As to the sources, there are in the Islamic community the Koran, the authenticated Traditions of the Prophet (*sunna bi-l-naṣṣ*), the consensus of the community, and the supplementary additions (*ilḥâq*) (by analogy, etc.) to these three sources.[2] In order to utilize fully these sources for determining precisely what actions are prescribed and commanded, various sciences are needed and have been developed in connection with each of them: To understand the Koran, we have the sciences of koranic exegesis and koranic readings. To ascertain the true Traditions of the Prophet, we have the sciences of Tradition dealing with abrogating and abrogated Traditions, the character of Traditionists and their links, the unusual words and expressions occurring in Traditions, etc. And in order to know the proper rules of consensus and of the supplementary additions, we have the fundamentals of jurisprudence. The true end of all these sciences is the legalistic (*shar'î*) interpretation of the Law or the science of jurisprudence (*fiqh*) which consists of knowing the specific commands concerning specific acts. To jurisprudence, in turn, are attached various secondary disciplines dealing with the problems of inheritance (*farâ'iḍ*, or how to divide the inheritance of a deceased person), the way of discussing matters controversial among the various schools of jurisprudence (*khilâfiyyât*), the

[1] To the extent that Ibn Khaldûn was concerned with the rise and development of the sciences actually existing in the Islamic community, his account of these sciences can be called 'historical' and 'objective'. To the extent that he was interested in explaining the social uses and abuses of these sciences, his study can be called 'sociological'. But to accept such adjectives without qualification in defining Ibn Khaldûn's study of the sciences, is to miss the philosophic principles according to which these sciences are organized, discussed, and evaluated. These principles, i.e., the nature of philosophy and the Law, and his theory of prophecy and the social order based upon it as discussed above (pp. 73 ff.), are more important in explaining Ibn Khaldûn's account of the sciences than its 'historical', 'objective', or 'sociological' character.

[2] *Q* II 386: 1–3.

rules of analogy, and the rules of dialectical discussion of legal matters (*jadal*, or how to defend or disprove a legal opinion).[1]

Since in addition to prescribing certain acts, the Law prescribes certain beliefs concerning the nature of God and His attributes, the resurrection, heaven and hell, and predestination, and since these beliefs have to be explained and defended against innovations, we also have dialectical theology.[2] For the majority of believers, jurisprudence and dialectical theology are sufficient, since the majority live by the rules of conduct ascertained by jurisprudence and the beliefs explained by dialectical theology. There are some, however, who have the aptitude for, and the interest in, devoting themselves to spiritual exercise and devotional piety with the hope of attaining an intuitive knowledge of things divine. This is the way of the mystics who, starting with the externals of the Law, have devised certain practical exercises through which they attain direct knowledge of what the prophets have taught and what the community as a whole accepts on faith. These practical exercises have been systematized in the science of mysticism (*taṣawwuf*).[3] Finally, there is the phenomenon of dreams, through which some of the believers gain direct knowledge of the things beyond the senses. Dreams are usually remembered in the form of sense representations which are posited in common sense by the imagination, e.g., the sea representing power and the snake an enemy. There were developed general rules of interpreting such representations. These rules are the object of the science of dream interpretation (*ta'bîr al-ru'yâ*).[4]

All these sciences presuppose some knowledge of the language in which the sources have been revealed or written. Thus the

[1] *Q* II 386, 388 ff., III 1–26.

[2] *Q* II 386: 15–18, III 27 ff.

[3] *Q* III 60–65.

[4] *Q* III 82–83, 84–86. It is important to notice at the outset that Ibn Khaldûn considers dialectical theology, mysticism, and dream interpretation, positive sciences that are the speciality of a certain community, and not universal rational sciences. In the introductory summary schematism in *Q* II 385–87, of these three sciences Ibn Khaldûn mentions dialectical theology only (*Q* II 386: 17). Apparently, he did not think that mysticism and dream interpretation were important enough to be mentioned in a summary account of the positive sciences. At the beginning of the two chapters dealing with mysticism and dream interpretation, he says: 'This science is a legal science and it is new in the community. . . .' (*Q* III 59, 80). By saying that they are new (*ḥâdith*) in the community, he is indicating the fact that the early generations of Islam led a perfectly pious life without them. This is true, according to Ibn Khaldûn, of dialectical theology also (*Q* III 36: 15, 51: 14–16).

linguistic sciences (*'ulûm lisâniyya*) are in a sense necessary tools for all the positive sciences and are grouped with them.[1]

Although these positive sciences are primarily concerned with transmitting and ascertaining prescribed commands concerning practical matters, they contain some measure of rational thought which is apt to increase with the growth and complexity of social life. This is true, for instance, of jurisprudence and dialectical theology which deal with practical matters and with beliefs respectively. The use of personal prudential elaboration and analogy, which are, to a certain extent, rational efforts on the part of the jurisconsult, had been recognized by all the four orthodox schools of Islam long before Ibn Khaldûn's time. The same was true of some of the sciences closely connected with jurisprudence. Thus, the fundamentals of jurisprudence deal with the problem of how to deduce legal injunctions from the various sources of the Law, including personal prudential elaboration and analogy;[2] the science of controversial matters is concerned exclusively with rational rules for argumentation among the exponents of the various schools of jurisprudence; and the science of dialectical discussion of legal opinion is, formally at least, a purely rational discipline.[3] The rational element in dialectical theology, on the other hand, is all too clear, since the function of dialectical theology is to defend religious beliefs by rational arguments.[4] Ibn Khaldûn's analysis of the nature and function of the positive sciences, therefore, recognizes the existence, and to some extent the necessity, of a rational element in these sciences.[5] The crucial problem is, however, to define the nature of that rational element, to limit the extent to which it needs to be used, and to explain the possible danger of its excessive use.

The nature of the rational element used in the positive sciences is defined by the primary end of these sciences. This end, as we

[1] This is true only of the general schematism presented in *Q* II 386: 18–20. In the actual detailed account of the sciences, however, Ibn Khaldûn discusses the linguistic sciences after the rational sciences (*Q* III 278 ff.).

[2] *Q* III 17 ff.

[3] *Q* III 26.

[4] *Q* III 27 ff.

[5] Cf., e.g., Ibn Khaldûn's assertion of the necessity of arithmetic for dividing the inheritance of a deceased man in accordance with the prescriptions of the Law (*Q* III 14–15).

have seen, is practical: it is to ascertain and apply the commands of the Law. Consequently, whatever rational knowledge may be needed or used in these sciences must be strictly governed by, and directed to, that end. The jurisconsult may have to elaborate and to use rational rules of personal prudential elaboration, the rules of discussing controversial matters, or the rules of dialectic, for defending or disproving legal opinions. The dialectical theologian may find it necessary or useful to explain rationally and defend the beliefs commanded by the Law, or to disprove contrary beliefs or the innovations of sectarians and deviationists. In so doing, they all must recognize the pragmatic end to which they are utilizing rational argumentations, i.e., that their use of reasoning is a tool for applying the Law and defending the beliefs of the community.[1]

The extent to which reason is to be utilized in these sciences would, therefore, have to vary with the practical needs at particular times and places. The early generations of Muslims in Medina, for instance, led a pious life in full accord with the Law without the need to use reasoning by analogy, dialectical theology, or mystical exercises. The rise of new practical problems resulting from the expansion of the Islamic empire, and the rise of sectarians and innovators as a result of contact with other cultures, necessitated the use of reasoning by analogy and dialectical theology.[2] The spread of worldly pursuits and mundane luxury during the ninth century and after, on the other hand, made a special order of those who consecrated themselves to a life of piety and devotion; and they organized the life of the spirit in accordance with rationally specified rules, practices, and exercises, known as mysticism.[3] But in all these positive sciences the rational element should be limited by the immediate practical purpose for which it is used. Thus, the problems discussed in the fundamentals of jurisprudence, in legal controversies and dialectic, and in mysticism, must be full of practical examples, and limited to the field of legal matters and devotional practices. They need not become rationally elaborate and abstract. The juridical sciences, for instance, need not deal with the whole range of rational analogy or dialectic as such.[4]

[1] *Q* II 127, III 1 ff., 16–17, 122, 123–24.
[2] Cf. *Q* III 2 ff., 44 ff.
[3] *Q* III 59–60, 62–63.
[4] *Q* III 22, 26.

Dialectical theology should concentrate on explaining to the community as a whole the beliefs contained in the Law, and ensure the continued existence of the 'state of possession' and the unity of beliefs; it must use simple arguments that could be understood by all, and at the same time emphasize the necessity of accepting beliefs without too much rational enquiry, the shortcomings of human reason, its inability to know the true meaning of beliefs, and the necessity of actually living by beliefs rather than simply uttering them.[1] Mystics should not pervert their practical exercises by attempting to demonstrate their intuitions and visions. They should, rather, practise their way of life and concentrate on the acquisition of the proper qualifications leading to mystical knowledge.[2] In the only rational argument which Ibn Khaldûn himself uses in this connection, his argument on the unity of God (*tawḥîd*), these ideas are prominently and effectively emphasized in a manner proving that he has mastered to the last detail the technique advocated by Averroes as most fitting for addressing the many.[3]

Restricting the use of rational argumentation in the positive sciences to the indispensable minimum is necessary because of the practical dangers that will inevitably result from superfluous abstractions in these sciences. The most immediate danger is that the author will lose sight of the practical purpose of these sciences and waste his efforts in elaborating useless argumentative schemes.[4] In dialectical theology, the practice of reckless rational

[1] *Q* III 30–31.

[2] *Q* III 61, 63–64.

[3] *Q* III 27 ff.; cf. Averroes *Manâhij* 43 ff.; above pp. 93 ff. Ibn Khaldûn starts his argument by saying: 'Let us start here with a *winning argument* [literally, a witty saying: *laṭîfa*] and a rational proof that discloses for us the unity of God *in the simplest or shortest way*.' (*Q* III 27: 5–6. Notice the use of 'disclose' [*kashf*] here and in the title of this chapter, and the use of the same word in the title of Averroes' *Manâhij*.) He then proceeds to show what the constituent elements of this simple or short way are. First he uses the argument from causation used by Averroes (except that Averroes gave the argument the more popular name of invention [*ikhtirâ'*] [*Manâhij* 43: 6]). Throughout the whole argument, the stress is on the necessity of abstaining from investigating the matter and following the Legislator in beliefs and actions. He even defines the unity of God as 'our inability to comprehend causes and the way they operate, and our delegation of that [knowledge] to their Creator' (*Q* III 31: 9–10, cf. also 51: 15–16.) He concludes by saying that the recognition 'of the inability to comprehend is comprehension' (*Q* III 31: 13), and appends a long argument on the necessity of having belief as a 'state of possession'.

[4] *Q* III 21–23, 26. This has been the case, for instance, in the treatises written by dialectical theologians like Juwaynî (d. 1085/478 [*GAL* I 388–90]), Ghazâlî,

argumentation about beliefs has been not only useless, but socially destructive. It has been the source of the various disruptive sects and dissensions that broke the spell of the Law, confused the community, and jeopardized its solidarity.[1] Finally, taking rational argumentation too seriously in the positive sciences is dangerous because none of the rational disciplines used in these sciences are true rational sciences. Therefore, their conclusions are never rationally demonstrated. When not checked by the prescriptions of the Law, they are apt to be false.[2] Considered rationally, the results of such faulty methods are simply opinions and have no intrinsic grounds for certainty. The positive sciences cannot, therefore, use the authority of rational demonstration to defend their conclusions. That is why they should keep away from the use of rational argumentation except when deemed necessary either for the explanation or for the defence of the prescriptions of the Law. In such cases, they must keep close to these prescriptions, for they are the only authority for their conclusions. To do otherwise is injurious to the health of the community, to the many and the few alike. It leads to the confusion between the proper methods of the legal sciences and those of the rational sciences, a confusion which Ibn Khaldûn thought to be the most important single characteristic of the sciences of his time.

The confusion between the positive sciences and the philosophic sciences was not, however, limited to the confusion between their methods but included their subject matter and problems. Indeed, the confusion was so widespread that it had become impossible to distinguish one group from the other.[3] The problem was particularly serious in the case of dialectical theology and mysticism on the one hand, and philosophy on the

---

and Râzî, on the fundamentals of jurisprudence, and 'Âmidî (d. 1233/631 [*GAL* I 393]) and Nasafî (d. 1142/537 [*GAL* I 427–28]) on legal dialectic.

[1] *Q* III 36 ff.

[2] When investigated from the standpoint of demonstrative science, the syllogisms employed in legal dialectic are for the most part 'fallacious and sophistical' (*Q* III 26); the logic employed by the 'ancient' school of dialectical theologians is naïve and not in accordance with the strict rules of reasoning; and the logic employed by the 'moderns' is only formal and, therefore, not productive of demonstrable conclusions (*Q* III 40–41, cf. 112–16, 123–24; cf. Averroes *Tahâfut passim*).

[3] *Q* III 42, 121.

other.[1] Ibn Khaldûn's attempt to reintroduce the distinction between dialectical theology and mysticism, and between both and philosophy, was ostensibly aimed at defining the proper object of the positive sciences and redirecting them to their practical end. But behind this practical purpose, his distinctions were directed toward another, more theoretical end, i.e., that of defining the proper sphere and object of philosophy.

In order to understand the predicament in which Ibn Khaldûn found dialectical theology, mysticism, and philosophy, we must consider his analysis of the post-Ghazâlian development of these sciences. In the case of the 'ancient' or Ash'arite school of dialectical theology, the relation between dialectical theology and philosophy was relatively simple and clear-cut. The ancients rejected the posterioristic logic of the philosophers and, consequently, denied the objective existence of universals to which the universals in the mind were to correspond. They refuted the very principles of essence, of nature, and of natural and rational causes. Instead, they started with principles of their own, especially designed for the defence of religious dogmas, like asserting the existence of the atoms and the vacuum, and the dissolution of time into time-atoms, and like holding that accidents do not endure through two time-atoms and that no accident can subsist in another accident.[2] In short, they rejected philosophy and its method; and having rejected nature and causes, they almost rejected reason itself.[3] From the standpoint of demonstrative science, their method was naïve and their principles were false. But this did not matter, since they clearly

[1] This problem concerned Ibn Khaldûn to such an extent that he felt it necessary during his stay in Egypt to add a new chapter dealing with 'the equivocal expressions of the Koran and Tradition' (*Q* III 44–59). This chapter is not in *Bq* which means that it was written after 1393/796–1396/799, the period during which the Marînid king 'Abd al-'Azîz, to whom this version was dedicated, ruled. Cf. *T* pp. *w–z*. In attempting to interpret these expressions, the Islamic community was led to great confusion. It is significant that he inserted this chapter between his discussions of dialectical theology and mysticism, as if to suggest that these two disciplines had been responsible for that confusion. The chapter contains nothing new, except for the analysis of the states of the intellect *habitus* discussed above. What Ibn Khaldûn had in mind, then, was to explain in clearer terms what he had already stated repeatedly in his discussions of the various positive sciences, i.e., that their ultimate source is the saintly intellect of the prophet, and that they should not, therefore, be confused with theoretical knowledge properly so-called, which is the object of philosophy.

[2] *Q* III 40, 114–15; cf. Maimonides *Dalâla* i. 63.

[3] Cf. Averroes *Tahâfut* 522: 7–8, *passim.*

differentiated themselves from the philosophers, did not place much faith in reason, and deliberately used it as a tool to defend the beliefs of the community—a task in which they were successful so far as the community accorded them victory over the innovators.[1]

A new trend, initiated by Ghazâlî, and developed by Râzî and his successors, appeared with the ' moderns '. The ' moderns ' refuted the method and principles of the ' ancients ' with proofs based on Aristotelian logic and borrowed from the physical and metaphysical doctrines of the philosophers. Thus arose the serious problem of a dialectical theology which continued to start from non-philosophic premises—the religious beliefs revealed in the Law—yet tried also to prove them rationally with philosophic demonstration, considering this to be the true task of philosophy in opposition to the philosophers who were considered the adversaries of belief.[2] Averroes' attack on Ghazâlî as a thinker who had ' confused the sciences considerably and had led them away from their source and path ',[3] had not been effective. On the contrary, it strengthened the position of post-Ghazâlian dialectical theology, which attempted to avoid the criticisms of Averroes by becoming more rationalistic. In fact, this tendency went so far that it became impossible to distinguish dialectical theology from philosophy. Dialectical theologians from Râzî onward became the philosophers of the community:

' The " modern " dialectical theologians mixed the problems of dialectical theology with the problems of philosophy because of the [doubtful] resemblance of the two in the questions [they treat], the resemblance [between] the subject matter of dialectical theology and the subject matter of metaphysics, and [the resemblance of] their problems.[4] The two have become as if they were one art. They [the dialectical theologians] have altered the arrangement of the philosophers in the problems of physics and metaphysics, mixing them [i.e., physics and metaphysics] into a single art which they introduced with a discussion of general matters, followed by [the discussion of] physical beings and

[1] Cf. *Q* III 39–40, 49.

[2] *Q* III 41: 13–14.

[3] Averroes *Tahâfut* 437, cf. 108, 454, 491, 587.

[4] Insert *wa* (and) at the beginning of *Q* III 122: 1 with MS C of *Q*, *Bq*. Cf. De Slane *Prolégomènes* III 167 n. 3.

related subjects, and then the spiritual beings and related subjects to the end of the science. That is what Ibn al-Khaṭîb [Râzî] did in the *Oriental Disputations* (*al-Mabâḥith al-mashriqiyya*) and *all* the dialectical theologians who came after him. Dialectical theology is mixed with the problems of philosophy and its books stuffed with [such problems] as if the purpose of their subject matter and problems were one. This [confusion], which is wrong, has misled the public.

. . . . .

'Know this that you may distinguish between the two arts, for they are mixed up among the "moderns" in theory as well as in writing. The truth is that each is different from the other in subject matter and problems. The confusion has resulted from the identity of their questions in the process of demonstration. As a result, the arguments of the dialectical theologians have become as if they were constructed to seek beliefs through demonstration. This is not the case. [Dialectical theology] is but the refutation of infidels and [its] questions are already known [through the Law] and posited as true.'[1]

The confusion between dialectical theology and philosophy had been intensified further with the development of rational mysticism, which attempted to make 'intuitive comprehension scientific and theoretical', and prove through 'theoretical reasoning' the object of spiritual exercises.[2] The result was a combination of rhetoric, and vague and misty talk, whose real meaning and purpose no investigator could understand.[3] It led some of the mystics to rationally indefensible positions like solipsism and the identification of 'the Creator with His creatures in essence, existence, and attributes'.[4] Others strayed from the right path by making their equivocal intuitive knowledge the object of supposed rational demonstration, using the arguments of the later dialectical theologians and borrowing others from the philosophers. Thus, after dialectical theology, rational mysticism was the most important element in the confusion of the proper object of the positive and the philosophic sciences:

'And there also came the "modern" extremist mystics who talk about intuitions. They mixed the problems of the two arts

[1] *Q* III 121–23. [2] *Q* III 65, 68. [3] *Q* III 69–70, 73. [4] *Q* III 67, 72.

[dialectical theology and philosophy] with their art. They argued about all these things indifferently, like their arguments about prophecies, Identity [of man and God], Pantheism, Monism, etc. But [the fact is that] comprehensions in these three arts [dialectical theology, philosophy, and mysticism] are different and distinct. The perceptions of the mystics are the farthest removed from the species of arts and sciences because they claim intuition in them but run away from demonstration—and intuition is far [removed] from scientific comprehension.'[1]

With the post-Ghazâlian development in dialectical theology and mysticism, then, Ibn Khaldûn was faced with a new attempt to reconcile the Law and philosophy. This was more serious and more dangerous than the attempt of the 'ancient' school of dialectical theology because it was not simply a pious attempt to defend the beliefs of the community and refute philosophy, but an attempt to demonstrate rationally revealed dogmas about subjects like the essence and attributes of God—a thing which philosophy had not attempted and had considered beyond the sphere of demonstrative proof. Philosophy, true Aristotelian philosophy and not the false doctrines of the 'ancient' dialectical theologians, had become a captive of dialectical theology and mysticism: they had become its champions and its only representatives in the Islamic community; they had rearranged its subject matter and problems and were using it to demonstrate what it was not intended to demonstrate, and indeed what it was incapable of demonstrating. The noblest of sciences has thus been

[1] *Q* III 123: 17 ff., 124. Cf. Miya Syrier 'Ibn Khaldûn and Islamic Mysticism' *IC* XXI (1947) 264–302. Syrier presents in this article an exhaustive study of Ibn Khaldûn's attitude toward the various schools of Islamic mysticism with a fine comprehension of the delicate problem of Ibn Khaldûn's style, and correctly notices Ibn Khaldûn's 'bias' toward the '*principle*' of Monism (cf. *ibid.* 267, 294; *Q* III 68). We do not think, however, that Ibn Khaldûn's adherence to this principle is a sign of his gradual acceptance of mysticism or that he adhered to it as a substitute for philosophy. On the contrary, the principle of monism as explained in this context (i.e., the distinction between the Creator and things created, and attributing true existence to the former only) was a central doctrine in the Islamic philosophic tradition. That the prophet and the mystics could know this principle intuitively is consistent with Ibn Khaldûn's theory of prophecy and the intellect *habitus* (cf. above pp. 85–86, 88–90), and so is the fact that he does not think that *that* type of knowledge should be made the object of theoretical science. If this is the case, there is no need for supposing that there was any development, or 'earlier' and 'later' phases, in Ibn Khaldûn's doctrines concerning these matters.

defaced and absorbed into rationally baser sciences. The most universal science has been made a handmaid of sciences which are the property of a particular community. 'The science of divine beings . . . to which the greatest of attention should be paid' has been on the decline: 'its air has been stagnant and its light has been dim'.[1]

The only philosophy existing in Ibn Khaldûn's time in the Islamic community was that mixture of dialectical theology, mysticism, and philosophy, which he has described for us. To salvage true philosophy from this unholy alliance, to redirect philosophy to its proper end, he had first to expose and refute *this* philosophy and to show it for what it was, a theoretically fruitless and a practically dangerous venture.

Dialectical theologians and mystics are handled with care and kindness by Ibn Khaldûn. In effect, he gently points to the hopeless confusion of their principles and the failure of their methods, and shows that by attempting to use philosophy in demonstrating religious beliefs, they have blurred its principles and rendered it impotent and unable to arrive at certain and necessary demonstrations of any kind. He urges them, therefore, to refrain from the fruitless use of philosophy as a tool in their disciplines and to concentrate on pursuing their former useful function in the community: to obey the Law and follow its directives, to overlook its equivocal expressions and delegate their interpretations to God relying on the authority of His Prophet, and to cultivate that practical piety or 'state of possession' which characterized their universally respected and revered ancestors, the early generations of Islam.

But toward the philosophers, or rather the pretenders to philosophy, he is merciless in his criticisms and refutations. Nor is his criticism restricted to the philosophers of his time. He investigates the whole history of philosophy as he knew it and tries to find those elements or tendencies within philosophy which had, either in appearance or in reality, led to, or facilitated the emergence of, the confusion in which philosophy found itself in his time. His description of the philosophy which he singles out for refutation leaves no doubt as to what it is: Neo-Platonism, the apparent Neo-Platonic tendencies of Fârâbî, and

[1] *L* fols. 3v–4r.

the Neo-Platonic doctrines of Avicenna.[1] This is the philosophy which he refutes, showing its doctrines to be false; this is the philosophy which he considers as harbouring 'great dangers to religion'; and this is the philosophy whose true nature he intends to expose:[2]

'[They] claim that the *essences, properties, and proximate and distant causes, of all beings*, sensible as well as those that are beyond the senses, can be perceived by theoretical investigations and rational syllogisms. [They claim] that the dogmas of faith are to be established by [rational] investigation and not through hearing [transmission], since they are among the things to be perceived by reason. . . . They claim that happiness lies in the

[1] Cf. *Q* III 121, 210 ff. Aristotle figures prominently among those whose doctrines concerning divine beings are criticized by Ibn Khaldûn, who calls him the 'leader in these doctrines' (*Q* III 212: 14–15). But it is Aristotle the supposed author of the *Theology* (*Uthûlûjiyâ*), a work which is in fact a paraphrase of parts of the *Enneads* of Plotinus (cf. P. Kraus 'Plotin chez les Arabes' *BIFAO* XXIII [1940–41] 263–95). The doctrines of Aristotle included in this work are clearly distinguished by Ibn Khaldûn from the doctrines contained in his logical works and what 'Aristotle and his companions really meant'. The latter doctrines are approved unqualifiedly (*Q* III 213: 1, 217: 16). Fârâbî and Avicenna are frequently criticized by Ibn Khaldûn, but almost always in connection with Neo-Platonic doctrines held by them or attributed to them (cf., e.g., *Q* II 331–33, 371, III 57, 73, 213, 217, 219). It is of crucial importance that Ibn Khaldûn never criticizes Averroes or his doctrines on basic philosophic issues.

Ibn Khaldûn's criticism of specific philosophers and philosophic doctrines is based on philosophic principles; it is invariably the criticism of a philosopher and is never founded on anti-philosophic or non-philosophic principles. The critique of false philosophic doctrines is a constant theme in Islamic philosophy: Ikwân al-Ṣafâ' frequently criticize the philosophers who doubt the utility and secrets of prophecy (*Rasâ'il* IV 22 ff.). Fârâbî frequently attacks popular, false, amputated, spurious, vain, and pretentious philosophy (*Taḥṣîl* 40, 44–47), and emphasizes the proper limits of theoretical reason (*Ta'lîqât* 4, 5, 12, 20, 24). Avicenna attacks the 'infidels and riff-raff among those philosophers' (*Ishârât* 222: 9–10). But it is in the critique of Islamic philosophy by Averroes that we find the true precedent for Ibn Khaldûn's position in its doctrinal aspect. Both Averroes and Ibn Khaldûn attempt to rescue philosophy from dialectical theology and mysticism, and direct it to the true path of the ancients, i.e., the true doctrine of Aristotle. (Cf. Averroes *Faṣl* 20–21, 25, 26, 29, 32, *Manâhij* 113 ff.) They attack the attributed or real Neo-Platonic doctrines of Fârâbî and Avicenna, and criticize both for confusing their art with that of the dialectical theologians and mystics. (Cf. Averroes *t. Mâ ba'd al-ṭabî'a* I 313: 6–9, *Tahâfut* 54: 13–15, 274.) Finally, they criticize both, and especially Avicenna, for altering the philosophy of the ancients in metaphysics, and for departing from the 'way of demonstration' and ending with rhetorical and dialectical conjectures and opinions alien to philosophy, thus justifying Ghazâlî's criticism of that art (cf. Averroes *Tahâfut* 67, 92, 163, 173, 179, 182, 184, 239, 245–46, 252, 270, 274, 276, 295–96, 302, 320, 325, 371). For Avicenna's own statements on his departure from the ancients, cf. *Shifâ'* fol. 2r (I. i. i. 1).

[2] *Q* III 209–10.

comprehension of all beings, sensible and those that are beyond the senses, through this investigation and those [logical] demonstrations . . . together with the expurgation of the soul and its embellishment with virtues. This [they claim] is possible for man in accordance with his reason, speculation and disposition toward praiseworthy acts, and abstention from the reproachable, even if no Law is revealed to distinguish between virtuous and vicious acts. [They claim] that when the soul acquires this [happiness], it acquires joy and pleasure, and that ignorance of that [happiness] is eternal misery. This, according to them, is the meaning of felicity and torment in the world to come.'[1]

These doctrines, according to Ibn Khaldûn, 'are false in every respect'.[2] In the main, he has two objections to them, one theoretical and the other practical. Against the possibility of a theoretical and demonstrative knowledge of the essence of divine beings, he upholds the Aristotelian-Averroestic doctrine that the essences of divine beings cannot be directly and fully comprehended by reason. The essences of physical beings can be comprehended because these beings can be perceived by the senses. From such perception their essences are abstracted. Beings that are beyond the senses, however, cannot be rationally comprehended except through their effects in physical beings, i.e., as causes. But the knowledge of a being as a cause is not coextensive with the knowledge of the essence of that being. Hence the rational demonstrative knowledge of divine beings is limited to certain aspects of their essences only.[3] All that, says Ibn Khaldûn, 'has been declared by those among them [the philosophers] who have investigated the truth', and it is in this connection that he quotes Plato as saying that no certainty can be reached concerning divine beings but only probabilities and conjectures.[4] But the philosophers who have not heeded Plato, had tried to acquire demonstrative knowledge concerning such things. It was this tendency of overstepping the limits of reason that was adopted by the later dialectical theologians and mystics, and made the primary object of philosophy or the mixed science which they created. This tendency was especially strong among the Neo-Platonists or the philosophers who claimed that metaphysics

[1] *Q* III 210–12. [2] *Q* III 213: 11. [3] *Q* III 211–12, 214–15. [4] *Q* III 215: 9–13.

deals with 'the principles of beings [claiming] that they are spiritual, and with how [other] beings *emanate* from them, with the gradation of beings, and with the properties of the soul after it departs from the body and returns to the Source'.[1]

Ibn Khaldûn's practical objection to such a philosophy is based on his theory of prophecy and the distinction between the few and the many. Those who have held such false doctrines were dangerous to the community because they have been disclosing their doctrines to the many and openly preaching opinions that 'contradict the Laws and their external expressions'. They have been, in effect, telling the many that the Law is not necessary and that what it preaches and commands could be known as well by human reason alone. They have, further, confused the many by asserting that the happiness attained by the sole agency of reason is the *same* as the happiness promised by the Legislator.[2] All this has led the many away from seeking the happiness promised them by their Legislator, which they could attain only through forsaking theoretical knowledge (including the true and perfectly demonstrable)[3] and concentrating on the necessary tasks of seeking a living and performing their devotional duties. Instead:

'. . . you find the expert among them indulging in [the study of] *On Healing*, the *Directives*, and the *Deliverance* [*Najât*], [of Avicenna], and the summaries of Aristotle's *Organon* by Averroes, etc., scattering around their pages and making sure [of learning] their demonstrations, seeking that form of happiness among them, and not knowing that they are multiplying the obstacles in their way to it. But they rely in this matter on what *they relate* of Aristotle, Fârâbî, and Avicenna: that he who acquires the knowledge of the active intellect and conjoins it in this life has acquired his share of happiness.'[4]

Such doctrines had been responsible for many of the dissensions in the Islamic community, and they had resulted in numerous sectarian movements that were partly responsible for its decline. These doctrines are false as well as dangerous. Philosophy must not openly oppose the Law, to say nothing of

[1] *Q* III 121.
[2] *Q* III 217–18.
[3] Like physics, cf. *Q* III 214.
[4] *Q* III 217: 6–13. Cf. pseudo-Aristotle *Uthûlûjiyâ* 14 ff.

misleading the many into fruitless and socially harmful doctrines and ways of action. The philosopher should uphold the Law, and assert that a great deal of what it has brought forth cannot be known by reason, that ' the universe is too wide to be embraced or to be known exhaustively in its totality ',[1] and that the happiness promised to all by the Legislator is the true happiness. He should assert that doctrines like the resurrection of the body cannot be known demonstratively but should be accepted as explained by the ' true Law '. And finally, the philosopher should preach that the believers must first and foremost study the sciences of the Law and act according to its demands—praying, fasting, and turning their faces toward God.[2] These are the practical matters which Ibn Khaldûn himself repeatedly emphasizes throughout his work, and especially in the chapter on the ' refutation of philosophy'.[3]

[1] *Q* III 218: 9.

[2] *Q* II 372, III 214, 215–20. Cf. Ikhwân al-Ṣafâ' *Rasâ'il* I 108–9, IV 301.

[3] This chapter on the refutation of philosophy is the fifth of ' seven ' discussions of pseudo-rational sciences. (*Q* III 121–241: Metaphysics [the science of divine beings: *ilâhiyyât*], magic and talisman, the occult properties of the alphabet, alchemy, the refutation of philosophy, the refutation of astrology, and the refutation of alchemy. Cf. Ikhwân al-Ṣafâ' *Rasâ'il* IV 32 ff., where some of these sciences are included within the domain of philosophy; Averroes *Tahâfut* 509–11, where many of these sciences are criticized in a manner not very different from that of Ibn Khaldûn.) The central, i.e., the fourth, of these seven discussions is an exposition of the science of alchemy and the last, i.e., the seventh, is on the ' rejection of the fruit of alchemy . . . and the corruption resulting from practising it '. (*Q* III 191 ff., 229.) The first four of the seven discussions do not bear the title of ' chapter '; while the last ' three ' are set apart and given more prominence by inserting the word ' chapter ' in their titles. The first of these latter three ' chapters ' is on the refutation of philosophy. Like its counterpart, the third ' chapter ', its title includes the word ' corruption ', but in the singular and followed by the phrase ' of its doctrines '. The second or central ' chapter ' deals with the ' refutation of the art of astrology, the weakness of its perceptions, and the corruption of its end '. (*Q* III 209, 220.) Taking the two arrangements together, it appears that Ibn Khaldûn's criticism of philosophy is related to the common object of his criticisms in all the seven discussions, which is to distinguish the positive element from the truly philosophic element in these sciences. (*Q* III 108, 124: 2–5, 125, 133, 137 ff., 146, 191 ff., 220 ff.) But it seems to be more particularly related to his discussion of the nature of alchemy in the central and last parts of the seven discussions, and of astrology in the central ' chapter ' of the three ' chapters '.

Both alchemy and astrology could be perfectly legitimate rational sciences if the subject matter and end of each is properly limited and defined. When properly defined, alchemy would be reduced to chemistry, which deals with ' the nature of matter ' (*Q* III 191), and astrology to astronomy, a noble art dealing with the movements of the stars (*Q* III 105, 106). But these two sciences in Ibn Khaldûn's time were confused and corrupt. Alchemy was dedicating itself to the production of gold from baser metals through magical incantations,

IV

Philosophy and Style

1. Ibn Khaldûn's main activity as a mature author was the writing of the *'Ibar*. In writing the *'Ibar* he chose a specific medium of communication and a specific subject matter: he chose not only to *write* but also to write about *history*. The specific style[1] of

and astrology was trying to foretell future events by guesses and conjectures. (*Q* III 209, 221–25; cf. Averroes *Tahâfut* 511.) It is possible that gold could be produced from baser metals and that future events could be foretold, but there are two distinct ways of accomplishing these ends: the rational way, which is an arduous task because its object is the perfection of man's rational faculty, and the magical way which by-passes reason. (*Q* III 125, 209, 221, 225, 235, 239.) The drawback of alchemy and astrology as they existed in Ibn Khaldûn's time was that they confused the two ways; while the alchemists and astrologers were for the most part practising a prophetic-magical art, they thought they were practising rational disciplines. The result was that most practising alchemists and astrologers had neither the prophetic-magical powers nor the rational powers. They were pretenders to both, deceived the vulgar by selling them conjectures for truth, and diverted students from the search for knowledge to the easier path of making a living through deception and corrupt practices. *Q* III 92.

These are the same criticisms that Ibn Khaldûn directs against the philosophy existing in his time. What philosophy, alchemy, and astrology, seemed to have had in common, then, was the theoretical confusion between rational enquiry and prophetic-magical powers, and the practice of deceiving and misleading the community. Like chemistry, true philosophy is a rational enquiry into the nature of things and it should search for gold by travelling its own legitimate, though long and arduous, path. Like astronomy, philosophy is a noble art concerned with heavenly things. But like alchemy and astrology, philosophy has chosen a short-cut to its goal and ended by travelling a theoretically confused and a socially dangerous path.

[1] The problem of Ibn Khaldûn's style can be studied from several points of view, all being necessary for the precise comprehension of his meaning. From the literary point of view, his style is characterized by a conscious effort to write in a simple, free, and flowing manner in contrast to the prevalent use of flowery rhymed prose by his contemporaries. (Ibn Khaldûn uses rhymed prose in the opening passage of the *'Ibar* [*Q* I 1–6] and the *Lubâb* [*L* fols. 3v–4v.]) From the historical point of view, it must be recognized that he used some words and expressions whose precise meaning cannot be understood without reference to the particular usage of his time in western Islam. (Cf. De Slane's philological notes in *Prolégomènes* I–III, *Histoire des Berbères et des dynasties musulmanes de l'Afrique Septentrionale* [4 vols.; Alger 1852–56] I–IV; R. Dozy's review of *Prolégomènes* [*JA* VI xiv (1869) 133–218] concentrates on the philological problems of the text. Dozy incorporated most of the material of this review in his *Supplément*, a work indispensable for the student of Ibn Khaldûn's style.) From the biographical and psychological points of view, we have to understand the peculiar way he constructs his phrases, the historical and literary events associated with his expressions, and the time-sequence during which the work was written. Interesting and important as such studies could be, they are essentially of no philosophic relevance. The problem of style is philosophically relevant only when it is concerned with, and is designed to solve, theoretical and practical philosophic problems.

writing and the subject matter he chose presented possibilities as well as problems to Ibn Khaldûn—possibilities of reaching a large audience and of influencing it in certain directions, and problems inherent in the mode of communication he had chosen. The literary character of the *'Ibar* is the result of his attempts to solve these problems.

Language, according to Ibn Khaldûn, is not a product of nature, but, like other arts, a *habitus* (*malaka*).[1] To express meaning through words is to clothe mental images with external forms.[2] The spoken word mediates between the speaker and the hearer. It interprets meaning but also conceals it, it is simultaneously a bridge and a veil.[3] Understanding is a struggle with words and meanings, and a continuous exploration of the relationship betweeen them. To understand the meaning we have to understand the word that expresses it, and to understand the word we have to understand the meaning for which it stands. Through this process, meanings, words, and their relationship, become more precise, the veil recedes, and we progress to knowledge.[4]

This can be done best through direct teaching and conversation: the primary means of communicating ideas.[5] But direct communication is possible only with those whom one can meet. To communicate to persons not present in the same place or not yet born can be done only through writing, a medium decidedly inferior to direct conversation. Therefore, a new and additional veil, the written word, mediates between the reader and the mental images of the writer. The reader has to struggle twice: first, to reconstruct the spoken word from dead letters, and, second, to arrive at its meaning. The written word is less penetrable; it conceals meaning more effectively.[6] For, in addi-

[1] Goichon *Lexique* 384–85 (No. 676).

[2] *Q* III 242, 244, 257, 297, 313, 332, 334.

[3] We have already met this dual character of the word *'ibra*, cf. above pp. 65–66, 70–71.

[4] *Q* III 255–58, 275.

[5] Fârâbî *Aflâṭun* 16: 3–4. This idea was traditionally ascribed to Socrates and Plato in Islamic and Christian literature alike. Cf. Bîrûnî *Hind* 81; Ibn Abî Uṣaybi'a *'Uyûn* I 43; F. Rosenthal *The Technique and Approach of Muslim Scholarship* [' Analecta orientalia; commentationes scientificae de rebus orientis antqui,' 24] (Roma 1947) 69; Jerome *Contra Rufinus* iii. 40; Augustine *De consensu evangelistarum* I 7; Otto of Freising *Two Cities* ii. 19.

[6] *Q* III 242–43, 267, 275–76. The first text is definitely corrupt in at least one place (*ibid.* 243: 2–3); and because it is neither in the *Bq* nor in *TT*, it could

tion to the difficulties just mentioned, the reader has to surmount the difficulties of differences among various languages, the differences in the meaning of words from place to place and from time to time within a single language, and the differences of the meanings of words in different sciences and, especially, in the positive sciences and the historical sciences (*'ulûm ta'rîkhiyya*) which differ from one community to another.[1]

In the universal philosophic sciences these difficulties are easier to surmount. The technical terms they employ are precise, and once the logical tools are grasped and applied in the exposition of these sciences, error can be avoided and the communication of meaning becomes less hazardous.[2] The reader can examine for himself the validity of their arguments, accepting what he finds to be true and rejecting what is erroneous.[3] Explicit logical reasoning is not, however, sufficient for the achievement of true knowledge, for one must also have intuition. Thus, personal intuition of truth is the final stage in the process of exploring the written and spoken word.[4] Intuition and logical exposition are the two foci between which thought must move. They are emphasized throughout the Introduction and Book One of the *'Ibar* as the characteristic features of the work, and the reader is invited to examine the work accordingly.[5] Nor does logical exposition automatically overcome all the difficulties inherent in communication through writing. To write is to undertake the risk of being misunderstood both in the sphere of thought and the action to which thought leads. Ibn Khaldûn was not in favour of satisfying the urge to write except when there was a purpose which could be fulfilled only through writing, a

not be collated or corrected. De Slane's conjecture (*Prolégomènes* III 265 n. 1) is probably correct. However, all doubt as to the superiority of direct teaching and conversation over the written word is ruled out because of the supporting texts mentioned above. The chapter in which this text occurs was most probably written in Egypt toward the end of Ibn Khaldûn's life. According to De Slane (*loc. cit.*), it is included in only one of the MSS upon which Qatremère based his edition, i.e., MS ' A '.

[1] *Q* III 243: 9–13; cf. above pp. 75–76.
[2] *Q* III 87, 255.
[3] *Q* III 108 ff., 255.
[4] *Q* I 66, where Ibn Khaldûn's discovery of the science of culture is attributed to intuition (*ilhâm*). *Ilhâm* also means inspiration when used in connection with prophetic knowledge and that of the saints.
[5] *Q* III 255–57.

purpose important enough to counterbalance the risks of misunderstanding.[1]

But Ibn Khaldûn could have written the *'Ibar* for a small group of specialists like 'the learned few' (*al-'ulamâ' wa-l-khâṣṣa*)[2] or for a special social class such as rulers and princes only. This would have simplified the problem of communication through writing. By limiting his audience, a writer could presuppose a certain amount of theoretical or practical knowledge in the reader. The undesirable reader could be excluded by writing in a technical language that none but the specialist could understand. This was not merely a theoretical possibility. The practice of eliminating the undesirable reader was common in Islamic mystical and philosophic literature. It was made possible through an art of writing whose difficulty and ambiguity automatically excluded all except those for whom it was intended.[3] In contrast, Ibn Khaldûn chose to write for all people, for the chosen few and for the many, for the learned and for the ignorant, and for the rulers and for the ruled. Such a choice presented difficulties as to the subject matter to be chosen, the way of its treatment, and the literary character of the work.

History seemed to be the ideal subject through which ideas could be communicated both to the few and the many in the Islamic community. Unlike philosophy, it was not avoided by the many, suspected by the pious, or condemned by accepted opinion. Unlike entertaining poetry and story-telling, it was not derided and disliked by the few. It was of interest alike to rulers and princes, and to the ruled. It was a practical discipline useful for immediate political action, and a theoretical discipline investigating the nature and causes of human things. It was simultaneously a discipline which the Islamic community considered its own, and a universal discipline transcending national boundaries. It included in some fashion all other subjects; yet was recognized as an independent discipline.[4] In characterizing their discipline, Muslim historians had already emphasized the comprehensiveness and diversity of its subject matter, and its

[1] *Q* III 242: 5, 243: 3–4.
[2] *Q* I 6: 2–3.
[3] Fârâbî *Ta'allum* 53–54 (secs. 6–7); Avicenna *Ishârât* 222.
[4] Cf. Ghazâlî *Iḥyâ'* I 5 'Introduction', where he relates that some authors wrote about medicine under the guise of astrology in order to attract readers.

uses for the various classes of people. Theologians, mystics, philosophers, and literateurs, studied history, and each class tried to learn from its *'ibra* in their respective fields. Common people enjoyed its pleasant and dramatic stories, and its memorable events. Rulers and princes cultivated and encouraged it because it was a field through which they could learn the policies of their predecessors and gain competence in the art of ruling.[1] It is this comprehensive character of history, and its diverse uses for the few and the many, that Ibn Khaldûn also emphasizes in the opening passage of his work.[2] History can be understood by the few and the many, he explains, because of a duality in its subject matter. There is the external aspect which calls for the simple narration of events. This is the only aspect in which the many are usually interested, and it is in this sense that the historical sciences are relative to a particular community and differ from one community to another.[3] But there is also an internal and philosophic aspect in history which calls for insight into, and the critical examination and evaluation of, the inner causes and remote origins of historical events.[4] In this second sense, history is a rational and philosophic science, and thus universal and not relative to a certain community. This is the science which Ibn Khaldûn intended to communicate to the 'learned few'.[5] In order to communicate simultaneously the externals of history to the many, and the nature and cause of historical events to the few, it was necessary for Ibn Khaldûn to use a specific style of writing through which he could successfully impart to the intimate circle of the few the doctrines intended for it without allowing the many to suspect even the existence of such doctrines in the *'Ibar*.[6]

[1] Sakhâwî *I'lân* 7 ff., 17 ff., *passim*.

[2] *Q* I 2: 9–13.

[3] This is explicitly stated by Ibn Khaldûn. The historical sciences differ among different communities, he says, 'because of differences in the external[s] of narration' (*li-ikhtilâf khârij al-khabar*) (*Q* III 243: 14).

[4] *Q* I 2: 12–19. Cf. above p. 48 n. 3.

[5] *Q* I 6: 2–3. It was for these learned few that Ibn Khaldûn wrote about the science of culture, the theoretical and philosophic portion of the *'Ibar*, in which he followed the method of 'demonstration' which investigated the truth about the 'ideas of the few and the many, and through which illusions are rejected and doubts are resolved'. (*Q* I 66: 17–19.) The few are also referred to as those who have a profound knowledge of things (*ahl al-rusûkh*) and the true investigators (*muḥaqqiqûn*). Cf. above pp. 91 ff.

[6] The literature on the exoteric-esoteric art of writing as practised by Muslim

2. It is essential for the success of this style that the fact that an author is employing it should be communicated indirectly.[1] Nor should we expect it to be uniformly employed, for that would defeat its very purpose. For its effectiveness, it would be preferable if an author could devise innumerable variations of its basic principles. A master of this art writes in such a way that each passage presents difficulties which only the initiate could overcome. What is, then, the object of the student who makes such texts the object of his study? Is he to 'explain' the art employed in the text, saving the initiate the effort of encountering it for himself, and breaking its spell on the many? Or could he exorcise its secrets without jeopardizing the efficacy of its intended purpose for the few and the many? Ibn Khaldûn himself has shown the way out of this dilemma in his study of the 'equivocal expressions of the Koran':[2] The proper way to explain such texts is to explain them according to the principles of the art they employ. We shall follow this precept by attempting first to comprehend the art Ibn Khaldûn employs in order to be able to meet adequately the problems we are bound to encounter in the *'Ibar*.[3]

One of the main devices of Ibn Khaldûn's technique of

authors is very limited and inadequate. Cf. E. Blochet 'Études sur l'ésoterisme musulman' *JA* IX xix (1902) 489–553, *ibid.* xx (1902) 49–111. Blochet misses the mark when he says that Muslim philosophic texts 'n'offre point de difficultés insurmontables'. (*Ibid.* xix [1902] 490.) Further, the description of their technical terms as 'obscur' is incorrect; the proper term being 'ambiguous'. For the distinction between the two terms, cf. W. B. Stanford *Ambiguity in Greek Literature: Studies in Theory and Practice* (Oxford 1939) 73 ff., 181–82.

[1] The most common way of hinting indirectly at the use of the exoteric-esoteric style by a writer is to speak about other writers or works which have employed that style, and use this opportunity for the purpose of indicating the techniques he himself is using. Fârâbî follows this method and talks about the exoteric-esoteric style of Plato and Aristotle (*Jam'* 5–6). Ibn Khaldûn follows it by referring to the interpretation of the Koran and Tradition (*Q* II 391–92, 395, III 19–20, 44 ff., 54–59), and of dreams and alchemic texts (*Q* III 85–86, 209). In 'documenting' the following remarks on Ibn Khaldûn's own style, we shall, therefore, refer to such texts as well as to examples in which Ibn Khaldûn applies these stylistic techniques.

[2] Above pp. 102–3.

[3] Ibn Khaldûn's work presents the student with a challenge that has not been adequately met by those who look for his doctrines in the most prominent places, accept the doctrines which he repeats most frequently as his original contribution, and select, paraphrase, and rearrange them to prove the modern 'scientific' character of his thought. As this problem has not been recognized before, all previous studies of Ibn Khaldûn remained oblivious to its implications. This was to a large extent due to the modern rationalistic and positivistic approaches of these studies; for modern rationalism and positivism stand for complete exotericism.

exposition is to give a rational proof of a proposition, e.g., the necessity of a ruler, and then turn to a koranic text or a Tradition and inform his reader that the real meaning of the text in question conforms to what had been rationally proved in spite of the fact that its literal meaning may not.[1] What he intimates is this: Had the reader, like Ibn Khaldûn, been in possession of certain knowledge not contained in the text, yet related to its subject, he would have been able to understand a deeper or an alternative meaning in that text. Or, had the reader known a certain truth related to the subject of the text, e.g., the truth about human nature, he would have understood the *purpose* or *intention*[2] of the text rather than simply accepting its apparent meaning. The hidden and the apparent meanings of the text are not contradictory. The apparent meaning remains true for those for whom it was intended. We can, therefore, expect to find in Ibn Khaldûn's writing many passages with various levels of meaning. We can also expect that the deeper the level of meaning, the deeper the previous knowledge required for understanding it should be. The use of the word *'ibra* in the title is of that order.

There are various ways in which the different levels of meaning can be linked together, and the initiate is usually given clues indicating their existence and helping him to move from one to the other. For example, the initiate can be aided by the insertion of terms or phrases containing hints that will escape the many, but which will remind him of other contexts in which he had met that particular word or phrase. The initiate may stop to reflect, and it may dawn upon him that the text may mean something different from, or contradictory to, the first impression it made upon him. The author can also help the initiate by inserting an apparently harmless phrase, and this may in turn be a quotation from the Koran or Tradition, to the effect that those who look deeper will find *the* answer, or God likes and aids those who *use* their reason *rightly*, or one must refer to God's grace for the *right* answer, or the reader must reflect upon the *'ibra* of the event or the story, or he must seek to understand the *secret* of what has been said.[3] The reader may disregard these

[1] Cf. esp. *Q* I 346–48, 364–66.
[2] *qaṣd, murâd. Q* I 347–48, II 226–27.
[3] E.g., *Q* I 172, 173, 180, 239, 243, 245, 247, 267, 344, II 370, 374.

hints as do some of the editors of Ibn Khaldûn who ' modernize ' his text by dropping out such phrases. He may consider them merely as signs of the writer's piety and intellectual humility, as they sometimes are. But the initiate will stop and reread the passage, or lay it aside and try to think about the subject and the purpose of the writer.

This is the stage in which the author can aid him by the insertion of contradictory, equivocal, and extremely brief, involved, or perplexing statements.[1] Such statements will simply confuse the many, and Ibn Khaldûn explicitly advises them not to attempt to explain them or penetrate to the truth that may lie behind them.[2] But the initiate will feel the urge to explain and understand them. When he studies the text again with this intention, he will usually find that some of these statements can be explained through the commonly accepted linguistic interpretations and easily defined within the apparent context (*qarîna*) in which they occur.[3] Yet others may still remain ambiguous and in need of explanation. As he further examines these, he may find that some of the crucial words employed in them admit of two or more meanings, one of which is concrete while the others are figurative (*majâzî*). By choosing the proper figurative meaning he will find the statements clarified. He can also be aided in the choice of the proper figurative meaning, if these happen to be many, by the context or by special hints that specify the one intended.[4]

Another aspect of Ibn Khaldûn's art of writing is to alternate the exoteric texts, clearly intended for the many, with esoteric texts intended for the few. The latter are usually few and inserted unobtrusively so that the many will pass by them without noticing them. He embarks on a long discussion of a subject, giving undue space to traditional and popular views, and elaborating on them in a traditional way, frequently quoting passages from accepted authorities and passages by others praising these authorities. The reader becomes more and more convinced that he is reading another version of a traditional subject treated in a

[1] *Q* II 391, 395, III 45, 53, 59: 13–14.
[2] *Q* III 27 ff., 44–45.
[3] *Q* II 391–92, 394–95, 397, III 19–20, 38: 10–11, 85–86.
[4] *Q* III 35: 14, 50–51, 53: 10, 54–55.

traditional way.[1] Suddenly, there comes a break in the type of vocabulary used, in the ideas, or in the method of treating them. Even the subject matter is sometimes forgotten and a new problem is introduced related to the previous discussion only externally or not related to it at all.[2] The inserted passage is sometimes also a quotation and a commentary upon it, but it is quoted from a remotely related field or from an author who was not usually accepted as an authority on the subject under discussion.[3] Such passages are usually short, cryptic, and at first generally confusing.[4] They are, however, carefully worded. Invariably they deal with very crucial points concerning basic religious and philosophic doctrines or with Ibn Khaldûn's own method and purpose.[5] Then, again with the same suddenness, the discussion of the previous subject is resumed and carried to a conclusion.

The first impression that such a treatment gives is the utter lack of formal style and organization in the discussion.[6] There are no clear premises, no demonstrations, and no clearly formulated conclusions. On the surface, there is no significant addition to the traditional and accepted views expressed by his predecessors. Yet, upon the reconsideration of the meaning and purpose of the inserted passage, and upon determining its relation to other parts of the work, the initiate may find that it does throw light upon the discussion and give it inner coherence and purpose.

A variation of this technique is to add an important passage as

[1] Many doctrines are repeated by Ibn Khaldûn simply because they are 'commonly known' (*'alâ al-mashhûr*), e.g., *Q* I 24, 338, II 40. On the conflict between philosophy and the commonly known arts, cf. Fârâbî *Aflâṭun* 16–17 (sec. 23).

[2] Cf., e.g., *Q* I 329: 10 ff., 343–44, 394: 1–7.

[3] Cf., e.g., *Q* I 173 ff., II 128–42.

[4] Cf., e.g., *Q* I 63: 6–9 (the end of the science of culture).

[5] Cf., e.g., *Q* I 173 ff. (the nature of prophecy), 329: 10 ff. (the method of the science of culture), 415: 8 ff. (Islam vs. Judaism and Christianity), II 3: 12–15, 19: 4–5 (the distinction between the science of culture and jurisprudence), 75: 17–18 (the meaning of chance), 127: 6–14 (political philosophy), 365 (theoretical reason), III 44 ff., esp. 47: 9–12, 57: 4 ff. (prophecy and dreams), 68: 12–16 (mystical knowledge), 92: 10–13 (the persecution and decline of philosophy).

[6] Cf., e.g., the description of Ibn Khaldûn's style by Silvestre de Sacy in *Anthologie grammaticale arabe* (Paris 1829) 433: '. . . son style verbeux et surchargé de répétitions inutiles'; and in his article on Ibn Khaldûn in *Biographie universelle* XXI (1818) 155*b*–56*a*: 'Son style est serré, et quelquefois un peu obscur. Les idées manquent assez souvent des liaisons nécessaires, ou des développments que le lecteur pourrait désirer; les chapitres, aussi, ne sont pas toujours liés par des transitions bien sensibles.'

a mere appendix, a marginal note, or a related problem, leading the careless reader to think that it is only of secondary importance.[1] This technique has been so successful that many of Ibn Khaldûn's modern students have assumed that his work could be divided into two categories: one in which he writes his original thought (usually about history and the science of culture), and another in which he merely rehashes the thought of other authors.[2] In disregarding the second category, many of the important passages and their significance are also disregarded, with the result that many of the clues to the basis of Ibn Khaldûn's thought and his intentions are missed.[3]

So much for the direct and positive aspect of Ibn Khaldûn's art of writing. Another major device of his is indirect communication. This is usually achieved through the discussion and critique of doctrines contained in the writings of others. A large part of Book One of the *'Ibar* is dedicated to the treatment of various authors: theologians, mystics, philosophers, literateurs, and men of political experience. Ibn Khaldûn also reproduces various letters, and recites diverse stories and parables.[4] To these we should add the numerous words and phrases repeated in a formal and traditional way. These are words and phrases that have been accepted as the proper thing to say in certain contexts. For example, the name of the Prophet is usually followed by the phrase 'may God have mercy upon him', a certain learned man is usually called 'the leader of the community', philosophic doctrines are usually called 'erroneous', and a discussion is preferably concluded with the phrase 'and God knows best'.[5] The apparent meaning of these phrases has been determined by tradition and consensus, and they have become inflexible. Their use in Arabic follows the principle of 'as the

[1] E.g., *Q* III 27 ff., 254–58.

[2] 'Umar Farrûkh *Kalima fî Ibn Khaldûn wa-muqaddimatihi* ('A Word on Ibn Khaldûn and His Introduction') (Beirut [1943]) 19.

[3] Notice, e.g., the omission of practically all of the sixth section of Book One ('On the Sciences') from the selections of Annemarie Schimmel *Ibn Chaldun: Ausgewählte Abschnitte aus der Muqaddima* (Tübingen 1951) 218–19.

[4] Cf., e.g., *Q* I 170 ff., II 94–95, 128–41, 215, 216, 272, 300, cf. *T* 130, 147.

[5] The cumulative impact of such stylistic devices has led some modern scholars to conclude precisely what Ibn Khaldûn intended his orthodox contemporaries to conclude. Cf., e.g., T. W. Arnold *The Caliphate* (Oxford 1924) 74: 'He [Ibn Khaldûn] attached himself to no philosophic system, but relied upon revelation in matters of belief.'

story goes '.[1] Consequently, it is not always clear, without a careful study of the context and the general position of the author regarding the problem under discussion, whether or not they are purely conventional.

Ibn Khaldûn's treatment of other authors' ideas deserves special attention. On the surface he follows a traditional method. Religious leaders are praised; and philosophers, heretics, and alchemists, are duly condemned and the pious are warned against them. There are long chapters in the sixth section of Book One of the *'Ibar* that appear as if they were objective accounts of the origin and development of the sciences. Yet, no sooner do we approach the text with a critical mind than we find that there is hardly a discussion of an author or an account of the history of a science which is not intended for another purpose.[2] This purpose can only be understood when we study the apparently unimportant remarks Ibn Khaldûn makes about the authors or the ideas he discusses, the minor words or phrases which he takes the liberty of adding or omitting, and the problems which he emphasizes and those he passes over with little or no comment. It is particularly important to notice those passages in which he uses another author as a mouthpiece for expressing his own ideas. When he is giving an account of the ideas of an author whose doctrines he has already mentioned as his own or as the basis upon which he will conduct his investigation, it is easy to detect such passages.[3] But when this is not the case, they are not as easy to detect. Nevertheless, they remain crucial, especially when dealing with problems concerning the nature of philosophy and the Law. When studying Ibn Khaldûn's discussion of such subjects, it is important to ascertain whether he is treating them from the point of view of the Law and the interest of the many, or from the point of view of philosophy. Only through such distinctions can contradictory statements like the condemnation of many rational sciences, including philosophy, and their praise as realizing the ' true essence of man ', be reconciled.[4] It must

[1] *'alâ al-ḥikâya*. Jurjânî (*Ta'rîfât* 41) defines *ḥikâya* as follows: ' [1] it is the transposition of a word from one place to another without changing a vowel or altering [its] case . . . [2] using a word by transposing it from [its] first position to the next position while preserving its former condition and form.'

[2] Cf. above pp. 73 ff.

[3] E.g., *Q* I 166, 170–71, 175 ff., III 133–34.

[4] Above pp. 76–77, 108–12.

also be noticed that it is in connection with such crucial subjects that Ibn Khaldûn communicates important esoteric doctrines, and in some cases most effectively, in a negative way. Some doctrines are rejected silently by not being mentioned at all, through reference to doubts about them expressed by commonly accepted opinion or accepted authorities, or by hints made by the author himself. Others are concealed through intentional ambiguity, reticence on important issues, lack of a clear plan for an argument, apparent contradictions, and inexact and confusing repetitions.[1]

This brings us to the well-ordered portion of Book One of the *'Ibar* in which the new science of culture is methodically treated starting from explicit premises, proceeding through the construction of syllogisms according to the rules of scientific demonstration, and ending with conclusions derived from such syllogisms.[2] Ibn Khaldûn takes pride in, and repeatedly mentions the fact that he has followed the method of scientific demonstration in organizing his new science.[3] But this does not mean that *all* the premises and arguments necessary for understanding the new science are to be found in the text.[4] This is especially true regarding its philosophic foundation. The science of culture is a special science dealing with a particular subject matter: human society. This means that the author was at liberty not to treat explicitly problems of a more general philosophic nature whose conclusions he needed as principles and methodological tools for the particular science he was discussing. Thus,

[1] E.g., *Q* I 165–73, 177–78, 205–7, II 370–72. There are instances where Ibn Khaldûn himself defends his silence on fundamental issues, cf. *Q* II 66: 4, 365, 370, III 53: 10, 59: 13–14.

[2] *Q* I 68 ff.; cf. below pp. 171 ff.

[3] E.g., *Q* I 66.

[4] Cf. Fârâbî *Jam'* 5 ff. Fârâbî argues that Aristotle's apparent intention to be clear and well ordered should not deceive his reader. He gives numerous examples of intentional omissions by Aristotle and tells of his answer to a letter from Plato in which the latter is supposed to have blamed him for writing well-ordered and complete treatises. Aristotle tells Plato that he (Aristotle) too had written his works and organized them in such a way that only the initiate would understand them (*ibid.* 6–7). The important techniques in Aristotle's exoteric-esoteric writings, according to Fârâbî, are the omission of the necessary premises in many of his syllogisms on physics, metaphysics, and ethics; the omission of the names of many of his masters; confining himself to one of two related principles, like mentioning justice and omitting injustice; and mentioning the two premises of a syllogism and following them with the conclusion of another syllogism, and then mentioning the premises of a new syllogism and following them with the conclusion of the former premises (*ibid.* 6).

although we encounter concepts taken from metaphysics, politics, and logic, e.g., ' nature ', ' cause ', ' end ', ' the good ', and ' demonstration ', we find no elaborate and independent discussion of these concepts. This is proper, since Ibn Khaldûn has written a work on history and not on metaphysics, politics, or logic. But he goes further. In order to avoid being condemned as a philosopher, he usually does not mention the sources from which he derived these concepts, whether from a philosophic tradition, from particular authors, or from the masters under whom he studied. For instance, throughout the work there is not a single reference to Averroes or Âbilyy concerning any of the *major* philosophic problems which he discusses.[1] However, to understand the precise meaning he assigns to many of the key philosophic concepts, like those mentioned above, it is important that we ascertain the philosophic tradition he followed. This has to be based largely on indirect evidence utilizing the meagre information we possess about his early training and writings, comparing his explicit statements with those of major Muslim philosophers, and ascertaining his position concerning the nature of philosophy and the Law. The reader, who has come with us thus far, has already been afforded numerous illustrations of this procedure,[2] of which more are to follow.

V

The Regime of the Solitary

1. Having investigated Ibn Khaldûn's purpose in writing the '*Ibar*, his conception of the nature of philosophy and the Law, of the role of the philosopher in a community based on the Law, and the style through which he chose to communicate his ideas about important philosophic problems, we are now in a better position to understand the real significance of the outcome of the long period of reflection and study following his repeated failures in practical politics.[3] At the end of his retreat in the castle of Ibn

[1] Cf. above pp. 34–37. For the manner in which Ibn Khaldûn refers to Averroes, cf. *Q* I 87, 244–45. The latter reference is to Averroes' paraphrase of Aristotle's *Rhetoric*.

[2] Cf. above pp. 73 ff.

[3] Above pp. 37 ff.

Salâma, his vocation as an author and his role in society seem to have been decided for the years to come. He abandoned his early hopes of reshaping society through political action and ceased to consider it necessary to continue his attempts to realize the city of his hopes through a reformed ruler or through his own seizure of political power. He decided instead to lead the life of an investigator and to migrate to Egypt. There, he had a better opportunity to follow his scholarly interests, and could attempt, within the limitations imposed by the existing social order in which he lived, to contribute to the improvement of the community as a teacher, a judge, and an adviser to the rulers.[1]

His ideas concerning the nature of philosophy and its relation to a community based on the Law as expressed in the '*Ibar* seem to explain and furnish the theoretical framework justifying his new role in the community. Since they are also in agreement with the basic doctrines of the Islamic tradition of political philosophy inaugurated by Fârâbî and elaborated by Averroes, we can conclude that after his repeated failures as a political reformer, and the long period of anxiety and reflection upon the causes of these failures, Ibn Khaldûn arrived at a personal existential realization of the truth about the proper role of philosophy in society taught by Islamic political philosophy—a truth which he may have known since his student days but the full implications of which he had either missed or refused to accept as applying to his own personal life.

Since Fârâbî, whose doctrines were directly based on the political experience and teachings of Plato, Islamic political philosophy had taught that attempting a sweeping change in a mature community for the purpose of realizing the best or perfect community envisaged by reason was futile.[2] Having found that it was inherent in the nature of the perfect community to remain a community ' in speech ' (*bi-l-qawl*),[3] philosophy had to accommodate itself to the fact that it had to exist in imperfect communities, the communities ' in deed ' (*bi-l-fi'l*).[4] These communities are mixtures of the five cities described by Plato in the *Republic* and the majority of them are mixtures of the lower four.[5]

[1] Cf. above pp. 45 ff., 54 ff.
[2] Cf. Ibn Ṭufayl *Ḥayy* 148–54.
[3] Fârâbî *Aflâṭun* 20: 15 (sec. 26).
[4] *Ibid.* 21: 11 (sec. 29).
[5] Ibn Bâjja *Tadbîr* 11.

The Islamic community in which Ibn Khaldûn lived was such a mixture. With some adjustments, the Islamic Law could be considered the counterpart of Plato's second-best regime as envisaged in the *Laws*.[1] But the Islamic Law was not the sole basis of the Islamic community in Ibn Khaldûn's time. Ibn Khaldûn accepted the commonly held orthodox opinion that the sole rule of the Law ceased with the rise of the Umayyad dynasty (661/40–),[2] and that since then, Muslim monarchs had based their policies on a mixture of the Law and the demands of the natural, i.e., primitive and generally necessary, requirements for attaining and preserving power.[3]

In contrast to such an imperfect community based on a mixture of the regime of Law and the three lower regimes (the ignorant, the vicious, and the extravagant), political philosophy had envisaged the perfect community created and preserved by philosophy and in which philosophy is the most significant part, i.e., the ruler and the end.[4] In such a community, the philosopher achieves the most complete happiness possible for man, since he realizes the practical virtues as a ruler and the theoretical virtues as an investigator, and at the same time he properly subordinates the practical virtues to the theoretical.[5] But having decided that such a community cannot exist 'in deed', the question was posed by Muslim philosophers whether philosophy could exist at all, whether the philosopher could attain his proper happiness, and how he was to conduct himself within an imperfect community not created by philosophy and not ordered with a view to encourage, preserve, or further the ends of philosophy, and in which philosophy was suspected and persecuted.[6]

2. They found that the philosopher exists in an imperfect community as a solitary (*mutawaḥḥid*) individual. He is like the

[1] The relative merits of a law inaugurated by a legislator and based primarily on reason without explicit divine commission on the one hand, and a Law divinely inspired and legislated by a prophet on the other, and the relative merits of the communities based on each (or more specifically the relative merits of the *Laws* of Plato and the Laws of Moses, Jesus, and Mohammed) as conceived by Islamic political philosophy are interesting subjects that deserve further investigation.

[2] *Q* I 364 ff.

[3] *Q* II 128. Cf. below pp. 204 ff.

[4] Cf. below pp. 273 ff.

[5] Cf. Fârâbî *Taḥṣîl* 26–27.

[6] Cf. Ibn Bâjja *Tadbîr* 11, 61–62.

strange, wild flowers (or weeds: *nawâbit*), growing without being planted or cared for. Like the savages who live outside organized communities, and the madmen, criminals, and anarchists who live within them, he does not agree with the opinions of the citizens of imperfect communities. But, unlike these, he opposes the opinions of the citizens of imperfect communities, not with worse opinions, but with true knowledge.[1] He has to live in the imperfect community; yet he is not a true citizen of such a community. He has to order his life, and remove the obstacles that prevent the attainment of happiness, as a solitary individual; and when attained, his wisdom and happiness will be private virtues.[2]

If the philosopher's way of life is different in the imperfect community from what it would have been in the perfect, so are the objects of his investigation. The philosopher in the perfect community does not have to reflect upon false opinions or wrong actions. In the imperfect community, on the other hand, the philosopher has to start from the existing mixture of true and false opinions, and right and wrong actions, with the aim of eventually distinguishing between the true and the false, and between the right and the wrong.[3] He must also investigate the various arts of investigation common in his community and find out whether they do in fact attain what they are supposed to attain, what their limitations are, and how much and what kind of theoretical and practical knowledge they achieve. If the community in which he lives happens to be based on a religious Law, and its opinions and actions derived from such a Law, he will naturally pay special attention to the nature of religious investigation (*faḥṣ diyânî*),[4] to the knowledge of the prophet, and to the nature of the Law. According to Fârâbî, it was through the investigation of all the opinions and actions, and arts of investigation, existing in his time that Plato proceeded to the knowledge of the nature of things and of the best regime.[5]

The role of the philosopher in the imperfect community, therefore, is that of the arch-investigator (*fâḥiṣ*). He studies all

[1] Cf. Ibn Bâjja *Tadbîr* 6, 8, 10; Fârâbî *Siyâsât* 57–58, *Taḥṣîl* 41–44.

[2] Cf. above pp. 61–62; Ikhwân al-Ṣafâ' *Rasâ'il* IV 215; Fârâbî *Milla* fol. 56r; Ibn Bâjja *Tadbîr* 11.

[3] Cf. Fârâbî *Aflâṭun* 16–17 (sec. 23).

[4] Cf. Fârâbî *Aflâṭun* 6 (sec. 6); L. Strauss *Louis Ginzberg Jubilee Volume* 373.

[5] Fârâbî *Aflâṭun* 6 (sec. 6) ff.

existing opinions and actions and does not accept them 'without examining them and without seeking to attain virtuous things [whether] these are [in agreement with] the opinions of the people of his city and their ways of life, or contrary to them'.[1]

Since the true opinions and the virtuous way of life attained by the philosopher may differ from, or contradict, the opinions and the way of life of the imperfect community in which he lives, he might incur the wrath of the many and his life might be exposed to grave danger.[2] This was certainly the case in the Islamic community where philosophers were condemned and persecuted as sanctimonious unbelievers holding certain doctrines (e.g., the eternity of the world and the unity of the Intellect; the denial of the creation of Adam, of the resurrection of the body, and of God's knowledge of particulars) which the community and its orthodox leaders considered contrary to the texts or the approved interpretation of the Law.[3] How can the philosopher, then, protect himself against the community in which he lives, preserve his freedom as an investigator, and be useful in improving his community's way of life?

'It is evident from the situation of the solitary [philosopher] that he should not be in the company of men [whose end is] corporeal nor those whose end is spirituality adulterated with corporeality. He must accompany men of science. But men of science are numerous in some regimes and few in others. And in some regimes they may not exist at all. Therefore, the solitary may be obliged in some regimes to avoid people completely so far as possible, and not to associate with them except for indispensable things and to the degree of [strict] necessity. Or, he may [be obliged to] emigrate to regimes that cultivate the sciences, if [such regimes] happened to exist.

'This is not contrary to what has been said in political science and demonstrated in the science of nature. It has been

[1] Fârâbî *Aflâṭun* 16–17 (sec. 23).

[2] *Ibid.* 22 (sec. 32).

[3] Ghazâlî *Tahâfut*; *Q* II 393 ff., where Ibn Khaldûn doubts the biblical stories about the beginning of Creation and says that the study of such matters does not belong to the prescriptions of the Law. Concerning the resurrection of the body and the immortality of the soul, cf. *Q* III 55, 57–59; Fârâbî *Aflâṭun* 17–19 (sec. 24); L. Strauss *Louis Ginzberg Jubilee Volume* 371–72; Averroes *Aristotelis . . . Moralium Nicomachiorum . . . Expositione* in *Opera Aristotelis* III (Venetiis 1550) 182*c*: 40–45, 191*d*: 11–39, *Manâhij* 118–24.

demonstrated there [in the science of nature][1] that man is by nature political; and it has been demonstrated in political science[2] that all isolation is evil. But this is so *per se*, while *per accidens* isolation [could be] good, as it may happen with many natural things. For instance, bread and meat are naturally nutritious and useful, and opium and colocynth are deadly poison. But the body may be in unnatural states in which the latter [opium and colocynth] are beneficial and must be used, and natural diets harmful and must be avoided. Such states, however, are necessarily ailments and extraneous to nature. Therefore, they [the poisonous fruits] are beneficial in few cases and *per accidens*, and nutriments are beneficial in the majority of cases and *per se*. The relation of those states to bodies is like the relation of the regimes to the soul. Health is thought to be one in opposition to these numerous [sick states]. Health alone is the natural state of the body, while these numerous [sick states] are extraneous to nature. Similarly, the perfect regime[3] is the natural condition for the soul. It is one in opposition to other regimes which are numerous; and [these] numerous [regimes] are not natural for the soul.'[4]

Having decided that it is necessary for him to live in a community and having decided upon the community in which he is to live, the philosopher will have to deal with the non-philosophers not only in matters relating to his bodily and social existence, but also in matters relating to his knowledge and role as a philosopher. His solitary existence, though necessary for him as an investigator, has to be overcome if he is to play a useful

[1] Cf. Aristotle *Historia Animalium* i. 1. 488a7.

[2] Cf. Aristotle *Politics* i. 2. 1253a25 ff., *Nicomachean Ethics* ix. 9.

[3] *sîra iqâmiyya*. This is a rather unusual term for the perfect regime. M. Asín Palacios translates it as 'estable' adding the following note: 'Traduzco as íla voz "*iqámiyya*" ateniéndome sólo a la etimología; pero ignoro el sentido técnico que tenga en la mente de Avempace, imposible de adivinar por falta de contexto que lo explique . . .' (*El régimen del solitario por Avempace* [Madrid-Granada 1946] 91 n. 112). By saying that this regime is *one* and that it is *the* natural regime, by contrasting it to *all* other regimes and calling them unnatural, and by saying that this regime can never degenerate and that there are no causes of corruption in it (cf. *Tadbîr* 54), Ibn Bâjja sufficiently defines the technical meaning of the term in the surviving text. Etymologically, *iqâmî* means 'stationary' and 'established' (hence the lasting character of the perfect regime as against the changing and transitory character of the imperfect), and *aqâma* means to set upright, etc. Thus, the expressions: 'He put the affairs in the right state (*aqâma al-amr*)' and 'made it conformable with that which is right.' Cf. Lane *Lexicon* 2995*c*–96*a*.

[4] Ibn Bâjja *Tadbîr* 78–79; cf. Fârâbî *Milla* fol. 56r: 12–17.

role in his community. But how can the philosopher address the non-philosophers in matters which they do not understand; and who will decide the rules according to which he can address them, the many, the Law, or the philosopher himself? Being the royal art, philosophy could not accept limitations imposed upon it by inferior arts; it did itself formulate the provisions under which it was to function in an imperfect community.

Primary among these was a provision for the mutual protection of philosophy and the community, i.e., the provisional acceptance of the opinions of the community by the philosopher who does not thereby renounce his kingship but only conceals it; instead of manifest kingship, he assumes the role of a secret king.[1] In order to be effective in this new role, it would be best if the community accepted him as its leader, i.e., as the defender of the Law and the upholder of tradition (*sunna*).[2] The success of this venture will largely depend upon the art of writing he adopts. With the few, he must continue to follow the 'way of Socrates'. With the youth and the many, however, he must make use of the more successful 'way of Thrasymachus'. For Socrates, proficient as he was in the scientific investigation of justice and virtues, was deficient in his ability to convince the youth and the many.[3]

Thus, the function of the philosopher does not end with the attainment of the knowledge of the perfect community of which he is a true citizen. His knowledge of the perfect community qualifies him to study the character and shortcomings of the

[1] Ikhwân al-Ṣafâ' *Rasâ'il* I 62–63, 362–63, IV 179 ff., 198 ff., 214 ff., 220 ff.; Fârâbî *Taḥṣîl* 46–47: 'Thus, the king and the leader (*imâm*) is in his essence and art a king and a leader whether or not anyone exists who accepts him, whether or not he is obeyed, whether or not he finds a group to help him achieve his purpose—just as the physician is a physician in his essence and his ability to cure the sick, whether patients existed or not, there were tools for him to use in his practice or not, and whether he was rich or poor. His physicianship [*ṭibbuhu*, instead of *ẓannuhu* (his opinion) in the printed text (46: 19)] is not eliminated by the absence of any of these things. Similarly, the leadership of the leader, the philosophy of the philosopher, and the kingship of the king, are not eliminated by his not having tools to use in his acts and people to employ for attaining his purpose.' Cf. *Q* I 362–63.

[2] Thus the definition of the philosophers by Jurjânî (*Ta'rîfât* 41): 'Those whose speech and action conform with tradition'! Fârâbî (*Zaynûn* 9–10) says that the philosopher must 'restrain himself from [doing] what is forbidden in the community of his prophet and agree with the many in [following their] rules and habits'.

[3] Fârâbî *Aflâṭun* 21–22 (sec. 30).

imperfect community in which he lives. To perform this task, he needs hard and long training. To attain the ability of seeing higher things exposed in full daylight does not automatically render him able to see the shadows moving in the darkness of the cave. Nor is it enough for him to lay bare the true character and the shortcomings of the imperfect community. For in contrast to the perfect community, the imperfect community has an abundance of sickness and injustice; it is in urgent need of physicians and judges—and above all physicians and judges who have attained the knowledge of perfect health and true justice.[1] The philosopher is, therefore, also qualified to lead an active role in his imperfect community. But since he had abandoned trying to create a perfectly healthy and just community, he will have to confine his activities to piecemeal and gradual reform, yet reform that is directed to, and justified by, the perfect community.[2] Instead of creating a perfectly healthy body politic immune to disease, he will accept the role of the physician who diagnoses and tries to prescribe medicine for the diseases to which the body politic is subjected in particular times and places. Instead of creating a community harmoniously organized according to perfect justice and protected by it from the inroads of conflict and injustice, he will accept the role of a judge who removes injustice whenever and wherever it occurs.

Viewed within this tradition of Islamic political philosophy, Ibn Khaldûn's early philosophic training, his failures in politics, the long period of perplexity and reflection upon these failures, his turning to the philosophic investigation of history, his doctrines concerning the nature and function of philosophy and the Law, his conception of the nature of prophecy, his distinction between the few and the many, the purpose of his critique of the mixed sciences, his adoption of the exoteric-esoteric style of writing, his cautious and conservative attitude to political life in Egypt, and, finally, the seriousness with which he performed his duties as a judge in that country, all fall into an intricate and complex, yet intelligible and ever-present, pattern.

[1] Fârâbî *Milla* fols. 56v–57r; Ibn Bâjja *Tadbîr* 8–9; Averroes *Aristotelis . . . Moralium Nicomachiorum . . . Expositione* in *Opera Aritotelis* III 194*b*, *Paraphrasis in libros Reipublicae Platonis* in *ibid*. 496*b–c*.

[2] Fârâbî *Aflâṭun* 22–23 (sec. 32), *Taḥṣîl* 34–35, 45; L. Strauss *Louis Ginzberg Jubilee Volume* 383, 383 n. 41.

CHAPTER III

From History to the Science of Culture

I

Faith, Traditionalism, and Rationalism in Islamic Historiography

1. Reflections upon the nature, purpose, and method of history in Islamic thought date back to the very beginning of Islam. They are to be found in the Koran and are among the actual and attributed sayings of the Prophet.[1] As is to be expected, these reflections are summary and general. They centre on the relation of God to human history, and emphasize the finite and transitory character of man's life on earth. They stress the religious, moral, and practical uses of history in furnishing reminders, exhortations, examples, and instructions. Muslims are directed to contemplate the vicissitudes of earthly life, the rise and fall of kingdoms, and the judgment of God upon the nations of old as revealed in their fortunes and misfortunes. As to method, they demand and commend veracity and exactitude in transmitting historical information derived, whenever possible, from primary sources or eyewitnesses.

With the spread of Islam during the seventh-eighth centuries and the production of a vast and varied historical literature, the seeds of historical thought contained in the Koran and the sayings of the Prophet blossomed. They thrived first and foremost under the care of professional historians who were led on by the practice of their profession to reflect upon its nature, purpose, and method. At first, these reflections were not explicitly formulated, but embodied in the product of their scholarship; and in order to understand them, the student must study these historical works and see for himself the assumptions underlying them.

[1] E.g., Koran 12: 111, 15: 57 ff., 47: 31, 99: 4; 'Creation', 'Prophet', 'Resurrection', 'Witness' in A. J. Wensinck *A Handbook of Muhammadan Tradition* (Leiden 1927). Cf. D. S. Margoliouth *Lectures on Arabic Historians* (Calcutta 1930) 74 ff.; H. A. R. Gibb '*Ta'rîkh*' *EI*(*S*) 234*b*–35*a*; F. Rosenthal *Muslim Historiography* 22–28.

History as a profession started in Islam with the search for, and the collection and transmission of, individual reports (*akhbâr, aḥâdîth*) about specific events. These reports were first transmitted orally, and when written records were gradually introduced, these were accepted at first merely as aids to memory. The historian took pains to learn about, and ascertain the competence of, the authorities who transmitted these reports, and used the sciences of biography (*'ilm al-rijâl*) and of authority-criticism (*al-jarḥ wa-l-ta'dîl*) as his main tools. He prefixed each of his reports with the chain of authorities transmitting it, and if a report came to him through different chains of authorities (*ṭuruq al-ta'rîkh*), he recorded the variants and indicated his authorities for each.[1] Having collected his reports from the best available authorities and according to the best standards of authority-criticism, he considered his task as a historian performed. He generally abstained from recording his opinions or transmitting those of others about his reports; these were not considered part of the historical material with which he should be concerned. (For instance, the fact that there was a flood was conceived by him as a historical event, but not the reasons for that flood.) This conception of the subject matter of history defined, in turn, the limits of its method. It was restricted to the criticism of the chain of transmitters (*isnâd*) and did not include the criticism of the content (*matn*) of a report, except so far as the content was related to the problem of authority-criticism.

The development of the explicit formulation of ideas and theories concerning history, whether by professional historians or by scholars in related fields, e.g., the science of Tradition, was due primarily to attacks upon the historical literature and its assumptions by theologians and philosophers during the ninth-tenth/third-fourth centuries when the uses and scientific character of history were questioned.[2] These attacks forced

[1] Cf., e.g., Ibn Sa'd *Ṭabaqât* III[1] 2; Balâdhurî *Futûḥ* 12 ff.; J. Horovitz 'Alter und Ursprung des Isnâd' *Der Islam* VIII (1917) 39 ff.; Goldziher *Muhammedanische Studien* II 143 ff.

[2] Cf., e.g., the criticism of Jâḥiẓ (d. 868/255 [*GAL* I 152–53]) in *Ma'âd* 6–8, 24–26, where he emphasizes the importance of the study of 'nature' and 'probability'; and the criticism of the method of early Muslim historians, i.e., narration by multiple witnesses (*tawâtur*), by Naẓẓâm (d. *ca.* 840/225) as reported in Baghdâdî (*Uṣûl* 11) and by 'Allâf (d. 840–41/226) as reported in Shahrastânî (*Milal* I 67).

historians to be more explicit in the formulation and defence of their assumptions. An increasing number of them started to write short introductions to their works in which they stated the religious, scientific, and practical uses of history, and defined and defended the method they followed in collecting and arranging the information contained in their works.[1] These introductions were too sketchy and unsystematic to deserve the name of historiography or theory of history. Yet they were, both in form and content, the prototypes of the subsequent historiographical literature that reached full development in the fourteenth-fifteenth/eighth-ninth centuries.[2]

As an example of these introductions, we may cite that of Ṭabarî (d. 923/310),[3] the most respected and most frequently imitated Muslim historian. Ṭabarî grew up in an atmosphere full of controversy between the traditional-theological school and the students of the newly translated Hellenistic rational sciences known as the Mu'tazilites.[4] He studied under prominent anti-Mu'tazilite masters, and is also reported to have acquired some knowledge of logic and mathematics.[5] He became a leading theologian and defender of traditional Islam. As a historian, he often stressed the belief that history is not a rational discipline and that human reason does not play a significant role in it. In the introduction to his *Universal History* he expresses himself concerning the proper subject matter and method of history as follows:

[1] E.g., Ṭabarî *Ta'rîkh* I 6 ff.; Mas'ûdî *Tanbîh* 1 ff.; Miskawayhi *Tajârib* I 1 ff.; Bîrûnî *Hind* 2 ff., *Âthâr* 4 ff.; Ibn al-Athîr *Kâmil* I 4 ff.

[2] They were particularly concerned with the formulation of the techniques of historical scholarship and the necessary qualifications of the historian, subjects which were also taken over by the historiographers of the fourteenth-fifteenth centuries. Cf. Subkî *Ṭabaqât* I 197; Ṣafadî *Fawât* I 1 ff.; and the quotations from the introductions of earlier historians in Kâfîjî (*Mukhtaṣar passim*); Sakhâwî (*I'lân passim*).

[3] *GAL* I 142–43; F. Wüstenfeld *Die Geschichtschreiber der Araber und ihre Werke* (Göttingen 1882) 31–32 (No. 94); *IHS* I 619–20, 622, 642–43. Ṭabarî was praised even by Muslim historians who differed from him in their approach to history. Cf., e.g., Mas'ûdî *Murûj* I 15–16; *C* II 426, 457, *T* 373, where Ibn Khaldûn invokes the authority of Ṭabarî when arguing with Tamerlane. He calls him '*the* historian and Traditionist of the Community', and tells Tamerlane: 'I will debate with you relying on Ṭabarî's account.'

[4] Cf. below pp. 137–38.

[5] Yâqût *Irshâd* VI 437, 438, 445, 450–51. Ṭabarî founded a 'liberal' theological school which lasted to the eleventh century and was the reason for his persecution by the ultra-orthodox Ḥanbalites. He was classified as a Shâfi'ite by later theologians (cf. F. Kern's preface to his edition of Ṭabarî's *Ikhtilâf* 15, 17 ff.; Subkî *Ṭabaqât* I *passim*).

'The knowledge of the events of past nations, and of the information about what is currently taking place, does not reach one who is not contemporary to, or does not observe, such events except through the reports of historians and the transmission of transmitters. These [historians, transmitters] should not use rational deductions and mental eludications. Now if there happens to be in this book a report that I have transmitted from some past authority to which the reader objects or which the hearer detests because he does not see how it could possibly be true or correct, let him know that this report did not originate with me, but came from some of those who transmitted it to me and all I did was to deliver it as it was delivered to me.'[1]

Such a conception of the method of historical research raised another problem, that of the nature of the sources of historical events. Since not all historical reports could be traced back to the time of their occurrence through a reliable chain of transmitters (and this was true of most pre-Islamic events), who, then, could be the authority for such events? Ṭabarî solved this problem by recourse to the 'Prophet and the pious predecessors'.[2] But he also had to resort to the Old and the New Testaments, Jewish and Christian historians, and Persian chroniclers.[3] Not all of these sources could claim divine origin; nor could the Muslim historian apply his technique of authority-criticism to authors about whom he knew little or nothing at all. Here, at least, was a major problem which traditional historiography could not solve.

In order to understand the subsequent discussions of such problems, the student of Islamic historical thought should consider the contribution of the Islamic philosophic tradition and of Islamic dialectical theology. This contribution is twofold: Philosophers and dialectical theologians considered history in their study of the organization of the sciences and especially in their treatment of the practical sciences. They adjudged the claims of history to be a science, the character of the information

[1] Ṭabarî *Ta'rîkh* I 6–7, cf. 55–56. Ṭabarî's historical method as expressed here was a special instance of his general approach to religious problems (cf. his *Tafsîr* I 2–3, 26, 28–29).

[2] *Ta'rîkh* I 55–56, 79. On the merits of the tribe of the Prophet, Quraysh, and of his Companions, cf. Baghdâdî *Uṣûl* 20; Subkî *Ṭabaqât* I 99.

[3] Ṭabarî *Ta'rîkh* I 17, 174 ff., 201. The authenticity of many of the stories furnished by Jewish and Christian historians was questioned by the Muslims (cf. Gibb *EI*(*S*) 233*b*–34*a*, 235*b*, 236*b*–37).

it supplied, and its uses for theoretical knowledge and practical action. Their ideas on these subjects influenced professional historians and in many cases directed the course of their research.[1] It is also important to note in this connection that the most prominent Muslim historians were at the same time either prominent theologians (e.g., Ṭabarî), accomplished philosophers (e.g., Miskawayhi [d. 1030/421][2] and Bîrûnî [d. 1048/440][3]), or had at least some philosophic and theological training (e.g., Mas'ûdî [d. 956/345][4] and Ibn al-Athîr [d. 1233/630][5]). Philosophers and dialectical theologians influenced historical thought through another, indirect channel. Their consideration of the nature, purpose, and method of the sciences in general, and of the practical sciences in particular, were studied and partially adopted by practising historians. Consequently, Islamic historical thought developed parallel to Islamic philosophy, and to the reaction of Islamic religious thought to philosophy as expressed in Islamic dialectical theology.

2. The Mu'tazilites were the first to question the principles of the traditional historical school represented by Ṭabarî. Their attack on the sources and method of the then prevailing historical scholarship was part of their general attack on the conservative and traditionalist religious attitude. They stressed the necessity of rational understanding and of the exploration of the nature and causes of things,[6] and refused to accept reports whose only claim to truth was the multiple chain of authorities prefixed to them. They asserted that 'the whole [Muslim] community

[1] Cf. below pp. 142 ff.

[2] *GAL* I 342–43; *IHS* I 687–88.

[3] *GAL* I 475–76; *IHS* I 707–9.

[4] *GAL* I 143 ff.; *IHS* I 637–39.

[5] *GAL* I 345–46; *IHS* II 682–83.

[6] C. Nallino 'Sull'origine del nome dei Mu'taziliti' *RSO* VII (1916–18) 429 ff.; Shahrastânî *Milal* I 32–34, 53 ff. The Mu'tazilites are said to have preferred the doctrines of the 'naturalist philosophers' to those of the 'theological philosophers' (*ibid.* 71–72, 95–96). 'The root and the foundation of their beliefs,' says Shahrastânî, 'is that they seek causes in everything.' (*Ibid.* 15; cf. J. Obermann 'Das Problem der Kausalität bei den Arabern' *WZKM* XXIX (1915) 325 ff., and *ibid.* XXX (1917–18) 36 ff.) It is well known that the Mu'tazilites were considered by the philosophers as dialecticians, and in this respect they can be grouped together with the Ash'arite and other schools of dialectical theology. To avoid confusion, however, we shall reserve the term 'dialectical theologians' to describe the Ash'arites and subsequent dialecticians who upheld the tradition of the Islamic community in contrast to the Mu'tazilites who were considered innovators. *Q* III 38–43.

could agree on what is false' and that 'it is possible that an infinitely numerous group of people would lie'.[1] They demanded that conviction be based on rational grounds and not solely on authority. Applied to history, this meant the acceptance of what is inherently reasonable and the rejection of what is not.

The Mu'tazilites were the forerunners of the philosophers who continued to introduce, and elaborate on, Greek philosophy, and the dialectical theologians who used the rational sciences to defend traditional Islam. The attitude of the philosophers and the dialectical theologians to history is a clear example of their basic point of view concerning the major issue on which they opposed each other, i.e., the relation of reason to the accepted views of the Muslim community regarding the nature of Islamic revelation and of the tradition of the community.

Following Aristotle, the philosophers did not consider history a science and did not mention it as such in their classification of the sciences.[2] In his discussion of the various sciences in Book Six of the *Nicomachean Ethics*, which served as a basis for the later classification of the sciences by Muslim philosophers, Aristotle distinguishes between (1) the *theoretical* sciences whose proper object is demonstrative knowledge (*epistēmē*) of necessary, eternal, and universal things that are or come into being in accordance with nature; (2) the *practical* sciences whose object is prudence (*phronēsis*) or deliberation about perishable and particular things upon which man must act soundly with respect to an end which is goodness; and (3) the *productive* sciences whose object is the art (*technē*) of making or creating things through a correct course of reasoning.[3] The theoretical sciences, i.e., physics, mathematics, and metaphysics, aim at demonstrative and rational knowledge that is certain and explanatory. They proceed through the use of inductions and deductions that move from the particular to the universal or *vice versa*, and syllogisms that operate on the plane of the universals.[4] The practical sciences, i.e., ethics, politics, and economics, aim at sound deliberation about things conducive to the good life. Their objects are not necessary, but variable and capable of being

[1] Baghdâdî *Uṣûl* 11; Shahrastânî *Milal* I 67.
[2] Cf. Fârâbî *Iḥṣâ'*; Avicenna *Aqsâm*.
[3] Aristotle *Nicomachean Ethics* vi. 3 ff.
[4] *Ibid.* vi. 6, cf. *Posterior Analytics* i. 2.

otherwise. Their purpose should be the right use of means for the achievement of man's ends; consequently, they do not exist apart from moral virtue or the right direction toward true ends, and they are chiefly concerned with the perfection of man's use of his freedom in action, a perfection that can be achieved through nature, instruction, and habit.[1] The productive sciences also deal with things that come into being, change, and perish; but their end is the perfection of things made, e.g., a house or a poem. Because of the nature of their subject matter, the practical and productive sciences admit of an accuracy that is different and less complete than that found in the theoretical sciences.[2]

History is concerned with individual events taking place in particular times and places, and as such it is the very opposite of science; for according to Aristotle's theory of science, there is science only when a universal judgment is formed explaining the nature and causes of a class of objects.[3] History is not a theoretical science because its subject matter is mutable and changing. It ascertains, collects, and classifies data. On that level it is nearer to an art or a productive science. It may attempt to connect and explain these data, and produce a universal judgment about a class of objects through explaining their nature and causes. In so doing, it becomes a practical science (it is no longer concerned with individual events and hence no longer, strictly speaking, history) and it will have to deliberate about the data of human experience in terms of an end. Thus, there is here a mutual relation between history and the practical sciences: History is a material part of the practical sciences; it supplies the data upon which the practical sciences reflect. The conclusions of the practical sciences, on the other hand, can be used by the historian to explain his data. The object of the practical sciences is prudence or deliberation about experience. History, which supplies the data of experience, is, therefore, also an instrument of prudence, and as such useful for statesmen and political orators.[4]

Like Aristotle's theory and classification of the sciences, his

[1] *Nicomachean Ethics* vi. 4–5, 8–13.

[2] *Ibid.* i. 1. 1094^{b}19–26; cf. Fârâbî *Iḥṣâ'* 44: 1–3, *Milla* fol. 54.

[3] *Metaphysics* i. 1. 981^{a}5–6.

[4] Cf. *Poetics* 9. 1451^{b}5–7: 'Poetry, therefore, is more philosophical and a higher thing than history: for poetry tends to express the universal, history the particular.' (Butcher) *Rhetoric* i. 4. 1360^{a}30 ff. Cf. J. T. Shotwell *The History of History* (New York 1939) 227–29.

conception of the nature and use of history is present with little or no significant change in the writings of leading Muslim philosophers from Fârâbî on. These philosophers recommended that rulers learn from the experience of the past and referred to the writings of 'those concerned with [the events] that take place in a particular time and a particular regime' for illustrations of their political theories.[1] In so doing, they reaffirmed the importance of history as an instrument of prudence and as a material part of the practical sciences. These hints, however, are not elaborated anywhere in their writings. Unlike the Mu'tazilites who violently attacked the basic assumptions of traditional Muslim historical thought, the more prudent philosophers passed them by in silence.

It was to defend the traditional-religious approach against the Mu'tazilites and the philosophers, and to show that its underlying assumptions were rationally tenable, that dialectical theology rose in Islam.[2] Hitherto, the community had assumed that 'the good is the ancestral' and that a specific tradition, viz., that of the Prophet and the early generations of Islam, provided the surest source of knowledge and the best guide for action.[3] Islamic historiography, whose rise and development, and whose method, were intimately related to this assumption, tried to ascertain and preserve that tradition.[4] But the value of that tradition had now been questioned, and with it the principles and method of traditional historiography. In attacking traditional historiography, the Mu'tazilites were attacking some of the most fundamental beliefs of the community. Consequently, the attempt of dialectical theology to defend traditional historiography was part of a wider attempt to defend traditional Islam itself.

The defence of dialectical theology was based on an ontology and a theory of knowledge according to which all objects exist as the result of continuous creation by God in every instant of their existence, and all perception and reasoning consist of separate accidents directly created by God in the substance that is the knower.[5] These accidents were conceived as extrinsic both

[1] Ibn Bâjja *Tadbîr* 7, 8, 11; Fârâbî *Milla* fol. 52r–52v.
[2] *Q* III 27: 2–4.
[3] Cf. above p. 136 n. 2.
[4] Cf. Gibb *EI*(*S*) 234b–35*a*; Margoliouth *op. cit.* 54 ff.
[5] Baghdâdî *Uṣûl* 7 ff.

to the knower and the known; and as discontinuous, customary correlatives of things. Because they are not inherent in the knower or the known and because they do not reflect the nature of things or of the mind, the guarantee of their validity must rest: (1) objectively, on the repeated and uniform creation of the objective correlatives of the act of reasoning by God, and (2) subjectively, on His creation of the same accidents in the mind of the knower when apprehending or reasoning about the same objects.[1] Therefore, according to the dialectical theologians knowledge is concerned with the *ad extra* creation and relations of objects, and, consequently, it is deprived of all ontological significance. For the enquiry into the nature of things, they substituted the enquiry into the customary relations between objects that are directly created by God in every instance of their existence and the customary relations that are created in the mind when reflecting upon objects. On this central point, the 'ancients' and the 'moderns' among dialectical theologians were in essential agreement, although the 'moderns' tended to attribute more permanence to the customary relations of things, and Râzî, the dialectical theologian who came nearest to the philosophers in these matters, called this relation rational and tried to re-establish theology on a more properly demonstrative basis.[2]

The rejection of the quest for the nature of things by dialectical theologians meant the rejection of the principle of causality as understood by Aristotle and Muslim philosophers. For the dialectical theologians, a causal relation is simply the customary relation between accidents, and not a certain and explanatory relation between objects arising from their very nature. Hence the conception of what constitutes science underwent a basic change. For the philosophers, science par excellence is the certain and explanatory knowledge of nature and causes; with certainty and explanation as inexorably related, and neither of them alone constituting science. Thus, sense perception and history, understood as the knowledge of particular events, can be certain, as when we see a person or know the fact that a battle took place. But here, there is no certainty in explanation, since the consideration

[1] Cf. Îjî *Mawâqif* I 241 ff.

[2] Îjî *Mawâqif* I 241–42, 248; cf. L. Gardet and M.–M. Anawati *Introduction à la théologie musulmane* ['Études de philosophie médiévale,' XXXVII] (Paris 1948) 361–63.

of the causes of a particular perception or event may lead us back to an indefinite number of preceding events without the possibility of achieving a *final* explanation. The dialectical theologians, on the other hand, rejected the certainty of any explanation; for according to them, all explanations are only probable. Consequently, the only certainty they recognized was the certainty of primary or immediate knowledge which did not involve reasoning of the explanatory type, and they considered all knowledge involving explanation as secondary and less certain.[1]

The dialectical theologians considered history (*khabar*) as an extension of sense perception and, like the latter, necessary (*ḍarûrî*). Historical reports could be false and there were conditions which they had to fulfil before they could be accepted as necessary. These conditions included the fact that the original reporter must have had a necessary, i.e., a sensory, knowledge of the events he reported, and also the certainty of a reliable chain of the transmitters of these reports. This excluded all knowledge derived by reasoning from history, since according to them it was only probable and, unlike the sense perceptions of past events, did not need to be transmitted to be known.[2] Thus, through the arbitrary selection of certain philosophic principles regarding the nature of existence and of human knowledge, dialectical theology arrived at conclusions that reaffirmed and defended the traditional conception of the nature and method of history. With the support of dialectical theology, this conception of history continued, with minor changes, to dominate Islamic historical literature down to Ibn Khaldûn's time. It is true that many important historians departed from it, and attempted to follow the lead of the Mu'tazilites and the philosophers in searching for the nature of man and society. But their works served more as correctives to the traditional trend than totally new ventures in the field, and must be understood in relation to the traditional school which remained, throughout Islamic history, the main tradition of historical scholarship.

3. The acquaintance of the Muslims with the newly translated Greek sciences, especially in geography and natural philosophy, and the expansion of the Islamic empire which facilitated travel

[1] Baghdâdî *Uṣûl* 8–9, 14–16. [2] *Ibid.* 12–13.

and trade, stimulated fresh interest in the ideas and customs of other peoples and their comparative study. Such interest raised new problems for historical thought.[1] The historians who studied these problems either came under the influence of the Mu'tazilites and adopted many of their ideas, as Mas'ûdî did, or, like Miskawayhi and Bîrûnî, were independent philosophers and natural scientists who turned to history as a field related to their philosophic and scientific interests. Their contributions to Islamic historiography were as diverse as their backgrounds and interests. What binds them together is an attitude of the mind rather than a body of doctrine. They questioned many of the sources upon which traditional historiography relied, especially in relation to pre-Islamic history.[2] Mas'ûdî shifted the emphasis from political chronology to world cultural history. He discussed new problems such as the relation of the natural environment to human history and the analogy between the cycles of plant and animal life, and human institutions.[3] Miskawayhi elaborated on the rational use of secular history for ethical and political purposes. In the true Aristotelian tradition, history was for him the handmaid of politics, an art through which princes and high-ranking officials gain the prudence necessary for ruling well, and the vulgar learn about household management, friendship, and dealing with strangers.[4] Bîrûnî brought to history his knowledge of philosophy and the natural sciences, and was able to overcome the difficulties of studying the social structure, and the religious and scientific ideas, of the contemporary civilization of India, a civilization that differed radically from his own.[5] He proved that ' opinions ' could become the object of historical enquiry and be studied as objectively as the ' facts ' to which the traditional school confined itself.

In Muslim Spain, another philosopher and astronomer, Ṣâ'id (d. 1070/462)[6] wrote his *Classes of Nations*, a work similar to, though less detailed and more comprehensive than, Bîrûnî's *India*, in which he presented the history, learning, character,

[1] Gibb *EI(S)* 237–38; F. Rosenthal *Muslim Historiography* 117 ff.
[2] Cf. Mas'ûdî *Murûj* IV 111–14; Miskawayhi *Tajârib* I 5–6.
[3] Mas'ûdî *Tanbîh* 2 ff., 6 ff., *Murûj* IV 101–4, 179–286.
[4] Miskawayhi *Tajârib* I 1–5.
[5] Bîrûnî *Hind* 4, 9.
[6] *GAL* I 343–44; *IHS* I 776–77.

and social life of various nations.[1] He developed a general anthropology in which institutions are related to the various faculties of man. He considered the cultivation of the sciences, which are the expressions of the rational soul, a decisive moment in human history, and divided the nations, accordingly, into two broad categories: the civilized and the barbarous.[2] Muslim Spain also produced Ibn Ḥayyân (d. 1076/469)[3] one of the greatest political historians of all times. In his pensive, melancholy, and apocalyptic account of the downfall of Cordova, in his understanding of the psychology of the rulers and the masses, and in his analysis of the causes of the decline of Muslim Spain, he remains unexcelled among Muslim historians.[4] Ibn Ḥazm (d. 1063/456),[5] completes the triad of eleventh-century Spanish Muslim historiography with his attempt at a higher criticism of the Bible. Though a conservative religious scholar, his critique of the Bible is conducted for the most part on a purely rational basis. He resorts to proof and observation, and tries to analyse the content of the Bible by employing the criteria of internal consistency and the inherent possibility of the events reported in it.[6]

Finally, every study of Islamic historical thought should at least mention the appearance of, and characterize, the special works on historiography in the fifteenth century, notably, the *Short Work on Historiography* by Kâfîjî (d. 1474/879)[7] and the *Open Denunciation of the Adverse Critics of Historians* by Sakhâwî (d. 1497/902).[8] Both in their approach and content, these works belong to the traditional-religious school.[9] They contain little,

[1] Ṣâ'id *Ṭabaqât* 8–9. He drew some of his information from Mas'ûdî's works. Cf. the introduction and critical notes of R. Blachère to his translation, *Livre des catégories des nations* (Paris 1935) where the sources of Ṣâ'id are indicated.

[2] Ṣâ'id *Ṭabaqât* 9–11.

[3] *GAL* I 338; *IHS* I 734–35.

[4] Cf. Ibn Bassâm *Dhakhîra* I² 86 ff.; Maqqarî *Nafḥ* II 752 ff. (both quoting Ibn Ḥayyân's *Matîn*).

[5] *GAL* I 399–400; *IHS* I 713.

[6] Ibn Ḥazm *Faṣl* I 116 ff.

[7] *GAL* II 114–15. This work, *al-Mukhtaṣar fî 'ilm al-ta'rîkh*, was written in 1463/867 and has been edited and partially translated by F. Rosenthal (*Muslim Historiography* 468–501 [text], 181–94 [translation]).

[8] *GAL* II 34–35; cf. above pp. 69–70.

[9] By the fourteenth/eighth century, the 'introductions' to which we referred above multiplied and were augmented to such a degree that the mere collection of their content would have filled substantial monographs. A casual look at the introduction of the *Biographical Dictionary* by Ṣafadî (d. 1363/764) (cf. *GAL* II 31 ff.; *Fawât* 1–56; F. Rosenthal *Muslim Historiography* 178 n. 3) which was later extensively copied by Sakhâwî confirms this. Though technically

if any, new material on the subjects they treat, i.e., the origin, definition, and object of history; the techniques of historical scholarship; the qualifications of the historian; the defence of history against attacks by ' adverse critics '; the history of historians; and the enumeration of historical works on different subjects and different localities. The eclectic method used in these works is to a large degree responsible for this lack of originality. They quote the previous ' introductions ' and other sources extensively with little or hardly any analysis, synthesis, or penetration into the problems discussed in these sources.[1] In this respect, they definitely form part of the encyclopaedic tradition which was becoming increasingly prominent in Islamic scholarship during this period.[2] The purpose for which these works were written is also indicative of their character and true parentage. They are primarily directed against contemporary theologians who disclaimed history as a necessary, or even useful, science. Hence, Kâfîjî and Sakhâwî attempt to defend the flourishing historical literature of their time against these attacks and try to demonstrate the *religious* uses of history.[3] As a result, they are not only defensive in character, but they defend a specific tradition in Islamic historical thought, namely, the tradition of Ṭabarî and Ibn al-Athîr which conceived history as primarily the compilation of factual information, and not the tradition of Mas'ûdî and Bîrûnî which initiated philosophic or theoretical investigation in Islamic historiography.[4]

4. These are the major trends of Islamic historical thought in relation to which any single Muslim historian's thought must be studied. Since Ibn Khaldûn himself attempted to study Islamic historiography and give us a critique of it, we should not presume to determine his position within Islamic historiography without a careful consideration of his own discussion of the problem. This discussion presupposes a knowledge of the major trends of

still an ' introduction ', its content is independent of the work that follows it. It is no more an introduction to Ṣafadî's *Biographical Dictionary* than Sakhâwî's *Denunciation* would have been an introduction to his *Biographical Dictionary* (*Ḍaw'*) had it been prefixed to it.

[1] Cf. F. Rosenthal *Muslim Historiography* 177–79.

[2] Cf. Goldziher *Muhammedanische Studien* II 267 ff.

[3] Cf. F. Rosenthal *Muslim Historiography* 38.

[4] Cf. Mas'ûdî *Murûj* I 6 ff., 45–46, *passim*, *Tanbîh* 1 ff., 100 ff., *passim*; Bîrûnî *Âthâr* 4–5, 13–14; cf. above pp. 142–43.

Islamic historiography which we have presented above. With this knowledge as a background, we shall turn now to the study of Ibn Khaldûn's text. Ibn Khaldûn discusses history as a specific topic in a series of three consecutive 'introductions' in the *'Ibar*: the Preface, the Introduction to the whole work, and the first part of the introduction to Book One.[1] The subject is taken up and dropped three times without any apparent reason for such discontinuity; yet a close study of these introductions reveals an inner unity of content, method, and purpose, namely, to show that no previous historian known to him had attempted a systematic philosophic study of history, and to prepare for, and prove the necessity of, the science of culture. In the second part of the introduction to Book One, he examines sciences other than history,[2] both positive and philosophic, and shows that no previous writer on these sciences had attempted such a study either. It is our contention that the text of these introductions should be set apart from the rest of Book One as a 'dialectical' discussion which is designed to prepare for, and should not be confused with, the subsequent text which properly constructs the new science. Since this thesis runs contrary to accepted opinion, and since a careful study of the text under consideration is important for the understanding of the theoretical genesis of Ibn Khaldûn's science of culture, we shall present here an analysis of the text to provide a basis for our interpretation of its method and intention.

[1] *Q* I 2 ff., 8 ff., 56 ff. In designating the parts of the *'Ibar*, we shall follow Ibn Khaldûn's explicit division of the text in the 'Preface' and the corresponding titles inserted at the beginning of each part (*Q* I 8, *passim*). Thus, we shall distinguish between the 'Introduction' (*muqaddima*) and 'Book One' (*al-kitâb al-awwal*). These two parts together have been called the 'Introduction' (*muqaddima*) since Ibn Khaldûn's time (cf. Sakhâwî *Ḍaw'* IV 147; *Q* II 114: 4). From the beginning of the nineteenth century, French Orientalists invented the unfortunate title 'Prolégomènes' for the Introduction and Book One (cf. *JA* I iv (1824) 158, *ibid.* v (1924) 148, *ibid.* vi (1925) 106. This title was in turn adopted by the editor and by the translator of these parts, É. Quatremère and De Slane, and through them it crept into the English language (cf. A. Toynbee *A Study of History* [Oxford 1948] III 322; C. Issawi *An Arab Philosophy of History; Selections from the Prolegomena of Ibn Khaldun of Tunis (1332–1406)* [London 1950]). In spite of its frequent use, this title has little textual support and is misleading. The Introduction and Book One were clearly intended to serve two different purposes: they differ in their style, structure, and manner of argumentation. The Introduction introduces the *whole* work and not merely Book One. To confuse them may lead to serious misunderstanding of Ibn Khaldûn's procedure as well as his thought. Cf. below p. 148 n. 6.

[2] Cf. *Q* I 61–66.

II

Ibn Khaldûn's Dialectical Study of Islamic Historiography

1. The Preface poses the central problem of the *'Ibar* in a condensed and tentative form. This problem is described with the aid of a primary and four secondary sets of distinctions. There is first and foremost the distinction between the external form of history which is the compiled information about events of particular times and places, and the internal meaning of history which is a rational, theoretical investigation of origins and causes, and is called a scientific endeavour.[1] Ibn Khaldûn then turns from the characterization of history to the characterization of historians and distinguishes the few, commonly accepted and respected, authorities whom he calls experts and leaders (*fuḥûl*, *a'imma*) from the many childish dilettantes (*mutaṭaffilûn*), the imitators (*muqallidûn*), and the writers of skeleton summaries (*aṣḥâb al-ikhtiṣâr*). The works of both groups are subjected to a distinction in their method; and here Ibn Khaldûn differentiates the method of critical enquiry (*naẓar*) from mere copying (*naql*). This in turn leads Ibn Khaldûn to the distinction between two attitudes of mind among the students of history: the critical (*nâqid*) attitude which penetrates into the origins, nature, and causes of events and studies them on the background of their general properties (both constant and changing); and the uncritical (literally, stupid: *balîd*) attitude which compiles information with no regard to origin, nature, or causes. Finally, Ibn Khaldûn distinguishes between the *'Ibar* as a book of history from all previous histories. The *'Ibar* is concerned with both the external and internal aspects of history; it developed from its author's awakening to the necessity of a critical attitude toward historical information, and it employs the critical method. In contrast to all previous histories known to its author, it seeks the true nature and causes of historical events in an explicit and systematic fashion.[2]

Here ends the first movement of the argument. The simple distinction between the external and the internal aspect of history

[1] *Q* I 2. [2] *Q* I 5–6.

is pursued and related to the other four distinctions with the result that what appeared at the beginning as a formal and inconsequential statement is shown to be useful in classifying previous historians, in understanding their method and their attitude to history, and in judging and utilizing the product of their research. The simple concept of the internal aspect of history is shown through the subsequent distinctions to have various uses which deserve exploration and formulation. As the Preface closes, we are given a cryptic hint that this is to be done in the *'Ibar* and that a hitherto unknown field of knowledge is to be expounded.[1] The general table of contents which Ibn Khaldûn inserts in the text at this point reveals the fact that the first of the three books of which the work is composed is dedicated entirely to this task.[2]

2. The Introduction takes up all the problems posed by the Preface, but with differences in emphasis, method, and content. In contrast to the restrained and detached statements of the Preface, the Introduction indicates the merits or excellence (*faḍâ'il*) of history, the laboriousness and intricacy of its method, and the nobility of its purposes or uses.[3] The distinction between mere copying and critical enquiry is repeated, but the former is now specifically described as the cause of the numerous errors (*maghâliṭ*) and fanciful accounts (*awhâm*)[4] reported by leading historians, while the latter is definitely related to the principles (*uṣûl*) of action, the rules (*qawâ'id*) of politics, the nature of culture, and the comparison of analogous and varying conditions.[5] Critical enquiry becomes one with wisdom, philosophy, or science, i.e., with the exploration of the nature of things. In contrast to the Preface, the Introduction endeavours to explore the principles and method of history, and indicate that ignoring them leads to errors in historical accounts while knowing them can help the historian to detect and rectify such errors.[6]

[1] *Q* I 5–6, 7–8.
[2] *Q* I 6.
[3] *Q* I 8.
[4] Cf. *Bq* I 7, which adds *awhâm* after *maghâliṭ* in the title of the Introduction.
[5] *Q* I 8–9.
[6] This is indicated in the title Ibn Khaldûn chose for the Introduction by the phrase: 'and the scrutiny of its method' (*wa-taḥqîq madhâhibih*). The text that follows shows that this phrase in its context does not mean the 'establishment of principles' as De Slane chose to translate it (*Prolégomènes* I 13). The principles of the new science are not established prior to the first section of

This is done through twelve specific yet typical examples of reported information in which historians have erred according to Ibn Khaldûn. The examination of the causes (*asbâb*) of such error is intended to illustrate and bring to light the various phases of the relation between the knowledge of the *in*ternal and the *ex*ternal aspects of history. In most of them, criticism of the possibility or probability of the events themselves is coupled with the criticism of the authorities who transmitted them, their character, and their sources.[1]

The first nine of the twelve examples form a group that is concerned with: (1) ancient history (examples one to three), and (2) the behaviour, character, and ancestry of prominent Muslim rulers (examples four to nine). They all illustrate how error can result from the ignorance of the *permanent* aspect of history, i.e., the universal nature of man and society. However, this permanent aspect of history is not first formulated and then applied to these examples. The passage introducing these examples merely presupposes it and indicates that it could be formulated through critical rational enquiry, and through the comparison of events taking place in various times.[2] The examples are intended to show how this could be done. We shall illustrate Ibn Khaldûn's method through the analysis of the first example, and then indicate the additional contribution of the rest to the argument.

The first example is concerned with the number of the Israelites when they emerged from the desert. Mas'ûdî and others had reported that it numbered 600,000 or more male adults, twenty years of age or older.[3] According to Ibn Khaldûn, this number is exaggerated. He presents various arguments to

---

Book One (*Q* I 68 ff.). Ibn Khaldûn himself in the Introduction refers the reader to Book One for the establishment and demonstration of his principles (cf. *Q* I 10: 15 [adding *al-awwal* (the first) after *kitâb* (book) with MS C of *Q*, *Bq*]; cf. above p. 146 n. 1).

[1] In general, Ibn Khaldûn's use of authority-criticism in these examples is indirect. He does not attack the character, knowledge, or training of his authorities, but through criticising some of their reports and showing their inherent impossibility or improbability, he intimates that these authorities erred in specific instances and the reasons for their errors, viz., the fact that they did not consistently follow the method of critical enquiry and did not fully understand the underlying basis of history.

[2] *Q* I 9–10. 'The past and the future are more similar to each other than water is to water.'

[3] *Q* I 9 ff.; cf. Mas'ûdî *Murûj* I 92–94, where the number '600,000 adults' is reported; Num. 1: 46 reports 603,550 (cf. the round number in Ex. 12: 37; Num. 11: 21) with the important exception of the tribe of Levi (cf. Num. 1: 47).

support his contention. The first is drawn from the economics of war: such a large army, he argues, could not be adequately supplied either by Egypt or by Syria. The second is from military strategy: an army of that magnitude could not successfully engage in battle. The third is based on a comparative study of more recent armies that had conquered more extensive areas than had the Israelite army, and yet were far smaller. The fourth is based on genealogy: Moses was only four generations removed from Jacob (Israel), and no people can multiply so fast in four generations.[1] Then he proceeds to use this particular example as a basis for criticizing the general attitude of historians who are fond of exaggerating the number of various armies. He finds the reasons for such exaggeration to be ignorance of these arguments, psychological interest in the strange and the bizarre, prevalence of thoughtlessness, absence of a critical attitude relative to falsehood and fabrication, lack of moderation and justice in examining information, and lack of research which encourages acceptance of fabrication.[2]

The second and third examples deal with the supposed conquests of the Yemenite rulers, the Tabâbi'a, and the supposed existence of Iram, a town said to have been built by the ancient Arabs of 'Âd. Ibn Khaldûn criticizes the origin of the information, shows that its absence in accounts where it should have been mentioned casts doubt upon its authenticity, and discounts it as fabrication by mythographers. Philology and geography are the two new disciplines whose authority is invoked in the argument against these accounts.[3]

[1] *Q* I 9–12. The genealogy of Moses reported by Mas'ûdî (*Murûj* I 92: 5–6) is identical with that given in the Old Testament: he is the son of Amram (lived 137 years, Ex. 6: 20) the son of Kohath (lived 133 years, Gen. 46: 11; Ex. 6: 16, 18) the son of Levi (lived 137 years, Gen. 29: 34; Ex. 6: 16) the son of Jacob and Leah (Jacob lived 147 years, Gen. 47: 28 [Mas'ûdî reports 140 years]). The Book of Numbers (its authorship, composition, as well as the above-mentioned census) continues to pose numerous difficulties for Bible criticism. Counting women and children, the total number discussed here would be well over two millions which is larger than the estimated population of Egypt during that period. Modern students of the Bible prefer the theory that the above census was in fact the census of David (II Sam. 24) misplaced from its original context. Ibn Khaldûn knew of that theory (*Q* I 11) and thought that even for the time of David the number would be exaggerated. For literature on the analysis of the Book of Numbers, cf. F. H. Woods ' Hexateuch ' *Dictionary of the Bible* (New York 1903) II 363–76; G. Harford-Battersby ' Numbers ' *ibid.* III 567–73.

[2] *Q* I 11–12, cf. 51, II 78–79.

[3] *Q* I 13 ff.

Examples four to nine are primarily concerned with the criticism of the character of Muslim rulers. They deal with Islamic history which was familiar to Muslim historians and rulers who were interested in it for political, social, and religious reasons. Ibn Khaldûn uses these examples to illustrate new problems of the internal aspects of history. His procedure is similar to that used in the first three examples. He tries to shift the argument from the criticism of the authorities who transmitted the reports to the consideration of the content of the reports themselves. These accounts were reported by one or more of the most respected Muslim authorities whom Ibn Khaldûn accepts as generally reliable and whose works he uses extensively. The examples are, therefore, intended to illustrate how and why competent authorities go astray in reporting their information, and how their works should be studied by a historian who follows the method of critical enquiry.

In considering the content of these reports, Ibn Khaldûn studies the character of the rulers in question by referring to their words and deeds. He mentions the general conditions of religious sentiment, social behaviour, and political practice in the societies they ruled, explaining the nature and effectiveness of the religious and social restraints which condemned certain actions and sanctioned others.[1] Finally, he shows how circumstances gave rise to envy and discontent among groups which opposed these ruling families and how reports against them were fabricated and circulated. These reports were accepted by eminent historians who, through lack of knowledge of the internal aspect of history, committed the error of copying them uncritically. From this point of view, all previous historians were at fault, with the qualification that the leading historians were in general more reliable and their errors were the result of occasional blunders and slips (*zallât*), while the uncritical imitators merely copied and popularized these errors.[2] For the latter, true and false reports stand on the same level. That is why Ibn Khaldûn does not mention them except as a group and does not take issue with them on particular details. On the other hand, when a leading

[1] In some cases he quotes respected authorities to prove his contentions (cf. *Q* I 23, 27–28, 33–34).

[2] *Q* I 43.

historian like Ṭabarî or Mas'ûdî, a leading Koran commentator like Tha'âlibî (d. 1035/427)[1] or Zamakhsharî (d. 1144/538),[2] or a leading theologian like Bâqillânî (d. 1013/403)[3] commits an error, there might be reasons which, if explored, could throw light on the nature of the discipline under examination.

All this is intended to serve his primary purpose which is to explore the various aspects of the distinction between the external and internal aspects of history. Neither the specific errors nor the incidental reasons for committing them are the purpose (*gharaḍ*) of the discussion; it is, rather, the revelation of a secret (*sirr*) which according to him had hitherto gone unnoticed, namely, that the proper writing of history demands a knowledge of the nature of historical events and the constant examination of reported information on the basis of such knowledge, accepting what agrees with it and rejecting the rest.[4] Piecemeal historical information is the partial and external expression of something deeper and more general; and if a historian is ignorant of that deeper aspect of history, he cannot understand the external information reported to him or distinguish between true and false information.

While discussing the first group of nine examples illustrating how errors could result from the ignorance of the permanent aspect of history, another aspect emerges, namely, slow and gradual change (*tabaddul*) ending in relative heterogeneity.[5] That is why instead of closing the discussion, Ibn Khaldûn introduces a new distinction in which change is contrasted to permanence and heterogeneity to homogeneity. The second group of three examples is intended to illustrate this contrast by detecting errors of historians who ignored the idea of change, and who did not take into account the fact that forms of government, languages, arts, and the way of life are never the same in two periods.

From the discussion of change and its importance for understanding, and writing about, history, a transition is made to the discussion of the basic change taking place in the Islamic world since the tenth/fourth century. The new conditions prevailing in the fourteenth/eighth century are considered sufficient reason for writing the *'Ibar*. This is done in the form of an appendix (*fâ'ida*) which starts by stating the relation of universal to

[1] *Q* I 17; *GAL* I 350–51.
[2] *Q* I 17; *GAL* I 289 ff.
[3] *Q* I 32; *GAL* I 197.
[4] *Q* I 43–44.
[5] *Q* I 44–46.

specialized history and then elaborates the dissimilarity between the conditions prevailing in the Islamic world in the two periods, i.e., the tenth and the fourteenth centuries. The earlier period had been studied by many leading historians. From among these, Ibn Khaldûn singles out two: Mas'ûdî, who wrote a universal history called the *Meadows of Gold*[1] and who was considered by Ibn Khaldûn the most revered of Muslim historians,[2] and Bakrî (d. 1094/487)[3] who lived in a time when the conditions described by Mas'ûdî had not changed significantly and, therefore, wrote a work restricted to historical geography called the *Routes and Kingdoms*.[4] Both of these historians supply the reader with economic and sociological information and come nearer to what Ibn Khaldûn conceived to be the proper way of writing history. His praise of Mas'ûdî in particular is significant, since he was the most important representative of the philosophically oriented tradition in Islamic historiography. After a short description of the conditions prevailing in the Islamic world of the fourteenth century and after stating some of their causes, Ibn Khaldûn indicates the need for a history that will study these conditions and follow in the footsteps of Mas'ûdî.[5] Thus, the Introduction, like the Preface, ends with a statement about the '*Ibar*. In both cases, the work that is to follow and its character are organically related to the previous discussion of history; in both cases it is shown that there is a gap that needs to be filled in the historical literature of the experts.

3. Ibn Khaldûn takes up for the third time the discussion of history in the first part of the introduction to Book One which deals specifically with the science of culture. Before discussing this science, he sums up the conclusions reached in the previous discussions and relates them to the new science that is to be the subject of the book.

He begins with a new and more comprehensive definition of history. This definition does not invoke the distinction between the external and internal aspects of history. Nor does he allude to the excellence of history as a field of study. Having

[1] *Murûj al-dhahab*. *Q* I 51; cf. *GAL* I 145–46.
[2] *Q* I 51.
[3] *GAL* I 476; *IHS* I 768.
[4] *al-Masâlik wa-l-mamâlik*. *Q* I 51; cf. *GAL* I 476.
[5] *Q* I 52.

served in the development of the argument, the previous distinctions and ideas about history are now put aside. He simply states: ' History is *in reality* information about *human society* which is the *culture* of the *world* [in its diverse aspects].'[1] Next, he states that errors are inherent in historical accounts. This proposition is neither argued nor expounded. In the short and cryptic sentences that follow, *seven* causes for it are listed. The first six are related to the character of the historian—partisanship, overconfidence in the sources, failure to understand the intention of the reports, *unfounded credulousness*, failure to understand events in their proper context, and interest in gaining favour with the powerful and the influential. The seventh and last cause is related to the new science, being ' ignorance of the nature of the modes (*aḥwâl*)[2] of culture '. This cause is conceived as *prior* to all other causes, and as the most significant cause of error in historical works.[3]

A third group of four examples taken from the two historians who were singled out in the Introduction follow: the first, second, and fourth are from Mas'ûdî, and the third is from Bakrî.[4] They are designed to explain the following proposition:

' Every contingent being, whether an essence or an act, must have a nature proper to it and to its accidental modes. Therefore, if the hearer [historian] knew the nature of contingent beings and modes in existence, and what these involve[5] [e.g., their concomitants and consequences]—that would help him to distinguish truth from falsehood while examining [historical] information.'[6]

The examples are designed to demonstrate how such knowledge could be applied in specific cases to information in the fields of natural science, economics, and city planning. It is shown how the reports quoted cannot possibly be true when the nature of man and of economic life, and the quantity and the quality of the material used in building cities, are investigated.

On the surface, this may seem like a repetition of what has already been said twice. Yet, it serves a definite purpose in developing the argument a stage further. First, out of the rather confused discussion in the Introduction concerning the causes

[1] *Q* I 56.
[2] Cf. Goichon *Lexique* 98–99 (No. 198).
[3] *Q* I 57: 15–16, 58, 60, cf. II 78–79.
[4] *Q* I 58–60.
[5] *muqtaḍayâtihâ*. Cf. Lane *Lexicon* 2989.
[6] *Q* I 57–58.

of errors in historical reports, a definite distinction is made here between causes having their origin in the character of the reporter and the more important cause originating in the ignorance of the nature of events themselves. Second, the nature of things is now explicitly defined in terms of the science which is to follow.

The last question is that of method. Authority-criticism had already been developed by Islamic scholarship as a science auxiliary to the science of Tradition as well as to history. The next step for Ibn Khaldûn is, therefore, to delineate the proper object of the sciences of Tradition and history, both of which use authority-criticism as a methodological tool. According to Ibn Khaldûn, the science of Tradition is primarily concerned with legal prescriptions and commands to action, while history is primarily concerned with actual events (*wâqi'ât*). Therefore, the primary question in regard to the former is whether the prescriptions or commands were actually laid down by the proper authorities. The only way to ascertain such a fact is through the criticism of the reporters who transmitted these prescriptions.[1]

Historical reports, on the other hand, are not commands, but affirmative or negative statements about events. These statements are true or false in themselves. This is their grammatical and logical definition. The method for criticizing such statements should start by asking whether or not the events they describe could have taken place. This should be the primary question because once the impossibility of the events is established, it is useless to proceed with the criticism of the authorities who reported them.[2] Thus, while the science of Tradition confines itself to authority-criticism, history has to use both the enquiry into the nature of things and authority-criticism. History, then, needs two auxiliary sciences: the science of culture which deals with the nature of historical events and authority-criticism which deals with the competence, knowledge, motives, etc., of those reporting such events. Defined in terms of its result (*thamara*),

[1] *Q* I 60–61, cf. II 3–4, 18–19, 51 ff., 143, 340–45, where the distinction between the purpose and method of the science of Tradition and the legal sciences based upon it, and the purpose and method of the sciences that deal with events and their nature, is repeatedly emphasized. Ibn Khaldûn himself uses authority-criticism when the object is to ascertain what has been said, when the possibility of a natural event is granted, and when the problem is to find out whether the authorities reporting it can be trusted (cf., e.g., *Q* II 51 ff., 240–45, *passim*).

[2] Cf. *Q* II 143; below pp. 167–69.

the science of culture is the primary tool, but still a tool of history.[1] With this conclusion, Ibn Khaldûn ends his general discussion of history. Having shown the necessity of the science of culture for the understanding of history, and having shown, through the examination of concrete representative examples, that no previous historian known to him had developed or used such a science, he attempts in the second part of the introduction to Book One to define that science and compare it with related sciences.

4. Ibn Khaldûn starts his discussion of the new science with the following tentative definition:

'The criterion for distinguishing truth from falsehood in the [study of historical] reports according to [their] possibility and impossibility [is to be found] in our study of human society (i.e., culture). We must distinguish between: [a] the modes pertaining to its essence and involved in its nature, [b] that which is accidental and need not be reckoned with, and [c] that which cannot possibly occur in it. When this is done, we will have a criterion . . . demonstratively infallible.'[2]

The science of culture is an independent science because it treats the 'essential attributes' of a specific 'intelligible, natural reality'[3] which had not been studied before by anyone known to him. If nations other than the Greeks (notably the Persians, Chaldeans, Syriacs, Babylonians, or the Copts) had studied this science, the results of such a study did not reach the Muslims who inherited primarily the sciences of the Greeks.[4] But why did not the Greeks study this science? Ibn Khaldûn says that a possible answer is that the 'philosophers' were primarily concerned with the ends of science, and since the immediate end of the science of culture is the rectification of historical reports, which is not particularly noble, they ignored it.[5] Consequently, he claims that he could not have learned it from the wise men of antiquity, and that the principles of the new science dawned on him after personal search and long study.[6]

He does, however, admit that there existed sciences which

[1] *Q* I 60–62.
[2] *Q* I 61.
[3] *Q* I 63: 2–4.
[4] *Q* I 62–63.
[5] *Loc. cit.*
[6] *Q* I 62, 65, 66. In particular, Ibn Khaldûn denies that he had learned the new science from Aristotle or the Persian sage Mûbidhân. Cf. below pp. 166 ff.

were perhaps similar to the new science. He devotes the rest of the discussion to showing that this similarity is only apparent, and to explain the essential differences between these sciences and the science of culture. Specifically, he mentions five sciences: the first two, rhetoric and politics, of Greek origin; the third and fourth, the proofs of prophecy and the fundamentals of religious jurisprudence, are Islamic sciences; and the last, popular-wisdom-literature, which as he explains is not really a science, is common to most nations that have had wise men.[1]

He starts with rhetoric. Like other Muslim philosophers, Ibn Khaldûn considers the *Rhetoric* of Aristotle the seventh book of the *Organon*,[2] intimating that rhetoric is a logical method and, as such, has no particular subject matter. He defines it as ' speeches useful for swaying the multitude toward accepting or rejecting a certain opinion '.[3] Therefore, it could not deal in an essential manner with culture as an independent field of enquiry.

Politics, including ethics and economics, was considered by Aristotle and Muslim philosophers the supreme practical science.[4] As a practical science, the primary end of politics is the perfection of man's action. More specifically, it is concerned with ordering man's life as part of the household and the city. Ibn Khaldûn concentrates on this primary end and defines politics accordingly. ' Politics,' he says, ' is the ordering of the household or the city *as they ought to be* according to the requirements of ethics and wisdom so that the multitude could be made to follow a path leading to the protection and preservation of the species.'[5] The end of politics is, therefore, essentially different from the end of the science of culture; for while politics attempts to order society ' as it ought to be ', the science of culture studies society for the purpose of ascertaining historical events and of rectifying historical reports. The two sciences may deal with the same subject matter, but they deal with it from two different standpoints.

The proofs of prophecy and the fundamentals of religious jurisprudence, unlike rhetoric and politics, are essentially

[1] *Q* I 62 ff.

[2] *Q* I 62, III 111; cf. Aristotle *Rhetoric* i. 1, *Posterior Analytics* i. 1. 71^{a}8–9.

[3] *Q* I 62: 5–6; cf. Aristotle *Rhetoric* i. 2. 1355^{b}25 ff. History was grouped together with rhetoric by some Muslim writers, e.g., Ibn Abî al-Rabî' *Sulûk* 65. Cf. *Q* I 244–45, where Ibn Khaldûn refers to Averroes' epitome of the *Rhetoric*.

[4] Fârâbî *Iḥṣâ'* 102 ff.; Avicenna *Aqsâm* 107–8.

[5] *Q* I 62: 7–9.

non-rational sciences. Their ultimate source is not reason, but revelation. In their proofs, however, these sciences study problems similar to the problems of the science of culture ' in subject matter and point of departure '.[1] They explain, for instance, that prophecy is a necessary institution because men cannot live without a ruler, or that God orders the practice of justice because injustice destroys human society. But such proofs tend only to explain the ' purposes '[2] of prophecy and the Law. Such purposes are, however, accidental to these sciences, since their proper ends are to ascertain the historical facts proving the validity of the message of the Prophet, and the specific demands of the Law he initiated. The science of culture, on the other hand, is not contingent on revelation; it is a rational enquiry concerning the nature of man and society.[3]

Finally, Ibn Khaldûn compares the science of culture with, and distinguishes it from, the vast body of popular-wisdom-literature comprising the sayings of wise men. These sayings, general and epigrammatic in character, were collected and preserved by Muslims in handbook form for the use of princes, and were usually written in a rhetorical style full of exhortations.[4]

[1] *Q* I 63: 11; cf. Goichon *Lexique* 203 (No. 400).

[2] *maqâṣid*. *Q* I 63; cf. Goichon *Lexique* 304 (No. 583).

[3] *Q* I 63–64.

[4] *Q* I 65–66. The popular-wisdom-literature referred to here by Ibn Khaldûn can be divided into two traditions: The first is the ' Oriental ' tradition of the Egyptian Hermes, the Hebrew Daniel, the Persians Buzurjumhur and Mûbidhân, and the wise men of India. The condensed wisdom and the sayings of these wise men were made current in Arabic literature by Ibn al-Muqaffa' (d. 759/142 [*GAL* I 151]), Mas'ûdî (cf. *Murûj* II 106 ff., 134 ff., 152 ff., 193–94, 205–10), and Ṭurṭûshî (d. 1126/520 [*GAL* I 459]). The second is the Greco-Hellenistic tradition. Among other works, some of the *Dialogues* of Plato reached the Arabs in condensed form (cf. F. Rosenthal ' The Knowledge of Plato's Philosophy in the Islamic World ' *IC* XIV [1940] 392–94). The *Politics* (*Kitâb al-siyâsa*) to which Ibn Khaldûn refers in discussing popular-wisdom-literature has very little to do with the actual Greek text of the *Politics* as we know it today. Ibn Khaldûn himself doubted its authenticity and did not mention it as a work on political philosophy (*siyâsa madaniyya*). Nevertheless, he appears to have studied it carefully. He says that a portion of it is sound and that the book should be read by the initiates (cf. *Q* I 64: 17–19, 213). The work itself is in the form of an esoteric treatise intended for the use of Aristotle's student, Alexander the Great (cf. pseudo-Aristotle *Siyâsa* fols. 2r, 3v, 4v). It includes ten chapters on the art of ruling, the last of which deals, among other things, with magic, astrology, and medicine. The ' Oriental ' tradition and the Greco-Hellenistic tradition were related insofar as the Greeks were thought to have learned their wisdom from the ' East ', a tradition common both to the Muslim world and to Medieval Europe (cf. Mas'ûdî *Murûj* II 164–65; Otto of Freising *Two Cities* i. ' Prologue ', v. ' Prologue '; *Q* I 64–65, III 89 ff.; pseudo-Aristotle *Siyâsa* fol. 38v; Ibn Abî Uṣaybi'a '*Uyûn* I 6 ff.).

They included historical information about various social institutions, precepts for the public conduct of officials, and other subjects with which Ibn Khaldûn had intended to deal in his science of culture. The essential difference between the two disciplines, he explains, is that popular-wisdom-literature is not a true science: it does not fully cover any specific subject matter; it is invariably cryptic and does not explain what the sayings it reports concretely signify; and it never penetrates beyond the proximate causes to find the deeper causes that produce and necessitate the situations it describes and the prescriptions it recommends.[1] The science of culture, on the other hand, will cover the whole range of human institutions and attempt to explain demonstratively their nature, origins, and causes.[2]

III

The Need for a Science of Culture: Preliminary Statement of Its Principles

1. We are now ready to consider the method and purpose of Ibn Khaldûn's discussion of history and the science of culture in the text we have analysed. It is obvious from our analysis that adjectives like 'scientific' or 'true' do not tell us much about the method or purpose of the text. It is also clear that though Ibn Khaldûn's treatment of history may bear some outward resemblances to the general 'introductions' of Muslim historians and to the more specialized works on historiography, it differs from both in more than one respect. His discussion is more than an introduction in the usual sense because it does more than simply indicate a few principles of method and delineate the object of the work. It is not a work on historiography if we understand such a work to mean a systematic historical treatment of the development of historical thought based on principles of division according to time-sequence, subject matter, or the form according to which the data are arranged.[3]

[1] *Q* I 64: 5 and 18, 66: 3 and 9–10. Cf. *Q* I 281–82, II 77–78 (critique of Ṭurṭûshî); Ṭurṭûshî *Sirâj* 99 ff.; Ibn Bâjja *Tadbîr* 6–7, 8: 1–3.
[2] *Q* I 65–66.
[3] Cf., e.g., the use of these principles by Kâfîjî in his *Mukhtaṣar* and Sakhâwî in his *I'lân*.

Nevertheless, it is a history of historical thought, in spite of the fact that it follows a particular principle in organizing its subject matter and a particular method of argumentation. Ibn Khaldûn uses the same principle and method in discussing other intellectual disciplines including those disciplines similar to the science of culture: his treatment of history is a special case of his general approach to intellectual disciplines. In studying his approach to history as a discipline, therefore, we shall acquaint ourselves also with his general approach to the study of the history of ideas in general.

The term ' method ' as used here is coextensive with what Ibn Khaldûn knew as ' logic ' (*manṭiq*), i.e., a system of ' rules through which the correct [forms of reasoning] are known [and distinguished] from the defective in [the study of] the definitions (that define)[1] essences and in arguments that lead to judgments (*taṣdîqât*) '.[2] This is an art which was first elaborated by Aristotle in his *Organon*.[3] We may thus ask: Which of the logical methods among those contained in the *Organon* is used here by Ibn Khaldûn? Evidently it is not the sophistical, rhetorical, or poetic method. Consequently, we have to decide between the two major types of Aristotelian logic, namely, the logic of demonstration contained in the *Prior Analytics* and the *Posterior Analytics*, and dialectic which is contained in the *Topics*. The first aims at demonstrated conclusions, the second at conclusions of varying degrees of probability. This is how Aristotle defines demonstration:

' By demonstration I mean a syllogism productive of scientific knowledge, a syllogism, that is, the grasp of which is *eo ipso* such knowledge. . . . The premisses of demonstrated knowledge must be true, primary, immediate, better known than and prior to the conclusion, which is further related to them as effect to cause. Unless these conditions are satisfied, the basic truths will not be appropriate to the conclusion.'[4]

The primary requirement of demonstration (*burhân*), as Ibn Khaldûn observes in his paraphrase of this passage when

[1] For *ma'rûfa* (known), read *mu'arrifa* (defining) with MSS C, D of *Q*, *Bq*, *TT*.

[2] *Q* III 108: 9–10.

[3] *Q* III 110, 212–13.

[4] Aristotle *Posterior Analytics* i. 2. 71ᵇ19–23 (Mure); cf. the commentary of W. D. Ross in his *Aristotle's Prior and Posterior Analytics; a Revised Text with Introduction and Commentary* (Oxford 1949) 507 ff.

describing the nature of the method of the *Posterior Analytics*, is that its syllogism should be based on premises that are true, self-evident, and primary.[1] Conclusions based on such premises could then be used as premises for other syllogisms. If we examine Ibn Khaldûn's discussion of history as expounded above, we find that this condition is not satisfied. He does not start from the type of premises defined here, does not construct syllogisms, and does not end with a set of demonstrated conclusions.

By elimination, only dialectic is left. Dialectic (*jadal*), says Ibn Khaldûn following Aristotle, is that type of syllogism whose purpose is to silence a contentious opponent. Its premises are commonly accepted opinions (*mashhûrât*). For the conditions of using such arguments and the 'places' (*mawâḍi'*, *topoi*) from which they are derived, Ibn Khaldûn refers the reader to the *Topics*.[2] But we know that Ibn Khaldûn does not use dialectic primarily to silence an opponent; he intends to impart knowledge and is preparing the ground for introducing a new philosophic science. These are also, however, among the major uses of dialectic as expounded in Aristotle's *Topics*: it is useful in searching for the difficulties of, and detecting the truth about, the various problems, and it can contribute to the collection and classification of the relevant materials, the discovery of principles, the discovery and formulation of problems, and the refutation or defence of propositions, relating to a science.[3] This is the end to which dialectic is used by Ibn Khaldûn. For such purposes, it is not necessary to start with self-evident, true, and primary premises, or from premises that have already been demonstrated. A dialectical argument can start with opinions, or premises used as opinions. These opinions may have been held

[1] *Q* III 111: 2–8.

[2] *Q* III 111: 8–14; cf. Aristotle *Posterior Analytics* i. 1. 71a5–7.

[3] Aristotle *Topics* i. 2. 101a32 ff. The function of dialectic is, in short, to test and criticize rather than to properly know. Cf. *Metaphysics* iv. 2. 1004b25–26. It should be noted that dialectic has not meant the same thing in the history of thought. According to Plato, for example, dialectic is the method of philosophy par excellence (*Republic* vii. 535A). This is not the meaning of dialectic as used here. Ibn Khaldûn used dialectic in the Aristotelian sense as a method inferior to demonstration. But though inferior to demonstration, dialectic in Aristotle and Ibn Khaldûn has certain uses, and is necessary in dealing with certain problems and in certain stages in the development of a science. Cf. Richard McKeon 'Philosophy and Method' *Journal of Philosophy* XLVIII (1951) 653 ff.

by all, by the few, by the wise, or by the experts in the field. They may, in themselves, be true or false; it is the purpose of the dialectical argument to scrutinize them. It either refutes them or convinces the reader to accept them, and it does so by showing how absurd they are or by refuting opinions contrary to them. Nor is it necessary that the premises of a dialectical argument be exhaustive, or that they be applied consistently.[1]

A dialectical argument moves on a purely *logical* plane. We have seen that one of the primary conditions of demonstrated knowledge is the identity of the definitions and the defined objects. In demonstration, we start with premises that are true, and, if our reasoning is correct, our argument proceeds on a logical plane identical with the real. That is what gives our conclusion its demonstrated character. In dialectic, however, we start with opinions and manipulate them according to a logical art. We make distinctions, formulate propositions and problems, and apply these in various ways to detect error and to determine their component parts. We substitute a logical procedure for science. This means that from beginning to end we may operate on a plane *extraneous* to the nature of things; or it may have some relation to the nature of things, but it is a relation that is not guaranteed throughout the argument. As a result, instead of a set of demonstrated conclusions, we arrive at a set of merely probable and tentative conclusions. There is certainty in dialectic, but it is a formal certainty confined to the logical art: We can define without qualification its 'places' and forms of argumentation. This certainty cannot be transferred to the nature of things treated.[2]

2. We can now examine Ibn Khaldûn's treatment of history in the light of these remarks. He starts with a set of simple and commonly known distinctions: the 'external' and 'internal' aspects of history; 'leading' historians and 'dilettantes', 'imitators', and 'copyists'; and 'critical' and 'uncritical' students of history. Then, he introduces the problem of the enquiry into the nature of historical events and calls it a philosophic science.[3] He does not proceed to establish his claim. Nor

[1] Aristotle *Metaphysics* i. 4. 985ᵃ 10 ff.
[2] Cf. Aristotle *Posterior Analytics* i. 6. 75ᵃ22 ff.; Ross *op. cit.* 530; Thomas Aquinas *Commentary on the Metaphysics* iv. les. 4 (ad. iv. 2. 1004ᵇ25–26).
[3] *Q* I 43–44, 56.

does he refer to anyone else who might have established it before him. Soon, a new distinction between the ' permanent ' and the ' changing ' aspects of history is introduced. At another point, he introduces the proposition that the criticism of the nature of historical events is prior to the criticism of the authorities who reported them. The only argument he presents to convince his reader of the validity of this proposition is that it is ' similar ' to another proposition hitherto commonly accepted by previous investigators:[1] if the literal or interpreted meaning of the content of a report is found to be impossible, it should be rejected without investigating the reliability of the authorities transmitting it. The reason for the inconclusive and tentative character of Ibn Khaldûn's arguments is simply this: these arguments cannot be developed any further on the dialectical plane. They have to be accepted as probable opinions. These opinions were implicit in the thought of the ' leading ' Muslim historians. It was because of them that the ' learned men ' of the Islamic community engaged in studying history.[2]

In order to find demonstrations for these propositions, the reader will have to study Book One of the '*Ibar* which is specifically designed for that purpose.[3] Here, Ibn Khaldûn proceeds differently. He picks up, casually and apparently at random, passages from different historians most of whom had nothing in common except that they were all well known and had been accepted as authorities in their field. There is no attempt at an exhaustive enumeration of examples. On the contrary, Ibn Khaldûn expressly says in the title of the Introduction that he intends merely to allude (*ilmâ'*) to the error of past historians and to find the cause of these errors.[4] Some of the passages are quoted verbatim, others are paraphrased. There is no indication that he is attempting to give his reader an objective picture of what their authors really thought about their contents or that he is presenting these passages in their proper contexts. In some instances there is no specific mention of the authors at all. He merely refers to what a few, the majority, or all, reported, said, or did.[5] In such cases, it seems to make little difference to him

[1] *Q* I 60; cf. Aristotle *Topics* i. 10.
[2] *Q* I 44.
[3] *Q* I 5: 2–6, 61: 12 and 17.
[4] *Q* I 6, 8.
[5] *Q* I 26, 29, 39.

who it was that held the opinions he is trying to refute. What matters is that such opinions were actually held; for there is no reason to refute propositions that nobody ever accepted.[1] In refuting them, Ibn Khaldûn uses other opinions explicitly or implicitly accepted by all, by most, by some, by a few, by the most notable among philosophers, by authorities in the field of history, or by the religious scholars who had been accepted as the leaders of the community in their specialities.[2] In some instances he uses commonly accepted opinions to refute other commonly accepted opinions or to refute the opinions of the authorities.[3] For example, in defending the noble descent of the 'Ubaydî (Fâṭimid)[4] rulers of North Africa and Egypt, of Idrîs II, the ruler of Morocco (d. 828/213),[5] and of the Mahdî[6] of the Muwaḥḥids, he resorts to the opinions of their supporters and followers to prove his contentions. He argues that these supporters and followers would not have defended the cause of these rulers had they not 'believed' in their noble descent.[7] Thus, popular opinions and the opinions of the authorities seem to serve the same dialectical purpose. Ibn Khaldûn does show a preference for using the opinions of certain philosophers, historians, and theologians, but on the dialectical level such preferences can only be expressed by the choice and use of such opinions. In this fashion, Ibn Khaldûn shows his preference for some leading Muslim historians, especially Mas'ûdî, who attempted to use the philosophic method in studying history. This preference is, however, qualified to the extent that these historians, including Mas'ûdî, used the philosophic approach implicitly, and did not formulate it or apply it explicitly. It is precisely the function of the dialectical argument to bring this problem to light and to explain it. This is the reason why Ibn Khaldûn's attitude toward Mas'ûdî is a mixture of admiration and fault-finding.[8]

[1] Cf. Aristotle *Topics* i. 10. 104^{a}5–6.
[2] *Q* I 3, 27–28, 33–34, 44.
[3] Cf. Aristotle *Topics* i. 10.
[4] *EI* III 119–21.
[5] *EI* II 451.
[6] *EI* II 425–27.
[7] *Q* I 31, 38, 46.
[8] Cf. above pp. 151–52; *Q* I 157, 196, 319–20, 368–69, 373. The same is true of Bakrî (cf. *Q* II 211). The problem of Ibn Khaldûn's relation to these and other historians is not, therefore, adequately posed when treated on the simple

The truth of the content of the reports also seems to be incidental to the purpose of Ibn Khaldûn's argument. Whether the specific events in the examples quoted were in fact true or false, whether they did in fact take place or not, and, consequently, whether the historian in question was right or wrong, seem to make little difference for what he is trying to prove. This can be shown through the examination of a curious passage, evidently inserted in the text in Egypt to meet the criticism of the theologians who were appalled by the conclusion of Ibn Khaldûn's first example which clearly contradicted the explicit text of the Old Testament.[1] They argued that God had promised Abraham and his sons prolific progeny and that the number of the Israelites had to be accepted as the result of a divine miracle. They explained away the rest of the difficulties raised by Ibn Khaldûn as follows: the Israelites did not engage in battle; they were not an army or a garrison; and the land of Canaan was prepared for them as a place of settlement. Although in quoting these criticisms, Ibn Khaldûn starts the passage with the ambiguous phrase ' and it may be said ', he does not take issue with his critics. It is possible, he says, that a miracle did take place and that these explanations answer the rest of his objections. The Old Testament and the Muslim historians who reported the number may not have erred after all. However, what is important is the way Ibn Khaldûn reports these criticisms and what he concludes from them. He makes his critics concede every detail of his previous argument. They are made to prove the veracity of the number not by questioning any of his *reasons* for rejecting it, but by explicitly accepting them and introducing other factors, supernatural and natural, to show that the reported number could have been true. This shows that it was not the reported number that interested Ibn Khaldûn, but the proposition he was explaining and trying to define. ' This prodigious

level of ' direct influence ' and ' indirect influence ' (cf. M. Kamil Ayad *Die Geschichts- und Gesellschaftslehre Ibn Haldûns* [Stuttgart 1930] [' Forschungen zur Geschichts- und Gesellschaftslehre ' 2. Heft.] 24–25, 38 ff. 48). A critique of Ayad's work was attempted by Alessio Bombaci (' La dottrina storiografica di Ibn Haldun ' *Annali della Scoula Normale di Pisa* XV [1946; fasc. iii–iv] 159–85) whose own conclusions, however, suffer from a vagueness about Ibn Khaldûn's philosophic position which is then attributed to Ibn Khaldûn himself (*ibid.* 185).

[1] *Q* I 12–13. This passage, which is also included in *TT* (8–9), is not in *Bq.*

growth among the sons of Israel,' he says, ' would therefore be a supernatural miracle. But the natural course of events (as [the previous] proofs indicate) would prevent such [growth] among others.'[1]

It should be noticed, further, that Ibn Khaldûn deals exclusively with what he considers false reports. In every case he is trying to disprove rather than prove the historicity of an event. For in order to demonstrate that an event is true, he would have had to show that it was in conformity with the conclusions of the science of culture, and the nature of man and society as demonstrated in that science. As that science had not yet been developed, it would have been impossible for him to supply a positive proof of the truth of an event at this stage. Error, on the other hand, can be detected by dialectic, which, as already stated, does not have to be based on demonstrated conclusions. In addition, negative criticism serves one of the major purposes of a dialectical argument, i.e., it contributes to the knowledge of what propositions should be chosen or accepted, and what propositions should be avoided or rejected.[2]

Having started from a set of propositions and distinctions, Ibn Khaldûn uses his examples to amplify and specify them. He shows how these propositions and distinctions can be fruitfully applied in the field of history. He is thus able to discover difference where likeness was supposed to have prevailed, as in applying the distinction between change and permanence, and likeness where difference was supposed to exist, as when he shows that error in reporting historical information is common to respected authorities, to mythographers, and to popular opinion. He is able to show throughout his argument the necessity and usefulness of knowing the nature of man and society, and how errors in historical reports can be traced in most cases to the lack of such knowledge.[3]

3. Ibn Khaldûn's comparison of, and distinction between, the science of culture and the related sciences is in form essentially similar to his critique of historiography. It carries the argument a step forward by progressively defining the four essential principles of the new science, namely, its ' subject matter ',

[1] *Q* I 13: 4–5. [2] Cf. Aristotle *Topics* i. 11. 104^{b}1 ff.
[3] *Q* I 56–57; cf. Aristotle *Topics* i. 13.

'problems', 'method', and 'end'.[1] The definition that opens the new discussion makes the following assertions concerning these principles: (1) the subject matter of the new science is human association (i.e., culture), (2) its problems are the essential modes of culture, (3) its method is demonstration, and (4) its end is marking off truth from falsehood in historical reports. The rest of the discussion indicates that these are four integral aspects of the same science. Other sciences may deal with human association, consider some of its essential modes, employ demonstration, or be useful in marking off truth from falsehood in historical reports; what characterizes the new science is that it does all of these simultaneously.

The fact that Ibn Khaldûn tries first to distinguish the new science from rhetoric and politics is of particular importance. The new science had been characterized as a rational and philosophic discipline dealing with an intelligible, natural reality. In order to explain its specific approach, Ibn Khaldûn compares it with, and distinguishes it from, the rational and philosophic sciences nearest to it, and these he conceives to be rhetoric and politics. In defining these sciences, Ibn Khaldûn does not state their specific subject matter, but simply their ends and more specifically their supreme practical ends, i.e., to convince the multitude, and to order the household or the city as they ought to be ordered. He does not, for instance, mention that rhetoric may study human passions, or that politics may study existing regimes.[2] His emphasis upon the supreme ends of these sciences seems to suggest that he considered the end, and not the subject matter, as the most important element in defining a science; it is the end, and particularly the supreme end, that determines the choice of the subject matter, method, and problems of a science. Since the end of the new science is essentially different from the ends of rhetoric and politics, the science of culture should be accepted as an independent science, despite the similarities between it and these sciences. If the new science is to accomplish its proper end, it will have to determine its subject matter, problems, and method, with the intention of understanding and rectifying historical reports; and because historical reports deal

[1] *mawḍû'*, *masâ'il*, *manhaj* or *burhân*, and *ghâya*. *Q* I 8, 63: 10–11; cf. Akfânî *Irshâd* 26 ff.

[2] Cf. Aristotle *Rhetoric* ii. 2–11, *Politics* iv. 3. 1289^b26 ff.; Fârâbî *Madîna* 90 ff.; 106 ff.

with events that manifest the essential modes of culture as it is and not as it ought to be, the new science will have to investigate the nature and causes of culture as it is and not as it ought to be according to the dictates of ethics and wisdom. If that is the end of the new science, is it worthy of being studied? In answering this question, Ibn Khaldûn shifts the argument back from the end to the problems which the new science will investigate, asserting that though the practical end of the new science may not be very worthy, its problems are worth studying 'in themselves and in their "proper sphere"'.[1]

The clarification of the principles of the new science is carried a step further by comparing it with, and distinguishing it from, the positive or legal sciences which are similar to it in certain respects. These sciences, particularly jurisprudence, are concerned with the study of society to find out the intentions or purposes of the Law in order to be able to judge how the Law should be applied in concrete instances. However, they never made society the subject of an independent science; the study of society remained subordinate to their main purpose which was to expound the demands of the Law, what it approves and disapproves. For, once the demands of the Law are determined, they become obligatory and should be obeyed. This purpose in turn defined the method of the legal sciences, and it was primarily that of authority-criticism through which they could determine whether a certain command was in fact laid down.[2] The jurisconsult (*faqîh*) may, therefore, study the origin and the nature of society, he may describe the development of Islamic institutions, and he may use rational arguments in his explanation of the purpose of the Law. But ultimately, his study of society is incidental to his main purpose, and unlike the student of culture, he is not primarily concerned with the essential modes of society as such. His method, too, is radically different from the method of the new science, since the latter is concerned with the rational demonstration of its conclusions regardless of the demands of the Law; and while the jurisconsult is usually intent on showing the compatibility of the nature of society and the demands of the Law, such compatibility is extraneous to the new science.

[1] *khâṣṣ, appropriatum. Q* I 63: 6–7; cf. Goichon *Lexique* 107 (No. 215).
[2] *Q* II 3–4, 18–19, 52.

The distinction between the science of culture and jurisprudence is essential for Ibn Khaldûn, since he is asserting that the new science can be used as an auxiliary tool for history. This assertion may lead to confusion; for if the science of culture is an auxiliary science, would not its relation to history be the same as that of the study of society conducted by the jurisconsult to the sciences of the Law? The difference, according to Ibn Khaldûn's analysis, seems to lie in the fact that though the new science had its genesis in the study of the shortcoming of historiography and though it has been designed to rectify historical reports, it will nevertheless be studied as an independent science. It will start from rational premises and will demonstrate its own conclusions. Such a science could have been developed by the jurisconsults, but it never was. Their study of the purposes of the Law led them to reflect upon the nature of society, but these reflections remained unsystematic. Jurisconsults invariably started from the demands of the Law and attempted to explain the nature of society accordingly; their reflection and proofs remained essentially dialectical, since they always started from the rationally undemonstrated or indemonstrable commands of the Law and tried to show that the nature of society necessitates such commands.[1]

Unlike the philosophic and legal sciences mentioned above, popular-wisdom-literature does not employ any strict method of proof. It may cover the whole range of social institutions with which the science of culture will be concerned; but the similarity between the two disciplines does not go beyond the similarity of their subject matter. What popular-wisdom-literature asserts about culture may be true, but that has to be demonstrated. The essential difference between popular-wisdom-literature and the science of culture is that while popular-wisdom-literature employs exhortations and may occasionally make assertions about apparent and proximate causes of social phenomena, the science of culture will attempt to demonstrate its conclusions through the exploration of the true causes of the essential modes of human association.

To sum up and conclude: Ibn Khaldûn's treatment of history in the text analysed in this chapter is a dialectical history of

[1] Cf. above pp. 155–56.

historical thought in general and of Islamic historiography in particular. It is intended to show the necessity and usefulness of the science of culture for the rectification of historical reports. It is also a dialectical comparison of the new science with related sciences intended to define and elucidate the principles of the new science. The whole discussion comes *before* the science of culture is properly developed. It does not start from primary or demonstrated premises, but with a set of propositions and distinctions that are opinions or used as such. These propositions and distinctions are applied to a set of examples for the purpose of discovering and tentatively formulating the principles of the new science. The comparison of the new science with related sciences is intended to specify and clarify these principles. Such a procedure is useful in introducing the new science. Its conclusions are, however, only probable. They cannot be used as principles in developing the new science; for the proper principles of a science have to be either true, primary, and self-evident, or demonstrated premises. The proper procedure of science, according to Ibn Khaldûn, is not that of dialectic, but of demonstration. The introductory dialectical treatment of history and of the new science is the *way* leading to the new science; it is an introduction in the proper sense of the term. It must not be confused with the following discussion in which the proper premises will be proposed, data newly amassed, definitions established, and conclusions demonstrated.[1]

[1] Cf. above pp. 146 n. 1, 148 n. 6. The expression ' and we shall now explain [or demonstrate] ' (*wa-naḥnu al-âna nubayyinu*) occurs at the end of the dialectical discussion and at the beginning of the text where the principles of the new science are expounded (*Q* I 66: 15–16). It is obvious that Ibn Khaldûn is not writing a ' history ' of Islamic historiography and related sciences by juxtaposing the opinions of others about these subjects according to time-sequence. This was not a true alternative for him because he did not believe that time-sequence *ipso facto* meant either progressive revelation of the *core* truth about a problem or the deeper penetration into its significance. He knew of instances when ignorance displaced knowledge, imitation displaced intelligent enquiry, and scientific traditions disappeared (cf. *Q* I 3, 4–5, 43, 44, 56–57, 62). This does not mean, however, an outright rejection of the possibility of scientific progress. Through happy chance, new data can come to light and, if intelligently used, they might lead to the augmentation of previously known theories or furnish additional proofs for them. Ibn Khaldûn believed that the history of the Islamic world from the eleventh/fifth century to his own time did present such data (cf. *Q* I 51–53). Therefore, he set himself to explore the theories of his predecessors, with the purpose of checking these theories and correcting them with the help of the new data.

CHAPTER IV

The Science of Culture: Its Subject Matter and Problems

I

Human Nature and the Nature of Culture

1. Ibn Khaldûn thought that the way out of the dilemma presented by the inadequacy of the traditional method of expert historians lay in the investigation of the nature of man and society, an investigation which led him to the discovery and construction of the new science of culture. The object of the new science, the examination of the nature and causes of human society, is to reveal the internal aspect of the external events of history. History and the science of culture study two aspects of the same reality. History ascertains external events while the science of culture explains the nature and causes of these same events. Consequently, the science of culture and history, in this limited sense, are related in three ways. In the sequence through which the mind achieves knowledge, the science of culture comes *after* history: it reflects on, and explains the external events ascertained by history. The historian cannot, however, ascertain external events without a minimal acquaintance with their nature and causes. In the art of the historian, history and the science of culture should be combined. Finally, in the order of being, the object of the science of culture comes *before* the object of history. Historical events are the product of the nature and causes underlying them. Ibn Khaldûn chose the third relation for the pedagogical presentation of the two disciplines. Our study will proceed by asking and attempting to answer the following questions concerning the science of culture: (1) what are its subject matter and problems, (2) what are the principles underlying it and what is the method according to which it proceeds, and what is its end and how is it accomplished? The rest of this study will deal with these questions in this order.

Ibn Khaldûn starts his enquiry by positing certain principles (*muqaddimât*) whose demonstration does not fall within the scope of the new science. But since they are used in the demonstration of the conclusions of the new science, it becomes necessary to state and explain them. The first of these principles is that society is necessary; the second is that man and society are internally—through man's physical constitution—and externally related to the physical environment; and the third is that man and society are related—through man's rational faculty—to the spiritual world, the world beyond perceptible natural beings. Although Ibn Khaldûn does not think that the proof of these principles falls within the scope of the new science, he attempts to prove the first. As to the second and third, he simply presents and explains the conclusions arrived at by other sciences, e.g., geography, astronomy, medicine, and prophetology, and shows how such conclusions are pertinent to, and must be used as premises in, the arguments of the new science.

The exploration of the nature and causes of culture, which begins after these principles are established, proceeds by dividing the subject matter into five major problems, examining them separately and indicating their interrelation. These problems are: (1) primitive culture and its transition into civilized culture, (2) the state, (3) the city, (4) economic life, and (5) the sciences. This is the basic structure according to which Ibn Khaldûn organizes his subject matter.[1] In order not to do violence to it, and to be able to follow the steps of his argument, we shall start with defining the nature and general characteristics of culture, and then proceed to give an exposition of the three principles mentioned above and the various problems of the new science in the order given by Ibn Khaldûn.

[1] Book One of the *'Ibar* is planned with exceeding care by its author; yet its structure, the arrangement of its sections and chapters, and their titles have received little attention in previous studies. Cf. especially the basic technical terms employed in the titles of its six sections: section i is made up of 'premises' (*muqaddimât*) only (*Q* I 68 ff.), section ii of 'principles' and 'preliminaries' (*uṣûl, tamhîdât*) (*Q* I 220 ff.), section iii of 'fundamental laws' and 'supplementary [enquiries]' (*qawâ'id, mutammimât*) (*Q* I 277 ff.), section iv of 'preliminaries' and 'addenda' (*sawâbiq, lawâḥiq*) (*Q* II 201 ff.), section v of 'problems' (*masâ'il*) (*Q* II 272 ff.), and section vi of 'a premise' and 'addenda' (*muqaddima, lawâḥiq*) (*Q* II 363 ff.). Notice also the repetition of the phrase 'and the modes inherent in [all] that' (*wa-mâ ya'riḍu fî dhâlika* [*kullihi*] *mina-l-aḥwâl*) in the title of all of these sections except the first.

2. Culture is not an independent substance, but a property (*khâṣṣa*)[1] of another substance which is man. Hence the natural character of culture must have reference to what is natural to man, i.e., to his nature and to what differentiates him from the rest of the animal world.

The essential differentia of man is the power or faculty of intellect or mind (*quwwa nâṭiqa, virtus rationalis*),[2] reflection (*fikr, cogitativa*)[3] or deliberation (*rawiyya*).[4] Through his intellect man can understand; he can know both particular objects embedded in matter and universals abstracted from matter.[5] Of the two faculties of the intellect, the theoretical and the practical, it is the practical which emerges first and is at the root of what man makes and does, which constitute culture. Like Aristotle in his discussion of the intellectual virtues in the *Nicomachean Ethics*,[6] Ibn Khaldûn divides practical reason into two faculties: one whose object is making and which Aristotle calls art, and another whose object is doing and which Aristotle calls practical wisdom. Ibn Khaldûn, however, attempts first to describe only the most elementary functions of these two faculties and, consequently, calls them by two simpler names: *discerning* and *experiential* reason. He orders them as follows:

'First, understanding things ordered, either naturally or conventionally (*waḍ'î*), outside [the self] with the intention of realizing them by his [man's] powers. This reason is mostly[7] [made up of] conceptions. It is *discerning reason* (*'aql tamyîzî*) which acquires his utilities and living, and prevents [things that] harm him.

'Second, the reason through which he learns opinions [about], and rules [relative to] dealing with members of his species and to governing them. Most of these are judgments gradually acquired

[1] *Q* I 67: 1 and 10 ff., II 367: 9–10. Cf. Goichon *Lexique* 108–9 (No. 217).

[2] *Q* I 175: 14.

[3] *Q* I 174: 6 and 7.

[4] *Q* I 174: 6 and 7, 176: 10.

[5] *Q* I 173–77, II 363–64. 'The human mind,' says Ibn Khaldûn, 'is a specific "nature" that God has created as He has created the rest of His creation.' *Q* III 254.

[6] *Nicomachean Ethics* vi. 3–5, esp. vi. 4. 1140a4.

[7] For *akthar* (more), read *aktharuhu* (mostly) with *TT* and De Slane (*Prolégomènes* II 427 n. 1).

through experience until their use is perfected. This is what is called *experiential reason* (*'aql tajrîbî*).'[1]

Because he possesses these two practical faculties, man has the capacity of bringing into existence the two separate, yet related, realms of his making and doing. Like those of other animals, man's actions are intentional (*maqṣûd*); but while the acts of animals are not orderly or organized, those of man are:

' [Discerning][2] reason apprehends the rational or conventional order of events. When it [reason] intends to bring something into existence it has to notice readily its [proximate] cause or its [remote] cause, or its condition, and these on the whole are its principles. For it [the thing] does not exist except as the result of them; and the anterior cannot be made posterior or the posterior anterior. . . . For example, if [a man] thought of making a roof to protect him, he [has to] move through his understanding to the wall which supports it and to the foundation upon which the wall stands, and this is the end of [the process of] thought. Then he starts to work on the foundation, then the wall, and then the roof which is the end of his action. This is the meaning of their [the philosophers'] saying:[3] " The first stage of action is the last [in the process of] thought and the first [in the process of] thought is the last in action." . . . It is because of the recognition of this order [among things] that human acts are orderly; while because of the lack of reason by which the actor finds out the order which he [must] follow, there is no order in the acts of animals other than human beings.'[4]

In addition to his capacity for making things by the agency of his discerning reason, man has the capacity of ordering his

[1] *Q* II 364: 18—365: 5, 365–70.

[2] After the chapter in which human reason in general is discussed and divided into two practical faculties and a theoretical faculty (*Q* II 364–65), two chapters follow dealing with the two practical faculties in the order quoted above. The first (*Q* II 365–67) deals with the human acts (*ḥawâdith fi'liyya* [De Slane's reading of *'aqliyya* (rational) instead of *fi'liyya* (relating to acts) has no textual support and confuses rather than explains the meaning of the title of this chapter [*Prolégomènes* II 428: 1 and n. 1]). Its content (building a roof, etc.), clearly indicates that it is *discerning reason* which is meant to be discussed. The second deals with *experiential reason* and how it comes-to-be (*Q* 368–70). At the end of this chapter Ibn Khaldûn avoids the discussion of *theoretical reason*.

[3] Cf. Aristotle *De Anima* iii. 10. 433a17–18, *Nicomachean Ethics* iii. 3. 1112b19–20, 23–24.

[4] *Q* II 365–67.

relations with others with a view to realizing some good not in things made but in action:

'You read[1] in the books of the philosophers[2] [that] man is by nature political. . . . The reference is to the *polis*, which is a metonymy of human association. The meaning of this saying is that the life of the solitary human being is impossible; and the existence [of man] cannot be complete except together with the members of his species because of his incapacity to perfect his existence and life. Therefore, he is by his nature in need of co-operation in absolutely all of his needs. In this co-operation there has first to be negotiation, and then partnership and such things as follow from it. Such dealings may, upon the combination of accidents, lead to disputes and contentions. Thus results discord, companionship, friendship, and enmity, leading to war and peace among nations and tribes.

'This does not happen fortuitously[3] as is the case among uncontrolled animals. Among human beings, because God has given them organized and ordered actions through reason as mentioned above, [action] is performed in an organized way, and [God] has made it possible for them to perform it in accordance with political [maxims] and scientific [or wise] rules through which they turn from what is evil to what is good and from the ignoble to the noble,[4] after they discern the ignoble and the evil by what results from practising them. [They know these things] through correct experience and habits well-known among them. Thus they are distinguished from uncontrolled animals, and the result of reason becomes apparent among them in the organization of actions and their remoteness from evil.'[5]

Man is thus distinguished from the rest of the animal world by certain activities that are unique to him and are the result (*natîja*) of his reason. In their most elementary form, these activities are common to all men, who differ in performing them in degree only: (1) They can deliberate about variable and perishing things which they produce and do, and whose existence

[1] Literally : 'you hear in . . .' *Q* II 368: 2.
[2] Cf. Aristotle *Politics* i. 2. 1253a3.
[3] Correcting the sequence of the words in *Q* II 368: 12 from *ayy*/*'alâ*/*wajh* to *'alâ ayy wajh*. Cf. De Slane *Prolégomènes* II 431 n. 1.
[4] Correcting the sequence of words in *Q* II 368: 16 from *'an al-ḥasan ilâ al-qabîḥ* to *'an al-qabîḥ ilâ al-ḥasan*. Cf. *TT*, De Slane *Prolégomènes* II 431 n. 2.
[5] *Q* II 368.

is dependent upon their wills. (2) They can discern causal connections among things natural and conventional, and deliberately produce things according to a regulated rational course of action. (3) They learn from experience. They accumulate the results of experience and deliberately choose and transmit rules of conduct. (4) They can discriminate good from evil in the various ways of conduct. They can learn what is good and bad for them, and what they ought to do or ought to avoid. Thus, apart from its use in enabling man to devise means indispensable for his survival like seeking and preparing his food and co-operating with others, reason is also the 'principle of man's perfection'.[1]

3. Although reason is the noblest part of man, it is not the whole of man. To understand the nature of man's conduct and the nature of what he creates, we have to study also the relation of reason to the other faculties of the human soul in co-operation with which or in opposition to which reason operates. Apart from reason, the main faculties of the human soul are the vegetative, served by the faculties of generation, nutrition, and growth; the sensitive, including common sense and imagination; and the appetitive, served by the concupiscible and irascible faculties which have at their disposal the motive faculty residing in the muscles.[2]

These human faculties are innate *capacities* to desire. The desires of the human soul are capable of infinite variation from the simplest instinctive urge for the satisfaction of hunger and thirst to the most intricate, complex, and specialized desires developed in a highly civilized social order. All of these desires are natural in the sense of being related to human nature, the faculties which constitute the human soul, and the activity which characterizes it. There are, however, certain desires which Ibn Khaldûn is more apt to call natural either because they are more fundamental, are implanted in human nature and exhibit themselves from the very beginning of man's activities in primitive cultures, or because they are more vehement and overpowering.[3]

First among these are the lower desires springing from the

[1] *Q* I 70–71 (cf. Aristotle *De Anima* iii. 12. 434^{b}22 ff.), II 364: 6, 407–8.

[2] Cf. below pp. 190–92; Avicenna *Najât* 274–75; Averroes *Nafs* 12 ff.

[3] *Q* I 67: 12, 221–23, 332–33, 338, 365, II 202: 1–2, 249, 265, 272 ff., 307. The desires and emotions mentioned by Ibn Khaldûn belong to Aristotelian psychology as developed by Muslim philosophers.

needs of the nutritive (*ghidhâ'î*) part of the soul. Ibn Khaldûn calls them bodily appetites (*shahawât badaniyya*).[1] They are hunger and thirst, or the desire for food and drink;[2] the desire for bodily comfort, including the desires for warmth and coolness expressing themselves in the need for clothes and shelters or homes;[3] and the desires for sexual intercourse and for reproduction.[4] These desires are there at the very outset of man's social life; indeed, they are one of the factors necessitating the formation of social relationships.[5] Being absolutely necessary for the very existence of man, they are not subject to significant variation like some of the other less necessary desires; and when they vary from time to time and from place to place, the variation is for the most part connected with the form and degree of satisfying them.[6] Close to the bodily appetites in their strength and fundamental permanence are anger (*ghaḍab*) and the desire for vengeance (*intiqâm*).[7] Its opposite is calmness (*sukûn*), the feeling present in the soul in the absence of obstacles, or when such obstacles are conquered and man is able to satisfy his desires. Calmness through victory is, therefore, the end toward which anger moves.[8] Next come fear (*khawf*)[9] and its opposites, confidence (*thiqa*)[10] and hope (*amal*),[11] or the expectation of safety, prosperity, calm and, in general, the absence of serious causes of alarm.[12]

Another fundamental instinct in man is the desire for affiliation (*ṣuḥba*)[13] with other men who are related to him or who resemble him in certain ways. It includes a number of related desires such

[1] *Q* I 278: 9, II 272 ff., 307: 15. Cf. Aristotle *Nicomachean Ethics* iii. 11. 1118b17–18, vii. 4. 1147b25–27.
[2] *Q* I 69: 1–2, 70: 17–18, 221: 3, 222, II 272 ff.
[3] *Q* I 221: 3, 222, 223: 4, 318: 2, 319: 10, 326.
[4] *Q* II 260: 3–4.
[5] *Q* I 220: 10–12.
[6] *Q* II 256, cf. I 225: 14–15, 226: 5, 264–65, 309: 17, 316: 17–18, 317, 335, 365 ff.
[7] *Q* I 338, 342: 7, 343: 9–10, 365: 8–11, II 65: 10.
[8] *Q* I 365, II 210, 299, 301.
[9] *Q* I 231: 3 and 15, 234: 6 and 12, 262: 2, 268–69, II 81, 84, 93.
[10] *Q* I 229: 8–9, 230: 7.
[11] *Q* II 80–81, 124.
[12] *Q* I 156: 16–18, 157: 1, 252, II 124, 129, 204, 210 ff. Cf. Aristotle *Rhetoric* ii. 5. 1383a1–5.
[13] Using 'affiliation' to translate *ṣuḥba* and its Greek synonym *philía* (usually translated as 'companionship', 'friendship', or 'affection'). *Q* I 332: 7 ff. Cf. Aristotle *Nicomachean Ethics* viii–ix, *Rhetoric* ii. 4.

as the desire for living together in companionship and fellowship; of co-operating; of sharing the experiences of life and death by helping and defending those near to one; and the desire that such feelings be reciprocated by one's friends.[1] These are the basic desires which lead to the formation of human society and help sustain it. They are strongest when concerned with the family and one's immediate relations, and are the sources of the strong *solidarity* in clans and tribes.[2] The opposite of the desire for affiliation is failing others (*takhâdhul*),[3] hatred, and the desire to harm. This is one of the natural sources of enmity and the desire to annihilate others.[4]

Less fundamental and less necessary for man's survival is another group of desires which express themselves, after the formation of human associations, as modes of relations within society. Foremost among these is the desire to obtain victory (*ghalab*)[5] and superiority (*ri'âsa*)[6] over others. Like anger, the desire for victory is attended with a vehement disturbance (*sawra*)[7] in the soul. Man is by nature a domineering being; and his desire to overcome (*qahr*)[8] others, and subdue and coerce them, is the source of wars and of trespassing the properties of others.[9] It moves those desiring victory to struggle for political supremacy and for establishing the state in which they intend to be leaders. Those who are conquered and enslaved, on the other hand, wither away, since to be enslaved is contrary to human nature and leads to the loss of hope.[10] Victory and superiority are in most cases sought to satisfy other desires, namely, glory and honour (*'izz, jâh*),[11] distinction or nobility (*sharaf, ḥasab*),[12] and reputation (*bu'd al-ṣît*).[13] Like victory and superiority, these desires are related to the desire to control others, but they are higher because they express themselves in doing right or good

[1] *Q* I 67: 11–12, 234: 6, 235, 236, 238, 278: 6–7, 332: 7 ff., II 267: 3.
[2] Cf. below pp. 196 ff.; Aristotle *Politics* i. 2. 1253ᵃ6 ff.
[3] *Q* I 234: 12, 253: 7.
[4] *Q* II 249, 265.
[5] *Q* I 71: 18–19, 239: 14, 240, 251, 252, 263, 332: 4.
[6] *Q* I 336–37.
[7] *Q* I 264: 9–10.
[8] *Q* I 230: 9, 233: 10–12, 252: 17–18, 253: 1, 340: 11.
[9] *Q* I 71: 13 and 19, 233: 6, 268–69, II 65: 15, 249: 12–13, 265.
[10] *Q* I 71: 18–19, 236–37, 252, 299.
[11] *Q* I 241: 17 ff., 242, 262: 2, II 279: 12, 287–88.
[12] *Q* I 240: 15, 242: 17 and 19, 248.
[13] *Q* I 315: 20.

or great things (e.g., ruling well, defending one's country, and building extensive public works) with the hope of being loved, respected, and flattered.[1] Between these desires and the desire to possess wealth (*taḥṣîl al-mâl*)[2], there seems to be a reciprocal relation. The desire for possessing wealth may be for the purpose of spending it to gain honour, distinction, and reputation. Yet the desire for honour, distinction, and reputation may aim at using them as instruments of gaining wealth.[3]

The satisfaction of these desires by some individuals in society gives rise to a new set of relations and feelings between those who have satisfied them and those who have not. Among these is the feeling of pity (*shafaqa*)[4] and the desire to help those who are less fortunate (*rifq*);[5] and its opposite, contempt (*iḥtiqâr*),[6] which is a kind of slighting others and considering them of no importance; and also emulation (*tanâfus*)[7] or the desire to be equal to others, and the desire for imitating (*taqlîd*)[8] those in power or who possess any other desirable good. Finally, there are the desires connected with leisure. In the main they include three sets of desires: First, the desire for amusement (*ṭarab*),[9] relaxation, and laughter. Second, the desire to hear rhythmic tunes (*alḥân*) and experiencing all objects of hearing, tasting, touching, smelling, or seeing, which are harmonious and lead to the experience of delight and delectation.[10] And thirdly, the feeling of wonder, and the desire for learning and for knowledge (*ma'rifa*).[11]

4. Man's faculties are actualized and his desires are satisfied through activity in accordance with his nature, i.e., with his faculties and desires. Since his desires are natural and fundamental, the need for activity recurs. Because he can discern causes and what is good and evil, man can learn from the

[1] *Q* I 315: 20, 316, II 42: 6, 289 ff.
[2] *Q* I 315: 19–20.
[3] *Q* II 42: 6, 287–88.
[4] *Q* I 234: 4.
[5] *Q* I 230: 5, 340: 11 and 18–20, II 1 ff., 124 ff.
[6] *Q* I 249: 4.
[7] *Q* I 259 ff.
[8] Other terms used by Ibn Khaldûn are: *iqtifâ'*, *iqtidâ'*. *Q* I 248: 13–14, 266 ff., 316: 13–15. Cf. Aristotle *Poetics* 4. 1448b5 ff., *Shi'r* 224: 15 ff. The Arabic translation of the *Poetics* uses the terms *tashbîh* and *muḥâkât*.
[9] *Q* I 155: 9 ff., 156: 11–16.
[10] *Q* II 42: 16–17, 43, 352–61.
[11] *Q* II 363 ff.

consequences of his action and gain experience (*tajriba*).[1] Through experience he learns better and more efficient ways of making things, and more virtuous ways of action. The repetition of actions demands concentrated effort and strain, and these are necessarily painful. But repetition also leads to the formation of habit (*'âda*) as man becomes accustomed to act with little effort if not with the pleasure resulting from the confident anticipation of accomplishment. For instance, through experience, the desire to be cool or warm is satisfied by building a house, the desire to live together by the establishment of a political organization, and the desire to survive by the habit of courage. The result is fixed ways of satisfying some of man's desires. In addition, habit leads to fixed ways of desiring. For it is through experience and habit that man follows certain desires and not others, and certain desires rise in him and others do not.[2]

Through frequent repetition a habit is deeply rooted in the soul and becomes a *habitus* (*malaka*).[3] When this stage is reached habit has already transformed nature by the addition of new factors to it which express themselves in the form of arts, customs, and conventions. Neither activity, habit, *habitus*, art, custom, nor convention rise in man and human society by nature alone. Thought and deliberation, rather than nature, determine the concrete ways in which man acts;[4] and the stabilization of action in various habitual forms is the product of experience and learning in addition to nature.[5] But although, strictly speaking, man's activity and its products are not natural, they are not contrary to nature. Since nature has given man the faculties and the power for acquiring them, nature has intended man to acquire them. In other words, although they are to a large extent man-made and artificial, and despite the fact that they supplant man's original nature, they are nevertheless in accordance with nature and can be called another or second nature.[6]

[1] *Q* II 362–63, 375–76, 381; Aristotle *Metaphysics* i. 1. 981a3–7; Fârâbî *'Aql* 41; Ibn Bâjja *Tadbîr* 24–28; Avicenna *Ṭabî'iyyât* 33: 16, *Najât* 93–95, *Ishârât* 56–57; Averroes *Nafs* 76–77.

[2] *Q* I 266 ff., III 244: 5–6, cf. 34, *passim*.

[3] Cf. above p. 90.

[4] *Q* II 290.

[5] *Q* III 244: 4–6, cf. I 225–28, 228–29, 251–52, 269–77, II 80, 81, 306–7; Fârâbî *Jam'* 16–19, *Tanbîh* 8 ff.

[6] *Q* I 229: 1–2 and 14–16, 279, II 5, 80, 88, 107, 333 ff., III 117–19.

To say that habits are in accordance with nature means that man has the natural capacity of acquiring, and living by, habits. In that sense every habit can be called natural. Thus it is natural for man to acquire good habits as well as evil habits;[1] it is also natural that some men have the skill to build and others do not; and it is natural that some groups should be able to form a stable political organization and others should not. But since man is able to know and devise means to attain what is useful and good, and avoid what is injurious and evil, it could be said that the proper nature of man, that which is in accordance with his rational power, is the perfection of man.[2] When nature is also understood to mean this possible perfection, we could say that although in one sense habits, conventions, and in general all artificial things that transform the original powers of man through the addition of new factors, are all in accordance with nature (i.e., can be explained as the results of some of man's desires), they can also violate, deviate from, and sometimes even transgress nature. For instance, in the habits of character (courage, liberality, etc.) it is commendable to follow the mean (*wasaṭ*) while both excesses and defects (rashness, cowardice; prodigality, illiberality or meanness, etc.) are deviations (*inḥirâf*).[3] Hence, the explanation of things artificial in reference to one meaning of nature is not incompatible with judging them in reference to another meaning of nature.

However this may be, it is clear that without actual activity, experience, and the modification of man's primitive nature, without something done by man and without things created by man, no mode of culture can arise.[4] Culture is neither the faculties nor the desires of man considered in themselves, but precisely the habitual and conventionalized forms of social institutions and artistic productions. The relation of human culture to human nature is, therefore, the same as the relation of habits, conventions, and artificial creation, to man's nature. And culture can be called natural and artificial in the same way.

[1] *Q* I 223, 225–28, 233 (quoting Koran 90: 10, 91: 8), 259–60, 273. Cf. 225: 9–10, 274: 1, II 362, 364 ff., 367, 375–76, 380–82, III 225; below p. 195 n. 4.

[2] *Q* I 67: 10, 72: 6–7 (quoting Koran 20: 50 in both places), 192–94, 295, III 225: 14–16.

[3] *Q* I 341: 18–19, 342: 1–3, cf. 158: 9–10, 159: 4.

[4] Cf. *Q* II 279, 309–11, 313–14, 338, 364: 6, 407–8.

Consequently, although the science of culture is interested in the natural faculties and desires that lead to the formation of habits, it is essentially concerned with these habits themselves; for culture consists of these habits.[1] The study of the nature and causes of culture is, therefore, the same as the study of the nature and causes, the development, and the interrelationship among these habits.

Following Ibn Khaldûn's distinction between discerning reason and experiential reasons, the habits produced by these two faculties can be divided into those concerned with things made or produced and those concerned with things done. The first would include the habits concerned with all the arts (*ṣanâ'i'*) which deliberate on the means of producing things. The second would include the habits of conduct (*af'âl*).[2] The habits of the arts are judged to be good or bad according to whether the artist possesses a true course of reasoning or not, and to what degree; and this can be done through examining the things produced. As to the habits of character, or virtues (*khilâl*), which are capacities to act regarding what is good and useful for the actor, their end is not the perfection of things made, but of the doer himself. Habituation in them does not lead to well- or ill-made things, but to good or bad character. This is why Ibn Khaldûn states that ' perfection in the arts is a relative (*iḍâfî*) and not an absolute (*muṭlaq*) perfection, since its defect does not result from the defect of the self in religion or [moral] virtues '.[3] In contrast, the perfection of the habits of character are absolute in the sense that they are the result of what man is: his moral character; and it is in their repetition that good or bad moral character is formed.[4]

But habits, both of the arts and of character, do not depend merely upon the experience of the individual, and their formation and change are not wholly the result of an individual's stage of development. There are causes that determine the habits of an individual which are beyond his control. These causes invite some of his desires to develop in certain directions, and form certain habits and repress others. The practical disciplines concerned with what individuals make and do (e.g., architecture and

[1] *Q* II 250: 8–9.
[2] *Q* II 304, 343.
[3] *Q* II 343: 4–6.
[4] *Q* II 304, III 31.

ethics) take these causes and their operation for granted; they presuppose existing conditions, circumstances, or an environment, in which man acts, and judge his success or failure, his goodness or badness, accordingly. The science of culture, on the other hand, is concerned in an essential manner with exploring all such causes and their interrelationships, finding out whether they remain the same throughout or change, and determining whether such a change follows a discernible pattern and has discernible causes.[1]

This presupposes, of course, that there are such things as collective habits, and Ibn Khaldûn thought that this necessarily follows from the necessity of human society and the fact that men have to act in unison both in war and in peace, in producing their means of living, in organizing a political regime, and in developing the arts and the sciences.[2] It presupposes, further, that both the permanent and the variable causes of collective habits can be known by reason. Ibn Khaldûn thought that such causes, both those which are outside man (climate, etc.) and inside him (desires, reflection, etc.) can be known rationally by observing their operation in human society. Finally, it presupposes that such knowledge is not of individual events, but can have a relatively general character, i.e., that collective action is the result of relatively stable causes and is to a certain extent uniform in character. Hence, general rules of conduct and general rules of change could be discerned under specific environmental and social conditions. Ibn Khaldûn thought that this was possible because culture comes into existence to satisfy definite needs. Cultural habits are the *product* of human desires and reason, which can lead to, or devise a limited number of basic means of satisfying man's needs. Therefore, collective human action takes place according to a pattern discernible to human reason,[3] and the phenomenon of culture can be made the object of a rational science.

[1] Consequently, the science of culture does not enquire into the precise intention (*qaṣd*) of an individual or the precise determination of his will (*irâda*), for these may be caused by others and their causal explanation may thus regress *ad infinitum*. *Q* III 27–28.

[2] *Q* I 67, 68–73, 342, II 265–66.

[3] *Q* I 70, II 234–39, 289–90, 363–64, 368–70. Cf., e.g., the collective habits of Arab nomads, *Q* I 154: 18, 270, 273.

5. To describe this phenomenon, its various modes, and its complex structure, Ibn Khaldûn chose the Arabic word *'umrân* which we translate as 'culture'[1] because of the manifest correspondence between almost all the meanings of the Arabic verb-root *'-m-r* and Latin *colo* from which *cultura* and English 'culture' are derived. *'Umrân* is an abstract substantive derived from the triliteral verb *'-m-r* whose principal meanings are: (a) to live, inhabit, dwell, continue, and remain in a place; (b) to become inhabited, stocked, or cultivated (with people, animals, or plants), to be in good repair, i.e., the contrary of desolation, waste, or ruin; and (c) to cultivate, build, institute, promote, observe, visit, or aim at, a thing or a place. The first two usages describe a place (various parts of the Earth, agricultural land, village, town, fortress, and parts thereof like a house or a marketplace), while the third refers to both places and abstract concepts, e.g., 'to *promote* (or *observe*) the good'.[2] Prior to Ibn Khaldûn, the various forms of *'-m-r* are most frequently used in the works of Muslim geographers, and in particular in the *Book of Roger*[3] written by Idrîsî (d. 1166/560)[4]

[1] The practice of translating the technical term *'umrân* as 'civilisation' in French has the disadvantage of blurring the distinction between primitive and civilized culture (cf. below p. 193 n. 7). The latter, which is an advanced stage of culture, is also called *ḥaḍâra* which etymologically corresponds to 'civilization'. De Slane who usually translates *'umrân* as 'civilisation' and 'société' (*Prolégomènes* I 71, cf. 86 n. 1) translates *ḥaḍâra* as 'la civilisation de la vie sédentaire' or simply 'la vie de villes' (e.g., *Prolégomènes* II 300) as well as 'civilisation' (*ibid.* 301). This confusion has survived in later works on Ibn Khaldûn written in French (cf. T. Hussein *La philosophie sociale d'Ibn-Khaldoun—Étude analytique et critique* [Paris 1917] 65, 183 ff.; Bouthoul *op. cit.* 24, *passim*). In contrast, works written on Ibn Khaldûn in German have been more consistent in translating *'umrân* and *ḥaḍâra* as 'Kultur' and 'Zivilisation' respectively (cf. Ayad *op. cit.* 204–5; E. Rosenthal *Ibn Khalduns Gedanken über den Staat* [München 1932] 4, 94; Schimmel *op. cit.* 9, 177). It is perhaps useful to note here that *'umrân* does not usually apply to a single man as does 'culture' in expressions like 'a cultured man'. Rather, it means the cumulative social heritage (ideas, attitudes, and activities) of a group as objectified in institutions and conventionalized activities in a particular time and place. In this respect, its meaning is extremely close to that of 'culture' as used in modern sociology and anthropology. Cf. Malinowski 'Culture' *Encyclopedia of the Social Sciences* (New York 1935) I 621; R. Redfield *The Primitive World and Its Transformation* (New York 1953) 85, *passim*. This does not mean, however, that Ibn Khaldûn had the same conception of the nature and causes of culture as that of modern social science.

[2] *'amara-l-khayr*. Lane *Lexicon* 2153*c*–55; Dozy *Supplément* II 170*b*–72.

[3] *Nuzhat al-mushtâq*. Except in *Q* I 93: 5 ff., Ibn Khaldûn calls this book: the *Book of Roger* (*Kitâb rujâr*). *Q* I 75, 81, 87, 96.

[4] *GAL* I 477.

for Roger II, the Norman king of Sicily, in 1154/548.[1] In his section on geography, where Ibn Khaldûn summarizes this book,[2] the various forms of '-*m-r* occur frequently also; and by studying them we can form a precise notion of the usages which Ibn Khaldûn found current among the geographers, and which most probably suggested to him the choice of '*umrân* as a technical term to describe the subject of his new science.

In general, the geographers' use of the word is characterized by concreteness, and even when they use it as a general term it continues to refer to a particular place or state of things rather than to an abstract concept. They divide the Earth into almost two halves, one covered by water, and another uncovered and ready for ' culture ',[3] i.e., offers the possibility for the generation and continued existence of living beings, and for habitation and cultivation. But they found that three-fourths of this uncovered half is waste and desert because climatic conditions prevent the generation of plants and animals in it, and they called it the ' uncultured '[4] part, or the part without culture, in contrast to the ' cultured '[5] part of the Earth in which minerals, plants, and animals are generated and can continue to exist. In this context, ' culture ' usually indicates the existence of living beings generated from the elements;[6] and the adjective ' cultured ' indicates a place in which living beings can be generated, and can be further specified by adding to it words such as ' by plants ' (i.e., a cultivable or cultivated land) or ' by men ' (i.e., a habitable or an inhabited place).[7]

[1] Idrîsî *Nuzha* 6; *Q* I 93.

[2] *Q* I 73–148, esp. 73: 7 (cf. 51: 4–5) where Ibn Khaldûn describes the content of the works of the geographers. Cf. Idrîsî *Nuzha* 6.

[3] *Q* I 74: 4–5, cf. 88, 129, 137, 139, 145, 148; Râzî *Mabâḥith* II 198: 3.

[4] *ghayr ma'mûr, lâ 'amârata fîh.*

[5] *ma'mûr, 'âmir, dhû 'amâra.*

[6] *Q* I 82: 8–11, 83: 13 and 20, 86: 12 and 17, 87: 2 and 3 and 12, 88: 8 and 11 and 15 and 16 and 18, 89: 8 and 13, 91: 19, 95: 15, 98: 13, 146: 3–4, 148: 18. The ' modes ' (*aḥwâl*) of culture, and adjectives like ' more ' and ' less ', in such contexts refer to this general meaning of culture (*Q* I 71, 82: 2 and 4–5) except when further specifications are made, as when ' man ' (*Q* I 71: 4–5 and 11–12) or another living species is mentioned. Cf. Râzî *Mabâḥith* II 198 ff., 218; Idrîsî *Nuzha* 8: 12–13, 9: 3, 14: 5–6.

[7] *Q* I 73: 6, 74: 13, 75: 5 and 7 and 12, 79: 8 and 14–15, 81: 13, 82: 14, 83: 17 and 18, 84–85, 86: 3–4, 87, 88: 3 and 4 and 9–10, 89: 1 and 19, 91: 9 and 19, 93: 16, 98: 16, 120: 17, 148: 14. The contrary of this meaning of culture is emptiness (*khalâ'*), waste (*qafr*), and ruin (*kharâb*), cf. *Q* I 74: 5, 75: 7 and 8, 77: 15, 82: 5–6 and 8–9 and 11, 88: 10–11 and 13, 89: 9, 98: 5; Râzî *Mabâḥith* II 199; Dozy *Supplément* II 172*a*.

From this general meaning, the following, more restricted meanings emerged: (a) a place *well* peopled and more specifically (b) *well* cultivated, constructed, adorned, equipped, stocked, preserved, promoted, and in general in a flourishing state resulting from man's labour and industry, and from the use of his intelligence and art. The verbal adjectives *'âmir* and *ma'mûr* (is cultured) point to the existence of the various results of man's labour without further specification, and are equally applicable to a land, a house, a fortress, or a marketplace, and indicate a flourishing state or a general state of prosperity.[1] They can become more specific in two ways. First, by the object described. Thus, when a house is called *ma'mûr*, what is meant is that it is inhabited, taken care of, and in a good state of repair; while when the same adjective is applied to a harbour, what is meant is that it is bustling with merchants and ships.[2] Second, through the use of additional defining words or phrases. Thus a marketplace is said to be '*well-stocked* with *goods*' or '*frequented* by *merchants*'.[3] What has been said of the verbal adjectives is also true of the substantive *'umrân*.

Ibn Khaldûn's contribution to the meanings of the word is in singling out its most abstract sense and defining it as a technical term to describe the subject of his new science. As a technical term, he used it consistently to mean the diverse arts and institutions of social life and the modes pertaining to them, beginning from the moment man invents them through the exercise of his rational faculty and throughout the various stages of their development. Thus, at the beginning of social life, culture means 'living together, and being housed alongside each other in a city or a tribal community for the pleasure of companionship and the satisfaction of their needs because of their natural propensity for co-operation in acquiring their subsistence'.[4] As society

[1] Cf. above p. 185 n. 7; Mas'ûdî *Murûj* II 152, 162, 172, 174, 210; Idrîsî *Nuzha* 25: 18, 31: 2, 32: 5, 42: 11–12, 45: 1, 46: 14, 51: 4–5. Whether a place is inhabited or not is usually expressed by the word *maskûn* which indicates this fact without the additional implications contained in the adjectives *'âmir* and *ma'mûr* (cf. *Q* I 105: 3–4, 120: 16). In *Q* I 95: 14–19, Ibn Khaldûn describes a place which is inhabited, but because the conditions of its inhabitants are nearer to those of animals than to human beings, they hardly possess any culture. Cf. Idrîsî *Nuzha* 8: 5 and 12–13, 41: 16–17, 42: 11–12, 52: 13.

[2] Cf. Idrîsî *Nuzha* 28: 6, 32: 6 and 17–18, 32: 15–16, 40: 9, 41: 15, 42: 7.

[3] Cf. *ibid.* 32: 7, 52: 10.

[4] *Q* I 66–67, cf. II 363–64.

develops, the social habits pertaining to the various arts and institutions are formed, and the various aspects of social life are differentiated and become more complex. The culture of a society is these habits, and the objects (e.g., tools, buildings, and sciences) created by, and the institutions (political, economic, urban, and scientific) resulting from, the exercise of these habits.[1] To understand the detailed and more specific contents of the term 'culture', we must proceed now to give an account of the subject matter of the new science and the problems into which it is divided.

II

The Origin of Human Culture

1. Ibn Khaldûn proves the necessity of human society or culture through an enquiry into its origins and an attempt to reconstruct the stages through which man passed before the rise of culture. He tries to show that man's physical needs lead him necessarily to associate with others, and that once society comes into existence, it has to proceed through certain stages leading to the formation of culture as the only type of association through which man can successfully satisfy his needs and desires.

The most necessary and simple needs of men are those which they have in common with the plants: food and procreation. To satisfy these needs they have to come together, to specialize, and to produce the tools and perform the many tasks required

[1] *Q* I 56: 7, 61: 8–9 and 18, 66: 16–17, 67–68, 69–73. *Culture and human association.*—Ibn Khaldûn says that culture is the same as 'human association' (*al-ijtimâ' al-insânî*) (*Q* I 68, II 126). Yet he did not choose 'society' as the central term to describe the object of his new science. It is possible that he thought it is not precise enough, since it means simply association (men living together), while the new science is concerned with the coming-to-be and passing away of certain social habits and devices or inventions (e.g., arts, implements, and political organizations).

Culture and the 'polis'.—Ibn Khaldûn also says that the general significance of the term culture is the same as the *polis* (*madîna*) (*Q* I 68, II 126, 368). He adds that in the technical usage of the philosophers, the *polis* is a metonymy (*kinâya*) of human association. Thus, according to him, the science of culture, like the science of the *polis* (*politics*), deals with human society as a whole. It is, however, interesting to note that in spite of his knowledge of an existing and well-established technical term, he chose to coin a new term to describe his new science. Perhaps he thought that the *polis* and politics could be misleading because of their apparent emphasis on the city (and on politics in the narrow sense of political organization or constitution).

for the acquisition or production of food. Through the division of labour, they can satisfy needs which no individual can satisfy by himself. The second set of necessary needs rises out of the faculties man has in common with other animals: the appetitive and the choleric. The animal desire of attacking others and destroying them or becoming their master confronts man with the need of defending himself against wild animals which could destroy him if he lived alone. Man can protect himself only through organized communal defence. Instead of physical power, of which he possesses less than many other animals, he has to utilize the power in which he excels other animals, namely, the power of thought and practical reason. These faculties help him to become dexterous in shaping tools and to organize communities for producing them.[1]

Thus, on this simple and most primitive level, and in what we may call the community of necessity, it can be shown that human society is natural and necessary. It is necessary in an absolute sense because the existence of man is not possible without it: what he seeks in this form of association is not luxury or the good life, but the preservation of life without further qualification.[2] It is natural because the need for food and self-defence are imbedded in the constitution of man; they are part of his physical nature. Man cannot survive or lead the most primitive life intended for him by nature without actualizing some of the potentialities with which it had endowed him: co-operating with others and organizing the institutions of primitive economic life and defence.[3]

When the community of necessity, which provides food and safety, is established, it generates the force leading to its destruction. Men have to co-operate to feed themselves; but their co-operation and the division of labour lead to producing more than what is necessary for sheer survival.[4] Economic opulence

[1] *Q* I 67: 2, 69–70, 337–38, II 201–2, 234–35.

[2] *Q* I 68, 71, 220–23, II 126, 234–35, 289. Cf. *Q* II 290, where Ibn Khaldûn states that a single person cannot exist at all and that even if he happened to exist, he could not preserve himself.

[3] *Q* I 68, II 265, 272.

[4] *Q* I 69: 16–17. Cf. *Q* II 234–35: 'A single human being cannot by himself acquire the necessities of his livelihood. All [men] have to co-operate in society (*'umrân*) for that purpose. The need[ed goods] produced by a small group of them when co-operating can supply the necessary needs of [a group] many times as numerous as they. For instance, no one can independently produce

transforms the community of necessity to a community of luxury. In that community, men are no longer dedicated to the mere preservation of life. The animal motives that have always been latent in their nature, but had hitherto been subordinated to the supreme motive of preserving life, start to play their part. Men start 'transgressing' the property of others and 'over-reaching' the limits of their own.[1] The injured, driven by the equally natural motives of anger, pride, and revenge,[2] refuse them their property, fight them, and try to turn them away. The result is conflict, bloodshed, and confusion.[3] This war of all against all is carried out with the weapons men had forged to defend themselves against wild animals. Having produced more weapons than necessary for such defence, these are now used against their fellow men. They were adequate for turning away wild animals, but since all men possess them, they are not adequate to defend man against man.[4]

We have again come to a point where men's existence is threatened. In order to preserve life, it becomes necessary to curb their animal motives and order their relations. They must be made to live together and co-operate in spite of the disappearance of the earlier conditions which forced them to live peacefully together. The motives of transgression and over-reaching are curbed, and the community can be preserved, only when men are ruled by the most powerful and the most able (*wâzi'*) among them who has the capacity to restrain and reconcile them.[5] He forces them to follow his

---

enough wheat for his subsistence. But if six or ten (including a blacksmith and a carpenter for fashioning tools, and somebody to take care of the cows, to work on the land, to harvest the ears of corn, and do other jobs of cultivation) [come together] and if they divide the work among themselves or do it together and produce food through that labour of theirs, it will then be enough for many times their number. Therefore, after [men live in] society, products exceed the needs and necessities of those who labour.'

[1] *ẓulm*, *'udwân*. *Q* I 71: 13, 233: 6, 338: 4, II 249: 12, 265: 1, where *ta'âwun* (co-operation) should read *'udwân* (over-reaching) with *Bq* I 315: 1.

[2] *Q* I 338: 5, II 65: 10–14.

[3] *Q* I 338.

[4] *Q* I 71: 13–15. Man was given the tools for life. They were intended for his good. But like every good, this could not be actualized without some evil which exists accidentally in the material part of the process of actualization. Cf. *Q* II 290: 15–19.

[5] *Q* I 71, 233: 8, 338: 10, II 304. These two conditions are expressed by Ibn Khaldûn through the use of the Arabic word *wâzi'* which is related to *fâri'*.

directives,[1] and in so doing he becomes their ruler and institutes kingship (*sulṭân* or *mulk*) and the state (*dawla*).[2]

The state is, thus, natural and necessary because society is natural and necessary, and because society cannot continue to exist except through the state. It is true that man did exist prior to the formation of the state, but his existence was more animal- than human-like. Through the state man expresses his peculiarly human nature, namely, his rational power as against the vegetative desires that motivated the establishment of the community of necessity, and the violent animal motives of transgression and over-reaching that resulted from the community of luxury.[3] We may call this third and final stage in which men have come to live the community of the state. Through the study of the rise and transformations of society leading to the coming of the state, Ibn Khaldûn shows the necessity and natural character of this community, or culture properly so-called, which is the totality of the actualized forms of human endeavour resulting from the interplay of vegetative needs, animal appetites, human reason, and—in some cases—the divine Law.

2. According to Ibn Khaldûn, the study of man and society should start with a consideration of the place of man within the universe; for man is part of the universe, and his body and soul (*nafs*) are closely linked to the rest of the physical-perceptible world or the world of becoming, and to the world of intelligences. Within the universe, man occupies an intermediate position, and the various elements of his body and his soul are related to the various parts of the universe below and above him.

Ibn Khaldûn's physical-perceptible world (*'âlam jismânî-*

Both have the dual meaning of surpassing others in strength, and of restraining and reconciling them. Cf. Zabîdî *Tâj* V 448 ff., 540 ff.; Lane *Lexicon* 3378*b*–80*c*. Consequently, the term does not necessarily imply the idea of a despotic ruler. In translating it as *Machthaber* (cf. E. Rosenthal *Ibn Khaldun* 8–9; Schimmel *op. cit.* 20) this point must be clearly stated. Further, though Ibn Khaldûn almost always speaks of the *wâzi'* as a person, and, therefore, the term could be translated as 'sovereign' (cf. Issawi *op. cit.* 100), the reservation must be made that Ibn Khaldûn conceived of the possibility of a social group restrained by, and acting in obedience to, its elders (e.g., *Q* I 233: 16 ff.). The difficulties of translating the Arabic term result from its abstract character; it means the power of restraint without further qualification (cf. *Q* I 345–46).

[1] Having the ability to choose, they may choose not to co-operate with others. This creates the need for a ruler. Cf. *Q* II 290.

[2] *Q* I 71–72, 338, II 264–65.

[3] *Q* I 259, 338.

maḥsûs) is the Ptolemaic universe. It is made up of concentric spheres beginning with the four elements that ascend from earth, to water, to air, and to fire. These elements are arranged in a sequence of progressive refinement, and have the potentiality of turning into each other as they ascend or descend. The upper limit of the region of fire is connected with the beginning of the world of the spheres which is also arranged in ascending regions of progressive refinement.[1] The physical-perceptible world of the elements and the spheres partially determines and limits man's activity. Human society is intimately related to the natural environment within which it grows. The land, its latitude, its fertility, and the type of food it produces; the air, its temperature, and humidity; and the seasons—all exercise an influence on society: they determine the action of man and set limits to what he can do. Internally, they determine man's physical qualities: his colour, character, temperament, and humours. Externally, they condition his ability to control nature and to form cultural institutions, and the degree of his success in cultural endeavours.[2] Culture can only come into being in certain geographical regions. It cannot exist in regions where cold temperatures and snow defy man's ability to cultivate the land; nor does it develop in regions where food is abundant and the temperature too warm to allow man to work. In such regions, man is forced to continue living in a state nearer to that of wild animals. He cannot lead a properly human existence, since he is either forced to spend all his time seeking food with primitive tools or prevented from work altogether.[3] Where the natural environment does permit the growth of culture, it channelizes that growth in certain directions. The desert, for instance, prescribes the modes of association and the economic activity, and shapes the social character, of those who roam in it.[4]

[1] *Q* I 173. Cf. D. B. Macdonald *The Religious Attitude and Life in Islam* (Chicago 1909) 54 ff. Macdonald's partial translation of, and commentary on, Ibn Khaldûn's cosmology and prophetology had no impact on subsequent studies of Ibn Khaldûn. This may have been due to the fact that Macdonald and others have not recognized the crucial point that Ibn Khaldûn's cosmology and prophetology are integral parts of his theory of culture. Cf. above pp. 89 ff., below pp. 237 ff., 267 ff., 280 ff.

[2] *Q* I 148 ff., 156–57, 160 ff., II 125–26, 210, 211–12, 333. Cf. Ikhwân al-Ṣafâ' *Rasâ'il* I 85–86, 110 ff., 227 ff., III 373.

[3] *Q* I 82 ff., 156–57, 269, *passim.*

[4] *Q* I 157 ff., 225 ff., II 318.

Then, there is the world of becoming or organisms (*'âlam al-takwîn*) whose parts (or regions: the minerals, plants, animals, and men) are not only arranged in an ascending sequence, but also shade off from one to the other. Thus, the highest mineral forms are 'joint' (*ittiṣâl*) to the lowest forms of plants, the highest forms of plants to the lowest forms of animals, and the highest forms of animals to the lowest form of man. 'The meaning of "joining" in these organisms,' says Ibn Khaldûn, 'is that the highest form[1] [of each species] has an extreme[2] readiness to becoming the lowest form[3] of the [species] that comes after it.'[4] Man, for instance, 'lifts himself out of the world of apes, which has intelligence and apprehension, but has not yet reached [the stage of] deliberation and actualized thought.'[5]

To this organic world, man is related in two ways. Externally, he depends on it for his food and shelter. The character of its materials determines his tools, and the type of food it provides or enables him to cultivate may determine his social habits and cultural institutions. Internally, man has preserved in his soul the powers and desires of the plant-soul and the animal soul. He has his vegetative soul in common with the plants; like them, he is in need of nutrition, growth, and generation. He has his animal soul in common with the rest of the animal kingdom; like them, his appetites and choleric power seek actualization. These needs and desires are strong drives that direct human action and intention. They may be elemental and primitive, but they are powerful and persistent.[6]

3. Together with his intimate relation to the physical-perceptible world and the world of organisms, man is related to the world of intelligences (*'uqûl*). The rational faculty of man, when sufficiently developed or aided by supernatural help, can

[1] Literally: 'last region'.
[2] *qarîb*. Cf. Dozy *Supplément* II 323.
[3] Literally: 'lowest region'.
[4] *Q* I 173–74, cf. II 373, III 124 ff.; Ikhwân al-Ṣafâ' *Rasâ'il* III 64; Averroes *Nafs* 87. Minerals have souls according to Ibn Khaldûn (*Q* III 203: 2, 236 ff.).
[5] *Q* I 174. Cf. Aristotle *Metaphysics* xi. 12. 1069^{a}5 ff., *Historia Animalium* viii. 1. 588^{b}4 ff., iv. 5, *De Generatione Animalium* iii. 11. 761^{a}15 ff. For an account of the genesis and development of the 'idea' of continuity in the cosmos and related 'ideas', cf. A. O. Lovejoy *The Great Chain of Being* (Harvard 1950) esp. 54 ff.
[6] *Q* I 69, 175, 300–1, II 201–2. Cf. Ikhwân al-Ṣafâ' *Rasâ'il* II 325 ff.; above pp. 176 ff.

communicate with the unseen world of angels (i.e., separate intelligences),[1] demons, ghosts, jinn, and other spirits. Through them, man can foretell the future and generally know 'secret things' not knowable through the senses.[2] This can be done either through natural endowments or artificial means as in soothsaying, magic, talisman, or astrology. Prophecy is the most important of these phenomena because of its decisive role in the development of culture.[3] The purpose of the prophet is primarily practical. He is sent to communicate a message (*tablîgh*) and to 'instruct men in what is best for them and take pains to guide them'.[4] The Law initiated by him is designed to preserve and protect human society. Thus the appearance of a prophet and a Law in a community is liable to be of fundamental cultural significance, since they can change its ideals and ways of life, and impose new attitudes and create new institutions.[5] Although the explanation of the nature and powers of the prophet is not part of the object of the science of culture,[6] this science should use the result of such explanation as a basic principle in its study of society and its development.

III

Primitive Culture and Civilized Culture

1. The most important distinction made by Ibn Khaldûn in his study of the development of culture is the distinction between 'primitive culture' (*'umrân badawî*) and 'civilized culture' (*'umrân ḥaḍarî*) or 'civilization' (*ḥaḍâra*).[7] Primitive culture is

[1] Cf. above pp. 85 ff., 88 n. 3.
[2] *Q* I 181 ff.
[3] Cf. above pp. 84 ff.
[4] *Q* I 165.
[5] Cf. below p. 201.
[6] It belongs to philosophy. Cf. above pp. 84 ff.
[7] The full significance of this distinction has escaped most of those who have hitherto attempted to study Ibn Khaldûn's social thought because of their failure to distinguish clearly among the various meanings of the word *badawî*, and especially between its principal meaning (which is 'primitive') and the other derivative meanings like 'nomadic', 'countryside' life, etc. (cf., e.g., Hussein, *op. cit.* 123–26; Bouthoul *op. cit.* 63–64; Ayad *op. cit.* 187 ff.; E. Rosenthal *Ibn Khaldun* 6–7). The Arabic *badawî* is from *b-d-'(w)* (beginning, appearing, initiating [Koran 9: 13, 24: 31, 85: 13; Dozy *Supplément* I 59; Lane *Lexicon* 170*b*–72*a*; *Q* I 252]) and it stands first and foremost for 'primitive' societies, i.e., societies in which man concentrates on satisfying limited and necessary needs (*Q* I 252, II 307: 19). As a stage of culture, it can thus be

defined primarily in terms of an economic way of life, which, in turn, colours the other aspects of a community, and distinguishes it from civilization.

Primitive culture concentrates on the cultivation of land and/or taking care of domesticated animals whether in one locality or while roaming the wide deserts.[1] It is characterized by the relative dominance of simplicity in the various aspects of life and the satisfaction of the most simple and necessary needs only: Communities are small and self-supporting; the foodstuffs are simple and are eaten with little if any processing; clothes are made of animal skins or hand-woven materials; and men shelter themselves in caves, tents, or simple huts.[2] All but the most

---

contrasted to 'civilization' or the culture characterized with life in big cities with its complexity, luxury, advanced technical skills, etc. (*Q* II 250–51, 255–61). Primitive culture thus defined, need not be nomadic. Nomadic primitive culture is only one of the forms of primitive culture. There are primitive peoples living in mountains and caves (*Q* II 203: 3: 'the culture of the mountains' [*'umrân al-jibâl*]), living on, and cultivating, the land (*Q* II 317, cf. *B* I 5), living in small villages and towns (*Q* II 237), as well as primitive peoples roaming the desert. These peoples have in common a way of life which Ibn Khaldûn calls 'primitive culture' applying the word 'primitive' also to its constitutive parts, e.g., 'primitive [political] rule' (*mulk badawî*) (*Q* I 230–34, *C* I 27: 4), 'primitive building' (*binâ' badawî*) (*Q* II 234) and 'primitive industries' (*ṣinâ'a badawiyya*) (*Q* II 317).

Such a way of life admits of degrees depending on the complexity of the social heritage. Thus, the nomads are more primitive than mountain-cave dwellers, and both more primitive than village and small-town dwellers (*Q* I 224–25, II 313–14, 317). Similarly, 'civilization' is not simply living in big cities, but leading the way of life characteristic of civilization, i.e., concentration on the production and consumption of luxuries, the concentration of absolute political power, the practice of the complex arts, and the knowledge of highly sophisticated sciences (*Q* I 223–25, 235–37, 250–51, 256. In some cases Ibn Khaldûn uses 'culture' to mean this civilized stage of culture, cf. *Q* I 270). There are great cities that do not possess civilized culture because those living in them concentrate on the production and consumption of the necessities of life; such uncivilized cities 'become civilized' (*tatamaddan al-madîna*) only when their inhabitants develop a civilized mode of life (*Q* II 237, 307: 10–11, 309, 343, 383: 14–15, III 265). Like primitive culture, civilized culture also admits of degrees depending on its complexity and persistence in a certain region (*Q* II 250–51, 255–61).

It must also be emphasized that Ibn Khaldûn is devising and using technical terms to describe the relationships among types of social phenomena which he had abstracted from the concrete data of history and made the object of a theoretical science. Consequently, the reduction of the technical meaning of his terms to one or more of their non-technical meanings, like the reduction of 'primitive' to 'nomadic', can lead to serious misunderstanding of his thought.

[1] *Q* I 220: 9–10 and 12 ff.
[2] *Q* I 220 ff., II 296.

necessary tools and arts are absent.[1] There are no cities or public works, and no market economy or taxation. There is hardly any literacy, the arts are based on fragmentary and insufficient experience, and there is no body of organized rational knowledge.

This simplicity of economic and social life engenders in primitive peoples certain physical and moral virtues. Physically, they are healthy and strong because they eat the simplest of foodstuffs, live in the open air, and do hard physical labour.[2] They have to stand the hardships of adverse environmental conditions, and to live in continuous vigilance, since they are not guarded or wall-defended.[3] As a result, they are daring, brave, and confident. Being nearer to the original state of human nature (*fiṭra*) they are more prone to lead a virtuous life when it is preached to them. Unlike city dwellers, they have not gone far in the practice of vice. They may be as eager for vice as city dwellers, but because they never had the opportunity to practise it, their original nature remains pure and more receptive to the good.[4] Their simple life leads them to form habits conducive to the practice of virtue, and these habits become a second nature with them and characterize their social action and psychological attitudes.[5]

Yet the mode of life dictated by the method of production in primitive culture has the serious shortcoming of not being conducive to the well-organized political institutions necessary for the full realization of the potentialities inherent in human nature. Having been forced to live in small bands of nomadic groups or small communities in agricultural villages, and having been reared in an atmosphere of independence and self-reliance, primitive peoples are not amenable to the regimentation and hierarchical subordination which political rule necessitates. They possess only the simplest form of social solidarity. It is in

[1] *Q* II 201, 230, 233, 296, 307, 313–14, 392–93, III 2, 91, 118–19.

[2] *Q* I 158, 160–61, *Bq* V 505, 527. Cf. Suyûṭî *Ḥusn* II 199, quoting the following Tradition: 'When God created things . . . misery said: "I will go to the desert." And health answered: "I will follow you."'

[3] *Q* I 228–29, *Bq* III 450, IV 173, *B* I 106, 126 ff.

[4] *Q* I 225 ff., 273–74, II 337. Cf. *Bq* I 371. Ibn Khaldûn quotes (*Q* I 225) the famous Tradition: 'Every infant is born in conformity to the original state of human nature (*fiṭra*) and his parents make a Jew, a Christian, or a Magian out of him.' Cf. Lane *Lexicon* 2416*c*.

[5] Cf. *Q* I 229, 233.

the study of the origin and nature of this communal ethos, community of sentiment, or social solidarity (*'aṣabiyya*)[1] that Ibn Khaldûn explains the nature and characteristics of the state in primitive cultures.

2. The most elementary form of social solidarity originates in the natural desire to be compassionate toward, and to help and defend one's immediate relations.[2] Out of this tendency, the nucleus of a social group is formed—a number of individuals identifying themselves as a single group bound together by a common familial bond. Familial relations, however, admit of degrees, and so does the solidarity they engender. With this natural desire as its source, solidarity takes a more concrete social form under the impact of external necessity. An individual cannot live without a group to protect and defend him; and an isolated primitive group, whether cultivating the land or roaming the desert, finds such life impossible without internal social cohesion in the face of groups encroaching upon it from the outside.[3]

Common ancestry, common interests, and common experiences of life and death reinforce each other in developing the

[1] *Q* I 235 ff. We shall use 'solidarity' to translate *'aṣabiyya*, a word whose meaning will be progressively defined in the following pages. It must be noted, however, that this term, which embodies one of the key concepts of Ibn Khaldûn's science of culture, is elusive and cannot be defined apart from the context of his discussion, which is for the most part sociological. 'Solidarität' has already been used by L. Gumplowicz (' Ibn Chaldun, ein arabisher Soziolog des XIV. Jahrhunderts' *Ausgewählte Werke* IV [Innsbruck 1928] 102–3) and by Issawi (*op. cit.* 103) as a technical term to render *'aṣabiyya*. In German, *Gemeinsinn* and *Gemeingefühl* have also been used (cf. Ayad *op. cit.* 175 ff., 203; Schimmel *op. cit.* 37; other terms suggested by E. Rosenthal *Ibn Khaldun* 1 ff.). *Ésprit de corps*, used by De Slane in his translation (thus, the unhappy translation 'public spirit' used by R. Flint in the *History of the Philosophy of History* [London 1893] 167) is still used in French studies of Ibn Khaldûn (cf. Bouthoul *op. cit.* 56 ff.). T. Khemiri (' Der 'Aṣabîja-Begriff in der Muqaddima des Ibn Haldûn' *Der Islam* XXIII [1936] 163–88) undertook a detailed study of the word and its various uses prior to Ibn Khaldûn and in Ibn Khaldûn's writings. He pointed out that Ibn Khaldûn sometimes uses the word loosely. He did not notice, however, that in such cases Ibn Khaldûn is not using it as a technical term and that, consequently, it should be translated, as De Slane did (*ibid.* 173–75), according to the particular context in which it occurs. That the term when properly used by Ibn Khaldûn, meant 'Nationalismus' and that all of its other connotations are 'foolish and worthless' (*ibid.* 181–82) is certainly based on a different conception of culture than that of Ibn Khaldûn. Cf. F. Gabrieli ' Il concetto della 'aṣabiyyah nel pensiero storico di Ibn Haldûn' *Atti della Reale Accademia delle Scienze di Torino* LXV (1929–30) [Classi di Scienze Morali, Storiche e Filologiche] 474–75. It must be added that this is true even when nationalism is defined, as by Khemiri (*Der Islam* XXIII [1936] 183), to mean ' Nationalismus der einfacheren Vorkriegsform.'

[2] *Q* I 235.

[3] *Q* I 234.

feeling of solidarity.[1] In time, the latter factors overshadow common ancestry. Persons outside the blood-relations of a group are adopted and become part of it; common ancestry remains an important factor, but in reality it has become a mere figment. Some isolated tribes do continue to possess solidarity based on true common ancestry, but in most primitive groups genealogies become confused and a common ancestry is adopted as a means of attaining solidarity.[2] Solidarity comes into being as a result of common ancestry, but it is usually sustained by external factors: the feeling of relatedness is dictated by the necessity of co-operation and self-defence.

These factors, as well as the method of production, determine the size of primitive groups and the character of their political institutions. Because men come together to satisfy the simple necessities of life which require the co-operation of relatively few persons, the size of the groups they form is normally small. Primitive people do not usually submit to others except by force, necessity, or the hope for some reward. The political institutions of these groups are, consequently, simple and based essentially on kinship, and the respect of, and obedience to, their elders.[3] Defence is usually entrusted to the brave and dependable young men; the group is ruled by those who are considered noble because of their ancestry or deeds; and differences are solved by resorting to the judgment of the old and wise among them or from the outside.[4]

3. But primitive culture does not remain static within these conditions. The small groups may increase in size and their solidarity may be shaken because of dissensions within the ruling family, leading to conflicting loyalties and struggle for undisputed power.[5] The sub-group with the strongest inner solidarity overcomes other sub-groups and rules them through coercion and suppression. This is natural, since, like the elements that constitute a natural body, a multitude of powers cannot form a harmonious whole except when arranged hierarchically with an undisputed leader at the top.[6] When this transformation

[1] *Q* I 332: 7–9.
[2] *Q* I 236–39, 332, 333. Cf. Khemiri *Der Islam* XXIII (1936) 169; Ayad *op. cit.* 178–79.
[3] *Q* I 233, 239, 252, II 175: 12–13.
[4] *Q* I 233–34.
[5] *T* 131, *Q* I 239, *Bq* I 110–11.
[6] *Q* I 294, 299–300, 314, III 236.

of political rule takes place, chieftainship (*ri'âsa*), based on voluntary common consent, becomes kingship based upon the destruction of other loyalties and the threat of force.[1] Thus, solidarity creates the conditions that make the acquisition of absolute power possible, and kingship is the goal toward which solidarity moves. The love of power, especially of absolute power, and of coercing and suppressing others, are the manifestations of the irascible, animal faculty of man.[2] Consequently, kingship and solidarity have their origin in the animal faculties of man, and are not the product of voluntary choice only. Human reason and the divine Law may limit, supplement, and direct them toward rational ends. But throughout the course of social life, solidarity and kingship continue to be essential for the formation and sustenance of all political regimes.[3]

The power of kingship in primitive culture is circumscribed by the primitive mode of economic activity which does not lend itself to luxurious living or to amassing large fortunes. It is also limited by the unruly character of the subjects who still remember their freedom and have to be manipulated with caution. Consequently, unlike civilized kingship (*mulk ḥaḍarî*), primitive kingship (*mulk badawî*)[4] cannot completely satisfy man's lust for absolute power and even less his desire for riches. Such drives can be satisfied only through the conquest of other primitive or civilized groups, and the creation of a civilized culture. Hence, this is the next step in the development of culture.

Although primitive groups are isolated, their isolation is not complete. Nomadic tribes in particular cross each other's paths and may have to struggle for the same pasture land. They come in contact with other primitive groups settled in villages and with the civilized nations on whose fringes they roam. To satisfy their lust for riches and for more power, they engage in endless petty wars among themselves and with neighbouring civilized nations.[5] These wars often prove inconclusive. Instead of accomplishing the ends for which they are fought, they create a state of anarchy whose only result is loss of men and substance.[6] This confused state of affairs can be ended when the many loyalties that divide

[1] *Q* I 252.
[2] *Q* I 342, cf. 278, 352–53, 364.
[3] *Q* I 364.
[4] *C* II 41.
[5] *C* II 41, 46 ff., *Bq* V 429.
[6] *Q* I 270 ff.

them into numerous independent and warring groups are overcome by the superior power of one of them. This process is natural. Once a superior solidarity emerges within a group, it tends to subdue the lesser solidarities and bring them under its control. The result is a greater solidarity (*'aṣabiyya kubrâ*) that unites the conflicting factions and directs their efforts to fight and subdue other groups.[1] This process of expansion and unification continues until a point is reached when the newly formed solidarity is able to conquer the dominions of a civilized state or to establish new cities and the institutions characteristic of a civilized culture.[2]

Primitive culture is driven toward civilization by the desire for power, riches, and leisure. Its members are able to conquer an existing civilized state, or to create one, because they have strength, courage, endurance, and, above all, inner cohesion and solidarity. These virtues are necessary for the new adventure. Yet, it is not always easy for a primitive group to travel the road to civilization. The virtues of its members can be a source of new dissensions and conflicts. Its solidarity is not stable, and once its members have achieved certain objectives, they may resist further demands from their ruler. They may then be dominated by a strong civilized state, lured by its ways, and become content with small remuneration for serving it as mercenaries.[3] Further, their primitive mode of life was such that they have acquired habits contrary to the ways of civilization; and these habits[4] may have become second nature. They may have developed social and psychological attitudes preventing them from creating a civilization and driving them to destroy the civilization they may dominate. This is particularly true of nomadic primitive cultures like those of the Berber and Arab nomadic tribes.[5] Nomadic life engenders the love of personal feuds and indifference to authority, the habit of continuous movement and lack of attachment to certain regions, and the habit of appropriating whatever is in sight regardless of the

[1] *Q* I 253.
[2] *Q* I 252–53, II 203.
[3] *Q* I 254 ff., 276–77, 297–99.
[4] *'awâ'id*. *Q* I 229, 270.
[5] Ibn Khaldûn's study of the psychological and sociological aspects of the phenomenon of nomadism has been made the basis of a campaign against and an apology for the 'Arabs' (Hussein *op. cit.* 126–32; Muḥammad 'Abd

rights of others; and civilization cannot exist without respect for authority, attachment to a certain locality, and deference to the rights of others.[1] The virtues of primitive culture are thus

Allâh 'Inân [Enan] *Ibn Khaldûn, ḥayâtuhu wa-turâthuhu al-fikrî* [Cairo 1933] 112–14; Sâṭi' al-Ḥuṣrî *Dirâsât 'an muqaddamat Ibn Khaldûn* [2 vols.; Beirut 1943–44] I 107–34. Ḥuṣrî's is the most careful discussion of the problem. The following remarks concentrate mainly on the sociological aspect which he did not treat in detail). The above discussion concentrates on Ibn Khaldûn's abstract formulation of the nature and characteristics of nomadic primitive life as a universal cultural type without limiting the discussion to a single example of that type. Ibn Khaldûn himself attempted to disengage his type from as wide an area of experience as he could. Thus he cites, together with Arab and Berber nomads, Turkish and Mongol nomads as examples and evidence for his theories (cf., e.g., *Q* II 229–31, *T* 358 ff., 382), and his characterization of these latter nomadic groups is not essentially different from that of the Arab nomads. In addition, there are four points which deserve some explanation:

(1) Ibn Khaldûn's assertion that Arab nomads are more deep-rooted in nomadism (*a'raqu fi-l-badwi, ashaddu badâwatan*) than other nomadic groups (*Q* I 223, *C* II 163, *B* II 1, 4). This statement has to be qualified by another in which Ibn Khaldûn groups Arab nomads and Berber nomads as equally deep-rooted in nomadism (*Q* II 230–31). The reason for the extreme nomadism of the Arabs, according to Ibn Khaldûn, is their economic mode of life, since Arab nomads are characterized by attending to camels and living in tents only. Arab nomads interested him because they represented 'pure' nomadism; for they are not bound to a certain locality which is necessary for those who herd other animals or have more permanent dwellings. This is why Ibn Khaldûn sometimes used the word 'Arab' to describe the phenomena of 'nomadism', hence simultaneously (a) applying it to peoples who are not linguistically or racially (in the restricted sense used in biblical genealogies [cf. *C* I 22 ff.]) Arabs and (b) restricting its meaning in such a way as to exclude the Arabs who did not lead a nomadic life. Thus, the word 'Arab' as employed in such cases is the same as 'Arabism' (*'urûbiyya*), the 'meaning and symbol of Arabism' (*ma'nâ al-'urûbiyya wa-shi'âruhâ*), or 'the ways of life of Arabism' (*madhâhib al-'urûbiyya*) (cf. *C* II 163, 166). In this abstract sense of a general type, he could talk about Zanâta (a Berber tribe) as 'adopting the symbol of Arabism' and having the character of 'Arabism' (*B* II 1, 4), and of 'Arabization' to mean 'coming to live in the desert' (*Q* I 226).

(2) This usage of the word 'Arab' as a mode of primitive culture does not mean, however, that Ibn Khaldûn does not simultaneously use 'Arab' to mean a specific linguistic and racial group. He uses both and does not fail to distinguish between the Arabs who live in the desert (whom he sometimes calls 'nomadic Arabs' [*'arab bâdiya*] [*C* II 2 ff.]) and those who do not live in the desert (cf. *C* II 81, 101).

(3) The association of the Arab with the desert (and thus restricting the word to the inhabitants thereof and the herders of camels) is an ancient one. The word *'arab* is a Semitic word which means 'desert' and the inhabitants of the desert with no specific reference to a genealogical-racial or linguistic group. We find it used in this restricted sense in the earliest (Assyrian) text referring to the Arabs as well as in the Old Testament and the Koran (cf. Hitti *op. cit.* 37, 41). In Ibn Khaldûn's time, the use of 'Arab' to mean 'nomadic Arab' was common (cf. *Bq* V 415, 427, 429, 436, 450, *B* I 2 ff.).

(4) Nomadism is a natural phase of primitive culture (*Q* I 223: 15) which entails certain natural virtues as well as vices. Whether a nomadic people is virtuous or vicious depends on how far they follow the rational-ethical norms, or the prescriptions of the Law, when these are preached to them. Cf. below pp. 201 ff.

[1] *Q* I 270–72. Cf. *Bq* V 429.

counterbalanced by shortcomings that diminish the ability of many primitive peoples to found a new civilization, and handicap them when attempting to wrest the dominions of a civilized state. Such primitive peoples may create the rudiments of civilization in a restricted region or conquer a weak civilized state.[1] But usually the civilization they found does not last long and the state they conquer decays.

In order to be able to found a great civilization, or to conquer or build a great empire, they may need an additional force to eliminate their shortcomings, and to buttress and enhance their solidarity. This force is religion. Religion, like any other *social* cause, needs solidarity to establish it. It has, therefore, to rise, and it usually does rise, among a group with strong solidarity that propagates it by fighting for it.[2] Once a religion is adopted and supported by such a group, it becomes a highly effective force. It creates a new loyalty: absolute belief in, and obedience to, the demands of the Law and the religious leader. This is the source of a solidarity superior to, and more lasting than, the solidarity based merely upon natural kinship and worldly desires. Religion does away with the competitiveness and envy resulting from pursuing worldly purposes, restrains its followers from immoral and unjust practices, commands them to obey their superiors, and establishes a divine Law regulating their political life.[3] Those who believe in it act from inner compulsion and are motivated by the hope for the rewards it promises them in the world to come. Second to natural solidarity and based upon it, religion is the most powerful force in the creation of civilization and its commands are the most effective instruments for preserving it.[4]

4. Civilization, or the culture centred around life in cities, is the natural completion of the life begun in primitive culture and the end to which human nature has been moving ever since the creation of the most simple forms of communal life.[5] Viewed in relation to that end, primitive culture is an incomplete culture. It merely satisfies man's necessary needs. In contrast, civilization

[1] *Q* I 269 ff.
[2] *Q* I 168, 286 ff., 364, II 172.
[3] *Q* I 231–32, 273–76, 284–86; cf. below pp. 206–9, 213–16, 219–21, 223–24.
[4] *Q* I 276; cf. below pp. 237 ff., 267 ff., 280 ff.
[5] *Q* II 203 ff.

tends to satisfy needs and desires that may not be necessary for survival, but are nevertheless natural and necessary because they are latent in the human soul, waiting for an opportunity to assert themselves. The city is the place where these desires, such as lust for power, love of luxury and sensual pleasure, and yearning for rest and leisure, can be satisfied.[1] Hence, once solidarity and a religious cause supply the necessary force for establishing or conquering cities, primitive culture necessarily moves toward civilization and the creation of the civilized political, economic, and scientific institutions destined for the satisfaction of these desires.

Compared to the circumscribed needs for food, shelter, and defence which are usually satisfied in primitive culture, the desires for which men come to live in the city are unlimited. They admit of infinite degrees, and men strive to create more and more effective ways of satisfying them. The result is the first essential attribute of civilization: its progressive development and growth. But in spite of the persistence of the desires for which civilization is created, invariably a stage will be reached when man's creative powers diminish due to factors generated during the process of growth.[2] The second essential attribute of civilization, therefore, is that it reaches an optimum point and a natural limit beyond which it cannot develop. Then, the powers that have brought civilization to this point start to decline. This is accelerated by new forces generated by the conditions of civilization at its height. The result is the dissolution of urban institutions and the disintegration of civilization. Thus, the third and last essential attribute: a civilization inevitably declines until it ceases to exist.

The characteristic feature of the new mode of culture is, then, a dynamic process of growth and dissolution.[3] Like natural living organisms, it has a beginning, it grows and develops, and it comes to an end. This life cycle is not essentially the product of chance and fortune, or of art and conscious construction. Chance and fortune are usually names given to hidden causes;[4] and art

[1] *Q* I 223, 299 ff., III 60: 2–3.
[2] Cf. below pp. 207–9, 214–16, 219–21, 222–24.
[3] *Q* I 247–48.
[4] *Q* II 75–79, *Bq* III 53, *B* II 138–40. Cf. below pp. 259–60.

learns from nature.[1] Chance and art may hasten the growth of civilization or may slow down its decline, but they can neither create it nor prevent its decline and death.[2]

Because of a fundamental unity in the manifold aspects of civilization, these attributes are true of civilization as a whole.[3] The principles that give rise to, and the laws that govern the development of, these aspects (i.e., the state, the city, economic life, and the sciences) are common to all of them: They all arise out of the basic human urge for power, riches, and leisure. They all start from a simple beginning, develop to an optimum point, and decline. There is an internal bond that unites them. During their rise and decline, they influence and causally determine each other. This causal determination differs in the various stages of the development of civilization. Therefore, to understand the complex dynamism of the rise and decline of civilization we need to inquire into the manifold relationships among its diverse aspects as they manifest themselves during the different stages of its development.

Yet within this fundamental overall unity, the state, the city, economic life, and the sciences, show a certain degree of independent development that can be disengaged and formulated. For instance, the rise and decline of economic prosperity could be shown to be governed by the laws of supply and demand, price-level, and cost of production.[4] This relative independence and semblance of unity within the various aspects of civilization is the justification for the division of the subject matter into a specific number of problems which is not wholly arbitrary.

Within the totality of civilization, the supremacy of the state and of political institutions remains uncontested by Ibn Khaldûn. The state builds the cities, and the extent of urbanization depends on the support and protection of a powerful state.[5] The state is the cause of the development and organization of economic institutions: it is the greatest of buyers, the greatest spender of money, and the largest monopoly; and economic luxury is dependent on the protection and policies of the

[1] Cf., e.g., *Q* II 333 ff., III 117–19 (on medicine); Averroes *Tahâfut* 413: 10.
[2] *Bq* I 110–11, *Q* I 299–300, 305, 314, II 255.
[3] *Q* II 254–55, *passim*.
[4] Cf. below pp. 218 ff.
[5] *Q* II 201–9, 254, 261–65.

state.[1] Finally, the state is the cause of the flourishing of the sciences, directly through its support of scientific institutions and indirectly as the cause of the other aspects of civilization apart from which the sciences could not exist.[2] The life of the state and the life of the civilization it brings into existence are coextensive. A civilization follows the rise of a powerful state, it is limited in space by the extent of the state, it flourishes when the state is at the height of its power, and it disintegrates with the state's disintegration.[3] Consequently, Ibn Khaldûn's study of the development of civilization is primarily a study of the development of the civilized state and an examination of the interaction of the other aspects of civilization within the state. The problems of the creation of the state, the stages through which it passes, its various forms, and the causes of its decline, are the central problems of Ibn Khaldûn's science of culture.

IV

The State

1. A civilized state comes into being through the establishment or conquest of cities by a primitive people welded together by solidarity and religion, and aiming at the satisfaction of their natural desires, the actualization of their potentialities, and the completion of the life begun in primitive culture. As is the case with other aspects of civilized culture, once a civilized state comes into being, it follows the natural and necessary law of growth, maturity, and decline. If not retarded by the lack of necessary initial force or some other accidental hindrance from outside, it passes through five distinct stages, each of which has its own essential attributes.[4]

[1] *Q* I 313, II 92, 234 ff., 244–46, 250–51, 255, 278 ff., 297, 303–4. Cf. E. Rosenthal *Ibn Khaldun* 71–92: 'Staat und Wirtschaft.'

[2] *B* II 144 ff., 305, *Q* II 383–84. Cf. E. Rosenthal *Ibn Khaldun* 92 ff.: 'Staat und geistige Kultur'; Flint *op. cit.* 167.

[3] Cf., e.g., *B* II 82, 85–86, *Q* I 317–29.

[4] *Q* I 308: 11–12, cf. 248–49, 305–9, II 236–37. We have chosen to concentrate on the stages of the state (*aṭwâr al-dawla*) (*Q* I 299 ff., 330 ff.). Ibn Khaldûn also talks about 'the generations of the state' (*ajyâl al-dawla*) (*Q* I 302 ff.), but adds that each of the stages mentioned above may take two or three generations (*Q* I 300).

The first stage is the period of establishment.[1] During this period, solidarity, based on familial ties and religion, continues to be essential for the preservation of the state. This is the period during which the ruled are forced to build the institutions necessary for a civilized culture or, when such a culture is already in existence, to submit to a new ruling class. There are, thus, new activities to be carried out and new political relations to be created. These cannot be accomplished except through a solidarity which generates sufficient power to force the subjects to accept the new ruler as their master and obey his directives.[2] When aided by religion, solidarity becomes more effective in establishing the state; since the subjects will then obey the ruler and his directives more willingly, convinced that in so doing they are obeying God.[3] Like other natural powers, the power generated by solidarity and religion has a limit beyond which it weakens and becomes ineffective. The united force of a people, when building cities or conquering them, weakens as they disperse to govern and defend the various parts of the kingdom. Soon a limit will be reached beyond which they can barely hold the new cities they have founded or conquered. This will determine the geographic boundaries of the state.[4]

During this first stage, solidarity is still largely based on a community of sentiment, and the ruler owes his position to his noble ancestry and the respect of his fellow tribesmen. His rule is dependent on their number, power, and assistance. He is still largely their chief rather than their master and king.[5] He has to accommodate their sentiments and desires, and to share his power with them. The same is true of religion. The ruler who is establishing a state with the aid of a religious message cannot act as a master and a king, since religion means the obedience of all to God and the religious Law.[6] The persistence of natural solidarity and religious sentiment during this period means the persistence of some of the primitive modes of life. The state is still in a period of transition. The primitive people that established it continue to preserve some of their primitive attitudes, including their attitude to authority. These attitudes handicap

[1] *ẓafar*. *Q* I 315: 1.
[2] *Q* I 279.
[3] *Q* I 284 ff.
[4] *Q* I 291–95. Cf. Gumplowicz *op. cit.* 94.
[5] *Q* I 252 ff., 315, 330, II 100 ff.
[6] *Q* I 367.

the development of civilization and the concentration of authority necessary for its development. In short, the forces that created the state become a hindrance to its growth.[1]

2. This condition is overcome when the ruler succeeds in monopolizing power and becomes an absolute master. The monopoly of power by the ruler is the natural and necessary end of the rule that began on the basis of natural solidarity. Like all well-disposed natural bodies, a well-ordered state should consist of a hierarchy of powers with an absolute commander at the top whose rule is not shared or disputed by anyone.[2] Further, the lust for power and mastery is innate in man's animal nature, and once a man is in a position where he can, he will try to obtain absolute power and mastery.[3] The ruler is now in a position to satisfy this lust and to build a well-ordered state. This he achieves through the destruction of those who share power with him, first by using some of them against others, and then by using paid mercenaries who are loyal to him as a person and not to a kinship-solidarity or a religious cause.[4]

The second stage in the development of the state is thus the period of consolidating the ruler's power and of creating absolute kingship.[5] Natural solidarity and religion are checked so far as they mean the sharing of power, and are used at the discretion of the absolute ruler. Solidarity is replaced by a paid army, and an organized administrative bureaucracy, that carry out his wishes. Natural solidarity becomes increasingly superfluous. The subjects gradually acquire the habit of obeying their new ruler. The impersonal organization of the army and the bureaucracy take care of the protection of the state and the development of the various institutions of a civilized culture.[6] The army and the treasury, and later a group of learned men, become the instruments of preserving the state.[7]

3. As the ruler's lust for absolute power is satisfied with the concentration of authority in his hands, he starts to use his

[1] *Q* I 302, II 100–101, 231.
[2] *Q* I 299–300. Cf. above p. 197 n. 6.
[3] *Q* I 252–53, 300.
[4] *Q* I 300, 330.
[5] *istibdâd. Q* I 315: 6, cf. 300, 330, 364 ff.
[6] *Q* I 279 ff., II 40 ff.
[7] *Q* II 19, 40 ff., 108 ff.

authority for the satisfaction of his other desires—he starts to 'collect the fruits of authority'. Thus, a third stage of luxury and leisure[1] follows. The ruler concentrates on the organization of the finances of the state and on increasing his income. He spends lavishly on public works and on beautifying the cities in imitation of famous civilized states.[2] He enriches his followers who in turn start living a life of luxury. Economic prosperity follows. The crafts, the fine arts, and the sciences, are encouraged by, and flourish under the care of, the new ruling class. The state has finally reached the stage where it is able to satisfy man's craving for luxuries and his pride in possessing them. This is a period of rest and self-indulgence in which men enjoy the comforts and pleasures of the world.[3]

Here ends the first phase of the development of the state. It has risen from primitive conditions and reached the end for which it has come into existence. Kingship has been established and the various ways of civilization perfected. The first three stages are periods of progressive accomplishment in which rulers are powerful, independent, and creative; they are able to consolidate their authority and satisfy their subjects' desires without either they or their subjects becoming the slaves of these desires. The economic prosperity they achieve is the expression of their power, and it is used by them to increase their followers, i.e., as an instrument of additional power.[4]

4. Having reached its zenith, the next stage is a period of contentment[5] in which the ruler and the ruled are satiated and complacent. They imitate their predecessors in enjoying the pleasures of life, ignorant of how these predecessors struggled to achieve them. They think that their luxurious life and the various advantages of civilization have always existed and will continue to exist forever. Luxury, comfort, and the gratification of their desires become a habit with them. They are completely dependent upon the continuous existence of what their predecessors had achieved and are powerless before forces that may lead to the disruption of their prosperity. The length of this

[1] *farâgh, di'a*. *Q* I 315: 18.
[2] *Q* I 309, II 82.
[3] *Q* I 300–301, 315–16, 320 ff.
[4] *Q* I 309, 313, 316: 8–10, 317 ff.
[5] *qunû', musâlama*. *Q* I 316: 11.

period depends upon the power and extent of the achievement of the founders of the state.[1]

5. During this stage, the state is already starting to decline and disintegrate, and the fifth and last stage of prodigality and waste[2] is setting in. The state has reached old age and is doomed to a slow or violent death. The very process of establishing it had destroyed the vital forces of solidarity and religion that were responsible for its existence. The rulers had destroyed the communal pride and loyalty of their kinsmen who, humiliated and impoverished, have lost the drive to conquer.[3] Instead, they chose clients and a bureaucracy whose services are completely dependent on generous remuneration, and whose loyalty does not extend to willingness to die for them. Their successors, having known only the life of luxury and surrounded by a prodigal entourage, continue to spend more and more on their pleasures. They increase taxes and these in turn discourage economic activity and lead to a decline in the income of the state which makes it impossible for the ruler to support his new followers.[4]

Further, the habits of comfort and luxury generate physical weaknesses and moral vice. The élite of the state forget the rough and courageous manners of primitive life. They are powerless before an outside invasion by a strong civilized state or by united primitive peoples.[5] Excessive taxes and the fear of invasion weaken the hopes of the ruled. Despair becomes so widespread that it halts economic activity and building. People no longer make long-range plans and the birth-rate drops.[6] The entire population, physically weak and living in large crowded cities, becomes subject to disease and plague. With the decrease of

[1] *Q* I 248, 300–301, 308, 316, 330–31, II 256, 278–79, 309–11 313–14. The relation between the life span of a ruling dynasty and that of a state is not very clear. In certain places, Ibn Khaldûn seems to think that they are one and the same. If this is the case, and since the power of a dynasty lasts only for three generations after it is founded (*Q* I 247–50, 308; cf. Gumplowicz *op. cit.* 100), the age of the state will then average one hundred and twenty years. But Ibn Khaldûn also states that within a large nation made up of many peoples (*shu'ûb*), various peoples (and hence dynasties) may follow each other in ruling the same state so long as the new rulers possess sufficient solidarity (*Q* I 264–66).

[2] *isrâf, tabdhîr. Q* I 316: 16, cf. 249, 305–8.

[3] *Q* I 302 ff., 332 ff., II 108 ff., *B* II 2 ff.

[4] *Q* I 332–34, II 82–83, 92–93, 100, cf. *Bq* IV 435.

[5] *Q* II 255 ff.; cf. the psychological effects of virtues and vices as explained by Averroes in his paraphrase of Plato's *Republic* (E. Rosenthal *JRAS* [1934] 743).

[6] *Q* I 268–69, 271, II 80 ff., 124.

economic activity and the depopulation of the cities, the state begins to disintegrate.[1] Starting from the outlying regions, princes, generals, and the dissatisfied kinsmen of the ruler, become independent. The rest of the state is then divided and subdivided into small provinces.[2] In the capital, the mercenary troops and the civil bureaucracy begin intriguing to wrest the actual power from the ruler, leaving him but the insignia and the name.[3] Finally, an outside invasion puts an end to the life of the state, or it may continue to decline until it withers away ' like a wick dying out in the lamp whose oil is gone '.[4]

V

The City[5]

1. The city exists for the satisfaction of man's desire for luxury, refinement, and leisure. These desires inevitably arise in men when their primitive needs are satisfied. Therefore, the city necessarily comes into being when men acquire the power of establishing it.[6] This power is the solidarity that had created the state. Since the city and its institutions are not indispensable for mere subsistence, men are not driven to build it out of the natural urge for survival. The initial establishment of the city requires the organization of a large group of men who must be either rewarded or forced to work, and who must be protected while working. The state is the only agency that possesses the

[1] *Q* II 336–37.

[2] Thus, the great empire (*mulk a'ẓam*) disintegrates into small kingdoms (*mulk aṣghar*) (*Q* II 268). These small kingdoms in turn pass through similar stages as the great empire, except that due to their small initial power of solidarity and their inappreciable dominion they do not live as long. Cf. *Bq* IV 16, 61, 211, 389, *B* I 237, 247–48, II 350 ff.

[3] *Q* I 291–92, 295, 302, II 100 ff., 114 ff., cf. *Bq* III 97 ff., 109, 280 ff., 401–2, 421, 478, 497, IV 175, 279.

[4] *Q* II 108, 113 ff.; cf. above pp. 25–26.

[5] The historical background of Ibn Khaldûn's thought concerning the subject is the Islamic city which is a continuation of the Hellenistic city (cf. W. W. Tarn *Hellenistic Civilization* [London 1936] 129 ff.) rather than the Greek city-state. Indeed, city-states existed in Islam, but they were the product of the disintegration of states that originally ruled whole empires or provinces. In contrast to the treatment of the city as a politico-ethical entity by classical authors (cf. Aristotle *Politics* iv. 1–3, vii. 5, 6) Ibn Khaldûn treats the city and its institutions as a single aspect of civilized culture dominated by a state that controls numerous cities.

[6] *Q* II 201 ff.

power and money to organize such a large group of men, to make them work from fear of punishment or love of reward, and protect them against invaders.[1]

The very fact that a powerful state has come into being leads to the establishment of cities, or their conquest if they already existed in the neighbourhood where such a state has risen. The new solidarity group now has the power to progress beyond the simple and austere modes of primitive life. The long struggle for building the state having ended, the group looks for rest and seeks the enjoyment of the fruits of its efforts; and it cannot achieve these objectives except by living in a place easier to defend and in which the luxuries of life can be produced. The city is the only place where this is possible. Hence the state naturally and necessarily engages in establishing cities if these did not yet exist.[2] If, however, there happened to be cities on its borders, then it becomes necessary to conquer them. Otherwise, these cities would be places of refuge for its enemies who, with few men and the additional protection provided by the walls of these cities, could contest its power and keep it harassed.[3]

The character of the city—its extent, prosperity, population, and the degree and duration of its civilization—depends on the power and extent of the state that establishes it.[4] If the state is powerful and has extensive possessions, then the cities it establishes, especially its capital, will grow rapidly; their population will increase, public works and monuments will be built, and their economic activity and scientific institutions will flourish. For the state will have the money to spend on, and encourage such growth. If the state continues to be powerful for a long time, this will give the cities under its hegemony an opportunity to grow and their institutions a chance to become firmly established.[5] On the other hand, if the state is made of a group of very primitive peoples who have no tradition or taste for civilization, the cities it establishes will be relatively primitive and impermanent.[6] If the state happens to be weak

[1] *Q* II 202.
[2] *C* II 342, *Bq* IV 15, *B* I 197, 221, 234, 290, 367, II 105 ff., 134 ff., 280, 282.
[3] *Q* II 203–5.
[4] *Q* II 263 ff.
[5] *Q* II 250 ff.
[6] *Q* II 213, 226, 232–33.

and unable to defend its cities against outside aggression, they will remain small and insignificant, and civilization will not take root in them.[1] In short, cities reflect the state that founds or conquers them. At first their rulers mould them with their way of life, their language, and their religion. They impress upon them their exuberance and create in them the atmosphere of safety and hope which encourage their population to work and produce more goods. Then, gradually the new rulers begin to succumb to the luxury and rest the cities provide, and become the slaves of the city and its way of life. When this happens, decline, both of the state and of the city, sets in.[2]

The location of the city and the manner of building it are determined by the ends which it is to serve: the satisfaction of man's desire for luxury, comfort, and protection. The degree to which a city can satisfy these desires depends on those who build it, on their knowledge and ability to foresee the proper means through which they can accomplish their ends. Thus, those who have foreknowledge of their ends, locate their cities in regions easy to defend and at the same time capable of supplying the needs of their inhabitants. They choose a location free from stagnant water that produces putrid and decomposed air and causes disease, endowed with a sufficient supply of fresh water, surrounded by pastures and arable fields, and accessible to foreign markets.[3] They fortify their cities with impenetrable walls and build their houses and public works of durable materials. But not all who establish cities foresee their ultimate needs or know the proper means to them. This is especially true of peoples who have known only the nomadic way of life. In conquering cities or building them, they cannot see beyond their immediate needs and those of their animals. Unwittingly, they destroy the public works they find in the cities they conquer, and when building cities, they confine themselves to the use of the most primitive and perishable materials and structures. Consequently, cities built by such peoples are not likely to endure.[4]

[1] *Q* II 205 ff., 229 ff.
[2] *Q* II 244–47, 269–72.
[3] *Q* II 201, 210 ff., 232–33, 237–38.
[4] *Q* II 226, 231–33. On the character of cities established by Arab invaders, cf. E. Reitmeyer *Die Städtegründungen der Araber im Islâm nach den arabischen Historikern und Geographen* (München 1912) 2 ff.

The interaction of primitive culture and the city is not, however, limited to the initial phase of conquest or establishment. After the city is conquered or established, a new set of relations comes to exist between its inhabitants and the inhabitants of the desert and the countryside which determines the character of both. The city is in continuous need of fresh supplies of inhabitants, and mercenary soldiers, who must be drawn from the desert and the countryside. It is also in need of the foodstuffs produced by the countryside adjacent to it. The inhabitants of the desert and the countryside, on their part, come to desire the enjoyment of some of the conveniences offered by the city. They offer their produce or services in exchange for these conveniences. Through their contact with the city, they come to learn about, or are forced to follow, some of its ways.[1]

Whenever possible, the more powerful civilized state attempts to dominate the primitive groups adjacent to the cities, especially when these groups are sedentary; since sedentary groups are at once easier to control and more important because the city needs their agricultural produce. As for the nomadic tribes, who are drawn to the city by the desire for procuring luxuries,[2] they may trade with the city, raid it, or be hired by it as mercenary troops. In any event, the city becomes a source of new desires for them, desires that will not be fully satisfied until they come to live in the city or conquer it. They compromise these desires so long as the state controlling the city is powerful, but they are always waiting for the opportunity to conquer it. When the state and the city start to decline, they prepare, whether by slow infiltration (as when the city becomes increasingly dependent on them for its defence) or by direct assault, to conquer the city and start leading a fully civilized life.[3] Once they begin such a life, they are carried through the same cycle of rise and decline inherent in the life of the city.[4]

The first stage in the life of the city is characterized by feverish expansion resulting from its establishment or restoration by its new masters. The influx of newcomers and the increase in the demand for permanent and elegant public works, private residences, and luxurious articles, lead to the increase of prices,

[1] *Q* I 223 ff., II 201 ff.
[2] *Q* I 276–77.
[3] *Q* II 119–24.
[4] Cf. above pp. 206 ff.

wages, specialization, and the development of diverse skills. Thus, a self-generating, progressive trend is started, leading to the growth of the city and the development of its various institutions. The state in turn benefits from this growth. It gains additional power because of the increase in its income which it can utilize, together with the skills of its urban population, to expand its territory and gain more booty.[1]

The development of civilization in the city is contingent on the continuous political patronage and protection that could be offered only by strong and stable political regimes. The perfection of specialized skills, of social and economic institutions, and of the sciences, is the product of slow and gradual improvement. It is only with the passage of centuries of uninterrupted development that civilization takes roots in a city. This process cannot be accomplished if the city is ruined every few generations, or if it is continuously threatened by raids from, or occupation by, primitive and other foreign peoples who have no appreciation for the type of culture it has developed. It is not important for that purpose that a city should remain under the rule of the same dynasty; but it is important that the successive dynasties ruling it should not interrupt the progress of its social, economic, and scientific institutions.[2]

2. As the city develops and becomes more and more prosperous, a new social structure, radically different from that of primitive cultures, emerges. The most important characteristic of the new social structure is the relative decline within it of the power and importance of natural solidarity based on true or imagined common ancestry, and common experiences of life and death, which had prevailed in small, closely-knit, and relatively isolated communities. This type of solidarity tends to disappear as the state, the city, and the urban mode of economic life, co-operate to destroy it. The ruler attempts to dispense with his previous helpers, who are usually his blood-relations, and to replace them by an efficient bureaucracy that has the necessary knowledge and experience to administer the various departments of a civilized state. The city tends to isolate the various families comprising the tribe. Individual families live in isolated residences and become strangers to each other. The

[1] *Q* II 234.

[2] *Q* II 203, 231 ff., 250 ff., 309 ff., 377–78.

highly differentiated demand for specialized goods and skills tends to create specialized groups of artisans and traders.[1] The various classes comprising the city, the rulers, the bureaucracy, the artisans and traders, and the learned, tend to group themselves according to their political and economic interests rather than their blood-relations.[2]

3. The expansion of the physical size of the city, the growth of its population, and the development of its institutions, prosperity, and luxurious manner of life, generate certain habits and attitudes among its inhabitants which inevitably lead to its decline and disintegration. The inhabitants of the city gradually become accustomed to satisfying their desires for luxurious living. Articles previously not considered necessary, become indispensable. Those habituated to using them cannot now dispense with them even when their prices rise as a result of increased demand and high taxes, and they cannot afford to pay for them any more. They begin to squander their substance on them and end in poverty. They have become the slaves of their habits. As the rich are thus pauperized, demand for such articles declines, leading to the decline of prices, profit, and production.[3]

Together with the loss of their fortunes, the inhabitants of the city start to lose their physical and moral virtues. They depend on the walls of the city and on paid mercenary troops for their defence, and become accustomed to expect others to defend them. They depend on the state and the law courts to protect their rights. They forget the use of arms and are helpless when the state becomes unjust and when mercenary troops betray them. They lose the courage and endurance which characterized the primitive peoples who established or conquered the city. As the city expands, its inhabitants are crowded together. They eat a variety of foodstuffs, weakened by cooking and seasoning, that do not always fit the humour of their bodies. Their professions do not lead them to live in the open, and they do not have the opportunity for enough physical exercise. Their bodies are weakened further by the stresses and strains of civilized life. All this tends to make them easy prey for plague and disease.[4]

[1] *Q* II 1 ff., 41–42, 265–66.

[2] *Q* II 249–50. Another substitute for natural solidarity in the city is the common fear of an external enemy (cf. *Bq* IV 173–74).

[3] *Q* II 255–57, 259.

[4] *Q* II 125–26, 336–37.

The life of the city forces its inhabitants to spend all their energies on the acquisition of the goods they have become accustomed to need. When it becomes impossible for them to acquire these goods through rightful means, they resort to all kinds of corrupt practices to acquire them. They strain their intelligence to invent new ways of lying, gambling, deceiving, stealing, and of avoiding punishment. They become masters in craft and treachery. Their desire for luxury starts to lead them to self-destruction. Religious commands lose their effectiveness. Prostitution and sodomy spread, leading to the decline of natural relations and compassion among members of the family, and to furthering the depopulation of the city resulting from disease and plague. In short, the inhabitants of the city become dehumanized. The physical, moral, and religious virtues that characterized them as human beings are lost. They have undergone a complete metamorphosis, and their nature has been transformed. That which held them together as a group has been dissolved. Their energies have been spent, and their bodies emaciated and deformed.[1]

4. Once this stage is reached, the decay and disintegration of the city is unavoidable. In most cases, the state that used to protect it is now also weak and helpless. A new state may arise among the neighbouring primitive peoples, and it may either destroy or take over the city and change its manner of life.[2] If not attacked from the outside, the city will slowly disintegrate. Depopulation continues and economic opportunities decline, skills in building and producing luxurious articles are lost, and the unattended public works are ruined.[3] The pace of such disintegration will depend on the persistence and vigour of the cultural life of the city. Thus, cities that have enjoyed centuries of continuous existence and development disintegrate at a slower pace than those founded only a few generations before their decline starts.

The last stage of the process of disintegration arrives when the city is forced, because of the decline of the state, to attend to its own defence. This leads to the rise of demagogues whose power

[1] *Q* I 230 ff., II 257–61, 289 ff., 304 ff., 336–37; cf. E. Rosenthal *JRAS* (1934) 743.

[2] *Q* II 261 ff.

[3] *Q* II 234.

depends on arousing the rabble and the dispossessed masses created by the city, and satisfying their hunger for booty and bloodshed. Factions arise in the city struggling to wrest power from each other. In that struggle they destroy what the plagues and conquerors have spared. Artisans and farmers, discouraged by the decline of demand and the threat of revolutions and transgressions, cease producing the necessary foodstuffs and other articles. The result is famine and the collapse of the structure that has characterized the city and distinguished it from a village. When the point is reached where the labour of the inhabitants of the city can hardly satisfy their needs for mere subsistence, the city has ceased to exist. It has either turned into a village whose inhabitants are leading a primitive mode of life, or into an unprotected and unprotecting heap of ruins.[1]

VI

Economic Life[2]

1. The economic life of the city is characterized by the gradual perfection of the methods of producing goods and services whose consumption and use differentiate civilized from primitive cultures. In contrast with primitive economic activity which concentrates almost exclusively on primary modes of production (farming, animal husbandry, and hunting), civilized economic activity is designed for the satisfaction of man's desire for luxurious goods and services. The modes of civilized economic activity (the use of money and exchange, trade, industry, and elaborate arts and skills) are the product of the demand created by this desire.

The gradual rise of civilized economic activity is intimately related to the rise of the state. The state attracts or forces people to come and live in the city in order to consolidate its power.

[1] *Q* II 237, 267 ff., *Bq* III 284, 291 ff., 412, 430, 441 ff., 473, 513 ff., IV 475, 493, V 28, 46, 54, 63, 68, 73 ff., 518 ff., *B* I 557.

[2] *Q* II 272 ff. Cf. R. Maunier 'Les idées économiques d'un philosophe arabe au XIVe siècle, Ibn Khaldoun' *RHES* VI (1913) 409 ff.; Hussein *op. cit.* 191 ff.; Bouthoul *op. cit.* 35 ff.; Sobhi Mahmassani *Les idées économiques d'Ibn Khaldoun, essai historique, analitique, et critique* (Lyon 1932) 181 ff.; M. A. Nash'at *Râ'id al-iqtiṣâd, Ibn Khaldûn* ('Ibn Khaldûn Pioneer Economist') (Cairo 1944/1363) 20 ff., 47 ff., 113 ff.

During this process, the ruler attempts to gain the loyalty of his followers by liberality, and to create an illusion of power through erecting public works and leading a luxurious life. The state thus creates the demand which leads to the development of the arts and of trade. This initial demand is the moving force that starts the process leading to the cultivation of skills and the production of highly specialized goods and services.[1]

Further, the degree and duration of civilized economic life are dependent upon the character, power, and duration of the state that brings it into being. Thus a powerful state that is able to consolidate its rule and develop an efficient bureaucracy, to institute laws protecting economic activity, and to create the demand for luxurious articles and specialized skills through large expenditures on public works, tends to stimulate and enhance the development of a civilized economy. On the other hand, a state that is not able to consolidate its rule, and lives in constant fear of dissension and conflict among the smaller solidarity groups within it, limits the development of economic life. If a state is made up of nomadic invaders who know little about the settled way of life and who are still dominated by the ideas and ideals generated by their nomadic existence, or who have been under the impact of a religion with ascetic ideals, the cities it establishes and the power and nature of the economic demand it creates are not likely to encourage the speedy development of a highly civilized economy. The primitive habits of the ruling class do not encourage the formation of an impersonal tax system or an efficient bureaucracy, and their frugality and simplicity do not encourage the rise of industry and commerce.[2]

In its turn, the rise of economic prosperity contributes to the strength and power of the state that has encouraged it. While establishing itself, the state is still relatively simple and is not in need of imposing excessive taxes. It is still partially based on natural solidarity and is not in need of an extensive bureaucracy or a large mercenary army. The ruling class has not yet been habituated to excessive luxury. The riches acquired by the state through conquests are spent on the consolidation of its power and for winning over its new subjects. This expenditure increases

[1] *Q* II 290 ff., cf. above pp. 206–7, 209 ff.
[2] *Q* II 205 ff., 229 ff., 250 ff., 313–14, 322–23.

demand and raises the price-level. Because taxes are still relatively low, there is great incentive to engage in economic activity and production. This incentive is strengthened when the state organizes legal and social institutions for the protection of its subjects and their freedom to produce. Such institutions, like the mint, the inspection of weights and measures, and just commercial laws, facilitate exchange and encourage entrepreneurial activity.[1] The expectation of profit leads to the expansion of production and eventually to the increase in the total taxes levied by the state. Thus the liberality of the state during the period of economic expansion adds to its total income and, consequently, to its strength; the power of the state and the economic prosperity of its subjects go hand in hand.[2]

The second important factor in the development of a civilized economy is the city in which such an economy develops. Since economic prosperity is to a large extent the product of highly specialized skills and since these skills result from a slow cumulative process, it is necessary that a civilized economy persist in a city whose growth should remain uninterrupted despite changes in the dynasties ruling it. Otherwise, these skills will vanish every few generations, will have to be learned all over again, and will never be perfected. That is why the economic prosperity of regions like North Africa could never rival those of Europe and the East where a longer tradition of settled urban life has existed undisturbed by the destructive forces of nomadism.[3]

2. The first stage in the development of civilized economic life is, then, its rise under the favourable conditions resulting from the establishment of the state and the building of the city. The state creates the demand leading to the rise in the prices of luxurious articles and services. Hope for remuneration attracts artisans and traders to the city, and they develop the skills and techniques of producing these articles and supplying the services demanded. The increase in the population of the city and the increase in their wages and profits lead to a further increase in demand. Elaborate arts, and highly specialized skills and professions are gradually perfected. Men exert themselves to create

[1] *Q* II 47 ff., 79–80; cf. Mahmassani *op. cit.* 139–63, 214.
[2] *Q* II 15–21, 79–80, 82, 87 ff.
[3] *Q* I 270 ff., II 229–30, 309 ff., cf. *C* II 2 ff., 81 ff.

new and more efficient ways of improving production.[1] The higher demand leads to further specialization within the city and among different cities. Such specialization creates the demand for the services of traders and other middlemen who offer to transport goods from one place to another and to store them, waiting for a change in the market, and the increase in demand and the rise of prices.[2]

The upward trend of prices is the key to the development of specialization and improved methods of production. Since demand for the necessities of life, like food, remains relatively stable, the impact of the new demand is mostly concentrated on luxury goods and services. Consequently, the rise in the prices of luxury goods and services is much greater than the rise in the prices of necessities. This price differential liberates human labour from primary production and leads to greater concentration on producing goods for exchange and supplying the services needed for the exchange of goods, i.e., industry and trade.

The basic principles underlying an expanding economy are thus made up of economic laws and psychological motivations. Prices rise primarily as a result of the increase in demand, though occasionally also as a result of the restriction of supply through monopoly. Profit is the primary motive of economic endeavour. Rising prices and lower cost of production (the cost of raw materials, wages, and transportation, etc.) resulting from specialization, fill entrepreneurs with the hope for, and certainty about, future profits, and encourage the production and perfection of luxury goods and services.[3]

3. As the power of the state reaches its summit, so does economic prosperity. The growth of absolute power in the state is the cause of the decline of economic prosperity and, consequently, of the state and the city. For, absolute power has to be preserved, as it has been established, by continuous expenditure

[1] *Q* II 301–2, 306 ff., 311 ff., 323, 361 ff.

[2] They may also resort to cornering the market and raising prices through the practice of monopoly. *Q* II 265–66, 297 ff.

[3] *Q* II 239–43, 276–77, 297, 299, 311 ff.; cf. Dimashqî *Maḥâsin* 10–12. Dimashqî's *Beauties of Commerce* is in general radically different in its treatment of economic life from that of Ibn Khaldûn. It concentrates on the praise and advantages of riches, on the description of various trades, and on the elaboration of the legal prescriptions concerning economic activity.

on a bureaucracy accustomed to a life of luxury and excessive indulgence in the civilized way of life. In order to continue to support this expanding bureaucracy and to satisfy the pleasures which the ruler and his aides have been accustomed to enjoy, taxes have to be increased until they reach a point where they discourage entrepreneurs from engaging in economic activity. This leads to a decrease in the total income of the state and new means of increasing its income have to be devised: taxes in kind, corvée, excise taxes, confiscation, and, worst of all, the direct interference of the state in economic activity by engaging in commerce. This last device is most destructive, since the state, with its power of coercion and its great financial resources, destroys the normal workings of a competitive economy by forcing producers and merchants to sell to it at a price lower than that of the current market and forcing buyers to pay whatever it chooses to charge them. Many producers and traders thus lose their capital, and others cease from engaging in economic activity. The result is a sharp fall in the total amount of taxes, the main income of the state. The state is now unable to meet its debts or to pay the bureaucracy. And when the state, the greatest single consumer, is thus financially ruined, demand falls and the resulting decline in prices forces most producers, who have now lost hope of making profit, out of business.[1]

With the decline of the state and of economic activity, the arts decline, the city is depopulated, and slowly the civilized mode of life, including civilized economic life, starts to revert back to primitivism.[2] First, the least necessary goods and services disappear, followed by the less necessary until economic activity is restricted to the production of the primary necessities of life. Unemployment and poverty make the city subject to disasterous famines and plagues. The life of luxury and pleasure had already destroyed the rational and religious restraint which had held the civilized culture together during the process of establishing it.[3] The decline of the power of the state and the disruption of the institutions of organized social life, coupled with these hazardous conditions, destroy the last vestiges of restraint in civilized life. Fraud, plunder, brigandage, and robbery take over the reins.

[1] *Q* II 92 ff., 256 ff.

[2] *Q* II 82 ff., 92 ff., 301–2, 312 ff.

[3] *Q* II 255 ff.

The cycle has reached its end. The desire for a luxurious mode of life had inspired men to perform heroic deeds, to fight, to overcome difficulties, and to build. Now that that superstructure has been destroyed, men fight again, but not for the hopes that they had once entertained. Motivated by the fear of hunger, they fight for mere existence, and like the primordial man who fought out of the same motive, they display the beast in man and return to the life of beasts.[1]

VII

The Sciences[2]

1. The establishment and subsequent growth of the state and the city, and the development of economic prosperity, enlarge the range of human experience. Their increasing complexity forces men to reflect upon the causal connections between the various stages through which the potential is actualized and ends are achieved in order to be able to produce the complex articles demanded in the city and to make plans for building, trade, and the organization of social life. Such knowledge is at first purely practical and experiential;[3] it is acquired through repeated trial and error and long practice during which men find out the right ways of doing things—whether producing goods or ordering their political and social relations—and the wrong ways that should be avoided. To achieve such knowledge, it is not necessary to penetrate into the ultimate causes of things, for it can be gained simply from the immediate data of experience. Through such experience, men learn to improve the methods of production, to perfect the arts, and to organize the political relation of rulers and subjects, and the social relations among subjects. It is also through such experiential knowledge that men learn the usefulness of the prophet as a legislator and the necessity of obeying the Laws he brings to them.[4]

[1] *Q* II 94 ff., 124 ff., 312–13.

[2] The treatment of the sciences in this chapter concentrates on studying them as an aspect of civilization and on their relations to other aspects of civilization. Ibn Khaldûn's treatment of the sciences includes, in addition, their study in terms of their principles (subject matter, problems, methods, and ends) which we have already discussed. Cf. above Chap. II.

[3] Cf. above pp. 173 ff.

[4] *Q* II 363–70, 407–8.

The growth of the sciences is, therefore, closely related to the growth of the state, the city, and economic activity. Like other specialized practical arts (for the teaching and learning of the sciences is a practical art), the sciences flourish only after the necessities of life have been provided. The degree of their advance is dependent on the fulfilment of certain conditions: the possibility of leisure, the continuity of a civilized tradition, the social demand for the services of the learned, and the appreciation and encouragement of the rulers of their profession as expressed in their generosity in establishing schools and founding endowments to maintain them. When these conditions come into being, it becomes possible for the sciences, and the arts that depend on the sciences, to grow and become more and more elaborate. In contrast, primitive cultures of the desert and the countryside, and the under-developed civilization of the small town, do not offer the necessary conditions for the development of the sciences. Those among their members who desire to acquire skill in the sciences have, therefore, to emigrate to highly civilized centres. For the same reason, a civilization newly founded by a people with a long tradition in primitive modes of living is unlikely to have as highly developed skills in the sciences as those civilizations that have had a long and continuous tradition of stable civilized life. Consequently, when primitive peoples come in contact with a civilized people through conquest, the subjugated people remain superior to their masters in their knowledge of the sciences.[1]

2. The accumulation of the data of experience, the need to reflect upon them for the practical purpose of producing the goods and services desired by a civilized people, and the need to order the relations of men within a civilized community, give rise to the practical sciences. Although these attain a certain degree of abstraction, they are essentially concerned with the order of doing and making. Thus, they are at the same time sciences (*'ulûm*) and arts (*ṣinâ'ât*). These may be common to all nations, like medicine, or special to one nation, like the positive

[1] *Q* II 182, 306–7, 376–84, 387–88, III 225–26 (cf. Averroes *Faṣl* 4–6, the necessity of a long tradition in the sciences is used by Averroes to establish the necessity of studying Greek philosophy), 270 ff., *B* II 85–86. Cf. above p. 195 n. 1. For the relation of political power to the rise of the sciences, cf. *Q* III 85 ff., *Bq* V 556.

sciences which consist of the sciences of the Law and of a particular language.[1] As a result of continuous experience in, and the practise of these sciences, men slowly acquire the *habitus* of the theoretical rational sciences and the ability to think in terms of cause and effect apart from the immediate experience of particular events or the application of such knowledge to particular situations for practical purposes.[2] It is only then that philosophic sciences come into existence.[3]

However, within the totality of culture, the position of the sciences, even at their highest stage of development, is of a secondary significance. The learned, absorbed in theories and abstractions, are not prepared by their profession to excel in the practical art of politics or in the acquisition of wealth. In these endeavours, they are surpassed by less theoretically minded persons who are more concerned with the immediate data of experience.[4] Further, since the sciences, especially the religious and philosophic sciences, are not necessary for social life, they are not in great demand. Consequently, those who practise them are usually of the lower income groups among the professions. Only the arts that are of immediate use in the administration of the state and in economic life are in great demand; and they are demanded only during the middle period of the life of the state, since at the beginning and at the end of its life the state has to rely on the sword and not on the pen to carry out its policies.[5]

As the state, the city, and economic life, start to decline, the demand for the sciences and the appreciation of the learned by the rulers and the subjects start to decline too. The sciences, being among the luxuries that are of little use when the ruler and the subjects are concentrating upon salvaging their declining power and acquiring the necessities of life, are neither encouraged nor pursued by a large number of the population when civilization is undergoing decline and disintegration. The modest position of the learned declines further. Their schools are ruined from neglect, and in the confusion that reigns during this period they

[1] *Q* II 316 ff., 376–77, 385–87, III 86 ff. Cf. above pp. 75–76.
[2] *Q* II 362–63, 365–70.
[3] Cf. above pp. 76 ff.
[4] *Q* III 268–69.
[5] *Q* II 40 ff., 295–96.

may be subjected to killing by the common people and persecution by the rulers.[1]

Confronted with such a situation, the learned react in various ways. Some may be in a position to counsel the ruler and help him to revitalize the state if its decline had been the product of injurious policies which can be corrected.[2] Others, especially the poor among them, may try to gain wealth through practising fraudulent sciences like geomancy and alchemy.[3] Still others may try to gain social prestige and money through arousing the masses against their legitimate rulers. They disclose to them their esoteric knowledge, pretend to be the defenders of the Law and the restorers of justice, and talk to them in a vague and incomprehensible language which the masses think to be a new revelation. Supposed mystics, jurisconsults, and prophets, arise to lead society to further confusion and hasten its decline. Having no knowledge of the basic requirements of political action, they espouse petty and inconsequential revolutions which are never successful and lead to nothing but defeat, disgrace, and bloodshed. Thus, the sciences that had once contributed to the progress and glory of a civilization turn now into a disruptive force in the service of the other forces of decline. Motivated by lust for power and gain, the learned lose their prudence, restraint, and moral judgment, and become rabble-rousers. Instead of using their knowledge and foresight to help the ruler who may try to prevent or delay the decline of the state, they contribute to its downfall.[4]

[1] *Q* I 259 ff., II 380, 384, III 118.

[2] *Q* II 107, 116, *C* I 257, *Bq* III 297, 421–22, 493–94. Cf. Ṭurṭûshî *Sirâj* 24 ff.

[3] *Q* I 203 ff., III 225, 229 ff., 231, 241. Ibn Khaldûn argues that the economic status of the learned is closely related to their practice of these sciences and even to their theories concerning their rational validity. Thus Avicenna, who was a rich vizir, thought that the art of alchemy could not produce gold, while Fârâbî, who was ' one of those poor people who are deficient in the lowest supply for a living or the way to it ', thought that the art of alchemy could produce gold. *Q* III 241.

For a study of the role played by alchemy, not in the history of chemistry, but in the history of religion and philosophy, and of its importance for modern psychology, cf. C. G. Jung *Psychology and Alchemy*, trans. R. F. C. Hull (New York 1953) 23 ff.

[4] *Q* I 201–2, II 172 ff., III 225, *C* I 257, *B* I 297, 337, 431. Cf. Ghazâlî *Iḥyâ'* I 60 ff.; Averroes *Faṣl* 28–29; L. Massignon ' *Zindîḳ* ' *EI* IV 1228–29.

CHAPTER V

The Science of Culture: Its Principles and Method

I

The Principles of the Science of Culture as Defined by Its End

1. Having described the phenomenon of culture and its parts, we shall proceed now to consider its nature and principles or the fundamental elements and causes that constitute it.[1] A thorough understanding of these principles cannot be separated from the precise determination of Ibn Khaldûn's position on major philosophic issues. We have examined at length Ibn Khaldûn's attitude to the various philosophic traditions in the Islamic community and explained that, both in theoretical and practical philosophy, he was deeply rooted in, and committed to, the tradition of the *falâsifa* (Muslim followers of Plato and Aristotle) who, broadly speaking, followed Plato in his political philosophy and Aristotle in metaphysics and physics.[2] Ibn Khaldûn's new science, therefore, cannot be explained as the product of a revolt against, or a rejection of, this tradition, but only as a minor addition to it in a field which his predecessors considered too humble to deserve the attention of philosophy.[3] This is of crucial significance for the understanding of the principles of the science of culture. Because Ibn Khaldûn followed the tradition of *the* philosophers, he did not find it necessary to discuss the general and basic principles of science or philosophy, like ' nature ' and the ' four causes ', which they had discussed at length and about which they agreed except for minor differences. The contribution he intended to make was in the application of these principles to a new field. Ibn Khaldûn made extensive use

[1] Cf. Aristotle *De Partibus Animalium* i. 1. 639^{b}6–12, ii. 1. 646^{a}6–12 and 25 ff.
[2] Cf. above pp. 73 ff., esp. 79–83, 84, ff.
[3] Cf. above pp. 167–68.

of these principles in the construction of the science of culture, but he did not repeat the proofs and elaborate theoretical discussions of these principles contained in the works of the philosophers. He could safely assume that the philosophically minded student would already know the precise philosophic meaning of these principles since they were discussed at length in every elementary work on philosophy. We cannot, however, make such an assumption in this study; for philosophy and philosophic principles do not mean in contemporary thought what they meant in Ibn Khaldûn's time, i.e., a body of demonstrated knowledge accepted as *the* true philosophic tradition, but a variety of systems which seem to have equal claim to truth. In order to avoid confusion, we shall state in the appropriate places in the following discussion the precise meaning of the principles used by Ibn Khaldûn according to the philosophic tradition which he followed, and then explain how he used these principles in the construction of the new science of culture.

The description of the subject matter and the problems of the science of culture have further clarified the basic principles of the new science. By observing how these principles were actually employed in the treatment of the subject matter and the formulation of the problems of culture, we have progressed a step beyond the tentative definitions of these principles in the Introduction. We can now restate these principles with greater insight into their real significance, and we shall begin by elaborating on the distinction between the science of culture and history.[1]

History, as Ibn Khaldûn defines it, is concerned with the nature and causes of *actual* existence. In attempting to understand actual events, the historian will have to ascertain and explain their causes in all their particularity and concreteness, rather than indulging in the consideration of the causes of events in general, or in the consideration of generalized patterns of events and the conformity of actual events with, or their deviation from, such generalized patterns.

The science of culture, on the other hand, by its very definition as a science, is not primarily concerned with actual historical existence, but with *real* and *possible* existence, namely, with

[1] Cf. above pp. 48–49, 70–71, 147, 148.

natures, causes, properties, qualities, and common accidents, which have relative permanence and change according to discernible patterns. It attempts to demonstrate that these exist, and that to some degree they are necessary and could not be other than they are.[1] For it, the knowledge of particular events, and their change and multiplicity, is not an end but a beginning from which to penetrate into a more intelligible frame of reference in the form of principles underlying and explaining these events. We thus have a subject matter for a science in the posterioristic[2] sense: a thing (in this instance, culture) of which the science will show that certain properties can be predicated.[3]

The same is true of the formulation of the problems of the two disciplines. History ascertains, selects, and groups events according to their existential dependence. The science of culture formulates its problems according to some intrinsic properties indicating essential distinctness in the way causes operate, and the way qualities or common accidents are related. In presenting these problems, it illustrates them by the description of a number of actual historical events. These events are not the proofs of a principle, nor are they the complete body of instances from which the principle was inducted. They are examples which embody it, but are not thereby fully explained by it. The full explanation of concrete events may require the consideration of other principles, the explanation of the concrete way in which all principles are embodied in the concrete events, and many other accidental causes.

As to the methods of the two disciplines, history is at best an art employing certain rules whose value can be demonstrated by their relevance and success in establishing the existential nexus of events and showing that certain consequences have followed upon certain antecedents. We say ' at best ' because such causal explanation is not always possible. And it is an ' art ' because it is a practical skill which aims at a perfect description and explanation of concrete events, and cannot disengage a general

[1] Cf. Aristotle *Posterior Analytics* i. 2. 71b8–15.

[2] Cf. *ibid.* i. 1.

[3] ' And if it is possible to investigate the properties [or accidents] pertaining to the essence of every intelligible reality (*ḥaqîqa* [*veritas*]), it becomes necessary to consider that there is a special science for every object of comprehension (*mafhûm* [*hoc quod intelligitur*]).' *Q* I 63: 2–4; cf. Goichon *Lexique* 82–84 (No. 171), 286–87 (No. 536).

rule or a constant pattern from such an explanation; it demonstrates that B followed upon A, but this is not a proper explanation of why it should have followed and why it could not be other than it was.[1] As an art, history cannot differentiate between accidental events and events exhibiting a more permanent nature or cause, or between what is rationally possible or probable and what is not. For instance, the historian, as a historian, cannot distinguish between past events that were, humanly and rationally speaking, possible, and events, like the creation of the world and Adam, which reason cannot explain. In this respect, the traditional-theological school of Islamic historiography was correct in reporting events like the creation of the world, since such reporting did not contradict their rules of collecting reports and ascertaining their sources; and it could reasonably argue that divine revelation is a more dependable source than a few mortal witnesses. In such cases, the function of the historian is further limited by the exclusion of the possibility of employing the existential causal explanation through which he could ascertain purely human events, and he is forced to describe events whose existence he is unable to explain.

In contrast to history, the science of culture is not an art, but partakes in science because it aims at the demonstrative knowledge not of the individual events themselves, but of the principles that underlie them and other similar events; it studies a class of historical events with the object of discerning and formulating universal judgments about them. And since there cannot be universal judgments concerning accidental or fortuitous events, except so far as their possibility can be seen and their relative importance determined, the science of culture is not essentially concerned with accidental or fortuitous events. Finally, the science of culture can only form judgments about, and demonstrate, what can be known by the agency of human reason.[2]

2. We have seen that the subject matter of the science of culture is inducted from historical events; that in the order of knowledge it comes *after* history.[3] Ibn Khaldûn also states

[1] Cf. Aristotle *Posterior Analytics* i. 2. 71^{b}12 and 15.
[2] Cf. above pp. 78 ff.
[3] Cf. above pp. 49–50, 171.

explicitly that the primary end of the science of culture is to serve as a tool for use in the rectification of historical reports. This is of crucial importance. For above all, it is the end of a science which determines the definition and operation of its principles.[1] We have also seen that of the three divisions of the sciences according to Aristotle, the end of the theoretical is the knowledge of truth, the end of the practical is good action, and the end of the productive is the perfection of things made.[2] If the science of culture is a rational philosophic science,[3] how is it then that its end seems to be peculiarly different from these three general categories of rational sciences? The answer is that we are dealing with a mixed science whose basic principles are not directed to a theoretical, practical, or productive end alone. This is a difficulty, however, in which to some degree all the Aristotelian practical and productive sciences share. We call politics a science; yet its final end is not theoretical knowledge, but practical action. Similarly, we call medicine a science; yet its end is healing. Such uses of the word 'science' are not purely equivocal. We call a practical or productive discipline a science because it possesses a degree of scientific or theoretical character.

In the science of culture we have the mixture of the three elements: the artistic or productive, the practical, and the theoretical. The immediate end of the science of culture is the rectification of historical reports. Since we have described history as an art and written histories as works of art, and since the immediate end of the science of culture is the perfection of the art of history, the science of culture seems here to be even lower in rank than an art. But the ultimate end of the art of history is practical action or the perfection of things to be done.[4] Thus the ultimate end of the science of culture is practical action also. This is not, however, an end with which the science of culture is directly concerned, but only indirectly through its contribution to the perfection of the art of history. And even when this indirect end is achieved, it will not by itself determine human action. For history and the lessons provided by past events are

[1] Cf. Aristotle *De Partibus Animalium* i. 1. 639^{b}14 ff., *Metaphysics* v. 2. 1013^{b}25–27.

[2] Cf. above pp. 138–39.

[3] Cf. above pp. 147, 148, 156–57.

[4] *Q* I 8: 4–5; cf. above pp. 139–40.

only one among the many elements that help man to deliberate about things to be done. Both the immediate and ultimate ends of the science of culture, therefore, do not seem to be noble or worthy. Ibn Khaldûn says that this is especially true of its immediate and more proper end, the rectification of historical reports.[1] Yet, it is evident that if the science of culture is to perform its function as a tool for the art of history, it has to achieve true knowledge of the nature and causes of historical events and of the principles underlying their change; and in order to truly understand these, human culture must be made the object of an independent theoretical enquiry. This enquiry is concerned with man and his acts which come-to-be, change, and pass away, and are not eternal or divine beings. Nevertheless, Ibn Khaldûn seems to think that in spite of the perishable character of man and his acts, the science concerned with them can be noble in its own way, and that in spite of the less ambitious character of its end, the problems of the science of culture are in themselves worthy of study.[2]

This does not, however, alter the subordinate character of the science of culture. Its end, which is admittedly less worthy than its subject matter and problems, nevertheless controls and directs the way the subject matter and problems are investigated. For it is ultimately this end which will determine to what extent the science of culture may proceed in its exploration of the nature and causes of man's actions, and the degree of theoretical completeness which it may attempt to reach: because its end is the rectification of historical reports for their use by men of action, the science of culture could not thoroughly explore the nature and causes of human action, or attempt a complete theoretical science of man. This will, of necessity, reduce its scientific character which is always proportional to the universality and eternity of the conclusions of a science.

Furthermore, since the science of culture is specifically concerned with the explanation and rectification of actual historical events, it could not properly concern itself with unrealized possibilities, i.e., with what men ought to do in the present and

[1] *Q* I 63: 7–8.

[2] Cf. above pp. 155–56, 166–68; Aristotle *De Partibus Animalium* i. 5. 644b24–645a4.

in the future.[1] More specifically, it cannot, by itself, demonstrate what must be done in a particular situation or what the best mode of conduct is regardless of circumstances. These will have to be decided by the man of action and demonstrated by political philosophy respectively. For instance, in studying political regimes, the science of culture is concerned with the consideration of that segment of the nature and causes of man's acts which lead to the establishment of the regimes known to have existed. If these regimes happened to be the product of man's lust for power, prosperity, or honour, then the science of culture will be concerned with these desires and how they lead to the establishment of political regimes. This is another limitation which prevents it from theoretical completeness. Many problems relevant to man and his social life will remain outside the scope of a science of culture whose immediate aim is to explain actual events and rectify reports about them.

Yet this very lack of theoretical completeness is an advantage so far as its use in understanding historical events and rectifying historical reports is concerned. By keeping close to historical events, it can help the historian to understand their proximate causes, it can direct his research to fields which he had hitherto overlooked because he had not thought of their relation to the events he was interested in, and it can provide him, besides the pragmatic principle of selection, another principle based on the nature of historical events themselves. What the science of culture loses as to the universality and eternity of its principles, it gains in its immediacy to, and grasp of, the nature of concrete events.

3. For Ibn Khaldûn, principles in general mean axioms that refer to, and have objective existence in, the reality which science investigates. They are not mere assumptions, postulations, or hypotheses.[2] Since the science of culture is not the first science, its principles are not first principles (namely, principles which absolutely speaking come first), but subordinate principles of lower rank which are principles only in certain respects, i.e., in respect to actual human action and production: they are the

[1] 'That we should understand this, after the occurrence, is—as I said before—no great mark of sagacity, since it is by no means difficult to draw an inference from an example of the past; but if, at that time, there had been anyone who foresaw the results . . .' Plato *Laws* iii. 692C (Bury), cf. 691B.

[2] *Q* I 329, III 114: 17–18; Aristotle *Posterior Analytics* i. 2. 71b24–25.

propositions lying at the foundation of culture and enjoying a fundamental priority (*qidam*)[1] to it, from which further, more detailed consequences follow.[2]

Priority, however, is an equivocal term. Most commonly it means priority in time. This is an important element which the science of culture considers, but it is by no means the most fundamental meaning of the priority of its principles. In posterioristic logic, priority is fundamentally dependent upon, and derived from, priority in nature. The principles which the science of culture seeks, therefore, are those fundamental elements which constitute the nature of culture.

II

The State and Culture: The Formal and Material Causes

1. By asserting that culture has a nature peculiar to its essence[3] and has natural modes,[4] Ibn Khaldûn intends to differentiate it from things whose essence and existence are one and the same. These latter either do not need or do not have in them 'a principle of motion and change'; they exist either in complete potency or in complete actuality with no need of passing from the one to the other. According to this most general meaning, nature is a principle and a cause of motion and change.[5] It means the same as essence (*dhât*) except that essence does not necessarily signify motion and development, while nature does. Nature, then, is a species of essence whose differentiae are motion and development. Since nature is a part of their essence, natural things have *within themselves* and as an immanent part this principle of

[1] *Q* III 27: 10 (*mutaqaddim*); cf. Goichon *Lexique* 299 (No. 569).

[2] Cf. *Q* I 2: 17–19, 5: 2–6, 7–8, 9: 9, 18–19, 43–44. *Mabda'* (pl. *mabâdi'*) (cf. Goichon *Lexique* 6–7 [No. 18]) and *qâ'ida* (pl. *qawâ'id*) (cf. Jurjâni *Ta'rîfât* 12: 18) are the Arabic words used by Ibn Khaldûn for 'principles'. The first is more technical, and the second means 'rules' rather than principles. Of course, Ibn Khaldûn also uses 'cause' (*sabab*, *'illa*) and the non-technical term 'reason of' (*dâ'î*, pl. *dawâ'î*) (cf. *Q*. I 43: 16) as equivalents of 'principles'. This is proper, since, as we shall presently see, a principle can also be a cause.

[3] *Q* I 57: 18, cf. 56: 12, 60: 11, 61, II 106–7.

[4] *Q* I 4: 1.

[5] Therefore the inclusion of 'movement' in the definition of essence in Aristotle's *Physics* ii. 1. 192^{b}23–24: '. . . nature is a source or cause of being moved and of being at rest in that to which it belongs primarily'. (Hardie and Gaye); Avicenna *Ṭabî'iyyât* 4–5, *Ḥudûd* 86.

motion and development. Of things that have their source of movement within themselves, some act in one direction only: thus a hot object generates heat in the object next to it and cannot do otherwise. Man, on the other hand, can act in a certain way at one time and in an opposite way at another, and he can do either of opposite acts at the same time. His actions, therefore, belong to that species of natural things that are the product of will and deliberation.

In order to know the nature of culture, as is the case with all composite things that come-to-be and pass away (*ḥawâdith*),[1] we have to know its causes or the principles and elements which constitute it.[2] It is these causes taken together that give the nature of culture and its various attributes an identity and an individual reality which can be defined and differentiated from others; and it is through the definition of this particular reality by the knowledge of its causes that reason knows culture and its attributes demonstratively: 'for knowledge and opinion about what comes-to-be result from the knowledge of all its causes: the efficient, the material, the formal, and the final'.[3] These causes are prior to the beings they generate, and are in turn the effects of other causes. Ibn Khaldûn, however, in conformity with the tradition of the divine philosophers (*ilâhiyyûn*, *theologoi*), and in opposition to the externalists and naturalists (*dahriyya*, *physikoi*),[4] denies the possibility of an infinite number of causes and affirms that they end in a first cause.[5] Within this hierarchy of causes, the science of culture is primarily concerned, not with all causes or the noblest and the first, but with those that are directly relevant for the understanding of history.

[1] *Q* III 27: 8. Cf. Avicenna *Najât* 357: 12, *Ishârât* 151: 2 ff.; Averroes *Tahâfut* 521: 12, cf. 488: 9–12.

[2] Concerning the relation of nature and the four causes, Kindî says: 'The philosophers call the matter nature, they call the form nature, they call the essence of everything nature, they call the ways to rest nature, and they call the power that orders bodies nature.' *Ḥudûd* 179. Cf. Avicenna *Ḥudûd* 86, *Najât* 343 ff.; Goichon *Lexique* 199 ff. (No. 393), 237–38 (No. 448).

[3] *Q* III 223: 2–4, cf. I 5: 2–6 and 16, 6: 5–7 and 13, 43–44, 56: 3–6, *passim*. On the theory of the four causes, cf. Aristotle *Physics* ii. 3, 7, *Metaphysics* i. 3; Avicenna *Najât* 343–47, *Ishârât* 138–46, *Ḥudûd* 100; Averroes *t. Mâ ba'd al-ṭabî'a* II 481–97, *Tahâfut* 238, 266, 274, 284, 322, 380, 388.

[4] Or *duhrîyya*. Shahrastânî *Milal*[2] II 104–7; Averroes *Tahâfut* 269: 12. Cf. I. Goldziher '*Dahrîya*' *EI* I 894*a*–95*a*.

[5] *Q* III 27: 11–14. Cf. Averroes *Tahâfut* 20: 6–7 (cf., however, 267–68, 284: 7–10), 269: 12, 274: 11.

In order to know the nature of culture, we have at least to know two of its causes, the material and the formal. These are the two immediate[1] and intrinsic parts[2] out of whose combination culture results. The material (*qâbiliyya*) cause is the matter or substratum of a thing, and it is usually identified with its parts. Thus Ibn Khaldûn calls the parts of culture, namely, economic activity, urban institutions, etc., the matter[3] of culture. The main characteristic of the material cause is that as a cause of a natural thing, it exists in potency, and its existence, alone, does not lead to the actual existence of its effect.[4] Consequently, the parts of culture, apart from their actual existence as parts of an organic whole with a form imposed upon them, do not enjoy actual existence, but only the potential existence of a heap of matter to be formed. It is then the formal (*ṣûrî*) cause which gives definition to a thing, and whose actual existence necessitates the actual existence of the thing of which it is a cause;[5] and the form of culture is that cause whose actual existence means the actual existence of culture, for in the order of being-actual, ' the form is prior to matter '.[6] Furthermore, it is the cause which organizes the material parts of culture, giving them a ' form ', a shape, or a character, within which they form an individual whole.

The formal cause of culture, Ibn Khaldûn says, is the *state*.[7]

[1] Cf. Avicenna *Najât* 346: 15–16.

[2] *Ibid.* 344: 3 ff.

[3] Cf. below n. 7; Aristotle *Physics* ii. 3. 195^a15–20, *De Generatione Animalium* i. 1. 715^a9.

[4] Avicenna *Najât* 344: 3–6; cf. Aristotle *Metaphysics* vii. 16. 1040^b5 ff., cf. i. 3.

[5] Avicenna *Najât* 344: 6–9, 345: 16; Fârâbî *Ta'lîqât* 21.

[6] *Q* II 270: 1.

[7] In concluding his discussion on the subject: ' That cities which are the seats of kings fall to ruins with the destruction and collapse of the state ' (*Q* II 261 ff.), Ibn Khaldûn says: ' The primary natural cause of this is, in short, that the state and domination is to culture what form is to matter. It is the shape that, through its species, preserves its [culture's] existence. It has been established in the philosophic sciences that they [form and matter] cannot be separated from each other. The state without culture is inconceivable; and culture without the state and domination is impossible, owing to the aggressive nature of man which necessitates a ruler. Thus, a regime (either [based on] the Law or kingly rule) comes to be. This is what is meant by the state. Since the two [the state and culture] are inseparable, disorder in one causes disorder in the other; just as the destruction of one would cause the destruction of the other.' *Q* II 264: 1—265: 4, cf. 96: 19, 255, 269–70.

The relation between the state and culture then is that of form to matter and the whole to its parts. Yet, we have already stated that culture is the whole of which the various aspects, including the state, are parts. (Above pp. 203–4.) The term ' culture ' is, thus, used equivocally. For, on the one hand it is used

It is the state, then, which is the principle of organization in culture, giving it the character of a natural whole within which the parts become actual functioning elements. Without the state as an organizing form, the material parts of culture, e.g., economic activity, cannot exist as actual parts of a whole, but enjoy potential existence only. At every stage in the development of culture, the actual existence enjoyed by the parts is proportional to the degree of actual existence enjoyed by their form which is the state.[1]

The proper method of investigating the formal cause of culture is the *analytical* method, i.e., the investigation of the parts or elements of culture and their relation to each other. Since

---

to mean the whole including the state, and on the other it is used to mean the 'matter' or the parts of which the state is the form or the organizing whole. This inconsistency will not confuse us, however, if we recognize the two senses in which the term 'whole' is used. Culture is the whole, if the whole is understood to mean the combination of various elements or principles. Within this whole, the state is one element or principle, the formal, besides which there are other elements or principles including the material, or the parts of culture. But when we analyse these principles, we find that one of them, the formal or the state, is the organizing principle apart from which the parts of culture do not have actual existence. In this sense, the state is prior to the matter or the parts. Since it is the principle of organization, it must also be the whole within which the matter of culture exists as actual parts. Ibn Khaldûn wanted to distinguish these parts from their form or the state. He needed a term that would stand for all of them, and he again called them 'culture'. (The distinction between the two senses of the term 'culture' becomes apparent when *Q* I 66–67 are compared with the references cited above.)

Considered in this latter sense, culture is not a wider term than the state. It does not include forms other than the state and it is not a genus of which the state is a species. They are coextensive in actual existence, and the state is the principle that identifies a culture and separates it from other cultures. At any given time, there are as many cultures as there are states, and the development and completion of a culture is determined by the development and completion of the state of that particular culture. For before the state is born and after it disintegrates, only the formless material parts of a culture exist. Further, concepts like primitive and civilized culture do not existentially divide cultures into groups and are not principles according to which each group could be considered as one whole. They are abstractions from the species 'culture' and are similar to concepts like youth and old age in psychology. This means that primitive cultures and civilized cultures are not two species of culture. Primitive cultures are incomplete cultures, like children who are incomplete human beings because they do not possess in act the powers of reproduction and reasoning characteristic of man. Children, however, do possess these powers in potency. They possess the form of a completed man without which they could not exist. Similarly, although primitive cultures do not actually have all the aspects constituting a developed political organization, their very existence presupposes that the state exists in them to some measure, and that they possess in potency the form of a completed state. To consider primitive and civilized cultures two distinct species would be like considering children and fully grown men two distinct species.

[1] Cf. above pp. 189 ff.

culture comes-to-be, passes away, and is subject to development, this method by itself is not sufficient to fully explain it. It disregards the element of development, concentrating on the analysis of culture when it is formed and has reached its full development.[1]

2. The character of the state cannot be judged apart from its relation to its matter or to the parts which constitute culture. Translated into political terms, this means that the character of the state is defined by the relation of the ruler and the ruled.[2] After investigating this relationship, Ibn Khaldûn finds that it is possible to distinguish more than one form of it, and his distinction among various states is based primarily upon the ends which they seek. We shall discuss these ends further when we analyse the final cause of culture.[3] At present, we shall confine ourselves to enumerating them and examining the forms of the state resulting from pursuing them. They are basically three in number: (1) The good of the ruled both in this world (*dunyâ*) and the next (*âkhira*). The regime based on this end pursues mundane (*dunyawî*) and other-worldly (*ukhrawî*) goods. (2) The good of the ruled in this world. The regime based on this end pursues mundane goods only. (3) The good of the ruler in this world. The regime based on this end pursues the mundane goods of the ruler only. Ibn Khaldûn calls the relationship between the ruler and the ruled based on the pursuit of any one of these three general types of ends a *regime* (*siyâsa*, *politeia*),[4] affirming that the regime is the basis upon which the rule (*ḥukm*) of the ruler rests.[5] There would therefore be as many forms of rule as there are regimes, and the character of each rule would follow the regime upon which it rests.

Since the last two ends have a common denominator which is

[1] Cf. Aristotle *De Partibus Animalium* i. 1. 640a13–14, *Politics* i. 1. 1252a20–23.

[2] *Q* I 339–41, cf. 64: 2; above pp. 207–9.

[3] Cf. below pp. 275 ff.

[4] The regime is not the laws of the land. Laws are the result of the regime. It is more fundamental than either laws or political leadership. In fact, it is the way of life (*sîra*) of the community, and particularly its political way of life. *Q* I 342: 18–19, II 128: 13, 265: 2–3. It must be observed, however, that Ibn Khaldûn also uses the term *siyâsî* to mean (this-worldly) *political* rule in opposition to natural rule (*mulk ṭabîʿî*) based on the desires of the ruler on the one hand, and to the rule of the prophet and his Caliphs (the regime of Law [*sharʿî*]) on the other. *Q* I 343: 12, 344: 3.

[5] *Q* II 126: 18. Cf. Fârâbî *Nawâmîs* 23: 9–11; Plato *Laws* iv. 714B.

the exclusion of the good of man in the world to come, we have two broad types of ends, those *both* of this world *and* the world to come, and those of this world *alone*, and the two broad forms of the state based on them are: (1) the regime of Law (*siyâsa shar'iyya*) or the religious regime (*siyâsa dîniyya*) and (2) rational regimes (*siyâsât 'aqliyya*) or regimes devised by man's practical reason without the 'light of God' to help it.[1] The latter is, subsequently, subdivided into the ends of the ruled and the ends of the ruler.

3. *The regime of Law.*—The main formal characteristics of the regime of Law follow upon its divine origin. It is a regime prescribed by God through the prophet who declares and legislates it.[2] The prophet-legislator, unlike a purely mundane legislator, 'knows best the common good of all concerning the affairs of their life in the world to come which is veiled from them'.[3] The belief of the ruled in God as the source of this regime, and in the trustworthiness of the prophet and the truth of his teaching concerning veiled or hidden things, leads to the first characteristic of the regime of Law, i.e., the bond of the ruler and the ruled is based on inner compulsion rather than on the hope of attaining some external good as is the case in rational regimes. Their belief in the rewards and punishments of the world to come as prescribed by the Law also marks them off as a community from all rational regimes not based on the certainty of life after death. Finally, the ruler (the Prophet, or his successor or Caliph) does not legislate with a view to promoting primarily his own or his subjects' mundane well-being, but rather their well-being in the world to come. To this end, he may prescribe moderation in the enjoyment of mundane goods or even the abandonment of some of them if these happen to run against man's well-being in the world to come.

Belief in rewards and punishments in the world to come creates in the community a 'state of possession' which is the inner

[1] *Q* I 342–44, II 126–28, cf. 128: 13, 265: 2–3, where regimes (*siyâsât*) are divided into two only: those of earthly kings (*mulkiyya*) and those of divine Law (*shar'iyya*). These, then, are the two general forms of regimes. In spite of the distinction between two sub-forms within the first, the fact that both pursue the goods of this world alone sets them apart as one general form.

[2] *Q* I 342: 18–19.

[3] *Q* I 343: 14–15.

power that explains the efficacy of legal obligation (*wujûb*).[1] The Law is obligatory because the community 'believes' in its prescriptions without further examination. Their divine source provides absolute certainty in their truth and absolute belief in their salutory effects. And it is the combination of these two factors which renders the prescriptions of the Law obligatory.[2] The ruled submit to them without hesitation and are ready to sacrifice all the goods of this world in implementing them.

It should not be concluded, however, that the regime of Law either eliminates or suppresses man's natural desires or the social institutions based upon them. This would be impossible, since man's desires are the necessary bases of all political regimes including the regime of Law. It merely controls and directs them to serve man's true end:

'Know that for the Legislator this world and its ways are all a vehicle for the world to come, and he who loses the vehicle cannot arrive at his destination. In what he forbids or condemns of evil deeds, or [what he] urges to be left alone, he does not intend that it be altogether neglected, or be torn up by the roots, and to render completely ineffective the powers upon which it grew. Rather, his intention is to direct them, as far as possible, toward true objectives.'[3]

The Legislator and his successors attempt to preserve and protect the well-being of man in this world and the world to come. Consequently, they legislate for, and govern in, both domains:

'As to religion [he governs] in accordance with the obligations of the Law which he [the Legislator] is ordered to convey and make people practise them. As to governance [in the affairs of] this world, [he rules] with a view to attending to their common

[1] *Q* II 126: 19, 127: 2, III 1: 1; or *taklîf*, *Q* I 348. Both of these terms are legal terms meaning 'obligation'. They are not to be confused with the philosophic meaning of necessity (*ḍarûra*).

[2] Cf. Strauss *Persecution* 10–11, 97–98, 115–17, 121 ff. Ibn Khaldûn's use of the term 'obligatory' in this context could be explained as follows. (1) On the surface, it is used as a legal term whose meaning can be explained within the domain of the (Islamic) Law. The commands of the Law are obligatory because they originate in the revelation in which Muslims believe. (2) From the point of view of the science of culture, the command of the various revealed Laws are obligatory because the various communities which believe in them submit to them unconditionally, while the submission of other communities to their rational laws depends upon the degree to which these laws fulfil their desires or prevent some evil they fear.

[3] *Q* I 364–65, cf. 346–47.

good in human culture. We have mentioned that this culture is necessary for men and so is attending to their common good. For, if this is ignored, culture would disintegrate. We have also mentioned that kingship and its power are sufficient for the realization of this common good. Yes, it would be more perfect if it were [in accordance] with the commands of the Law, since it [the Law] knows best what this common good is. Thus, kingship is below the caliphate and becomes one of its subordinate [functions] if it [the regime] were Islamic, but it may be separate if it were in another community.'[1]

The regime of Law, then, includes the principles of rational regimes, and covers all of man's actions, and social and political relations, both mundane and religious.[2] It is not a community within which mundane desires and other-worldly or 'spiritual' (*rûḥânî!*) ends are simply co-ordinated, and co-exist in peaceful harmony. Nor are religion and the affairs of the world simply twin-brothers.[3] The regime of Law is a single regime within which mundane ends are subordinated to man's end in the world to come.[4] It is superior to rational regimes because it widens the horizon of man's ends; and it is more effective than rational regimes in aiding man to acquire mundane goods too because it knows best what these goods are.

Once these principles of the regime of Law are grasped, the formal relation between the ruler and the ruled and the arrangement of offices in it can be easily shown to follow from them. The relation between the ruler and the ruled in the regime of Law is based on two basic political principles. The first is unqualified or pure justice (*'adl maḥḍ*) which does not exist except in such a regime, for in it justice is both commanded by the Law and upheld by the consensus of the community.[5] Further,

[1] *Q* I 393–94, cf. 72, 246. Thus, when Ibn Khaldûn says that the 'caliphate is religion and has nothing to do with a kingly regime' (*Q* II 6: 7–8), he does not mean that it has nothing to do with politics (because it *is* a political regime [*siyâsa*]), but that the ends of that regime are religious and not mundane.

[2] *Q* I 342–43.

[3] Cf. Ikhwân al-Ṣafâ' *Rasâ'il* I 255–56, IV 33, 186–87.

[4] *Q* I 415 ff., cf. 394: 3–7, II 2–3, *C* II 458–59, below pp. 280 ff.

[5] *Q* II 249: 16, cf. I 346: 10. On the purpose of the legislator in forbidding injustice (*ẓulm*) and the relation of justice and the flourishing of culture, cf. *Q* II 93–100. 'Umar, the second Orthodox Caliph (d. 644/23), is reported to have asked Salmân (d. after 656/35): '" Am I a king or a Caliph?" Salmân answered him: " If you collect from the land of the Muslims one *dirham* more or less

this supreme social virtue exists in the regime of Law in accordance with its most perfect definition, namely, rendering to everyone what is his due and what is good for him,[1] i.e., the good realized in this regime is total and not a partial good. The second is moderation (*qaṣd*), which is also commanded by the Law.[2] Like all the political principles of the regime of Law, justice and moderation are commanded in the context of the ends of man both in this world and the next. Thus, justice is intended to preserve society, and to aid man in attaining his well-being in this world and the next; and moderation is intended to protect society from the excesses of mundane desires which lead to its destruction, and to aid man in viewing mundane goods as parts within the totality of his ends.[3]

The most important office in any regime is the highest office with most authority, namely, the office of the founder or legislator and that of the ruler after him. This office is important in two respects. He who holds it represents the human character that the citizens of a particular regime respect most and try to emulate. Whether they have elected the man to that superior and dignified office or have passively acquiesced to be ruled by him is, of course, an important consideration. But in any event his superiority is explicitly or implicitly admitted by them. Furthermore, and regardless of how they have attained their office, the founder and the ruler create the regime and impress upon it their qualities and attitudes. Their public way of life or 'regime' is the essential factor determining the way of life in the regime which they rule,[4] for they control and

---

[than you should] and spend it wrongly, then you are a king and not a Caliph".' Suyûṭî *Ḥusn* II 91–92. Cf. Mâwardî *Aḥkâm* 16: 5–7.

[1] Cf. Aristotle *Magna Moralia* ii. 3. 1199^{b}10–35.

[2] *Q* I 339–42, 370 ff., II 231. Cf. *C* II 385–86. The third Orthodox Caliph, 'Uthmân (d. 656/35), is reported to have told the strict and ascetically orientated companion of the Prophet, Abû Dharr (d. 653/32–33): ' O Abû Dharr, people cannot be asked to lead an ascetic life; all I am supposed to do is to pass judgment among them according to the command of God and to attract them to moderation.' (*C* II 286.) Moderation as a principle of the regime of Law finds its counterpart in the ' moderate humour ' (*mizâj mu'tadil*) of the peoples that usually live under such a regime. Thus, Ibn Khaldûn finds that they are usually the people of the temperate zones (*Q* I 150, cf. 153–54).

[3] *Q* I 343: 1–3. For a more precise definition of the end of the regime of Law, cf. below pp. 280 ff.

[4] *Q* I 45: 11.

decide the most general and the most important policies of the state.[1]

In describing the regime of Law in the Islamic community, Ibn Khaldûn takes pains to distinguish between the rulers of the regime of Law and the rulers of the rational regimes, between the Caliph and the king.[2] The Caliph is the successor of the Prophet. The Prophet has founded and legislated the Law for a regime in which man can attain his well-being in this world and the next. If his regime is to continue, he must be succeeded by a ruler who is truly his successor, namely, who preserves his regime. But unlike the Prophet, the Caliph has no divine claim and was not designated by the Prophet as the heterodox Shî'ites assert.[3] Nor is his office deemed necessary by reason,[4] for there exist political regimes not ruled by Caliphs or originated by prophets.[5] The office of the Caliph owes its existence to consensus (*ijmâ'*);[6] and since consensus is one of the sources of the Law in Islam, the office can be called ' obligatory '. This obligation to recognize and obey the Caliph is ' legal obligation ' and not rational necessity.[7] Because its source is the consensus of the community, the true Caliph will have to rely on the active consent of the community.[8] But a community which consents to be ruled by a Caliph must be a community which admires and cherishes his

[1] *siyâsa 'âmma*. *Q* I 398: 16.

[2] *Q* I 343 ff., 393 ff., II 1 ff. Cf. Ikhwân al-Ṣafâ' *Rasâ'il* IV 31; T. W. Arnold ' *Khalîfa* ' *EI* II 881*a*–85*b*, *The Caliphate* 19 ff.

[3] *Q* I 355–64, 388. In the description of the office of the caliphate and the qualifications of the Caliph, Ibn Khaldûn's views conform in general to the orthodox tradition as formulated by Baghdâdî (*Uṣûl* 271 ff.) and Mâwardî (*Aḥkâm* 3–33). The difference between his approach and the orthodox views is not, therefore, apparent at first. Cf. below pp. 245–48, 280–84.

[4] This was the doctrine of the Mu'tazilites. Baghdâdî *Uṣûl* 271; H. A. R. Gibb ' Al-Mâwardî's Theory of the Khilâfah ' *IC* XI (1937) 295.

[5] *Q* I 344–46; cf. below p. 279 n. 1.

[6] *Q* I 378: 6 and 16–17. The explicit theory of ' consensus ' was not developed in the period of which Ibn Khaldûn is speaking, and he is referring to the factual consensus which existed among the Companions of the Prophet in Medina, the capital city. *Q* I 378–79.

[7] *shar'î taklîfî*. *Q* I 348: 17, cf. 345, 350, 377 ff. Of course the caliphate is both legally and, in a broad sense, rationally justifiable. The legality (*mashrû'iyya*) of the caliphate is shown by the fact that there is nothing in the Law to prevent the creation of such an office, and that it is in line with the interest or good of the community, since its function is to look after its common good (*maṣâliḥ 'âmma*) and the ' good of all ' (*maṣâliḥ al-kâffa*). *Q* I 343, 349, 377–78, 379, II 30–31, 32. The rational justification of the caliphate must be made, not in terms of its necessity, but in terms of its superior use in aiding man to attain his end. Cf. below p. 284.

[8] *Q* I 379; cf. Mâwardî *Aḥkâm* 6–7.

way of life. The office of the Caliph 'demands perfection in attributes and manners';[1] and only the community which can recognize and give allegiance to a man of this description is worthy of living under the regime of Law.

Under the Islamic Law, the Caliph must have four qualifications. First, he must have knowledge (*'ilm*) of the Law and be proficient in that knowledge to the extent of being able to interpret personally and elaborate on the Law (*ijtihâd*).[2] Second, he must be just. Justice (*'adâla*)[3] in this context includes both general and particular justice: the Caliph must be good or righteous as well as just in distributing offices and insuring that they dispense justice among the members of the community.[4] Thirdly, the Caliph must have competence (*kifâya*): he must be courageous in applying the Law. He must have courage in waging wars, know how to conduct them, and be able to arouse people to fight them. He must know the nature of solidarity; and must be shrewd, resourceful, and forceful in conducting the affairs of the state. It is primarily this quality of competence which Ibn Khaldûn emphasizes as leading to the protection of religion, the establishment of the state, and the management of public interests.[5] Finally, he must be free of bodily and mental defects, and of circumstances that may prevent him from the exercise of his powers.[6]

The various subsidiary offices of the regime of Law are

[1] *Q* I 349: 6.

[2] *Q* I 349: 3–6, cf. 278.

[3] *'Adâla* in this context evidently means more than simply legal justice (*'adâla shar'iyya*) (*Q* I 404: 19, 405: 18) or the complex qualities that may be summed up as the 'correctness and worthiness' present in a person whom a judge may recognize as legal witness (*Q* I 404: 11 ff., 405: 7–8 and 11). The Caliph must have these qualities, since he heads offices that require them.

[4] *Q* I 349: 6–9, cf. 393: 6–7, 404–5. Aristotle *Nicomachean Ethics* v. 1–2. Ibn Khaldûn does not confine this virtue to the Caliph. It is necessary for any king. *Q* I 394: 7–11.

Ibn Khaldûn reports in this connection that the question of whether 'doctrinal innovations' (*bida' i'tiqâdiyya*) constitute an impairment of this quality has been a subject of controversy (*khilâf*) (*Q* I 349: 10; cf. Mâwardî *Aḥkâm* 26), i.e., the question remains undecided and a Caliph could not be deposed on that account.

[5] *Q* I 349: 10–15.

[6] *Q* I 349: 15 ff., 350. The fifth of these qualifications or conditions (*shurûṭ*) is that the Caliph must be from the tribe of Quraysh. This condition was not accepted by all schools of jurisprudence in Islam, and Ibn Khaldûn attempts to show that the wisdom of accepting it as one of the necessary qualities of the Caliph is related to the quality of competence, since at certain times the tribe of Quraysh had the power of solidarity necessary for ruling. But, because 'the Legislator does not pronounce decisions for a specific generation or age or

designed to serve the Caliph in carrying out his functions. They include two types of offices: (a) Offices which are special to the regime of Law and do not exist in rational regimes, namely, those designed to promote man's well-being in the world to come. These offices may differ from one Law to another, but in every instance they are designed to preserve the Law and realize its ends through the execution of its commands.[1] In the Islamic Law, these offices administer the institutions of ritual public prayer (*ṣalâ*), of justice (*qaḍâ'*), of legal consultations or opinions (*fatwâ, fityâ*) given by those reputed for their acquaintance with the Law and works on jurisprudence, of holy war (*jihâd*), and of public morality and decency (*ḥisba*) by public magistrates (Muslim counterpart of Byzantine *agoranomos*) whose functions include judging offences involving public morality, weights and measures, and all other public utilities. Ibn Khaldûn enumerates all such offices existing under the caliphate and gives a detailed historical account of their functions and development.[2] (b) Offices which are common to the regime of Law and rational regimes.[3] The proper relationship of these offices in the regime of Law is prescribed by the essential character of that regime. The Law deals with 'all the actions of creatures' and, consequently, provides for all the offices related to man's actions.[4] Thus under the Islamic caliphate, the supreme authority, i.e., the Caliph, directly controls both sets of institutions. He appoints judges who act by virtue of the powers delegated to them by the Caliph; and the judge too is a religious and a lay personage, and many of his functions, e.g., the administration of public law

---

nation', it must be included under the general quality 'competence', and its necessity would then depend on the particular generation or nation in question. (*Q* I 352–54.) Cf. Ibn Khaldûn's enumeration of these conditions with Mâwardî *Aḥkâm* 5: 10 ff. Ibn Khaldûn combines the fourth and fifth conditions of Mâwardî under his fourth, and includes courage, etc., under 'competence' which is the fifth condition in Mâwardî who calls it 'sagacity' (*ra'y*) and defines it as 'ruling the subjects and ordering the common good'. Ibn Khaldûn paraphrases most of Mâwardî's discussion (*Aḥkâm* 3–33) on the Imâmate and refers to him in many places in his discussion of the various institutions. *Q* I 395, 399, II 3, 19. In the last two references he clearly distinguishes his purpose from that of jurists like Mâwardî.

[1] *Q* I 394: 19.

[2] *Q* I 394–408.

[3] Cf. below pp. 249–50. The distinction between these two sets of offices is regarded by Ibn Khaldûn as the main object of their enumeration and discussion in the '*Ibar*. *Q* II 3: 19—4: 1.

[4] *Q* II 2–3, 3: 2–4.

(*maẓâlim*),[1] demand good knowledge of the Law as well as political sagacity and power.[2] The Caliph also controls the institution of rendering legal opinions by the learned in the Law. He inspects the men of science and those teaching the Law in public mosques, helping those fit for that function, and punishing and preventing those not competent from assuming such a function in the community.[3] The Caliph, further, directly controls all functions which are deemed necessary for the well-being of the community and are not performed by any of the above offices.[4] It is not necessary, of course, that the Caliph perform any of these religious functions personally. It is more often the case that he must concentrate upon the most important affairs of state (*siyâsa 'âmma* or *kubrâ*)[5] like holy war and the conquest of new lands, and the protection of the frontiers and of his central domains.[6]

On the other hand, it is the Caliph, acting in accordance with the combined religious and mundane authority entrusted to him, who appoints the vizirs and emirs, the commanders of the legions, and tax-collectors. These offices, which exist in rational regimes also, are in the Islamic regime of Law part of an all-inclusive institution, of the caliphate. As the caliphate, and with it the regime of Law, declined and turned into a rational, i.e., this-worldly, regime, this arrangement of offices underwent a drastic change. The kingly offices were liberated from the control of the caliphate and became supreme, while the offices which were supreme under the caliphate either disappeared entirely or became subsidiary to kingly offices.[7]

Such a relation between the authority and offices concerned with the well-being of man in the hereafter and his well-being in this world is not, however, fully realized in all communities

[1] Cf. above p. 39 n. 1.
[2] *Q* I 399: 16–18.
[3] *Q* I 396–97.
[4] *Q* I 399–400. An example of such functions is the direct control of the means of preserving law and order, which the Caliph entrusted to the chief of the police (*ṣâḥib al-shurṭa*) who looked after criminal cases and executed judgments pronounced by the judges. *Q* I 406.
[5] *Q* I 398: 16, 399: 7.
[6] *Q* I 398–99. These functions predominate in the enumeration of the public functions of the Caliph in Mâwardî *Aḥkâm* 23.
[7] *Q* I 408: 1–9, cf. 364 ff. In his description of the formal characteristics of the regime of Law, Ibn Khaldûn seems to shift intentionally from the Islamic regime of Law to a more generalized regime of Law of which the Islamic is only one example.

created by divinely inspired prophets. While under the Islamic regime of Law it has been definitely realized, in other religious communities the two authorities and the two sets of offices may be separate.[1] In this connection, Ibn Khaldûn discusses the problem of the relation of the two authorities in the Jewish and Christian communities. After Moses and Joshua, the Jewish community did not pay much attention to kingly affairs. The two powers were separate during the centuries between Joshua and Saul, and only one of the two authorities has continued to exist since the Jews lost their political power and were dominated by the Romans.[2] In the Christian community, the two authorities were never united; and as they developed among the Franks, the Pope became the supreme authority in matters concerning the well-being of man in the hereafter, while the Emperor enjoyed the kingly authority based on the natural power of solidarity. It is true that, among other things, the Pope urged the Franks to obey one king and he crowned him as Emperor, but by the first he intended to concentrate political power in the hands of one king to avoid dissensions in the community, and the second was no more than a gesture through which that king obtained the Pope's blessing (*li-l-tabarruk*).[3]

The crucial difference between a religion like Islam in which the regime of Law has to actualize the proper subordination of the two authorities, and religions like Judaism and Christianity in which the two authorities can be separate, lies in the fact that in Islam there is a combination of a message intended for all *and* a legislation concerning holy war to force all (pagans) to follow that religion.[4] It is the combination of these two factors (with the legislation concerning holy war defining the way in

[1] *Q* I 394: 5–7.
[2] *Q* I 415–18.
[3] *Q* I 418–22.
[4] *Q* I 415: 8–10. The qualification 'pagans' is important because Islam differentiated between them and the people of the Book. Ibn Khaldûn seems to think that under the caliphate not only defensive but also offensive war was obligatory. This can be deduced from the fact that he differentiates the Islamic regime of Law from the Jewish and Christian by asserting that among the latter only defensive holy war is legitimate. *Q* I 415: 12–13. Cf. *Q* II 65: 15, 66: 4 and 7, where wars due to the desire for vengeance originating in 'anger for [the cause of] God and His religion' as well as anger aroused for mundane political power and in preparing the ground for establishing it are called '*jihâd and just*' in opposition to wars caused by envy, competition, and overreaching which are called wars of 'inequity and sedition'.

which the message is to be spread) which differentiates Islam from Judaism and Christianity, and not the universality of its message or the fact that it wages holy wars.[1] Islam legislated the institution of holy war in order to spread its message. Consequently, the religious leader of the Islamic community must concern himself with political power, the means of making war. This is why the Prophet originated both a religion and a state, and legislated for both. For if the central characteristic of Islam, the fact that it necessitates the use of political power as a means for propagating itself, is to find practical expression, the leader of the Muslim community must be the head of administration and the leader of the army (*amîr al-mu'minîn*),[2] as well as the leader in public prayer (*imâm*).[3] Hence, the supreme office in the Muslim community is the Great Imâmate (*al-imâma al-kubrâ*)[4] which includes all functions and controls all other

[1] *Q* I 415: 8–10 and 11–12. Holy war is an essential qualification of the 'call [of Islam] to all'. This does not of course preclude voluntary conversion and peaceful missionary work. Ibn Khaldûn is not contrasting Islam to Christianity and Judaism on the basis of their claims to being the only or the best religion. Nor is he contrasting Islam to Christianity on the basis that 'Islam aims at the conversion of the whole world' (Issawi *op. cit.* 136 n. 1), for he specifically refers to the proselytizing activities of Christians (*Q* I 418: 9–10, 420: 10–14, *C* I 305–6, 315, 322). Nor does he mean here (*Q* I 415: 9) to differentiate between Islam and Christianity because Islam 'seeks to regulate all aspects of life, while Christianity confines itself to spiritual matters'. (Issawi *loc. cit.*) The expression *'umûm al-da'wa* here means 'call intended for all [men]'. The fact that the Islamic regime of Law is concerned with the well-being of man in this world and the next had been already clearly and repeatedly emphasized. Ibn Khaldûn had also said that in other religious communities kingship may exist all by itself (*yanfarid*) (*Q* I 394: 6). In the chapter under discussion (*Q* I 415–22) Ibn Khaldûn is attempting to 'explain the terms "Pope" and "Patriarch" in the Christian community, and the name "Cohen" among the Jews' (*Q* I 415: 1–2). He subsequently explains that these three offices are concerned with the well-being of the members of these communities in the world to come only (except when the office of the Cohen was combined with that of the king during periods he specifies in the history of the Jewish community). What Ibn Khaldûn is trying to do in *Q* I 415: 8 ff. is to explain *why* Islam differs from other religions.

[2] *Q* I 409: 4 ff., cf. I 398: 15 ff., where Ibn Khaldûn emphasizes this function as the one to which the Caliphs gave the greatest amount of their time and care, and did not entrust to others as they did the less important functions of administering the Law.

[3] *Q* I 344: 16 ff., 394: 20. Cf. C. Huart '*Imâm*' *EI* II 473*b*–74*a*.

[4] *Q* I 394: 15–20. Here, *al-imâma al-kubrâ* is transposed by Ibn Khaldûn from its original meaning (*Q* I 344: 17), which alluded to the fact that the Caliph was *the* leader of public worship and that this position was 'greater' than the positions of the host of *imâms* who led public worship in mosques all over the Islamic world (*Q* I 395), to mean 'the great mother and comprehensive principle' from which all offices branch out and within which they are included. Cf. *EI* II 473*b*.

offices, religious and mundane. This is the religious principle behind the historical fact that the Prophet and his true successors in the leadership of the Islamic community aspired to have both religious and political authority,[1] while the leaders of other religious communities, not being in need of using political power for religious purposes, did not have to be concerned with political affairs.[2] In Islam, it is doctrinally essential that religion should not merely have an external concern with worldly affairs, define the conditions upon the fulfilment of which it may co-exist with kingly power, or clearly distinguish between affairs of the spirit and the affairs of the world. None of these would suffice. Religion itself must be politicized. This is the historical basis which led Muslim philosophers and Ibn Khaldûn to reflect upon Islam and the Islamic community as a political regime.[3]

Ibn Khaldûn does not explicitly and in detail evaluate the respective merits of the different institutional arrangements existing in Islam and Christianity. But he had posited the principle that God and the divine legislator know, and legislate for the ends of man in this world and the next, and that pure justice exists in the regime of Law (as defined in the Islamic sense) while rational regimes are for the most part unjust.[4] Thus, what he had already affirmed concerning the regime of Law, namely, that in it the common good is ' more perfectly ' realized,[5] is not subjected to any doubt throughout his discussion of the non-politicized Laws or the religious Laws that are not at the same time political regimes.[6] Nor is this judgment mitigated by any favourable observations about religions whose leaders are ' above ' the worldly rulers of the community and ' more remote from the turmoil of the masses '. We should not be led astray by the thought that Ibn Khaldûn is perhaps capitalizing on a minor difference between Islam and other religions and making it a central theme in the discussion, while in fact

[1] *Q* I 415: 10–11.
[2] *Q* I 415: 13.
[3] Cf. below pp. 281–82.
[4] *Q* II 249: 15–17.
[5] *Q* I 394: 4.
[6] Both Judaism and Christianity are of course based on divinely inspired Laws which Ibn Khaldûn called the Law of the Jews (*sharî'at al-yahûd*) and the Law of Jesus (*sharî'at 'Îsâ*) respectively (*Q* I 419: 8 and 15). He observes, however, that the New Testament is mostly made up of ' exhortations and stories ' and very few ' legal rules ' (*aḥkâm*). *Q* I 419: 4–5.

the real differences lie in certain doctrinal issues like the nature of God. This would lead to a complete misunderstanding of Ibn Khaldûn's purpose to which we shall have an opportunity to return at a later stage.[1] Suffice it here to say that throughout this discussion Ibn Khaldûn is not interested in religion as such, but in its political significance. It is politics (*siyâsa*) and not religion which is the central theme of Ibn Khaldûn's reflections on culture. Religion claims to know man's good in the world to come, while all existing non-religious (rational) political regimes are concerned exclusively with man's good on earth. Politically, religion can be the source of a regime with a wider horizon of man's ends. But such a wider horizon can exist only when it encompasses a hierarchy of related ends which includes ends higher than the highest ends pursued by rational political regimes, and not two separate schemes of ends, one of which could be entrusted to a rational political regime and the other to a religious authority. Ibn Khaldûn likens the relation between man's well-being in this world and his well-being in the next to a 'vehicle' and a 'destination'; and if his assertion that 'he who loses the vehicle cannot arrive at his destination' is taken seriously, religion cannot afford to lead men to their ends in the world to come without assuring the safety of the vehicle by sitting in the driver's seat.

4. *The rational regimes.*—Whereas the regime of Law is imposed upon men by God, rational regimes are imposed upon the ruled by other men, and more specifically by those in high places, the prudent, or the wise. These legislate certain rules which are 'imposed [upon, and] accepted by, all' who follow them 'for the acquisition of mundane ends'.[2] Since the state is made up of the ruler and the ruled,[3] and a rational regime may be directed to serve the interests of either, two types of rational regimes result:

(a) The rational regime whose end is the common good, and in which authority is exercised to further the common good.—

[1] Cf. below pp. 280–84.

[2] *Q* I 344: 3–5, cf. 342: 13–14, 343: 17, II 126: 19, 127: 1–3.

[3] The Aristotelian numerical basis for dividing regimes (according to whether they are ruled by one, few, or many [*Politics* iii. 7]) is thus lost sight of. Ibn Khaldûn conceives of the ruler (the true political ruler and not the primitive rule of elders, etc.) as a single man.

The primary concern of this regime is to 'to attend to the common good in general, and the interest of the ruler in [so far as it leads to] the righteousness [or correctness: *istiqâma*] of his [the ruler's] rule in particular'.[1] Such was the regime of the Persians,[2] and Ibn Khaldûn says that such a regime is 'on its way to being a philosophic' regime (*'alâ wajh al-ḥikma*),[3] namely, that it is the first step toward a regime in accordance with the teachings of political philosophy.[4]

Every office in this rational regime is a tool (*âla*)[5] for aiding the ruler in carrying out his functions. Thus all officers derive their power from him and are his assistants and helpers (*a'wân*).[6] They are not there to share his powers. It is the ruler alone who has the monopoly of power, and the power of his assistants, even if one of them happened to be given all the power in the state, is delegated to them by the ruler because he is a weak creature who is bearing a heavy responsibility which he cannot discharge by himself.[7]

These assistants can help the ruler with their sword, pen, or counsel and experience, or in all of these. Since these functions, in turn, have subdivisions, the offices based upon them are divided into various branches (e.g., in Islam the functions of the sword are divided into the command of war, the chieftainship of the police and of intelligence, and the governorship of the provinces) and each of these in turn may have subdivisions.[8] It is the supreme offices of the state and their relationship which are important for the study of the formal organization of the state. In Islam, these supreme offices were three:[9] the vizirate

[1] *Q* II 127: 15–17.

[2] *Q* I 342: 14, II 127, cf. 74: 17, 86. The tradition of praising ancient Persia as the model monarchy is classical in origin (cf. Plato *Laws* iii. 693D ff.; Aristotle *Politics* v. 10. 1310b36–1311a7). Ibn Khaldûn treats the history of ancient Persia extensively in the historical portion of the *'Ibar*, cf. *C* I 226 ff., esp. 256–57, 261, 264–65, 268.

[3] *Q* II 127: 17. The Arabic expression quoted comes nearest to the paraphrase given above (cf. Lane *Lexicon* 3040*c*–41*b*) than either 'ce système philosophique' (De Slane *Prolégomènes* II 142) or 'sie ist eine Art Philosophie' (Schimmel *op. cit.* 158).

[4] Cf. the expression 'political philosophy': *al-ḥikma al-siyâsiyya*, *Q* I 343: 11. The requirements of 'political philosophy' are distinguished from the requirements of a rational regime (*siyâsa*) (*Q* I 343: 11–12).

[5] *Q* II 40: 18.

[6] *Q* II 19: 8.

[7] *Q* II 1–2.

[8] *Q* II 2, 19, 30 ff.

[9] *Q* II 20: 9–11.

which involved assistance in all affairs of state and had varied functions which changed from period to period and place to place; the treasury which controlled the income and the expenditure of the state; and the office of correspondence and the secretariat. Ibn Khaldûn gives a detailed historical account of these offices and their function, tracing their development and how they differed from one Islamic state to another.[1] The first two he considers absolutely necessary for any state, while the third is necessary in civilized states only.[2] All of them exist in both rational regimes. However, in the rational regime whose end is the common good, they are directed to serve the common good, while in the regime whose end is in the interest of the ruler, they are directed to serve his interests.

Since the end of the first rational regime is the promotion of the mundane common good of the ruled, the principle of justice upon which it rests is that the ruler should not promote his own interests, but rule for the interests of the ruled. Thus the Persians used to stipulate that their monarch should be just (which meant that he should not confiscate the properties of others, engage in trade, or encourage increase in prices) and should not use slaves as servants because slaves do not counsel the monarch for the sake of the common good.[3] The character of the ruler, similarly, must conform to the end of the state and the functions he must perform. Thus the Persians would not let a man rule them unless he was a member of the ruling dynasty, and they chose him for his piety, virtue, gentlemanliness, liberality, courage, and generosity.[4]

When all these requirements relating to the character of the ruler and his relation to the ruled are met, a rational regime is just. But this is a qualified justice, and its shortcomings result from the limited nature of the end which the regime pursues. Since mundane ends and goods do not exhaust the true ends of man, and since this regime limits itself to the attainment of such ends, its just character is accordingly limited. It does not give to every man what is truly due him or what is good for him in this world and the next, i.e., the totality of the ends he must pursue. Further, even the qualified justice of this regime is not assured,

[1] *Q* II 4 ff., 15 ff., 21 ff.
[2] *Q* II 15: 19, 21: 15.
[3] *Q* II 86: 3–6, cf. 82 ff.
[4] *Q* II 68: 1–3.

since it is not always possible to ensure correct opinions concerning either the true ends of man in this world or the limitations of the rulers' powers. And it is a natural law of political development that, as a culture becomes more civilized, the ruler becomes richer and more powerful, and then it becomes hard to prevent him from becoming a tyrant who follows his own interests. Thus, Ibn Khaldûn's conviction is that most kingly rulers are for the most part unjust.[1]

(b) The rational regime whose end is the selfish interests of the ruler.—The principle upon which this rational regime rests is 'attending to the interest of the ruler and the way in which his[2] [absolute] power can be assured through suppression and contention. The common good has a subordinate position in this [regime]'.[3] It is clearly a despotic rule because its end is the personal interest of the ruler. Since the true end of a political regime is the common good, it is also a perverted or wrong regime condemned both by the Law and by political philosophy.[4]

The end of the ruler referred to here is of course a mundane end. More specifically, it is the satisfaction of his lower desires or appetites (*shahwa*). Consequently, it is ultimately a rule according to appetite. Yet, it differs from a regime in which the appetites are given free rein to rule unchecked in that it is also a rational regime or a regime in which reason has a voice.[5] But reason does not try to ascertain freely the proper end of the regime and the proper policies which the ruler must follow; it functions rather as a mere tool to augment and buttress the selfish interests of the ruler. It suggests the course he should follow to prevent the loss of power, and to that extent reason moderates the appetites of the tyrant. But in the last analysis, this is not real moderation, since it assures the fulfilment of his chief desire, namely, to continue to rule. Reason only helps the tyrant in attaining his selfish ends more efficiently. It assists him in organizing the offices necessary to wage war and collect taxes; and these and other offices, which in their form are similar to

[1] *Q* II 249: 16–17.

[2] *Q* II 128: 1, for *fîhi* (in which) read *lahu* (his) with *Bq* and De Slane (*Prolégomènes* II 142 n. 1).

[3] *Q* II 127: 20—128: 2.

[4] *Q* I 343: 9–11. Cf. Aristotle *Politics* iii. 6. 1279^{a}19–21.

[5] *Q* I 342–44, esp. 344: 2–5.

those of the first rational regime, are directed, not to serve the common good, but to serve the ends of the ruler and to increase his power to suppress, enslave, and exploit the ruled. This is an unjust regime; and injustice in it is all the greater and more ruinous to culture because it is practised by the ruler above whom there is no authority to check or punish his actions.[1]

5. These then are the forms of the state according to which the various parts of culture are organized. They have been discussed in the order of their excellence and not in the order according to which they come into existence[2] or the frequency with which they have existed. It should be noticed that Ibn Khaldûn knew only of one pure example of the regime of Law (the Islamic caliphate) and one pure example of the rational regime whose end is the common good (ancient Persia). He asserts that all other rulers, Muslim and non-Muslim, rule mostly according to the rational regime whose primary end is the private interest of the ruler.[3] However, he indicates that it is possible for a ruler to base his power on a mixture of these forms. Thus after the change of the caliphate into mundane rule, Muslim rulers followed the prescriptions of the Islamic Law so far as they were able (*bi-ḥasabi juhdihim*)[4] to do so in a rational regime based on the pursuit of the interest of the ruler. Their rule was based on a mixture of the demands of the Law, the teachings of ethics, the natural laws of social life, and the requirements of power and solidarity. Consequently, they emulated the Law, the teachings of wise men, and the conduct of other rulers.[5] But the nature of a regime based on a mixture of various forms of the state cannot be, as such, made the object of theoretical enquiry. This latter would proceed best if it attempted to elucidate the pattern of the pure forms, leaving it to the art of history to ascertain whether an actual state realizes one, or a particular mixture of such forms. In the latter case, it must be observed that a mixture does not mean that the pure forms of the state coexist on terms of equality. One of them is bound to bid for supremacy, relegating

[1] *Q* II 95–100 (esp. 97: 11–12), 132–35.

[2] The order in which they have been presented above is that given in *Q* II 126–28. In *Q* I 342–44 the three types of rule (*ḥukm*) are discussed in the order of their coming into existence, cf. below pp. 263 ff.

[3] *Q* II 128: 3.

[4] *Q* II 128: 5.

[5] *Q* II 128: 2–8.

others to subordinate positions and allowing them to exist only when their existence does not jeopardize that supremacy. Thus in the Muslim regimes after the decline of the caliphate, the interest of the ruler was supreme, and the demands of the Law and the teachings of wise men were followed only where they did not threaten that interest.

Finally, Ibn Khaldûn's enquiry into the forms of the state explicitly avoids the best or ' virtuous city ' (*madîna fâḍila*)[1] of the philosophers and *concentrates on the forms that have actually existed in known history*. Such limitation is clearly demanded by the end of the science of culture which is to aid history to understand actual historical events. What is important in this context is not the frequency with which a certain form has existed, but simply that it has once existed. Consequently, the fact that Ibn Khaldûn knew only of one pure example of the regime of Law and of the rational regime whose end is the common good, did not prevent him from enquiring into their character. Nor does Ibn Khaldûn simply describe these actual forms. For him, such description is only the point of departure toward the realization of the end for which it has been undertaken. He therefore proceeds immediately to give actual historical examples of the regimes he had described, showing through the description of the actual powers of various rulers, and of the organization of the offices in their regimes, how the theoretical enquiry into the forms of the state can help the student of history to understand these institutional arrangements.[2]

III

Solidarity: The Efficient Cause

1. To exercise their causality, the material and formal causes must be united and their union requires an efficient (*fâ'ila*)

[1] *Q* II 127: 10.

[2] That Ibn Khaldûn limits himself to a few examples drawn mostly from Islamic history, which is most familiar to his readers, is theoretically accidental, although it could be explained on practical grounds. It could, further, be justified by the end of the science of culture which is to aid the historian in perfecting his art. It performs this function by acquainting him with the principles underlying actual historical events and by illustrative examples from *familiar* historical events whose real character is made more plain when seen in terms of these principles.

cause.[1] Unlike the material and formal causes, the efficient cause is not a part of the effect and is often described as extrinsic. But since dynamism and change are inherent in the essence of a natural thing, and since the efficient cause is the primary source of change and the primary moving cause,[2] the relation between the efficient cause and its effect is not accidental. The efficient cause is that to which a thing owes its *actual existence*, which includes its generation as well as the succeeding changes through which it is progressively actualized; it is an existential cause which explains the actual existence of a being at the various stages of its development. It answers the question: How does a thing come to exist actually?

Culture and all its manifestations are in a constant state of change. Ibn Khaldûn accepts this proposition as self-evident, ascertainable by direct observation, and requiring no proof.[3] But like everything that comes-to-be and passes away, culture does not change in a haphazard way, but proceeds in a definite direction; for, as Aristotle says, nature flies from the infinite, from the unending and from the imperfect, and always seeks an end.[4] Within this overall direction toward an end, culture undergoes change in certain respects, and these can be divided into two types: (a) when a culture is generated and corrupted, and (b) when a culture persists but its properties or common attributes change.

(a) In the first type of change, nothing persists except unformed and un-individualized matter. In the generation and corruption of culture, that unformed matter is transformed, it takes a certain form and then it loses that form. This generation and corruption of culture does not refer to the species ' culture ', but to the individual cultures or the members of the species ' culture ', which means that the species ' culture ' is an abstraction, and only individual cultures enjoy actual existence. The continuous existence of the species ' culture ' is preserved by the

[1] For matter and form, by themselves, are not sufficient to bring things into existence; there must be present an originative source which causes movement. This is the efficient cause of which Aristotle says that his predecessors dreamed, but none of them definitely stated it. *De Generatione et Corruptione* ii. 9. 335b8–9, cf. i. 5. 321b7–8, ii. 9. 335a31.

[2] Aristotle *Physics* ii. 3. 194b29–31, ii. 7. 198a32, *Metaphysics* i. 3. 983a30. This definition of the efficient cause does not coincide with the definition of nature given above (p. 232). Nature is the first *intrinsic* principle of change, while the efficient cause is the first *extrinsic* principle of change.

[3] *Q* I 44 ff., 52, 155: 4–5, 247–50, 381 ff., II 125, 255–56, 306–7, 309–11.

[4] *De Generatione Animalium* i. 1. 715b15. Cf. *Q* III 238.

uninterrupted coming-to-be and passing away of individual cultures, and the cyclical life span of individual cultures is not the eternal and necessary being or cycle of *a* Culture. Culture is permanent and eternal only because of the continuous coming-to-be and passing away of individual cultures.[1] Ibn Khaldûn, consequently, rejects two alternative theories of culture, a linear theory and a cyclical, both of which asserted that there is one Culture or that all human history is one interrelated whole, and that the movement of culture is necessary and, consequently, can be determined and foreseen.

The first is the theory which Mas'ûdî took over from the philosophers.[2] This theory assumes that:

'When God created the world, Nature (which is the matter of bodies) was completely diversified, and most powerful and perfect. Because of the perfection of Nature, life expectancy was longer and bodies stronger. . . . Since then [the world] has been continuously diminishing because of the diminution of matter, until it has reached the state in which it is. It will also continue to diminish, until such time as the world will disintegrate and become extinct. This is an opinion which, as you see, has no support except capricious judgment. It has no natural cause and no demonstrative reason.'[3]

In rejecting this view, Ibn Khaldûn explicitly rejects the theory that history began with a golden age and has been regressing ever since.[4] The great monuments of antiquity are no proof that all men used to have larger bodies or that the biblical giant Og could fry a fish by holding it to the sun. The monuments of antiquity, Ibn Khaldûn explains, are witnesses to the power of the states that built them, their great dominion, large population, and their ability to organize a large number of their subjects to work on them.[5]

[1] Cf. the discussion on the eternity of the species, *Q* II 331–32; Aristotle *De Generatione et Corruptione* ii. 10. 336^{b}25 ff.

[2] Cf. Mas'ûdî *Murûj* I 152–53, IV 101–5; Hesiod *Works and Days* vss. 110–200. For the ancient Oriental and Greco-Roman sources of this theory, cf. 'Ages of the World' *ERE* I 182–210*a*.

[3] *Q* I 319–20.

[4] *Q* I 318–19. This statement does not contradict the fact that Ibn Khaldûn ascribes certain virtues to primitive peoples because: (a) primitive culture is not identified by Ibn Khaldûn with a certain stage in history and (b) the virtues of primitive peoples are imperfect. Cf. below pp. 276–77.

[5] *Q* I 317–18, 323. Cf. Ibn al-Athîr *Kâmil* I 138: 21–24; Num. 21: 33, 32: 33; *The Jewish Encyclopedia* IX 388.

The second is the cyclical theory of culture, held by the heterodox Shî'ites and many Muslim mystics. It asserts an eternal return or that all things return upon themselves and return to what they were.[1] The proponents of this theory, too, started with the golden age, declaring that there are three stages: prophecy, the caliphate, and unjust kingship, which follow each other in eternal cycles. Some of them even calculated the Great Year and gave precise dates for the appearance of the antichrist, the Mahdî, Christ, and Mohammed. Ibn Khaldûn first discounts all the legal support upon which such views are based by showing that all the Traditions cited in their favour are not based on reliable authority. He then gives his own interpretation of the possible return of any religious leader: He observes that many nations have become prominent since the rise of the Islamic empire, while no cohesive Arab group remains except for a few thousand tribesmen in Arabia. A Messiah might very well appear at some future time. But if he is to put into effect the expected reforms, he must come at the head of a powerful people with great solidarity. He might even need to bring a new religion to unite and inspire his people. Ibn Khaldûn thus intimates that such a Messiah could not appear among the Arabs where he is expected and might not even be a Muslim. At any rate, the expected Messiah will not come to power automatically because of the cyclical motion of the stars. He will have to possess the qualifications necessary for a leader and must be born in circumstances conducive to the creation of a powerful state, which in turn must follow the natural course of rise and decline. He ends the discussion with an attack on all those who have pretended to be the hoped-for Messiah, exposing their low motives and the social dangers resulting from believing in them and following them.[2]

[1] *Q* II 165: 19. Cf. Plato *Statesman* 269C ff., *Republic* viii. 548 ff. The adoption of the cyclical theory by mystics occurred in the Alexandrine age which is also rich in apocryphal works. *ERE* I 200. In *Q* II 332: 4–10, Ibn Khaldûn attributes a similar theory to Avicenna.

[2] *Q* II 142 ff. Cf. Fârâbî *Nawâmîs* 36: 3–14. Thus, both directly and indirectly, Ibn Khaldûn rejects the doctrine commonly held for ages among the many (*kâffa*) (*Q* II 142: 8) concerning the return of a Messiah. In so doing, he is rejecting the cyclical theory about the return of things upon themselves. Yet, he accepts some kind of return: the quasi-cyclical movement of various cultures when they are generated and corrupted. These two views are not, however, inconsistent. All things generated, man included, continue to exist by passing through a life cycle without 'returning upon themselves'. There are beings that do return upon themselves, e.g., the heavens, whose cyclical coming-to-be

(b) Apart from generation and corruption, culture changes during its life cycle. These changes effect only three of the common or essential attributes (*'awâriḍ dhâtiyya*)[1] or modes (*aḥwâl*)[2] of culture: quality, quantity, and place.[3] Examples of qualitative changes in culture are: the change from primitive to civilized culture; the change of solidarity from familial relations to tribal solidarity, to the greater solidarity of a whole people, to religious solidarity, and to solidarity among urban groups; and the change of the primitive, subsistance economy to the civilized economy of abundance. Examples of quantitative changes in culture are: the growth or diminution of the dominions, population, and income of a state; the growth of the cities; and the increase or decrease in the number of men dedicated to learning. And examples of changes in place are: conquests and the movement of population from the desert or the countryside to cities.[4]

2. These are all natural changes from potency to act or from the more potential and less actual to the less potential and more actual.[5] They are, further, gradual changes; they take place in time.[6] Finally, these changes are, in a sense, necessary,[7] but this

is necessary. Like the heavens, culture 'recurs', but culture and the heavens do not recur in the same manner. Properly speaking, only beings like the heavens whose substance is eternal return upon themselves: the same individual heaven recurs eternally in its sphere. But among things whose substance is perishable (and all things that come-to-be and pass away are such beings), the individual does not recur; what recurs is the species or the form (cf. Aristotle *De Generatione et Corruptione* ii. 10–11). Culture clearly belongs to that latter type (*Q* I 247–48).

[1] *Q* I 63: 3, 67: 17, 278: 1–2, 336. Cf. Aristotle *Posterior Analytics* i. 7. 75b1; Goichon *Lexique* 216 ff. (Nos. 421, 422). Ibn Khaldûn also uses the term 'necessary attribute' (*'âriḍ ḍarûrî*) (*Q* I 336: 5) to mean the same thing as 'essential attribute'. Cf. *Q* I 68: 14–16: 'Society is *necessary* for man. The philosophers express this by saying that man is political *by nature*, i.e., he has to live in society which is the *polis* in their terminology, and is what is meant [here] by culture.'

[2] *Q* I 61: 19, 63: 2–4, 67: 16–17: 'And in these modes there are things, which happen in the association [of men], that are essential attributes.' Thus, in this sense 'mode' is identical with essential attribute. Cf. Avicenna *Ishârât* 82: 11–14: 'And to each science pertains one thing or many things that correspond to it, and the modes of which we examine. *These modes are the essential attributes*; and that thing is called the object of that science like measurements for geometry.' *Najât* 109–10; *Q* I 317–19.

[3] Cf. Aristotle *Physics* ii. 1. 192b14, v. 1. 225b2 ff., v. 2. 226a25 ff., vii. 2. 243a6 ff.

[4] For further details about these examples, cf. above Chap. IV.

[5] *Q* I 221: 14–15, II 306–7, 313–14, 338.

[6] *Q* I 221, II 306–7, 309–11. Cf. Averroes *J. Mâ ba'd al-ṭabî'a* 43–44 (sec. 65).

[7] Like other natural things, culture follows in its movements a certain course or way (*sunna*) which is to some extent permanent and does not change. It is

necessity does not preclude the possibility of interference in the process of actualization, i.e., of failure in achieving a form, or the possibility of unintended results, i.e., of chance.

An examination of the term ' necessity ' (*ḍarûra*)[1] reveals that Ibn Khaldûn uses it to mean three different things. The first is *natural* necessity. It was explained that things that exist by nature have in themselves the source of their movement and change, or the capacity to actualize their forms and ends: a seed develops to a tree, a child to a man, and a primitive culture to a civilized culture.[2] This development of culture is necessary in accordance with its nature;[3] yet it is not absolutely necessary, for we know that not every primitive culture develops into a civilized culture.[4] Rather it is necessary in most cases or for the most part (*fi-l-aghlab*):[5] although not all primitive cultures develop into civilized cultures, they do in most cases.

Second, he calls a cause of culture or any of its parts ' necessary ' to indicate that it is necessary as a *condition*. Here, the effect necessarily requires a cause for its existence, but its existence is not necessarily determined by such a cause. Consequently, propositions expressing this kind of necessity are not convertible. Ibn Khaldûn says that if man is to survive, he must

---

determined by its nature, and since this nature is created by God, we can call it ' the way of God ' (*sunnat allâh*). Thus, Ibn Khaldûn identifies the way of God with the way of nature. The ' way ' of tradition, the ancestral and the conventional, can no longer claim to be the ' way of God ' without first proving that it is also the way of nature. The claim of the various traditions (*sunan*) to being *the* tradition or *the* way of God will have, then, to be tested by the way of nature. The road from tradition to God will have to pass through nature. All these undertones behind Ibn Khaldûn's use of the way of God will become immediately clear to the reader who substitutes the term ' natural ' for every single instance where ' the way of God ' is used. In each case, the meaning becomes clearer and more precise, since the context would indicate which of the ways of nature Ibn Khaldûn is talking about. Cf., e.g., *Q* I 155, 255, 265, 266, 300, 301, 331, 342, II 42, 63, 89, 93, 117, 121, 123, 176, 337. Cf. also Ibn Khaldûn's use of the term ' the secret of God ' (*sirr allâh*), e.g., *Q* I 282, and above pp. 70–71. Cf. Averroes *Tahâfut* 522–25, for the philosophic answer to the conventionalism of the dialectical theologians.

[1] In the following discussion of necessity, we shall not be concerned with its non-technical uses. Ibn Khaldûn's use of the term to indicate the indispensable conditions of mere life (e.g., *Q* I 67, II 307) is included in conditional necessity.

[2] Above pp. 197 ff.

[3] *Q* I 305 ff., 364: 7–8, II 106 ff., 255 ff.

[4] *Q* I 254: 8–9, 295–99. Cf. Aristotle *Metaphysics* v. 5. 1015^{a}33–34; Averroes *t. Mâ ba'd al-ṭabî'a* II 519: 6–9.

[5] *Q* I 189: 2, 249, 306 (*fi-l-akthar*), 307, II 103, 125, 208, *passim*. Ibn Khaldûn also uses the related expression: ' natural . . . but for few exceptions ' (*ṭabî'î . . . illâ fi-l-aqalli*). *Q* I 235: 3.

of necessity have food and shelter. But he does not assert that food and shelter lead necessarily to the survival of man. Similarly, he argues that if men are to survive in the desert, it is necessary that they have solidarity, and if they are to have solidarity, it is necessary that they have an actual or imagined blood-relationship; and that if a people is to achieve its desire for leisure and riches, it must necessarily establish or conquer cities, and encourage the development of urban institutions. In this sense, necessity holds even in the moral sphere in which man's freedom is most apparent and his decisions most decisive. Thus, Ibn Khaldûn argues that if a ruler is to become an absolute tyrant, he must necessarily murder all those who aspire to share his power; or if a ruler is to realize the common good, he must be kind, just, and beneficent to the ruled. In all such cases, he is merely saying that owing to the nature of such and such an aspect of culture, its coming into being necessitates the pre-existence of such and such antecedents. In no place does he say that because such and such antecedents exist, such and such aspects of culture shall of necessity come into existence.[1]

Thirdly, Ibn Khaldûn declares that culture or any of its essential attributes are caused by necessity to indicate that they happen by *compulsion*, or that a cause external to man or internal in him acts contrary to man's purpose and hinders him from achieving his end. Thus, the excess of heat or cold prevents man from creating the works of art and cultural institutions he needs to realize his ends; a tyrant forces the ruled to conspire against him; hunger forces men to rebel; man's desire for revenge makes him act contrary to his reason; and his desire for riches leads him to self-destruction.[2]

None of these three types of necessity precludes the possibility of chance (*ittifâq*) and fortune (*bakht*), or of unintended results.[3]

[1] *Q* I 67, 68: 14, 69, 70: 16–17, 71: 3–4 and 12–19, 220: 11, 224: 5–6, 239–40 272: 4–5, 276: 9 and 16–17, 338, 342, II 15: 19 (cf. 21: 15: unnecessary [*ghayr ḍarûrî*]), 126: 16–18, 212: 16, 213: 8, 272, 307–8, 324, 327, 333. Cf. Aristotle *De Partibus Animalium* i. 1. 639b25 ff., 640a33 ff., 642a9–14 and 33–34, *Physics* ii. 9. 200,a10 ff., *Metaphysics* v. 5. 1015a20–25.

[2] *Q* I 87: 3–4, 150–55, 221: 1–5, 222–23, 224: 11–12, 236: 14, 252–53, 301: 1, 372: 1, II 82: 18, 202: 1–4, 203–4. Cf. Aristotle *Metaphysics* v. 5. 1015a27–28.

[3] Ibn Khaldûn's conception of chance and fortune is restricted to practical matters involving human intentions (cf. below p. 260 n. 1). In *Q* II 76: 18, the expression 'as it has been shown in the proper place' (*kamâ taqarrara fî mawḍi'ihi*) refers to the discussion of the problem in philosophic texts, cf. Aristotle *De Partibus Animalium* i. 1. 640a24 ff., *Physics* ii. 4–6, *Metaphysics* vi. 3. 1027a29 ff., vii. 7. 1032a26.

Individuals and societies desire certain ends and plan the stages through which they hope to achieve them, taking into account the necessary conditions and existing circumstances. There are, however, other individuals and societies acting independently, and new conditions and circumstances continuously in the making; and these may either facilitate or hinder the achievement of the desired ends in unexpected ways. A multitude of efficient causes interfere with each other and result in events whose causes are indeterminate and cannot be explained. These are chance events. They are most apparent in war and the pursuit of victory. Victory cannot be foreseen with certainty because it is not primarily determined by apparent causes like the size of armies, and the quantity and quality of their weapons, but by hidden or unknown causes like strategic and psychological tricks which disappoint the calculations of the enemy. Fortune and misfortune are names given to the results of these hidden causes depending on whether they facilitate or hinder victory.[1]

Ibn Khaldûn's rejection of absolute necessity does not then mean that he refuses to give necessity a place in history, for that would have meant the reduction of all historical events to accidental events, i.e., to events that have no cause and, therefore, are unintelligible. Rather, he follows a middle course between two extreme and simple, though illusory, explanations: an explanation based on universal necessity and the negation of chance, and an explanation based on universal chance and the negation of necessity.[2]

3. The proper method of studying the efficient cause of culture is to consider its growth, and follow its development and formation.[3] This is the *genetic* method. In contrast to the *analytical* method which we applied in the investigation of the form and parts of culture, our investigation of the genesis and mutations of

[1] *Q* II 75–79, esp. 75: 17—76: 18, *Bq* III 53, *B* II 138–40, *passim*.

[2] The reduction of this complex relationship among free choice, natural necessity, conditional necessity, compulsion, and chance and fortune to the vague concept of ' social determinism ' by positivist sociologists has muddled rather than clarified Ibn Khaldûn's intention. Cf., e.g., Stefano Colosio ' Contribution à l'étude d'Ibn Khaldoun ' *Revue du monde musulman* XXVI (1914) 321–33.

[3] Cf. Plato *Laws* iii. 676C (Fârâbî *Nawâmîs* 16–17); Aristotle *De Partibus Animalium* ii. 1. 646^{a}15 ff., *Politics* i. 2. 1252^{a}24–25, *Physics* ii. 1. 193^{b}12–14.

culture will help us to see the causal determination of its various stages, starting from the most primitive, passing through the terminal stage or the most perfect and complete form, and ending in its decline and disintegration. In this part of our exposition, we shall *assume* the material, formal, and final causes.

According to Ibn Khaldûn, the primary cause that dominates the changes and movements of culture once human nature brings culture into existence is solidarity: 'The state in truth is the efficient cause in the matter of culture because of solidarity and [its] power.'[1] The state, with solidarity as its instrument, brings about all the changes in culture to which we referred above. The power, extent, and endurance of culture are caused by solidarity and depend upon its strength.[2] The relation between the formal and efficient causes of culture, or between the state and solidarity, is of the utmost significance for understanding Ibn Khaldûn's conception of culture.[3] Because solidarity aims at the formation of the state and political power, it is possible to explain the direction of the efficient cause and to investigate the changes of culture by concentrating on the actual operation of the existential cause without pretending that the investigation of the efficient cause, by itself, offers a complete explanation of the completed form of culture.

The enquiry into the genesis of the state must begin by ascertaining the pre-political state of society, i.e., when the scheme of social life was based on friendship and familial relations, and before the coming-to-be of the ruler-ruled relationship.

4. How did men, then, live at the beginning,[4] and how could their pre-political 'state of nature' (*fiṭra*) be described? According to Ibn Khaldûn, man's pre-political conditions were simple but not perfect. To begin with, men lived in a community of necessity. They came together for the sake of preserving life,

[1] *Q* II 265: 10–11, cf. I 278 ff., 286, 294, 295, 338: 12 ff., *Bq* I 110–11.

[2] *Q* I 294, 299–300, 305, 314, *Bq* I 110–11. Cf. above pp. 195 ff.

[3] The form, says Aristotle, 'is a kind of power immersed in matter—a duct as it were'. *De Generatione et Corruptione* i. 5. 322^{a}28–29 (Joachim).

[4] This use of 'beginning' does not necessarily mean historical beginning or beginning in time. Rather, it means the beginning of the individual members of the species 'culture' which as a species *may* be eternal (cf. above pp. 255 n. 1, 256 n. 2) or at any rate may have begun some time in the remote past, i.e., its beginning is unknown. Cf. Plato *Laws* iii. 676A–B, vi. 781E–782A. Ibn Khaldûn does not mention the temporal beginning or end of the species 'culture'.

and at best for the satisfaction of their natural delight in being together. But they did not lead a full life in accordance with their natural possibilities. They lived in small groups and were able to provide only the bare necessities of life. Fear strengthened their feeling of affection and mutual goodwill. Since they could satisfy only the necessities of life, there was no occasion for factions or quarrels; and since they had no opportunity to satisfy their immoderate desires for riches, power, and pleasure, they were forced to be virtuous and moderate. Yet, this pre-political way of life was primitive and imperfect because it satisfied the indispensable needs of the body and the appetites or of the irrational part of the soul only.[1]

Man's needs and desires were not the immediate cause of human association, not even of this most simple and primitive culture. Primitive culture was brought into existence and preserved by a primitive form of solidarity: the social bond that gave a concrete and institutionalized form to the desires of affection and fear, and the need for food and shelter. It is this bond which held men together, and made them follow certain habits and customs, and submit to the arbitration of elders and to the lordship of heads of large families. Without it, and in spite of the appetites that might have made them wish to the contrary, men would have remained isolated hunters or cave-dwellers. Thus, the appetites, which are present in all men all the time, do not explain the particular institutions through which desires are satisfied. On the contrary, the degree and manner of satisfying the appetites are dependent on the actual existence and operation of institutions whose character and extent are determined by the character and extent of the solidarity existing in a primitive culture.[2] If this solidarity is merely a familial bond, the group will not extend beyond the family; if it is the result of fear, it will lead to the production and perfection of weapons; and if it is an economic bond, it will lead to co-operation in the production of food.[3]

[1] Cf. above pp. 188–90, below p. 276 n. 2; Plato *Laws* iii. 677B, 678B ff. (Fârâbî *Nawâmîs* 17: 8 and 13. Notice the use of the word *bad'*, whence Ibn Khaldûn's *badawî* [primitive]); Aristotle *Politics* iii. 5. 1278^{b}20–29, vii. 15. 1334^{b}16 ff.

[2] Cf. *Q* I 314 ff.

[3] Cf. above pp. 196–98; Plato *Laws* iii. 680A, 680C–E; Aristotle *Politics* i. 3, iii. 9. 1280^{b}12–39, *Nicomachean Ethics* viii. 12.

Next, primitive solidarity leads to the increase of production and the size of primitive groups. It creates new opportunities for competition over material goods, and the causes of dissensions and conflicts within a group and wars among various groups. A new situation thus arises in which solidarity is put to a severe test. Hitherto, solidarity had meant a positive relation among the members of a group. In a state of war, another aspect of solidarity comes to the foreground: that of being against others, and of conquering others and dominating them.[1] As various groups contest for supremacy, it is again solidarity which is the immediate cause determining the survival of the way of life, the customs, and the laws of a certain group. Whether the conflicts are settled by open warfare or by arbitration, it is the group with the strongest solidarity which is bound to become supreme. The solidarity that proves itself in war becomes the source of the various types of civilized rule and the basis of various types of laws.[2]

In his study of the development and changes in solidarity and the state, which is brought into existence by solidarity, Ibn Khaldûn distinguishes three types of rule or ways of governing (*mulk*): (a) the rule based on natural solidarity alone, (b) the rule based on reason in addition to natural solidarity, and (c) the rule based on religious Law in addition to natural solidarity.[3] Natural solidarity is present in all types of rule, what differentiates them being the addition of practical rational precepts to solidarity in the second, and the addition of the religious Law in the third. As stated in the study of the regime of Law, ' addition ' does not mean a simple juxtaposition of two elements. The addition of rational precepts and the religious Law to natural solidarity introduces a basic change in the use made of natural solidarity and the ends which it is to serve.[4] Nonetheless, it is not the rational precepts or the prescriptions of the Law which are the immediate cause of any regime. These

[1] It is primarily in this sense that solidarity (*'aṣabiyya*) was used in Arabic before Ibn Khaldûn used it as a technical term. This is also the sense in which Fârâbî uses it in his compendium of Plato's *Laws* (*Nawâmîs* 18: 2 and 6; cf. Plato *Laws* iii. 682C–E).

[2] Cf. above pp. 197–99; Plato *Laws* iii. 680B ff. (Fârâbî *Nawâmîs* 17–18); Aristotle *Politics* iv. 11. 1296a30.

[3] *Q* I 342–44.

[4] Cf. above pp. 238 ff.

merely modify solidarity and direct it to particular ends, but solidarity remains the immediate cause which brings a regime into existence and preserves it. For as soon as men progress from the community of necessity and as soon as there is some surplus which one man could grab from another, injustice and over-reaching is bound to result because of man's animal appetites. Consequently, general confusion and war cannot be avoided except through a hierarchy of powers supported by force. This means that, at least during the establishment of the state, and before men are accustomed to obey their rulers and respect the rights of others, lower impulses cannot be restrained except by coercion. Since solidarity is the only natural source for such coercion, it is absolutely necessary for civil society no matter what end it pursues. Further, the exercise of coercion based on solidarity is neither contrary to the precepts of reason nor to the prescription of the Law. Nor is coercive rule necessarily unjust or sinful. On the contrary, it is an indispensable condition of justice and virtue.[1]

(a) Natural rule or governance (*mulk ṭabî'î*) is based on natural solidarity alone which is used by the ruler to further his own purposes and satisfy his own lower impulses. Paramount among these are his choleric desires which dominate the state. The ruled are oppressed and used merely as instruments to satisfy these desires. The ruler has ended the state of war among his subjects and checked their lower impulses for the sole purpose of waging a war against them and giving free rein to his own lower impulses. Ibn Khaldûn does not call this type of rule a

[1] *Q* I 252, 278 ff., 286, 295, 337–39, 342, 347, 364–66, II 265, 289–90, III 20–30, 236. Cf. above pp. 201–2, 204–6; *Bq* I 110 (where solidarity and society [*ijtimâ'*] are used almost synonymously), III 2–3, *C* II 384 ff.; Ikhwân al-Ṣafâ' *Rasâ'il* I 223, IV 33, 60; Plato *Laws* iii. 690A ff. (Fârâbî *Nawâmîs* 18: 13–16, 19: 21, 20: 15–18, 22: 16 ff., 27: 19–22); Aristotle *Nicomachean Ethics* x. 9. 1180^{a}18–22, *Politics* i. 5–6.

The Prophet's knowledge of these matters and the presence of solidarity as a condition for the rise of Islam is abundantly emphasized by Ibn Khaldûn in the historical part of the '*Ibar* (*C* II 168 ff.) where he states the principle: 'If God wills something He facilitates [the presence of] its conditions.' *C* II 168: 4. Thus the Prophet's economic condition is bettered by his marriage to Khadîja and by having rich followers like Abû Bakr (*C* II 188); he was an able general (*C* II 195 ff., 211, 234) and a persuasive speaker (*C* II 248); and he belonged to the powerful tribe of Quraysh (*C* II 247). Ibn Khaldûn was convinced of the fact that religion cannot come into existence without solidarity and political power to the extent of asserting that 'if it [solidarity] disappears, so will divine Laws'. *Q* I 366: 3.

'regime', and strongly condemns it as perverted and wrong. The reason is evident. It is not a regime, and strictly speaking not a political community, because it has no principle of justice. It is true that the rational regime whose end is the interest of the ruler comes close to this type of rule. Yet, there is an important difference between the two. The rational regime whose end is the interest of the ruler has a minimum of justice made necessary by the fact that the ruler does not give free rein to his lower impulses, but follows some rational precepts designed to protect and further his power, precepts which impose upon him a measure of moderation and justice. He is still a tyrant, and the laws he establishes are designed to further his own ends, but he is an enlightened tyrant who is able to preserve his power and the state he rules. The tyrant who rules in accordance with his lower impulses only, on the other hand, cannot preserve his rule. Soon his subjects are forced by his licence and unjust measures to rebel against him and destroy his rule. The outcome will be either the supremacy of a new group which rules according to reason or the Law, or constant war and confusion. Hence, the solidarity which was the basis of his authority is destroyed by his immoderate tyranny.[1]

In contrast to natural rule, the two rational regimes and the regime of Law enjoy relative permanence. This is due to the modification of solidarity by reason and the religious Law. In its modified form, solidarity is again the immediate cause which brings these regimes into existence and determines their character. In the two rational regimes, natural solidarity is strengthened by self-interest and the hope for achieving mundane ends. In the regime of Law, natural solidarity is strengthened by the inner compulsion to obey the Legislator which rests on the belief in the truth of his message and the certainty of the rewards promised in the world to come. We have seen how in each case the particular regime and the arrangement of its offices are determined by these ends. It is not these ends in themselves, however, which are the immediate cause of the regimes which pursue them. Rather, it is these ends as present in the souls of the citizens, as existential hopes and desires, which actualize the respective

[1] *Q* I 342–43. Cf. Plato *Laws* iii. 693E ff. (Fârâbî *Nawâmîs* 20: 19–20, 21: 2–3); Aristotle *Politics* iii. 6. 1279^{a}19–21.

regimes. The study of the actual rise and decline of these regimes, therefore, requires the study of the rise and decline of these hopes and desires.

(b) Rational regimes are brought into existence by natural solidarity modified by rational precepts concerning the ways and means of attaining worldly ends. What is added to solidarity and its power of restraint and domination in this case is an external bond. The ruled do not obey the ruler because of their belief in the goodness and the ultimate salutary effects of the Law, but because of forceful compulsion, the fear of immediate punishment, and the hope for mundane rewards. There are thus two causes leading to the decline and disintegration of solidarity in rational regimes: external compulsion weakens the solidarity of the ruled, and so does the gratification of the desires for mundane ends which the rational regimes pursue.[1]

It is inherent in the nature of solidarity that it leads to the concentration of power in the hands of an undisputed master. The ruler who first achieves his position because of the power of his kinsmen and tribe, finds it impossible to further the ends of a rational regime without the destruction of their power and the transformation of the state into an efficient impersonal machinery run by qualified functionaries who know how to organize the finances of the state and command its armics, and are versed in the ways of civilization: building cities, organizing economic activity, and encouraging the arts and sciences. Thus, the state is transformed from an aristocracy based on blood-relations to a civil and military bureaucracy which destroys natural solidarity and substitutes for it a rule based on force, and develops the ways of civilization to satisfy the mundane ends of the ruler and the ruled.[2]

Considering the ends of rational regimes, this transformation is necessary. It succeeds in creating the means for the satisfactions of man's desire for freedom from toil, ease, relaxation, rest, amusement, and other pleasures. But when the opportunity presents itself, men become habituated in the excessive gratification of their pleasures. Rational precepts do not seem to be as effective as the Law in educating men in good habits and good

[1] *Q* I 232, 233, 284–86.
[2] *Q* I 299 ff., II 1 ff., 79 ff. Cf. above pp. 196 ff.

character (*ta'dîb*, *paideía*) which lies in moderation and the choice of the mean. Without the moderating influence of the Law, civilization leads to luxury and excess, and excess leads to the disintegration and destruction of man and the state: ' the habits of character resulting from civilization and luxury are corruption itself '. Man's soul is ' coloured ' by these bad habits and he loses his humanity. In the progress of civilization to that end, natural solidarity is destroyed along with the destruction of other virtues. The common pursuit of worldly ends, which had become the substitute for solidarity, cannot preserve the state. On the contrary, it leads to its destruction by making men physically and spiritually impotent.[1]

(c) The regime of Law is brought into existence by a most vigorous and socially effective force which is indeed the cause of a miraculous transformation in social relations. Through the successive performance of amazing miracles, and other acts contrary to the normal operation of nature, the prophet creates in his followers that deep-rooted faith in the rewards and punishments of the world to come which greatly changes their social life. He gets rid of the low impulses which are the causes of factions and conflicts, and unites them for a cause superior to their individual appetites and interests. He induces them to get rid of their bad habits and to replace these with moderate and just habits. Since their hopes and desires are now directed to intangible and other-worldly ends like immortality and happiness in the world to come, they are able to be moderate in the pursuit of this-worldly ends, and their energies can be directed toward fighting for just and good causes. Finally, since the restraints against bad action and the desire to act in accordance with the prescription of the Law are the result of inner faith, the ruled do not need to be forced to obey the laws by threats of punishment in this world or the inducements of external rewards. They will obey the Law, and even die for it, for the sake of God, hoping that He will reward them for their piety in the world to come. The result is a strong, united, virtuous, and obedient group which can conquer and rule nations greater, richer, and

[1] *Q* II 256–61, cf. I 254 ff., 268, 300–303, II 307 ff.; above pp. 207–9. On moderation (*tawassuṭ*, *qaṣd*), cf. esp. *Q* I 271: 4, (*ḥadd* [limit]) 339–40, 341: 18–19 (*ifrâṭ* [excess]), 370, 372, II 130, 231. Mahmassani *op. cit.* 212.

stronger in all other respects except that inner faith which distinguishes a religious community.[1]

Yet, by its very nature and foundation this religious impulse is of short duration.[2] As the prophet dies and the generation which had known him and was directly influenced by him passes away, the miracles are forgotten and the impact of the extraordinary feats starts to decline. Since the regime of Law is not based on worldly interests but on inner faith, there is no external cause which can preserve the regime after the inner faith declines. The Law may remain, but once the inner impulse vanishes and the Law as a moving force in the hearts of men ceases to exist, the regime of Law as a dynamic reality ceases to exist. Natural solidarity re-emerges to assert itself, and unless a rational regime is substituted for the regime of Law, the latter is bound to degenerate into natural rule serving the lower impulses of whoever happens to have the stronger solidarity.[3]

5. The rise and decline of culture is thus caused by the interplay of external conditions and man's faculties, desires, and habits of character. Its various stages are characterized by the prominence of certain elements.[4] At the beginning, the hardships and challenges presented by the physical environment evoke in man fear, and the desire to live with his fellow men and to co-operate in the production of food and for defence. With the aid of practical reason, he develops the simple arts, forms the habits, and establishes the customs and conventions through which he overcomes the initial obstacles to the satisfaction of his elementary needs and desires. Solidarity is one of the habits which develop in this process. It is the socially institutionalized form of a simple desire: man's affection toward his fellow men, especially his blood-relations. This habit, in turn, becomes the cause of further development in culture. It creates the state, the

[1] *Q* I 172, 232, 233, 269 ff., 273, 278 ff., 352–55, 364 ff., 373, 374, 376, 380, 383, 390, 393, 418, II 6, 62, 65–66, 106–7, 124; Fârâbî *Nawâmîs* 11: 19–16: 11, 26: 24–27: 11; cf. Avicenna *Nubuwwât* 125: 6. Religion as moderation is the central theme of fifth-century Greek thought. Cf. Herodotus *The Persian Wars* ii. 78; Plato *Charmides* 164D–E, *Gorgias* 491E ff., *Laws* v. 732B–C (Fârâbî *Nawâmîs* 26: 24—27: 11).

[2] *Q* II 249: 17.

[3] *Q* I 275–76, 383–84, 387–90, 396. Cf. Ikhwân al-Ṣafâ' *Rasâ'il* III 170 ff. Consider Fârâbî's recommendations to the legislator on how to preserve the Laws, *Nawâmîs* 24: 14–25: 7, 29: 21–30: 2, 35: 16–36: 16.

[4] Cf. *Q* III 236–37.

form within which man can progress in the satisfaction of his desires. The state, with solidarity as its instrument, effects the change from primitive culture to civilization. Civilization presents man with new challenges and new possibilities. Man is again called upon to use his practical reason to choose among various ends and to devise new means to achieve them. It is man's natural tendency to succumb to his desires and use his reason to perfect the means for satisfying them. To that end he will exert his intelligence and direct all his energies, unless a religious Law intervenes to set his life in order, and guide him to be moderate in the satisfaction of his desires and direct his attention to other-worldly ends for the attainment of which mundane ends must take a subordinate position. In the absence of such a Law, man's desires will lead him to the immoderate enjoyment of riches and power. He becomes habituated in the new conditions of civilization which destroy his virtues and become his master.[1] But, the effectiveness of the Law is short-lived because the Law is doomed to oblivion by the generations following the prophet. Thus, while rational precepts are made ineffective by licentiousness, forgetfulness makes men heedless of the prescriptions of the Law. Hence, solidarity, in all its forms, is bound to disintegrate; and since it is the efficient cause of culture, culture disintegrates because it thereby loses the principle to which it owes its actual existence.

Theoretically, solidarity is only one of the elements which constitute culture, it is one of the four causes. If we consider the way Ibn Khaldûn treats the subject matter and problems of culture, however, we find that he lays so much emphasis on solidarity that it almost becomes the central theme of the new science. We shall attempt to explain the reasons for that emphasis more fully in the conclusion of this study. The most immediate reason for this becomes evident once we consider the immediate end of the science of culture and the character of the efficient cause. If the science of culture is to help in the rectification of historical reports, it has to explain how society actually comes to

[1] *Q* I 224, II 260–61, 272 ff., 307 ff.; cf. Aristotle *Nicomachean Ethics* vii. 1, *Rhetoric* ii. 5. 1382a28 ff. Bayhaqî *Ta'rîkh* 47: 1–2, where he reports the saying attributed to the philosopher Abû al-Faraj Ibn al-Ṭabîb al-Jâthlîq (*GAL*(*S*) I 828 [No. 95bb]): 'As the state rises, desires serve reason, and as it passes away, reason serves the desires.'

exist and what causes social change. But we saw that the efficient cause is precisely the cause that explains the actual existence of a thing and the change it undergoes. Since solidarity is the efficient cause of culture, it is only natural that Ibn Khaldûn should lay more emphasis on it in explaining how culture comes-to-be, the various stages through which it passes, and how it declines and disintegrates.

IV

The Common Good: The Final Cause

1. Like the efficient cause, the final cause or the end (*ghâya*) is not a part of its effect and is usually described as extrinsic to it. Yet upon close examination, it is found to be even more related to the being of a thing than all other causes. The final cause is defined as that for the sake of which a thing exists.[1] Thus, the actual existence of the final cause coincides with the achievement of its effect. How does it then exercise its causality? It exercises its causality through a mode of being which is actual existence in the soul by way of object. Avicenna called it 'intentional existence' (*shay'iyya*, *entitas*).[2] In intentional existence, the final cause or the end precedes its effect, exerçises its causality, and constitutes the starting point of all works of nature and art.[3] It also underlies and precedes all other causes, and explains how they acquire their causal efficacy. It is the primary cause for the sake of which all other causes exercise their causality.

This is particularly true in the case of culture where man acts and creates various institutions for an end which transcends the cultural institutions themselves. In this respect, man differs from the rest of the animal kingdom where the formal and final causes are one and the same, and the final cause is nothing more than existence in the most perfect form.[4] Human beings do not create urban institutions or the state for their own sake. The actualization of the form is not the end, but the means through which the

[1] Aristotle *Physics* ii. 3. 194^b32–195^a2, 23, *Metaphysics* ii. 2. 994^b9–16, v. 2. 1013^a32.

[2] Avicenna *Najât* 345: 1–11.

[3] Aristotle *De Partibus Animalium* i. 1. 639^b13–16.

[4] Aristotle *De Generatione Animalium* i. 1. 715^a4–5, *De Generatione et Corruptione* ii. 9. 335^b7 (where the end is said to be the 'figure' and the 'form'); Fârâbî *Ta'lîqât* 8.

attainment of the end, e.g., happiness and goodness, is made possible. Since in culture, the final cause is different from the formal, and since the final cause is the primary cause, we must not only attempt to know the final cause along with the other causes, but must ultimately explain culture in terms of final cause. By themselves the other causes cannot explain, for instance, why society takes certain forms and not others, and, consequently, why the human will is directed toward the actualization of these specific forms. Only on the basis of the priority of the end, and the subordination of other causes to the final, could such questions be answered.[1]

The problems posed for the science of culture in investigating the final cause could be formulated in a preliminary way as follows: Man is characterized by reason, his action is intelligent action, he acts for the sake of some ends. These ends are not given at the beginning, but are the objects of desire. Various men and various communities consider various ends good and seek measures to realize them. Further, individuals and communities attain their various ends in various degrees of perfection: ends are actualized in particular circumstances some of which are more and others less conducive to the actualization of what man desires. The science of culture is concerned with understanding the causes of man's actions; hence it cannot disregard the primary cause of man's action which is the desire to effect an end. It is also concerned with the understanding of the results of such action, i.e., the events of history. These too have to be understood in terms of the ends which they were intended to secure, or as ends in themselves. The study of the source which gives rise to culture and the study of culture itself, cannot thus avoid the consideration of the end or the good.[2]

Although the desire for ends, and actualized ends, are known by experience to be important constituent parts of culture, their nature cannot be known inductively. All that is found in culture is a diversity of desired or actualized ends, and a diversity of opinions asserting that some of them are more worthy than others, that some are apparent and others real, that some lead to

[1] This remains true in spite of the fact that in studying society we may start with the investigation of the efficient and formal causes. These causes are first in the order of knowledge but not in the order of being.

[2] *Q* I 31–32, 40–42, 259–62, *passim.*

true happiness and others to misery, and that some are virtues and others vices. Yet neither the factual existence of, nor the opinions about, ends are sufficient for the understanding of culture. The factual existence of diverse ends does not preclude the possibility that some of them are partial ends and others only means in relation to a supreme end. As to opinions, it is precisely the function of reason to penetrate beyond them and grasp the truth of which they are but imperfect reflections: diverse opinions about the end of man and society are indications pointing toward a supreme end which as a principle can be known by reason alone.[1] This principle defines the good of man as the perfection of his nature, absolutely speaking and without reference to particular circumstances. Since the end of society is but the existence of good men, it would also define the end of society. Once these ends are known, the particular desires and actions and opinions can then be measured against an unchanging standard, or they can be organized hierarchically depending on whether they serve or are served by other ends. Particular desires and acts and opinions can thus be judged in relation to this hierarchy of ends, i.e., they could be judged as good or bad absolutely speaking and without reference to particular circumstances. Similarly, the ends pursued by various communities can be judged with respect to how far they fulfil the possibilities of human nature as defined by man's end, and how near they come to the regime which fulfils all the possibilities of human nature and which can be called the best regime. Thus, it will be possible to establish a hierarchy of political forms according to their degree of perfection. Finally, it will be possible to judge whether particular cultural changes are toward a better or a worse regime, and hence whether they are good or bad.

The science of culture itself, however, cannot demonstrate the absolute end of man and society. This was not the end for which it formulated its principles and conducted its investigation. Its principles were formulated and its investigation conducted primarily for the sake of understanding the nature of historical events. In studying these events, it met with the necessity of knowing the absolute end of man and society in relation to which it must measure the particular ends pursued in various

[1] Cf. above pp. 161–63.

societies. This end cannot be inducted from the events; yet it is necessary for fully explaining them.

2. If the science of culture is to avoid the use of a dialectically or rhetorically formulated principle of finality, it will have to turn to a science where such a principle had been properly demonstrated,[1] that is, to a science whose main objective is the rational demonstration of the proper end of man and society absolutely speaking and without reference to particular circumstances. Since such an end is both the end of man and society, or the end of man living in society, this science must also explain the nature and the form of the perfect society in which the perfect end of man could be attained. Only political science or political philosophy (*siyâsa madaniyya*)[2] satisfies these conditions.

In order to avoid confusing the science of culture with political philosophy, Ibn Khaldûn must state simultaneously what political philosophy is and distinguish it from the science of culture by clearly stating the proper ends of the two sciences. In other words, the relationship between the two sciences can be best stated in terms of a distinction between them. This is what Ibn Khaldûn does in the two passages where he refers to political philosophy. The first of these occurs in Ibn Khaldûn's discussion of the subject matter of the science of culture. There he clearly indicates that the subject matter of political philosophy is man's life 'as it ought to be according to the requirements of ethics and wisdom'.[3] The second and longer passage occurs when Ibn Khaldûn discusses the forms and ends of actual regimes. After enumerating these regimes, and *before* explaining them and indicating their relative merits, he interrupts the discussion and almost parenthetically inserts the following remarks:

'The political philosophy you hear of does not belong to this category [of existing regimes]. Among philosophers, it only means what every single member of that society [of which they speak] ought to be in his character and conduct so that they can

[1] The science of culture has already used as principles the conclusions of various sciences including climatology, geography, and psychology. These could be used as principles because they were rationally demonstrated by sciences which had the demonstration of these conclusions as their main objective.

[2] *Q* I 62: 6–7, II 128: 6; cf. above pp. 157, 167–68.

[3] *Q* I 62: 7–8; cf. above p. 157.

dispense with magistrates[1] altogether. They call the society in which these required [conditions] are realized the " virtuous city " (*madîna fâḍila*), and the rules observed in the [organization or operation of that city] " political philosophy ". [By " political " (*siyâsa*)] they do not mean the " regime " which the members of society are made to follow with [positive] commands [or laws, prescribed] for the common good; for the latter [regimes] are different from the former [virtuous city].

' According to them [the philosophers], this virtuous city is rare and its realization is highly improbable. They *only speak* about it in the way of supposition and hypothesis.'[2]

The distinction between the virtuous city and actual cities or between the city ' in speech ' and the cities ' in deed ' is not, however, a sufficient ground for the creation of an independent science for the study of the latter. The distinction itself owes its origin to Muslim political philosophers and their Greek masters who studied the imperfect cities extensively,[3] but did not think that these cities could be made the object of an independent science. The extreme position against admitting the possibility or usefulness of such a science might be summarized as follows: The nature of actual and imperfect cities cannot be known except in relation to the perfect city. Political philosophy should, therefore, aim primarily at knowing the final end of man or his perfection. It must ascend from the ends pursued in existing and imperfect cities, and from the opinions held in them concerning the end of man, to the true knowledge of the end of man. It will then see the need for constructing another city in which man's perfection can be actualized. Once it achieves the true knowledge of all things in the full light of the sun, it can descend to the cave and study its shadows. When considered in relation to the perfect beings seen in the full light of the sun, the most important truth about the shadows in the cave is their imperfection, darkness, falsehood, and lack of real existence. Therefore, there can

[1] *ḥukkâm*. Dispensing with magistrates amounts to the same thing as dispensing with positive laws, which is a correct statement of the position of Plato and Fârâbî concerning the best regime. Cf. Plato *Statesman* 293E ff., *Laws* ix. 875D; Fârâbî *Nawâmîs* 41: 21–23.

[2] *Q* II 127: 6–14.

[3] Cf. Plato *Laws* iii. 678A ff. (Fârâbî *Nawâmîs* 17: 4 ff.), *Republic* ii. 369 ff., viii. 547 ff.; Fârâbî *Madîna* 90 ff., *Siyâsât* 57 ff., *Iḥṣâ'* 102–7; Avicenna *Aqsâm* 107: 16–17; Akfânî *Irshâd* 94–95.

be no independent science of these shadows. For, as soon as they are separated from the world of true existence and as soon as they are studied with any degree of independence, the student will fall back in a dark pit where he compares shadows with shadows and achieves, not real knowledge, but mere opinions. Such opinions will have little theoretical value and hardly any practical use.[1]

By venturing to create a new science of culture to study exclusively the imperfect cities and the shadows in the cave, Ibn Khaldûn accepted the basic premise but not all the conclusions of this position. Granting the distinction between the virtuous city, and the actual and imperfect regimes, and granting the need for the virtuous city as the valid standard against which actual regimes must be measured, it need not follow that the most important characteristics of actual regimes are their imperfection, darkness, falsehood, and lack of real existence. Sufficient experience and knowledge of actual regimes may reveal a delicate gradation in the shadows which can be compared and known with relative independence from the world of perfect and true existence. Such knowledge can be of practical use, not only to the historian whose purpose is to discriminate between these shadows, but also to the statesman who is chained in the cave and to the philosopher who ought to return to the cave and reform actual regimes as far as possible. In asserting that the two ways of studying actual regimes can, to a certain extent, be separated, Ibn Khaldûn is nearer to Aristotle than to Plato and Muslim Platonic political philosophers.[2]

In studying the final cause of actual regimes, Ibn Khaldûn usually defines it in terms of the common good (*maṣâliḥ ʿâmma*) and particular virtues, especially moderation (*qaṣd*) and justice (*ʿadl*).[3] But a careful study of the specific content of these terms shows that this content is not fixed. It changes from one regime

[1] This extreme position is represented by Fârâbî and Ibn Bâjja in particular. Cf. Fârâbî *Taḥṣîl* 12–16, 34–35, *Aflâṭun* 3 (sec. 1), 6 (sec. 6), 10–14 (secs. 12–15, 18–21), 16 (sec. 23), 20 (sec. 25), *Madîna* 79, 90–95, 108, 119; Ibn Bâjja *Tadbîr* 3–9, 13 ff., 29 (where he also denounces the preference of Muʿâwiya over ʿAlî), 37, 54, ff. Ibn Bâjja delegates the study of actual regimes, a subject which he holds in great contempt, to the historian (*Tadbîr* 11, cf. 6–7, 9, 22, 28, 36).

[2] Cf. Aristotle *Politics* iv. 1. Ibn Khaldûn was most probably not acquainted with Aristotle's *Politics*. But he almost reconstructs Aristotle's position on the possibility of a relatively independent study of actual regimes by utilizing the *Nicomachean Ethics*, the *Rhetoric*, and the physical treatises.

[3] Cf. above pp. 239 ff.

to another and from one situation to another. Therefore, it will be useful to proceed in our discussion by asking the following questions: (1) What is the specific end which a regime considers as the good? (2) What is the measure of goodness realized in each regime? The answer to these two questions will give the historian a standard by which to judge the relative goodness of each regime, and whether a change from one regime to another is good or bad.

3. In respect to the ends of existing regimes and the measure of goodness realized in each, three groups of regimes can be distinguished: (a) Primitive cultures whose end is mere life. (b) Civilized rational regimes whose end is the good of this world. (c) Civilized regimes of Law whose end is the good of this world and the next.

(a) The end of primitive culture is the preservation of life.[1] Mere life is undeniably good: it is preferable to lack of life in the estimation of man's desire and reason. The distinctive features of the common good in primitive cultures can be readily seen when viewed in relation to this end: they consist in assuring the indispensable conditions for the survival of the individual and the group. These include common defence, the essentials of economic intercourse like the production and exchange of necessary foodstuffs and household articles, and common agreement relating to disputes within the group. No elaborate and explicitly formulated legal code or any other institution is necessary. The precise content of moderation and justice in this context is similarly evident. Moderation simply means curbing the passions and desires that could not be satisfied in a primitive culture: no member of such a community should expect the rest of the community to starve to render him the services that might make him more comfortable; when a camel is needed for transportation and milk, he should not slaughter it for a banquet; and when the wheat is needed by his family for a week's sustenance, he should not distil it for drinking purposes. To be just means to fulfil his duties as prescribed by the common way of life necessary for survival: to defend his friends in times of danger, to abstain from acts that may endanger their lives and interests, and to help them in time of need.[2]

[1] *Q* I 221: 4–5, II 307: 9–11, 308: 1–4, 333.
[2] *Q* I 220 ff., cf. above pp. 193 ff.

(b) The end of rational regimes is the enjoyment of the full benefits of the advanced form of social life which is called civilized culture.[1] In addition to the preservation of mere life, they aim at the creation and the preservation of the indispensable conditions which make a full social life possible. These conditions include a civilized state under kingly rule, a large population occupied with diverse and specialized trades, large and well-defended cities in which the ruled can peacefully pursue their trades, and the development of the practical arts and sciences necessary for the regulation of the affairs of a large community.[2]

All of these conditions are good because man is by nature a social animal and by nature he is intended to live in such a society. The full enjoyment of social life is a higher good than the mere preservation of life; and so are the impulses that drive man to enjoy life in society and the conditions that promote it. They are the natural completion of the life begun in primitive culture; they are part of his nature as a human being, and by nature man is good.[3] However, by accident and as a result of man's animal impulses, evil is bound to be present in social life. Man's lower impulses lead him to injure his fellow men and drive him to the immoderate enjoyment of the goods of social life. There seems to be a conflict between man's rational desire to keep enjoying the pleasures of social life, which demands the preservation of society and moderation, and his lower impulses which drive him to destroy society and prevent him from enjoying its benefits.

A common system of laws and coercion by force exercised by an undisputed ruler imposing minimal justice and moderation is, therefore, necessary for insuring peace and order in society. Such laws and the coercion that ensures their application were invented by man's practical reason to ensure the preservation of the goods of social life. Practical reason, further, learned by repeated experience that the preservation of social life demands the existence of certain virtues in the ruler and the ruled alike. If man is to continue enjoying the benefits of social life, he must be just and moderate and prudent. The laws must be designed to ensure the common good of the whole society, and to encourage the

[1] *Q* II 250: 8 ff., 307: 11 ff.
[2] Cf. above pp. 197 ff., 248 ff.
[3] *Q* I 259–60, 342, II 290–91, 304; Fârâbî *Milla* fol. 55, *Taḥṣîl* 14–15; Ikhwân al-Ṣafâ' *Rasâ'il* I 62.

ruler and the ruled to cultivate these virtues; and the ruler and the ruled must obey these laws, promote the common good, and control their lower impulses. Consequently, the ruler and the ruled in rational regimes are deemed good by reason if they are able to live a just, moderate, and prudent life, and promote the common good. If, on the contrary, their lower impulses gain the ascendancy over their rational desires, they are bad. The same is true of the regimes and of their laws. They are good if they help man's rational desires to become supreme and bad if they encourage his lower impulses.[1]

The precise content of the common good and the other virtues in rational regimes is defined by the ends of these regimes: the preservation and enjoyment of the goods of social life. The goods of this life are usually contrasted by Ibn Khaldûn to the goods of the life to come. Since he does not explicitly define the goods of the life to come, at first his meaning is not clear. In contrasting the prescriptions of the regime of Law to the precepts of a rational regime, he indicates more clearly what he means by the goods of this life by saying that the prescription of the Law ' attend to the *external and internal* goods of culture '.[2] He also says that the ' Lawgiver knows best the good of the many in the affairs of the world to come which are *hidden* from them . . . while the commands of [rational] rule exhibit the goods of this world alone '. He then quotes the Koran: ' " They know the *appearance* of this life." '[3] Finally, he asserts that worldly ends are in fact sensuous desires, and a life given to pleasures.[4] Mundane goods, or the goods of this life, must then be defined further as external and apparent goods, and as sensuous pleasure or the pleasures of the body which include health, wealth, strength, and all that contributes to the delight of the senses. The good in rational regimes is identical with pleasure thus defined; and virtue is that habit of character which is useful or profitable, i.e., conducive to the greater and longer enjoyment of sensuous pleasures. In short, the ultimate end of rational regimes is the well-being of man's body only.[5]

[1] *Q* I 233–34, 243–44, 259–62, 346–47, II 94–95, 126–28.
[2] *Q* I 275: 6–7.
[3] *Q* I 343: 14–18. Koran 30: 7.
[4] *Q* I 373: 3–4 and 8–9, 375: 15.
[5] Cf., e.g., *C* II 332, 333, 336–37, 340, 343, 350–51, for historical instances where the ends of rational regimes are pursued. On the body, its goods, and the regimes that aim at the well-being of the body, cf. Plato *Phaedrus* 258E, *Republic*

The content and meaning of the common good in the rational regimes can thus be clearly defined, and also the moderation and justice conducive to it. To promote the common good in rational regimes means to ensure the greatest and longest possible enjoyment of sensuous pleasures to all the members of the community. To be moderate means to keep the enjoyment of these pleasures within the limits defined by the necessity of insuring similar pleasures for other members of the community, and of ensuring the prevention of pain, sickness, or premature death. To be just, similarly, means allowing others to enjoy the pleasures they are entitled to enjoy, deference to the laws which aim at providing the greatest pleasures to the members of the community, and obedience to the ruler who is trying to preserve and defend the community, and apply the laws.

In calling these regimes 'rational', Ibn Khaldûn did not mean that they are what human reason at its best (i.e., philosophy) considers the most perfect of regimes. They are rational because practical reason rather than man's lower impulses supplies the principles which order man's social life. But these principles ensure only the minimum conditions without which society could not continue to exist. Rational regimes lack many principles, the most evident of which is a prophetic Law which defines man's duties toward God.[1] At its best, human reason has

iii. 407; Aristotle *Politics* vii. 1. 1323^{b}7–21; Fârâbî *Madîna* 91–92, 99–102, 119–22, *Siyâsât* 57 ff.; Ibn Bâjja *Tadbîr* 37; Maimonides *Dalâla* ii. 39; Hallevi *Khazarî* iv. 19. Strauss *Persecution* 115 ff., 'Maimonides' Statement on Political Science' *Proceedings of the American Academy for Jewish Research* XXII (1953) 123–25.

[1] Yet Ibn Khaldûn asserts that prophecy is not 'necessary'. It is evident that all he means by this statement is that prophecy is not a necessary condition for the existence and preservation of society, and he proves this statement by pointing to the large number of societies that have existed for long periods without a prophet. Compared to them, societies ruled by prophets have been few and short-lived. (*Q* I 72–73, 346, 394.) Here, Ibn Khaldûn is not arguing against Muslim political philosophers, for none of them says that religion is rationally necessary in the sense that society cannot exist without it. Avicenna indeed argues for the rational necessity of prophecy (*Shifâ'* IV. x. 3; Muḥammad Yûsuf Mûsâ, ed. *al-Nâḥiya al-ijtimâ'iyya wa-l-siyâsiyya fî falsafat Ibn Sînâ* ['La sociologie et la politique dans la philosophie d'Avicenne'] [Cairo 1952] 8 ff., esp. 9: 11). But it is not certain that 'necessary' according to him means indispensable for social life. In fact he uses the legal term 'obligation' (*wujûb*) and not the philosophic term 'necessity' (*ḍarûra*).

Ibn Khaldûn agrees here with orthodox Muslim jurists that the necessity of prophecy is known through the Law (*Q* I 73: 4–5; Mâwardî *Aḥkâm* 3–4; cf. H. A. R. Gibb *BSOS* VII [1933–34] 26–28). This agreement is of little consequence, however, once we realize that all it means is that the followers of every envisaged a truly rational regime which is absolutely perfect. Compared to it, all existing regimes are imperfect. But there are among existing regimes various degrees of imperfection: primitive cultures are less perfect than rational regimes, and rational regimes are less perfect than the regime of Law. But if the regime of Law is more perfect than rational regimes, it must be nearer to the virtuous city, or the best regime envisaged by reason, and thus more rational when considered in the full light of reason. Hence, when compared to the virtuous city, or the community in which philosophy is the ruling principle, rational regimes are twice removed from the ideal or truly rational regime.

(c) The end of the regime of Law is the preservation of life, the preservation and the proper enjoyment of the benefits of social life, and, in addition, the enjoyment of the good of the world to come. Ibn Khaldûn indicates the specific meaning of the ' world to come ' in contrasting it to ' this world ' of externals, of appearances, of the body, and of the senses.[1] He describes it as the internal, the hidden, the permanent, and, above all, the final end, the true end, and truth.[2] In short, the good of the world to come is a religious expression whose philosophic equivalent and meaning is the good of the *soul*,[3] the true happiness and felicity of man.[4] The purpose of the regime of the Law, then, is to direct man towards this:

' Indeed, the purpose of human beings is not solely their mundane [existence], for it is all vanity and sham, and its end is death and evanescence. And God says: " What! did you think We have created you in vain . . . ? "[5] Truly the purpose of [God in creating] them is their religion which leads them to happiness in the life to come. " This is the path of God to whom Heaven and Earth belong."[6] Laws then come to urge men to follow this

---

Law must accept their Law as necessary, i.e., necessary condition for their salvation. I suggest that this is not the only argument presented by Ibn Khaldûn in defence of the superiority of the regime of Law to rational regimes, cf. below p. 284.

[1] In Arabic, ' this world ' (*dunyâ*) also means: near, narrow, covered, lowly, and few. Cf. Lane *Lexicon* 920*b*–22*a*.

[2] *Q* I 275: 6–7, 343–44, cf. above p. 278 n. 5.

[3] Cf. *Q* II 97: 4–5, where the protection of the soul is said to be among the essential intentions of the Law.

[4] Cf. Fârâbî *Milla* fol. 56, *Taḥṣîl* 20–21, *Madîna* 66–68.

[5] Koran 23: 115. The second part of the verse is: '. . . and that you shall not return to us? '

[6] Koran 42: 53. All this chapter of the Koran (' The Council ' [*al-shûrâ*]), of which Ibn Khaldûn quotes only the last verse, is important for the present

[path] in all their affairs: in their worship and in their dealings. Even the state which is natural to human society was channelled in the direction of religion, so that everything could come under the supervision of the Law.'[1]

Although man cannot normally attain true happiness except by being alive and enjoying the benefits of social life, it is possible that in certain cases it may be better for his soul if he dies and if he does not enjoy some of the benefits of social life. This is evident in the case of the martyr and the ascetic saint. Hence, although the Law does not altogether deny the natural desires for life and the benefits of social life, it imposes certain restrictions upon them and 'directs them toward true ends as far as possible'.[2] What is important in this respect is not so much man's action but its intention (*maqṣad*) and its direction (*wajha*). The intentions are good if they are all united and directed toward the true end.[3] According to the principles of the regime of Law, when man aims at a lower end as his final end, and his desires are thus directed away from the higher end, all his acts are bad and evil: they are the result of ignorance and can be rightly condemned. Compared to the regime of Law which is legislated by a prophet who knows best the common good of the community and who brings to it the light of God, rational regimes are 'devoid of light'.[4]

The regime of Law is not merely a collection of sermons and exhortations, or a creed denouncing the ways of the world and urging man to lead a moral or spiritual way of life, but an all-comprehensive code regulating man's private and public opinions and actions.[5] Nor is it merely a set of rules of conduct inspired by religion and defining the manner of worship and man's other duties to God. It is a complete social order within which religion in this narrow sense occupies a subordinate position. The regime

---

discussion. The religious Law is presented in a cosmological context, and God's mercy, justice, and forgiveness are emphasized.

[1] *Q* I 343: 1–9.

[2] *Q* I 365: 2–4.

[3] *Q* I 365: 5–8.

[4] *Q* I 259: 19—260: 2, 343: 11–14; Koran 24: 35. All of this chapter ('The Light' [*al-nûr*]) is of interest to the student of the Islamic regime of Law. Divine 'light' and 'power' are discussed as a preparation for urging Muslims to obey the Prophet.

[5] *Q* II 127: 19, *passim.*

of Law is the ' whole ' within which the various activities and institutions, including those relating to man's duties to God, exist as material ' parts ', which, however, do not enjoy actual existence apart from the whole.[1] This is what Ibn Khaldûn means when he says that ' religion is derived from the Law '.[2] Considered in this perspective, which is certainly the perspective in which Muslim philosophers, following Plato, considered it,[3] the regime of Law is essentially a political order. It is true that, among other things, the regime of Law is distinguished from rational regimes in that it prescribes opinions about remote and hidden things like God and Heaven and Hell, and prescribes man's duties toward God. This is why Ibn Khaldûn also calls it the ' religious regime '.[4] Nonetheless, it is a ' regime ' (*siyâsa*), and a regime is primarily a political order.

But if the regime of Law is primarily a political order, it follows that, first, within the social order it creates, the common good and the virtues cannot be defined apart from the particular hierarchy in which it organizes the various ends in general, and apart from the supreme end—the well-being of the soul—in particular. Here, the common good is whatever contributes to the proper ordering of the various ends of man, and, above all, whatever contributes to the well-being of the soul. There is then a clear distinction between the common good in rational regimes, where it meant merely whatever contributes to the well-being of the body, and to the preservation and continuous enjoyment of the benefits of social life, and the common good in the regime of Law, where it means the subordination of these ends to the well-being or the proper excellence of the soul and the enjoyment of true felicity. Secondly, there is a clear distinction between the content of moderation and justice in rational regimes and in the regime of Law. In the regime of Law, moderation means the limitation of the enjoyment of the goods of the body and the benefits of social life, not for the sake of the continuous enjoyment of these pleasures and of ensuring similar pleasures for other members of the community, but with the intention of

[1] Above pp. 234–35.
[2] *al-dînu innamâ yustafâdu mina-l-sharî'ati. Q* II 270: 1–2.
[3] Plato *Laws* iv. 723E ff., xi. 917D ff.; Fârâbî *Nawâmîs* 6: 17–19, 25–26, 27: 7–10, 34–35, 38–39; Avicenna *Shifâ'* IV. x. 2–3. (Mûsâ *op. cit.* 6–16), *Aqsâm* 107–8, *Nubuwwât* 124–25.
[4] Above pp. 236–37.

avoiding all pleasures except those necessary for the attainment of true happiness and the excellence of the soul. And to be just in the regime of Law does not mean not to transgress the rights of others to enjoy the goods of the body and the benefits of social life, and deference to the laws that aim at providing the greatest pleasure for the community as a whole, but piety, deference to the rights of others to lead a pious life and perform their duties toward God, and obedience to the divine Law and the divine ruler. In the regime of Law moderation and justice are not earthly, but divine virtues.

It is not true that in the regime of Law there is no distinction between earthly and divine things, or between mundane goods and the good of the soul; for without this distinction it would be impossible to distinguish between the regime of Law and rational regimes—a distinction which is basic for Ibn Khaldûn. What is true is that the Law provides the all-comprehensive principles and detailed prescriptions according to which all goods are properly organized with a view to man's supreme excellence. For given their ends, rational regimes cannot and do not properly order these mundane goods with a view to attain true happiness. Only a regime which aims at helping men to attain true happiness could undertake to place mundane goods in their proper position in the hierarchy of ends; only the light of God could illuminate the proper nature of mundane goods. It is, therefore, natural that the Law must be sovereign in all walks of life. To have a mundane government and a divine government side by side, entrusting to the one the care of earthly things and temporal goods, and to the other the care of spiritual things,[1] is not only

[1] Cf. Thomas Aquinas *De Regno* ii. 3 (I. 14.) frags. 105, 110 [as arranged in *On Kingship to the King of Cyprus*, done into English by Gerard B. Phelan . . . revised . . . by I. Th. Eschmann, O.P. (Toronto, Canada 1949)]. The basic principles of Aquinas' theory of government, of which *De Regno* gives only a summary presentation, are elaborated in *Summa Theologica*, esp. the distinction between theological, moral, and intellectual virtues, I–II q. 62 aa. 1–2, and *Summa Contra Gentiles*, esp. the discussion of the ultimate happiness of man, iii. 37–41. Aquinas' central argument in favour of the two ministries is the following: '*If this end could be attained by the power of human nature, then the duty of a king would have to include the direction of man to it* . . . . But because a man does not attain his end, which is the possession of God, by human power but by divine—according to the words of the Apostle: "By the grace of God life everlasting" [Rom. 6: 23]—therefore the task of leading him to that last end does not pertain to human but to divine government.' *De Regno* ii. 3. (I. 14.) frag. 108 (Phelan-Eschmann).

contrary to the prescriptions of the Law but also to the principles of reason and political philosophy.

As a political regime, the regime of Law is superior to rational regimes at least in two respects. First, it is superior to them in the nature of the opinions and actions it prescribes. A regime that prescribes opinions about man's soul, God, and things beyond the senses, is evidently superior to regimes that restrict themselves to opinions about the well-being of man's body and the benefits of social life. Similarly, a regime that prescribes actions conducive to the well-being of the soul, in addition to the preservation of life and the well-being of the body, is superior to regimes that prescribe actions conducive to the preservation of life and the well-being of the body alone. Second, the regime of Law is superior to rational regimes in the type of coercion it employs: In rational regimes the conflict between man's rational judgment and his lower impulses is resolved by the threat of physical force; in the regime of Law it is resolved by moral or religious persuasion. In rational regimes, the lower impulses are forced to serve rational judgment by external restraint; in the regime of Law, the faithful believe in the Law and obey its commands out of inner conviction or a ' state of possession ' and act voluntarily.[1]

In all of its essential aspects—its end, the opinions and actions it prescribes, and its method of coercion—it could be shown rationally that the regime of Law is superior to rational regimes[2] and that it comes nearer to the virtuous city envisaged by philosophy.[3] This means that this superiority is not based merely on the conviction of the members of a regime of Law, but also on reason. Therefore, when Ibn Khaldûn says that with the coming of the Islamic Law, and during the short period when the Islamic regime of Law truly existed in the Islamic community, Muslims could dispense with rational regimes,[4] he is expressing, not only a legal opinion, but a rational judgment as well.

[1] *Q* I 346: 1, 351, 366, II 126: 19—127: 1. Cf. above pp. 89–90, 237–38, 267.

[2] Ibn Khaldûn has already mentioned that the regime of Law exists in temperate zones, and among people who have temperate dispositions. *Q* I 150, 152, 153–54.

[3] The regime of Law is, of course, definitely inferior to the virtuous city. It needs laws and magistrates, and its members are not as they ought to be in their character and conduct, to say nothing of the fact that philosophy does not supply its principles and does not rule in it. The Law is only an imperfect substitute for the government of the perfect ruler or living intelligence. Cf. Fârâbî *Madîna* 90, *Siyâsât* 50–51, *Nawâmîs* 41: 21–23; above p. 127 n. 1.

[4] *Q* II 127: 18.

Summary and Conclusion

1. Ibn Khaldûn was a student of Classical and Islamic philosophy. The biographical, stylistic, and doctrinal evidence introduced in this study establish this point beyond reasonable doubt. It has been shown, in particular, that he articulately, though cautiously, defended the philosophy of Plato and Aristotle against Neo-Platonism, atomism, and logical nominalism; and that his study of prophecy, the religious Law, and the character of the Islamic community, prove that he was a true disciple of the Islamic Platonic tradition of political philosophy. Ibn Khaldûn was also seriously concerned with history and the study of society. His reflections on history and his study of social life command the admiration of modern social scientists to the extent of claiming him as their true predecessor and the originator of their science. Yet, he did not find it either useful or necessary to reject traditional philosophy. How was it possible for Ibn Khaldûn to consciously integrate traditional philosophy in general, and traditional political philosophy in particular, with the scientific study of history and society?

Historically, the relation between political philosophy, and history and a science of society which concentrates on explaining the nature and causes of human things as they actually are, has been extremely obscure. One has only to remember the derogatory remarks of Aristotle and Cicero about history. Many historians are known to have been followers of traditional political philosophy, but none of them actually elucidates the proper relation between history and the knowledge of the actual conditions of society, and political philosophy. Their summary introductions and remarks may imply or point to, but do not offer, a definite answer. Finally, it is well known that in modern times the enhanced interest in history, and in man and society as they really are, did not result simply from the attempt to apply the standards established by traditional political philosophy, but from doubting the whole framework of that philosophy. What was questioned was not only the applicability of the rational standards of traditional political philosophy, but also the possibility of establishing them, their relevance for understanding the actual conditions of man and society, and their validity. All these changes in perspective resulted in narrowing the horizon of science to what actually exists, and in accepting as standards the ends which are found to be actually pursued by most societies or which are deemed easy to realize.

Ibn Khaldûn seems to be the only great thinker who not only saw the problems of the relation of history and the science of society to traditional political philosophy, but also attempted to develop a science of society within the framework of traditional philosophy and based on its principles. One can go even further and state that, according to Ibn Khaldûn, traditional philosophy demands the study of man and society as they really are, and supplies the framework for directing such a study and utilizing its results. Therefore, far from being incompatible with traditional philosophy, for Ibn Khaldûn the study of man and society as they really are is necessitated by traditional philosophy and completes it. This study attempted to show how Ibn Khaldûn arrived at this conclusion, and how it influenced his conception of the nature of history and the science of society.

2. Ibn Khaldûn started as a student of religious and philosophic sciences. He studied under the greatest teacher of philosophy in North Africa, and his early works include numerous commentaries on Averroes. Although a profound student of Aristotle, Averroes, like his Muslim predecessors, followed Plato's political philosophy and actually wrote a paraphrase of Plato's *Republic*. Political philosophy was understood by Muslim philosophers to be a practical science. They called it 'the ordering of the city' (*tadbîr al-madîna*) or 'the ways of ordering political matters' (*siyâsât madaniyya*). Unlike physics or mathematics, it is not primarily a systematized body of theories or conclusions, but like medicine and sea-faring an art or a skill—it is the art of ordering a community of men. To excel in this art, i.e., to possess the practical wisdom necessary for ordering and guiding a political community, three things are required:

First and foremost, it is necessary to know the goal or the end to which the community must be guided. This goal need not be the best regime or the virtuous city (*madîna fâḍila*); it may be the second best or the third best, but it is important to know what the best regime is because it is the standard by which all other regimes must be judged. A statesman who pretends to guide a political community without even a glimpse of the perfect political order is like a physician who pretends to heal a sick man without even a vague idea of what perfect health is.

Second, it is necessary to know the actual conditions of the political community in which the statesman is to exercise his political art. Even if it were possible to know the perfect regime without an accurate knowledge of existing regimes, no statesman could guide his community toward it without first having dispassionately analysed and known the actual nature of his community and the forces that are moving it. For a statesman does not rule in a hypothetical, but in a particular community with particular problems, and he acts in specific and unique circumstances. Like a physician who must know the disease he intends to cure, the statesman must know, as profoundly as he can, the diseases of his community. An indispensable part of such knowledge is judging his community by the standards furnished by the best regime. The statesman who abstains from such judgment and declares himself ' neutral ' about what is good or bad, noble or ignoble, is like the physician who abstains from calling a disease a disease and declares himself neutral about sickness and health.

Thirdly, excellence in the art of ruling comes through experience in ruling. Like all other arts, it is acquired through practical experience. We do not call a man a skilled physician simply because he knows the nature of health and a few diseases. We judge a physician by his ability to heal the sick, a skill he acquires by practising his art. Similarly, an excellent statesman is he who through actual experience in the art of ruling has acquired the prudence or practical wisdom of deciding what is best under particular circumstances.

Early in his life, Ibn Khaldûn engaged actively in political affairs and showed an intense interest in revolutionary change in North Africa and Muslim Spain, a region where political confusion and decline in all aspects of life reigned unchecked. He was successively an advisor to the ruler of Morocco, a teacher who tried to impart philosophy to the ruler of Granada, and prime minister in Bijâya. These efforts ended in complete failure. Political philosophy had taught him the goal, but he failed to guide his community toward it because he lacked sufficient knowledge of the actual conditions and particular circumstances which he was trying to change. He identified that knowledge with history. Consequently, he turned to the study of the contemporary history of his region in order to understand what caused his failure.

There is absolutely no indication that Ibn Khaldûn turned from political philosophy to history because he doubted the validity of its standards, their effectiveness as such, or their value. Nowhere does he even hint that he expected history to replace political philosophy and supply him new and more effective goals of political life. Ibn Khaldûn's turning to history does not, therefore, indicate a *break* with political philosophy. It simply means he recognized that the realization of the standards already established by political philosophy requires knowledge of the actual circumstances in which they are to be realized. When studied for this purpose, history presupposes political philosophy. But in order to be of real value for the statesman, history must ascertain actual events and explain their specific nature and causes.

3. Ibn Khaldûn investigated the Islamic historical literature and found that no major historian had given an account of the history of North Africa and Muslim Spain in the thirteenth and fourteenth century. Personally and through informants he had collected valuable material for such a history, and he planned to write it himself. Writing a history meant for Ibn Khaldûn transferring isolated experiences and information into an intelligible whole. Relevant facts had to be first collected and verified. Otherwise the historian would be explaining fabrications of mythographers and prejudiced informants which are of little use to posterity and the man of action. But they must also be organized to reveal their nature and causes, and the lessons they can teach the man of action. A written history is a work of the mind through which the historian bequeaths to posterity not simply the facts but also his insights into their relationship, their meaning, and their value.

In order to perform his function, the historian will need various tools or subsidiary disciplines. Some of these depend on the nature of his material. Thus, a Muslim historian whose sources were for the most part transmitted orally, had to know the character and reliability of his informants. But regardless of the type of his material, the historian needs a systematically organized body of rational knowledge of the nature and causes of actual events in general, or of human culture (*'umrân*), by which Ibn Khaldûn meant the totality of conventionalized social habits, institutions, and arts. For according to Ibn Khaldûn, the selection, organization, and understanding of the events of history presuppose a theory of culture; and the implicit adoption of such a theory is more liable to lead to error in judgment than when it is explicitly formulated and examined. Ibn Khaldûn investigated all the sciences known to him, both religious and rational, and found that none of them could claim to have studied the nature and causes of human culture rationally and systematically. To be sure, some of the practical rational sciences, like political philosophy and rhetoric, and some of the religious practical sciences such as jurisprudence, had studied problems similar to the problems Ibn Khaldûn intended to investigate, but only incidentally since the end of political philosophy is the ordering of the city according to the requirements of philosophy, the end of rhetoric is swaying the multitude toward accepting or rejecting an opinion, and the end of jurisprudence is applying the prescription of the Law. Therefore, Ibn Khaldûn felt that he had to construct a new science to deal specifically with the nature and causes of human culture, in preparation for the writing of an adequate history of his time and region.

The rank of the new science of culture is clearly defined by Ibn Khaldûn: it is a tool for understanding and writing history. Since history is a practical art needed for the acquisition of excellence in the art of ruling, the ultimate end of the science of culture is to assist in the preparation of the history useful for the statesman. It thus belongs to that part of political philosophy concerned with understanding the particular circumstances in which the statesman must act. Although its object differs from that of political philosophy in that it restricts itself to the understanding of actual events, it is compatible with political philosophy and seems to be required by it. For the science of culture contributes to a sound knowledge of historical events which is necessary for guiding a political community.

But if the new science is so useful for political philosophy, why did not the ancients or the Greeks, who originated political philosophy, develop this science? Ibn Khaldûn, who of course raises this question, answers it as follows: The ancients judged the value of a science by its end or ' fruits '. When considered from this point of view, the value of the new science is ' feeble ' and not particularly noble. Therefore, the ancients did not concern themselves with it. He is thus aware that when considered philosophically, i.e., from a standpoint which compares the relative merits of the various sciences, the end of the new science—which is the understanding of actual events—is decidedly lower than many other sciences. Though definitely useful, the new discipline is not of paramount importance for acquiring excellence in the art of ruling. Since we saw that an excellent ruler needs to know the actual circumstances of his community, and therefore definitely needs a knowledge of its history, Ibn Khaldûn is also suggesting that a statesman with superior intelligence may be able to know the actual conditions of his community—may be able to grasp intuitively the nature and causes of the events around him—without the help of an elaborate discipline like the science of culture. Similarly, a historian of superior intelligence may be able to see the relationship among events and grasp their meaning without previous training in the science of culture. Finally, the nature and causes of the events of certain times and nations may be apparent and not in need of articulate formulation. This may have been the case of fifth-century Athens, and, therefore, the ancients did not feel the need for elaborating a science of culture to assist them in understanding their history.

However this may be, one thing is sufficiently clear. Ibn Khaldûn did not think that the new science was of supreme importance. And there might be times and places in which it was not even necessary. This was not the case in North Africa and Muslim Spain during his lifetime. The decline of the region was an apparent reality, but not the causes of that decline. To understand them, it was necessary to penetrate behind the external events of history and this required the science of culture. It is also clear that Ibn Khaldûn investigated the nature of culture for the explicit purpose of understanding and writing history, and that he turned to history because of its usefulness for political action. This has more than biographical significance.

It is true that as a rational science aiming at the explanation of the nature and cause of actual events, the science of culture is a universal and all-comprehensive science. Its material must be drawn from all known events; for it would be as absurd to have a science of culture based on the events taking place in North Africa and Muslim Spain in the fourteenth century as to have a zoology based on the animals of fourteenth-century North Africa and Muslim Spain alone. Consequently, Ibn Khaldûn abandoned his early plan for writing a contemporary history of this region in favour of a universal history. Further, the science of culture must study all aspects of social life and ascertain their intrinsic importance regardless of their immediate practical relevance. This may be called the theoretical aim of the science of culture. But for Ibn Khaldûn the science of culture is primarily a practical and not a theoretical science; it is a science in which theory is subordinated to practice. For its ultimate aim is to explain the factors that resist or prevent guiding actual communities in the direction of the best regime, and more specifically to explain the cause of the decline of his region, what prevented him from guiding his community in the direction of the best regime or the causes of his failure as a statesman, and to assist him in acting more prudently in the future. Ibn Khaldûn may not repeat this purpose on every page, and he is certainly not obsessed by it. He does not allow it to becloud his understanding or narrow his perspective. Yet it underlies the whole science and explains many of its characteristic features.

The main characteristic of the new science is that it concentrates on the study and explanation of actual events. Whether this is possible at all, whether there can be a science of the actual and the imperfect, is of course a crucial problem, especially within the Platonic tradition of political philosophy. Ibn Khaldûn thought that it was possible, and in this he was more of an Aristotelian than his Muslim predecessors. Furthermore, the new science emphasizes certain problems, certain aspects of the scientific method of investigation, and certain scientific principles:

A. Problems which had not previously received sufficient

attention from the practical sciences are given a prominent position in the science of culture. Thus, Ibn Khaldûn pays considerable attention to the influence of the environment on social life; to the relation of the climate, vegetation, and the fertility of the land, to the character and development of social institutions; to the basic needs and desires of man; and to the ways in which men earn their living.

B. Ibn Khaldûn pays considerable attention to the investigation of the origin and development of society, and to the primitive forms of social life, in the belief that they explain the necessary and permanent needs and desires of man. His investigation of how man lived at the beginning is not completely dominated by the principle of finality. Indeed, he does show that primitive culture is incomplete, and manifests a tendency to develop into the complete and more perfect community which he calls civilized. But he attempts also to show the nature of primitive culture, the elements which predominate in it (such as extreme environmental conditions, the desire for war, and tribal sentiments) and which may prevent the emergence of civilized culture and its more advanced forms of social institutions.

C. Finally, certain principles which were always known to be predominant in most societies, but which were not emphasized in the practical sciences because they were not considered particularly noble, or important with respect to man's perfection, receive considerable attention. Ibn Khaldûn emphasizes the material needs of most men, and the physical and psychological desires which compel them to act in certain ways and determine their social habits. He also emphasizes the conditions necessary for realizing man's ends and whose absence limits or prevents the actualization of what man desires. This emphasis on the material and efficient causes does not of course mean that Ibn Khaldûn ignores the formal and final causes. It is clear, however, that he pays less attention to the latter and that his summary treatment of them in the science of culture is always limited to their concrete manifestations: he is always interested in the forms of social life that have actually existed and not in the best form of society, and he is always interested in the ends of man which have been actually realized in known history and not in the ultimate end of man regardless of its actual existence.

The predominance of these features gives Ibn Khaldûn's science of culture a semblance of modernity. He is intensely interested in explaining actual events, in observing their relationship, in explaining their trends, and in analysing their regularity, with an extraordinary restraint and objectivity. He is interested in learning how most men live, their hopes and desires, their limitations and failings; and how societies develop and change, and rise and decline. To that extent Ibn Khaldûn resembles many a modern thinker. But we would be committing a grave error if we conclude from this resemblance that the *philosophic foundation* of Ibn Khaldûn's science of culture is that of modern social science. Ibn Khaldûn believed that the knowledge of the actual state of society demands an empirical method through which data must be gathered and organized. But he was not an empiricist. He did not believe that the nature and causes of things are mental constructions which have no ontological foundation. He believed that the understanding of the origins and various stages of social life could explain the existential character of certain habits and conventions, and even certain opinions. But he was not a historicist. He did not believe that the stages of development of a given society or the prevalent opinions in it offer a complete explanation of its institutions, artistic production, or way of life. He believed that physical, geographic, biological, psychological, and social factors determine, as conditions or by compulsion, the development and character of culture. But he was not a determinist. He did not believe that all of social life is governed by law, that all aspects of culture need be morphologically determined, or that all human decisions are determined by objective circumstances. He believed that disciplined reflection could reveal certain tendencies and regularities in social development. But he was not a positivist. He did not believe that reason is incapable of explaining the causes of these tendencies and regularities with reference to the nature of man and his perfection. He believed that the science of culture was, ultimately, a practical science. But he was not a pragmatist. He did not believe that success is the sole criterion of truth, or that man's concern with action exhausts the horizon of his knowledge and judgment. He believed in the necessity of knowing what man and society really are, and how they exist in fact. But he did not believe that such knowledge is possible without ' value-judgment ', or without knowing the true end of man and society as well as the degrees of their perfection. For only through such knowledge could he measure the actual, know and judge the degree of its imperfection, point out the factors that impede or prevent the actualization of the end of man and the best society, explain what measure of perfection is possible under various conditions, explain how far and in what directions these conditions must be changed in order to realize a higher degree of perfection, and explain under what conditions change for the better is impossible and need not be attempted by a prudent man.

4. Soon after Ibn Khaldûn completed his work on the new science of culture, he started to write his universal history. This is a clear indication that his original intention, which was to write a history, had not changed. He had turned to the science of culture because he thought it was a necessary tool for the writing of the contemplated history. The character and the structure of the new science was directed to, and largely determined by, this immediate purpose. And what is more important, the new science is actually utilized by Ibn Khaldûn in the writing of history. The subordination of the science of culture to history is thus demonstrated not only by words, but also by action; for Ibn Khaldûn spent the last three decades of his life writing a history. The study and understanding of history remains, then, essential for Ibn Khaldûn. The science of culture does not replace history or diminish its importance. The science of culture does not fulfil the functions previously fulfilled by history. The understanding of the general nature and causes of historical events is clearly subordinated to, and made to serve, the understanding of concrete events.

What this means becomes apparent if we consider the reason why Ibn Khaldûn turned to history and what he expected from it. He was concerned with guiding his community in the direction of the goal established by political philosophy. He had failed because he lacked the necessary knowledge of the particular circumstances in which he had to act. No science could supply this knowledge, for by definition a science cannot explain the specific and accidental causes of particular events. Only history can teach the man of action how others have acted in particular circumstances, the choices they made, and their success or failure. Only history can explain the particular causes of particular events, and whether particular choices and decisions were good or bad, well- or ill-done. Ibn Khaldûn turned to history to learn what prevents or impedes the realization of the common good. Only history could teach him how and why the realization of the common good has been prevented or impeded in particular circumstances. Ibn Khaldûn turned to history to understand the causes, the extent, and the direction of the decline of his region during his lifetime. Only history could ascertain what has happened or what is happening in particular times and places. Finally, he turned to history to assist him in acting more prudently and wisely. Only history could assist the man of action in seeing what alternative choices are open to him and what are the limits beyond which a prudent man should not hope to seek their realization. None of these could have been done by the science of culture; for it is history and not the science of culture which is most immediately related to political action.

5. This must not lead us, however, to exaggerate the value of history for Ibn Khaldûn. What he expected from history does not go beyond assisting him in applying the standards and goals he had already learned from political philosophy. Thus, Ibn Khaldûn's interest in application does not lead to abandoning or lowering his standards and goal. On the contrary, it seems that precisely because he was not ready to compromise his standards and goal, because he was not willing to follow the standards of his community or any other standard simply because it was easy to apply, he turned to history to learn how and to what extent he could apply the immutable standards which transcend history and which he knew to be difficult if not impossible to realize.

And so Ibn Khaldûn presents us with the continuing tension between the trans-historical standards and goals of political philosophy, and the imperfect standards and goals that are pursued in actual communities. Reflecting on his political activity in a letter which he wrote to his friend the vizir of Granada, Ibn Khaldûn described his hopes and his urge to reform his community as an ' incurable disease ' from which he could not free himself. It is true that his study of the nature of history and culture led him to realize the futility of his attempts in North Africa and Muslim Spain. He migrated to Egypt where conditions were more stable and where he could pursue his scholarly interests in peace. But his urge for action and his desire to confront his community with nobler standards than those it practised continued. Like Averroes, he assumed the office of judge. The Egyptians criticized him for his severity and his disregard for their conventions. But for Ibn Khaldûn, the new office meant upholding the divine Law, and reminding the community of its duties toward God. The Islamic community might not be able to realize the best regime, but it professed belief in a divine regime legislated by the Prophet. Ibn Khaldûn saw to it that it paid more than lip service to his Law.

Ibn Khaldûn did not turn to history to find his standards and goal, or to see how the Idea progressively realizes itself and learn its future course so that he could join the predetermined course of history. For him, future action cannot be determined by any science. It continues to be the product of an art which requires the knowledge of the end of man and society, and the knowledge of the actual circumstances supplied by history, but which must be perfected through experience. Having equipped himself with such knowledge, it remains the responsibility of the wise man to decide what is best under particular circumstances. He is not relieved of the task of making right choices. History, even when ascertained and explained in the light of the new science of culture, may help the wise man to make a better choice, but it does not and cannot choose for him.

Bibliography

The following list is composed of three sections:

1. Ibn Khaldûn's works.
2. Other primary Arabic sources.
3. Journals, Encyclopædias, and other reference works.

1. The complete and partial editions of Ibn Khaldûn's main work, the ' History ' (*Kitâb al-'ibar*), and the manuscript of his early work, the *Gist of the Compendium* (*Lubâb al-muḥaṣṣal*),[1] are arranged alphabetically according to the letter or letters by which they are abbreviated in the footnotes. We still do not have an *édition définitive* of all parts of the ' History '. *Bq*, which is the only complete edition, is inadequate; and apart from Volumes III, IV, V, of which there is no other edition, it was not used except for collation with the better partial editions *B*, *Ċ*, *Q*, *T*, and *TT*.[2]

2. The editions and manuscripts in this section are arranged alphabetically according to the name or surname by which their authors have been most widely known. Under each author, his works are again arranged alphabetically according to the abbreviated forms used in the footnotes. These are usually the forms in which these

[1] References to the unique MS can be easily located in the text of P. Luciano Rubio's edition (Tetuan 1952) which was received after the completion of this study.

[2] *Q* is now available in a complete English translation: Ibn Khaldûn, *The Muqaddimah—an Introduction to History*, trans. Franz Rosenthal [' Bollingen Series,' XLIII] (3 vols; New York 1958). It reproduces the original pagination of *Q* in the margin. Ṭanjî's edition of the text of *Q* has not appeared as yet (1964). Ibn Khaldûn's work on mysticism has been published: *Shifâ' al-sâ'il li-tahdhîb al-masâ'il*, ed. M. Ibn Tâwît al-Ṭanjî ['Ankara Üniversitesi Ilâhiyat Fakültesi Yayinlari,' XXII] (Istanbul 1958). The editor suggests that the work was written between 774 and 776 A.H. (see above pp. 44–48) or that it antedates the ' History ' (cf. above p. 107 n. 1). A comprehensive bibliographical work on Ibn Khaldûn has recently appeared in conjunction with a celebration held in Cairo (January 2–6, 1962; the speeches delivered on that occasion were published in *A'mâl mahrajân Ibn Khaldûn* [Cairo 1962]): 'Abdurraḥmân Badawî, *Mu'allafât Ibn Khaldûn* (Cairo 1962). It includes a useful collection of Arabic source material (pp. 241–313) about Ibn Khaldûn. Finally, another of Ibn Khaldûn's early works has been located in Fez. (Ṣalâḥ al-Dîn al-Munajjid, ' Nawâdir al-Makhṭûṭât fî al-Maghrib,' *Revue de l'Institut des Manuscrits Arabes*, V [1959] 167 [No. 88], see also 178 [No. 50]; cf. *ibid.* IV [1958] 355.) It is in the library of the Qarawiyyîn mosque and appears to be Ibn Khaldûn's commentary on Ibn al-Khaṭîb's didactic poem on the fundamentals of jurisprudence (above p. 35 n. 5 [No. 6]).

works are cited in classical Arabic literature. Each abbreviated form is followed by the complete title, and usually the subtitle(s) also. Whenever an editor supplies a translation of a title into a west-European language, it is given in parentheses. Further bibliographical data about the works cited, and biographical data about their authors, can be easily located in *GAL* through the use of the title index in *GAL*(*S*) III.

3. The entries in this section include only the items abbreviated in the footnotes by the use of letters. Bibliographical data about reference works not abbreviated, about secondary sources (including those in Oriental languages), and about Classical and Medieval Western texts for which no standard form of reference has been devised, are to be found in the places where they are first mentioned in the footnotes.

I

Ibn Khaldûn's Works

B — *Kitâb al-duwal al-islâmiyya bi-l-maghrib* (Histoire des Berbères et des dynasties musulmanes de l'Afrique Septentrionale), ed. William MacGuckin baron de Slane (2 vols.; Alger 1847–51). The two volumes correspond to *Bq* VI–VII.

Bq — *Kitâb al-ʿibar wa-dîwân al-mubtadaʾ wa-l-khabar fî ayyâm al-ʿarab wa-l-ʿajam wa-l-barbar wa-man ʿâṣarahum min dhawî al-sulṭân al-akbar*, ed. Naṣr al-Hûrînî (7 vols.; Bûlâq [1284/1867]).

C — *Kitâb al-ʿibar*, eds. ʿAlâl al-Fâsî and ʿAbd al-ʿAzîz Ibn Idrîs (2 vols.; Cairo 1355/1936). The two volumes correspond to *Bq* II.

L — *Lubâb al-muḥaṣṣal fî uṣûl al-dîn*, MS Escurial (cf. H. Derenbourg and É. Lévi-Provençal *Les manuscrits arabes de l'Escurial* III [Paris 1928] 163 [No. 1614]).

Q — *Muqaddimat Ibn Khaldûn* (Prolégomènes d'Ebn-Khaldoun), ed. É. M. Quatremère ['Notice et extraits des manuscrits de la Bibliothèque du Roi et autres bibliothèques, publiés par l'Institut Impérial de France.' t. 16–18, premières parties; also 'Tirage à part des . . .'] (Paris 1858). The three volumes correspond to *Bq* I.

T — *al-Ta'rîf bi-Ibn Khaldûn wa-riḥlatuhu gharban wa-sharqan*, ed. Muḥammad Ibn Tâwît al-Ṭanjî [' Âthâr Ibn Khaldûn ', Vol. I] (Cairo 1370/1951).

TT — *Tercümei Mukaddimei Ibni Haldûn*, trans. Perizade, eds. Elhac Abdurrahman Hâfiz Efendi and Muharrem Hâfiz Efendi (Cairo 1275 A.H.). The volume corresponds to *Bq* I. The Turkish translation of Perizade ends on p. 522 (corresponding to *Q* III 14). The rest is in the Arabic original.

II

Other Primary Arabic Sources

Akfânî, [Ibn] al- (d. 1348):

Irshâd — *Irshâd al-qâṣid ilâ asnâ al-maqâṣid*, ed. A. Sprenger, in *Two Works on Arabic Bibliography* [' Bibliotheca Indica ', Vol. VI [Fasciculus I] No. 21] (Calcutta 1849) 14–99.

Aristotle (d. 322 B.C.):

Manṭiq — *Manṭiq arisṭû*, ed. 'Abd al-Raḥmân Badawî (5 vols.; Cairo 1948——).

Shi'r — *Kitâb arisṭûṭâlîs fî al-shi'r*, in J. Tkatsch *Die arabische Übersetzung der Poetik des Aristoteles und die Grundlage der Kritik des griechischen Textes* (2 vols.; Wien and Leipzig 1928–32) I 220–82.

pseudo-Aristotle:

Siyâsa — *Kitâb al-siyâsa fî tadbîr al-riyâsa.* MS British Museum (cf. C. Rieu *Supplement to the Catalogue of the Arabic Manuscripts in the British Museum* [London 1894] 503 [No. 739]).

Uthûlûjiyâ — *Kitâb uthûlûjiyâ arisṭûṭâlîs* (Die sogenannte Theologie des Aristoteles), ed. Fr. Dieterici (Leipzig 1882).

Arisṭûṭâlîs, see Aristotle, pseudo-Aristotle.

Avempace, see Ibn Bâjja.

Averroes (d. 1198):

Faṣl — *Faṣl al-maqâl wa-taqrîr mâ bayn al-sharî'a wa-l-ḥikma min al-ittiṣâl* (Traité décisif sur l'accord de la religion et de la philososophie), ed. L. Gauthier [' Bibliothèque arabe-française ', 1] (3rd ed.; Alger 1948).

j. Mâ ba'd al-ṭabî'a — *Kitâb jâmi' mâ ba'd al-ṭabî'a* (Compendio de Metafisica), ed. C. Rodríguez (Madrid 1919).

Manâhij — *Kitâb al-kashf 'an manâhij al-adilla fî 'aqâ'id al-milla wa-ta'rîf mâ waqa'a fîhâ bi-ḥasab al-ta'wîl min al-shubah al-muzîgha wa-l-bida' al-muḍilla*, in *Thalâth rasâ'il* 27–128.

Nafs — *Kitâb al-nafs* (Hayderabad 1366/1947).

Tahâfut — *Tahâfut al-tahâfut* (Incohérence de l'Incohérence), ed. M. Bouyges [' Bibliotheca arabica scholasticorum, série arabe ', t. III] (Beirut 1930).

Thalâth rasâ'il — *Thalâth rasâ'il* (Philosophie und Theologie), ed. M. J. Müller [' Königlich-Bayerische Akademie der Wissenschaften: Monumenta Saecularia ', I. Classe [No.] 3.] (München 1859).

t. Mâ ba'd al-ṭabî'a — *Tafsîr mâ ba'd al-ṭabî'a* (Grand Commentaire de la Metaphysique d'Aristote), ed. M. Bouyges [' Bibliotheca arabica scholasticorum, série arabe ', t. V–VII] (3 vols.; Beirut 1938–48).

t. Nafs — *Talkhîṣ kitâb al-nafs* (Paraphrase du ' De anima '), ed. A. el-Ahwanî (Cairo 1950).

Avicenna (d. 1037):

Ajrâm — *Fî al-ajrâm al-'ulawiyya*, in *Tis' rasâ'il* 39–59.

Aqsâm — *Fî aqsâm al-'ulûm al-'aqliyya*, in *Tis' rasâ'il* 104–119.

Ḥudûd — *Fî al-ḥudûd*, in *Tis' rasâ'il* 72–102.

Ishârât — *Kitâb al-ishârât wa-l-tanbîhât* (Le livre de théoremès et des avertissements), ed. J. Forget (Leyde 1892).

Najât — *al-Najât* (Cairo 1331/1912).

Nubuwwât — *Fî ithbât al-nubuwwât wa-ta'wîl rumûzihim*, in *Tis' rasâ'il* 120–32.

Qiwâ — *Fî al-qiwâ al-insâniyya wa-idrâkâtihâ*, in *Tis' rasâ'il* 60–70.

Sa'âda — *Risâla fî al-sa'âda wa-l-ḥujaj al-'ashra*, in *Majmû' rasâ'il al-shaykh al-ra'îs*, No. 5 (Hayderabad 1353 A.H.).

Shifâ' — *al-Shifâ'*. MS Leiden, No. 1445. Numbers indicate the part, section, sub-section, and chapter (*jumla, fann, maqâla, faṣl*). Cf. M.–M. Anawati *Mu'allafât Ibn Sînâ* (Essai de bibliographie Avicennienne) (Cairo 1950) 30 ff., 76: 14–15.

Ṭabî'iyyât — *al-Ṭabî'iyyât min 'uyûn al-ḥikma*, in *Tis' rasâ'il* 2–38.

Tis' rasâ'il — *Tis' rasâ'il fî al-ḥikma wa-l-ṭabî'iyyât* (Cairo 1326/1908).

Baghdâdî, Ibn Ṭâhir al- (d. 1037):

Uṣûl — *Kitâb uṣûl al-dîn* (Constantinople 1346/1928——).

Bakrî, Abû 'Ubayd al- (d. 1094):

Masâlik — *al-Masâlik wa-l-mamâlik* (Description de l'Afrique Septentrionale), ed. William MacGuckin baron de Slane (2d ed.; Alger 1911).

Balâdhurî, al- (d. 892):

Futûḥ — *Kitâb futûḥ al-buldân* (Liber expugnationis regionum), ed. M. J. de Goeje (Lugduni Batavorum 1866).

Bayḍâwî, al- (d. *ca.* 1315):

Anwâr — *Anwâr al-tanzîl wa-asrâr al-ta'wîl* (Commentarius in Coranum), ed. H. O. Fleischer (2 vols.; Lipsiae 1846–48).

Bayhaqî, al- (d. 1169):

Ta'rîkh — *Ta'rîkh ḥukamâ' al-islâm*, ed. Muḥammad Kurd 'Alî (Damascus 1365/1946).

Bîrûnî, al- (d. 1048):

Âthâr — *al-Âthâr al-bâqiya* (Chronologie orientalischer Völker), ed. Ed. Sachau (Leipzig 1878).

Hind — *Ta'rîkh al-hind* (Alberuni's India), ed. Ed. Sachau (London 1887).

Dimashqî, Ja'far Ibn 'Alî al- (*fl.* 12th–14th c):

Maḥâsin — *Kitâb al-ishâra ilâ maḥâsin al-tijâra* ([Cairo] 1318/[1900]).

Fârâbî, al- (d. 950):

Aflâṭun — *Falsafat aflâṭun* (De Platonis philosophia), ed. F. Rosenthal and R. Walzer [' Corpus Platonicum Medii Aevi, Plato Arabus ', v. 2] (Londinii 1943).

'Aql — *Maqâla fî ma'ânî al-'aql* (Der Intellect), in *Rasâ'il* 39–48.

Iḥṣâ' — *Iḥṣâ' al-'ulûm* (La statistique des sciences), ed. Osman Amine (2nd ed.; Cairo 1949).

Jam' — *Kitâb al-jam' bayn ra'yay al-ḥakîmayn aflâṭûn al-ilâhî wa-arisṭûṭâlîs* (Die Harmonie zwischen Plato und Aristoteles), in *Rasâ'il* 1–34.

Madîna — *Kitâb ârâ' ahl al-madîna al-fâḍila*, ed. 'Îd ['Abd] al-Waṣîf Muḥammad al-Kurdî (2d ed.; Cairo 1368/1948).

Milla — *al-Milla al-fâḍila*. MS Leiden (cf. R. Dozy *et al. Catalogus codicum orientalium Bibliothecae Academiae Lugdono Batavae* [Lugduni Batavorum 1851–77] No. 1931).

Nawâmîs — *Talkhîṣ nawâmîs aflâṭûn* (Compendium Legum Platonis), ed. F. Gabrieli [' Corpus Platonicum Medii Aevi, Plato Arabus ', v. 3] (Londinii 1952).

Rasâ'il — *al-Thamara al-marḍiyya fî ba'ḍ al-risâlât al-fârâbiyya* (Philosophische Abhandlungen), ed. Fr. Dieterici (Leiden [1890]).

Siyâsât — *Kitâb al-siyâsât al-madaniyya* (Hayderabad 1346 A.H.).

Ta'allum — *Risâla fî mâ yanbaghî an yuqaddam qabl ta'allum al-falsafa* (Die Vorstudien zur Philosophie), in *Rasâ'il* 49–55.

Taḥṣîl — *Kitâb taḥṣîl al-sa'âda* (Hayderabad 1345 A.H.).

Ta'lîqât — *al-Ta'lîqât* (Hayderabad 1346 A.H.).

Tanbîh — *Kitâb al-tanbîh 'alâ sabîl al-sa'âda* (Hayderabad 1346 A.H.).

'Ulûm — *Risâla fî faḍîlat al-'ulûm wa-l-ṣinâ'ât* (2d ed.; Hayderabad 1367/1948).

Zaynûn — *Sharḥ risâlat Zaynûn al-kabîr al-yûnânî* (Hayderabad 1349 A.H.).

Ghazâlî, al- (d. 1111):

Iḥyâ' — *Iḥyâ' 'ulûm al-dîn* (15 vols.; Cairo 1356/[1937]–1357/[1938]).

Maḍnûn ṣaghîr — *Kitâb al-maḍnûn al-ṣaghîr*. On the margin of 'Abd al-Karîm Ibn Ibrâhîm al-Jîlânî *al-Insân al-kâmil fî ma'rifat al-awâkhir wa-l-awâ'il* II (1368/1949) 89–98.

Tahâfut — *Tahâfut al-falâsifa* (Incohérence des Philosophes), ed. M. Bouyges [' Bibliotheca arabica scholasticorum, série arabe ', t. II] (Beirut 1927).

Hajji Khalîfa (d. 1657):

Kashf — *Kashf al-ẓunûn* (Lexicon bibliographicum et encyclopaedicum), ed. Gustavus Fluegel [' Oriental translation fund of Great Britain and Ireland ', No. 42] (7 vols.; London 1835–58).

Hallevi, Judah ben Samuel (*fl.* 12th c):

Khazarî — *Kitâb al-ḥujja wa-l-dalîl fî naṣr al-dîn al-dhalîl* (Sefer ha-Kuzari, Das Buch al-Chazarî), ed. Hartwig Hirschfeld (Leipzig 1887).

Ibn Abî al-Rabî' (*fl. ca.* 1250):

Sulûk — *Kitâb sulûk al-mâlik fî tadbîr al-mamâlik*, ed. Muḥammad al-Samlûṭî (lith. [Cairo 1286 A.H.?]).

Ibn Abî Uṣaybi'a (d. 1270):

'Uyûn — *Kitâb 'uyûn al-anbâ' fî ṭabaqât al-aṭibbâ'*, ed. August Müller (2 vols.; Cairo and Königsberg 1299/1882, 1884).

Ibn al-Aḥmar (d. 1414):

Rawḍa — *Rawḍat al-nisrîn* (Histoire de Beni Merin, rois de Fâs), ed. G. Bouali and G. Marçais [' Publications de la Faculté des Lettres d'Alger. Bulletin de correspondance africaine ', t. 55] (Paris 1917).

Ibn al-Athîr (d. 1234):

Kâmil — *al-Kâmil fî al-ta'rîkh* (Chronicon quod perfectissimum inscribitur), ed. C. J. Tornberg (14 vols.; Lugduni Batavorum and Upsaliae 1851–76).

Ibn al-Furât (d. 1405):

Ta'rîkh — *Ta'rîkh al-duwal wa-l-mulûk* (The History of Ibn al-Furât), ed. Costi Zurayk and Nejla Izzedin [' American University of Beirut. Publications of the Faculty of Arts and Sciences. Oriental Series ', Nos. 9, 10, 14, 17] (3 vols.; Beirut 1936–42). Volume numbers refer to the series.

Ibn al-Khaṭîb (d. 1374):

Iḥâṭa — *al-Iḥâṭa fî akhbâr gharnâṭa* (2 vols.; Cairo 1319 [1901]).

Lamḥa *al-Lamḥa al-badriyya fî al-dawla al-naṣriyya*, ed. Muḥib al-Din al-Khaṭîb (Cairo 1347/[1938]).

Raqm *Kitâb raqm al-ḥulal fî naẓm al-duwal* (Tunis 1316/[1898]).

Ibn al-Qâḍî (d. 1616):

Durra *Durrat al-ḥijâl fî ghurrat asmâ' al-rijâl* (Répertoire biographique), ed. I. S. Allouche [' Institut des hautes-études marocaines. Collection de textes arabes ', Vol. IV] (Rabat 1934).

Ibn 'Arabshâh (d. 1450):

'Ajâ'ib *Kitâb 'ajâ'ib al-maqdûr fî akhbâr Tîmûr* (Ahmedis Arabsiadae vitae & rerum gestarum Timuri, qui vulgo Tamerlanes dicitur, historia), ed. Jacobus Golius (Lugduni Batavorum 1636).

Ibn Bâjja (d. 1138):

Tadbîr *Tadbîr al-mutawaḥḥid* (El régimen del solitario), ed. M. Asín Palacios (Madrid 1946).

Ibn Bassâm (d. *ca.* 1147):

Dhakhîra *al-Dhakhîra fî maḥâsin ahl al-jazîra* (vols. 1, 4; Cairo 1358/1939–1364/1945).

Ibn Durustawayh (d. 958):

Kuttâb *Kitâb al-kuttâb* (Le guide des écrivains), ed. L. Cheikho (2d ed.; Beirut 1927).

Ibn Ḥajar (d. 1449):

Durar *al-Durar al-kâmina fî a'yân al-mâ'a al-thâmina* (4 vols.; Hayderabad 1348/[1929]–1350/[1931]).

Ibn Ḥanbal (d. 855):

Musnad *al-Musnad*, ed. Aḥmad Muḥammad Shâkir (10 vols.; Cairo 1365/1946–1371/1951).

Ibn Ḥazm (d. 1064):

Faṣl *Kitâb al-faṣl fî al-milal wa-l-ahwâ' wa-l-niḥal.* On the margin of Shahrastânî *Milal.*

Jamhara *Jamharat ansâb al-'arab*, ed. É. Lévi-Provençal (Cairo 1948).

Ibn Maymûn, see Maimonides.

Ibn Rushd, see Averroes.

Ibn Sa'd (d. 845):

Ṭabaqât *Kitâb al-ṭabaqât al-kabîr* (Biographien Muhammeds), ed. E. Mittwoch *et al.* (9 vols.; Leiden 1904–40).

Ibn Sînâ, see Avicenna.

Ibn Taghrîbirdî (d. 1469):

Nujûm — *al-Nujûm al-zâhira fî mulûk miṣr wa-l-qâhira* (Annales), ed. W. Popper [' University of California Publications in Semitic Philology ' Vols. II, III No. 1, IV Nos. 1–4, VI Nos. 1–5, VII Nos. 1–4] (5 vols.; Berkeley, Calif. 1909–36). Volume numbers refer to the series.

Ibn Taymiyya (d. 1328):

Ma'ârij — *Kitâb ma'ârij al-wuṣûl ilâ ma'rifat anna uṣûl al-dîn wa-furû'ahu qad bayyanahâ al-rasûl* (Cairo 1323 A.H.).

Ibn Ṭufayl (d. 1185):

Ḥayy — *Risâlat Ḥayy Ibn Yaqẓân fî asrâr al-ḥikma al-mushriqiyya* (Roman philosophique), ed. L. Gauthier [' Institut d'études orientales de la Faculté des lettres d'Alger. [Publication,] ' III] (Beirut 1936).

Idrîsî, al-Sharîf al- (d. 1166):

Nuzha — [*min*] *Kitâb nuzhat al-mushtâq fî ikhtirâq al-âfâq* (L'Italia descritta nel ' Libro del re Ruggero '), eds. M. Amari and D. Schiaparelli (Roma 1883).

Îjî, al- (d. 1355):

Mawâqif — *al-Mawâqif* (8 vols.; Cairo 1325/1907).

Ikhwân al-Ṣafâ' (*fl. ca.* 1100):

Rasâ'il — *Rasâ'il Ikhwân al-Ṣafâ' wa-khillân al-wafâ'*, ed. Khayr al-Dîn al-Zarkalî (Cairo 1347/1928).

Jâḥiẓ, al- (d. 868):

Dalâ'il — *Kitâb al-dalâ'il wa-l-i'tibâr 'alâ al-khalq wa-l-tadbîr* (Aleppo 1346/1928).

Ma'âd — *Risâlat al-ma'âd wa-l-ma'âsh*, in *Majmû' rasâ'il* 1–36.

Majmû' rasâ'il — *Majmû' rasâ'il al-Jâḥiẓ*, ed. P. Kraus and Muḥammad Ṭâha al-Ḥâjirî (Cairo 1943).

Jurjânî, al- (d. 1413):

Ta'rîfât — *Kitâb al-ta'rîfât* (Cairo 1888).

Kâfîjî, al- (d. 1474):

Mukhtaṣar — *al-Mukhtaṣar fî 'ilm al-ta'rîkh* (Short Work on Historiography), ed. F. Rosenthal, in *A History of Muslim Historiography* (Leiden 1952) 468–501.

Kindî, al- (d. *ca.* 873):

Ḥudûd — *Risâlat al-Kindî fî ḥudûd al-ashyâ' wa-rusûmihâ* in *Rasâ'il* 163–79.

Rasâ'il — *Rasâ'il al-Kindî al-falsafiyya*, ed. Muḥammad 'Abd al-Hâdî Abû Rîda (Cairo 1369/1950).

Khwârizmî, al- (*fl. ca.* 975):

Mafâtîḥ — *Kitâb mafâtîḥ al-'ulûm* (Vocabula technica scientiarum), ed. G. Van Vloten (Lugduni-Batavorum 1895).

Lâwî, Abû al-Ḥasan al-, see Hallevi.

Maimonides (d. 1204):

Dalâla — *Dalâlat al-ḥâ'irîn* (Sefer Moreh nevukhim), ed. S. Munk (ed. and revised by Issachar Joël, Jerusalem 5691 *anno Hebraico*/[1931]).

Mas'ûdî, al- (d. *ca.* 956):

Murûj — *Murûj al-dhahab wa-ma'âdin al-jawhar* (Les prairies d'or), ed. C. Barbier de Meynard and Pavet de Courteille (9 vols.; Paris 1861–1917).

Tanbîh — *al-Tanbîh wa-l-ishrâf*, ed. 'Abd Allâh Ismâ'îl al-Ṣâwî (Cairo 1357/1938).

Maqqarî, al- (d. 1632):

Azhâr — *Azhâr al-riyâḍ fî akhbâr 'Iyâḍ* (3 vols.; Cairo 1358/1939–1361/1942).

Nafḥ — *Nafḥ al-ṭîb min ghuṣn al-andalus al-raṭîb wa-dhikr wazîrihâ Lisân al-Dîn Ibn al-Khaṭîb.* Vols. I–II (Analectes sur l'histoire et la littérature des Arabes d'Espagne), ed. R. Dozy *et al.* (Leyde 1855–61); Vols. III–IV (Cairo 1302–5 A.H.).

Maqrîzî, al- (d. 1442):

Khiṭaṭ — *Kitâb al-mawâ'iẓ wa-l-i'tibâr fî dhikr al-hkiṭaṭ wa-l-âthâr*, ed. M. Gaston Wiet [' Mémoire publiés par les membres de l'Institut français d'archeologie orientale du Caire ', t. XXX, XXXIII, XLVI, XLIX, LIII . . .] (Cairo 1911——).

Mâwardî, al- (d. 1058):

Aḥkâm — *Kitâb al-aḥkâm al-sulṭâniyya* (Constitutiones politicae), ed. Maximilian Enger (Bonnae 1853).

Miskawayhi, [Ibn] (d. 1030):

Tajârib — *Tajârib al-umam* (History). Reproduced in facsimile from MS at Constantinople in the Âyâ

Sûfiyya library, with a preface and summary by Leone Caetani [' E. J. W. Gibb Memorial series ', Vol. VII, 1, 5–6] (Leiden and London 1909–17).

Qifṭî, [Ibn] al- (d. 1248):
Ta'rîkh — *Ta'rîkh al-ḥukamâ'*, ed. A. Müller and J. Lippert (Leipzig 1903).

Qalqashandî, al- (d. 1418):
Ṣubḥ — *Kitâb ṣubḥ al-a'shâ fî ṣinâ'at al-inshâ'* (14 vols.; Cairo 1331/1913–1338/1919).

Râzî, al- (d. 1209):
Muḥaṣṣal — *Kitâb muḥaṣṣal afkâr al-mutaqaddimîn wa-l-muta'akhkhirîn min al-falâsifa wa-l-mutakallimîn* (Cairo 1323 A.H.).
Mabâḥith — *al-Mabâḥith al-mashriqiyya* (4 vols.; Hayderabad 1924–25).

Ṣafadî, al- (d. 1363):
Fawât — *Fawât al-wafayât* (Biographische Lexicon), ed. H. Ritter and S. Dedering [' Bibliotheca Islamica ', Bd. 6a, 6b] (2 vols.; Constantinople 1931–49).

Ṣâ'id, [Ibn Ṣâ'id] al-Qurṭubî (d. 1070):
Ṭabaqât — *Kitâb ṭabaqât al-umam* (Les catégories des nations), ed. L. Cheikho (Beirut 1912).

Sakhâwî, al- (d. 1497):
Ḍaw' — *al-Ḍaw' al-lâmi' li-ahl al-qarn al-tâsi'* (12 vols.; Cairo 1353/[1934]–1355/[1936]).
I'lân — *al-I'lân bi-l-tawbîkh li-man dhamma ahl al-tawârîkh* (Damascus 1349/[1930])=MS Leiden (cf. R. Dozy *et al. op. cit.* No. 746)=MS Berlin (cf. W. Ahlwardt *Verzeichnis der arabischen Handschriften der königlichen Bibliothek zu Berlin* [Berlin 1887–99] No. 9364).

Shahrastânî (d. 1153):
Milal — *Kitâb al-milal wa-l-niḥal* (5 vols.; Cairo 1317/[1899]–1321/[1903]).
Milal[2] — *al-Milal wa-l-niḥal*, ed. Aḥmad Fahmî Muḥammad (3 vols.; Cairo 1368/1948–49).

Subkî, al- (d. 1370):
Ṭabaqât — *Ṭabaqât al-shâfi'iyya al-kubrâ* (6 vols.; Cairo [1323/1905–1324/1906]).

Ṣûlî, al- (d. 946):

Adab — *Adab al-kuttâb*, ed. Muḥammad Bahjat al-Atharî and Maḥmûd Shukrî al-Âlûsî (Cairo 1341/1922).

Suyûṭî, al- (d. 1505):

Ḥusn — *Kitâb ḥusn al-muḥâḍara fî akhbâr miṣr wa-l-qâhira* (2 vols.; Cairo 1299/[1882]).

Ṭabarî (d. 923):

Ikhtilâf — *Kitâb ikhtilâf al-fuqahâ'*, ed. F. Kern (Cairo 1320/1902).

Tafsîr — *Jâmi' al-bayân fî tafsîr al-qur'ân* (30 vols.; Cairo [1321/1903]).

Ta'rîkh — *Ta'rîkh al-rusul wa-l-mulûk* (Annales), ed. M. J. de Goeje *et al.* (15 vols.; Lugduni Batavorum 1879–1901).

Tahânawî, al-Fârûqî, al- (d. *ca.* 1745):

Kashshâf — *Kashshâf iṣṭilâḥât al-funûn* (A Dictionary of the Technical Terms...), eds. Muḥammad Wajîh *et al.* [' Bibliotheca Indica . . . published by the Asiatic Society of Bengal. Old Series ', Vol. 17] ([Calcutta] 1853–62).

Ṭurṭûshî, al- (d. *ca.* 1126):

Sirâj — *Sirâj al-mulûk* (Cairo 1306/[1888]).

Ṭusî, Naṣîr al-Dîn al- (d. 1274):

Talkhîṣ — *Kitâb talkhîṣ al-muḥaṣṣal.* Printed as footnotes to Râzî *Muḥaṣṣal.*

Yâqût (d. 1229):

Irshâd — *Irshâd al-arîb ilâ ma'rifat al-adîb* (Dictionary of Learned Men), ed. D. S. Margoliouth [' E. J. W. Gibb Memorial series ', Vol. VI, 1–7] (7 vols.; Cairo and Leyden 1907–27).

Zabîdî, Sayyid Murtaḍâ al- (d. 1791):

Tâj — *Tâj al-'arûs* (10 vols.; Cairo 1307/[1889]–1308/[1890]).

III

Journals, Encyclopaedias, and Other Reference Works

BIFAO — *Bulletin de l'Institut français d'archéologie orientale* (Cairo 1901——).

BSOS — *Bulletin of the School of Oriental and African Studies* (London 1917——).

CEH — *The Cambridge Economic History of Europe from the Decline of the Roman Empire*, eds. J. H. Clapham and Eileen Power (Cambridge [England] 1941——).

CMH — *The Cambridge Medieval History*, eds. H. M. Gwatkin *et al.* (8 vols.; Cambridge, England 1924–36).

EI — *The Encyclopedia of Islam*, eds. M. Th. Houtsma *et al.* (4 vols.; Leyden 1913–34).

EI(S) — *Ibid. Supplement* (Leiden 1938).

ERE — *Encyclopedia of Religion and Ethics*, ed. J. Hastings (12 vols.; New York 1908–22).

GAL — Brockelmann, Carl. *Geschichte der arabischen Litteratur* (2 vols.; Weimar 1898–1902). The pagination of this edition is reproduced in the text of *GAL(S)* (below) and on the margin of *GAL(S^2)* (below). General references to *GAL* are intended to cover this original edition as well as the supplements.

GAL(S) — *Ibid. Supplementbände* (3 vols.; Leiden 1937–42).

GAL(S^2) — *Ibid. Zweite den Supplementbänden angepasste Auflage* (2 vols.; Leiden 1943–49).

IC — *Islamic Culture* (Hayderabad, Deccan 1927——).

IHS — George Sarton *Introduction to the History of Science* [' Carnegie Institution of Washington ', Publication No. 376] (3 vols.; Baltimore 1927–48).

JA — *Journal asiatique* (Paris 1822——). Capital Roman numerals refer to the number of the series; lower-case Roman numerals to the volumes within the series.

JRAS — *Journal of the Royal Asiatic Society of Great Britain and Ireland* (London 1834——).

OLZ — *Orientalistische Literaturzeitung* (Berlin [1898–1908]; Leipzig [1909]——).

REI — *Revue des études islamiques* (Paris 1927——).

RHES — *Revue d'histoire économique et sociale* (Paris 1908——).

RSO — *Rivista degli studi orientali* (Roma 1907——).

WZKM — *Wiener Zeitschrift für die Kunde des Morgenlandes* (Wien 1887——).

General Index

[All references are to pages; italic numbers refer to footnotes only. This index includes proper names, foreign technical terms (in italics), titles of books referred to in the text (under authors' names), and a selective analytical index of subjects. References to authors and their works in the footnotes are not indexed, except where the reference contains bibliographical information, or where the author is discussed or quoted. The Arabic definite article (*al-*) is usually not mentioned, and is never considered in alphabetization. For a complete list of Ibn Khaldûn's works and other primary Arabic sources, see Bibliography, pp. 297–310.]

A

'abbâr, *65*
'Abbâsids, *60*
Abbott, Nabia, 13
'Abd al-'Azîz, 47, *104*
'Abd al-Wâdids. *See* Ziyânids
Âbilyy, *33*, 34–37, 125
Abraham, 165
Abû al-'Abbâs, 45, 51–52, 57
Abû 'Abd Allâh, 38, 44–45
Abû Bakr, *264*
Abû Dharr, *240*
Abû Ḥammû, 39, 45, 47–48
Abû al-Ḥasan, 23, 28, 34, 37
Abû 'Inân, 23, 34, 37–38, *41*
Abû Isḥâq, 51
Abû Madyan, 47
Abû Sâlim, 38–40, 42
Accidents: 104, 140–41; common, 80, 227
'Âd, 150
'âda, 31, 180
'adâla, 242
'adâla shar'iyya, *242*
Adam, 129, 228
'adl, 275
'adl maḥḍ, 239
Admonition. *See* Warning
af'âl, 29, 182
Affiliation, 177
Africa, 36. *See* North Africa
aghlab, 258
agoranomos, 243
aḥâdîth, 134
aḥkâm, *247*
aḥwâl, 154, *172*, *185*, 257
a'imma, 147
aitia, 48
ajyâl al-dawla, *204*
akhbâr, 134
âkhira, 236
akthar, *258*
âla, 249
'âlam jismânî, 87
'âlam jismânî-maḥsûs, 190–91
'âlam al-mawt, 87
'âlam al-nawm, 87
'âlam al-takwîn, 192
Alchemists, 123
Alchemy, *112*, *118*, 224
Aleppo, 57
Alexander the Great, *45*, *158*
Alexandria, 22, 52–53, 57
Algeçiras, 25
Algeria, 21–22
alḥân, 179
'Alî, *275*
'Allâf, *134*
Allegories, 66
Allusions, 67–68
Alonso, P. Manuel, *36*
Alphabet, occult properties of, *112*
amal, 177
'Amar, 38–39
Ambiguity, 116, 124
'Âmidî, *103*
amîr al-mu'minîn, 246
'âmir, *185*, 186
'âmma, *67*, 91, *92*
Analogy, 30, 98–101
Anatolia, 20
Anawati, M.-M., *141*
Ancients (dialectical theologians), 32, 36, 80, *103*, 105, 107, 141
Ancients (philosophers), 7–8, 94, *109*, 290
Angels, 78, 88, 193
Anthropology, 144, *184*
Antichrist, 256
Appetites, 177, 190, 251
appropriatum, *168*
'aqâ'id, 78

Bergsträsser, G., *29*
Bible, 144, *150*
bida' i'tiqâdiyya, *242*
Bijâya, *38*, 44, 46, 51, 287
binâ' badawî, *194*
Bîrûnî: 137, 143, 145; *India*, 143
Blachère, R., *144*
Black death, 34, 37
Blochet, E., *118*
Bombaci, Alessio, *165*
Book, people of, 75, 245
Books, revealed, 75, *83*
Bourbon, Louis de, 25
Bouthoul, G., *18*
'-b-r, 65, *67*
Brockelmann, C., *18*
Brunschvig, R., *22*, *31*
bu'd al-ṣît, 178
burhân, 160, *167*
Bûṣîrî, *36*
Buzurjumhur, *158*
Byzantium, 17–18, 20

C

Cairo, 21, *44*, 55–57, 60
Caliph, *60*, *236*, 237, 239 ff.
Caliphate, 19, 239 ff., 256
Canaan, 165
Cardahi, G., *65*
Caskel, W., *68*
Castile, 41
Castilians, 24, 40
Causality, principle of, 141
Causes: 7–8, 48–49, 63, 76–78, 80, 95, *102*, 104, 109–10, 116, 125, 137, 139, 141–42, 147, 149, 154–55, 159, 169, 174, 182–83, 225, 227, 233, 261; efficient, 253 ff., 260; final, 261, 270 ff.; formal, 232 ff., 253–54, 261; material, 232 ff., 253–54, 261
Censorship, 72
Chaldeans, 156
Chance, *121*, 202–3, 258–60
Change, 152, 232, 254 ff.
Chemistry, *112*, *224*
Chicago, University of, 13
Christ, 256
Christian North, 25
Christian slaves, 42
Christian states, 22–23
Christianity, *121*, 245–47
Christians, 18, 24–26, 38, 40
Cicero, 285
City: 172, *187*, *194*, 195, 199, 202 ff., 209 ff., 257, 259, 286; character of, 210–11; establishment of, 209–10; habits in, 214–15; location of, 211; and nomadism, 211–12; planning, 154; and primitive culture, 211–12; social structure of, 213–14; stages in the life of, 212–16
City (state): *90*, 157, 167; in deed, 274; imperfect, 274–75; perfect, 274; in speech, 274; virtuous, 253, 274–75, 284, 286. *See* Community; *polis*; Regime; State
City-state, 25, *209*
Civilization: 53–54, *184*, 193–94, 201 ff., 269; aspects of, 203 ff.; essential attributes of, 202 ff.; rise and decline of, 202 ff.; stages of, 203 ff.
Climate, 183, 185, 292
Climatology, *273*
Coercion, 197–98, 277, 284
cogitativa, 173
Cohen, *246*
Collingwood, R. G., 7
colo, 184
Colosio, Stefano, *260*
Common good, 11, 31, 238–39, *241*, 247–51, 259, 270 ff., 275 ff., 295
Common sense, 87–88, 99, 176
Communication: 72, 114–16; indirect, 118, 122
communis consensus, 30
Community: 56, 75–76; best or perfect, 126–28, 131–32; in deed, 126–27; imperfect, 126–29, 131–32; nature of, 91; in speech, 126; virtuous, 83. *See* Islamic community; Regime; State
Conceptions, 76–77, 173
Consensus, 30, 36, 98, 122, 239, 241
Constantinople, 20
Controversial matters, science of, 98, 100–101
Convention, 56, 66–67, 180–81. *See* Habit
Conventionalism, *258*
Copts, 156
Copying, 147–48, 151
Cordova, 144
Cosmology, *191*
Croce, Benedetto, 7
Crusaders, 18, 20
cultura, 184
Culture: 154, 156–67, 173 ff., 184 ff., 234, 289, *passim*; causes of (see below); changes in, 254 ff.; civilized 172, *184*, 193 ff., 235, 257–58, 277, 292; cycles of, 255; cyclical theory of, 255–56; end of, 11, 270 ff.; form of, 11, 234 ff.; generation and corruption of, 254–57, 260 ff.; linear theory of, 255; matter of, 11, 234 ff.; modes of, 63, 154, 167–68, *185*, 232, 257; nature of, 11, 148, 171 ff.,

I

Q

R

T

PHOENIX BOOKS
in History

PHOENIX BOOKS
in Philosophy and Religion

P 1 *Ernst Cassirer, Paul Oskar Kristeller, and John Herman Randall, Jr.:* The Renaissance Philosophy of Man

P 5 *Jacques Maritain:* Man and the State

P 6 *Anselm Strauss,* EDITOR: The Social Psychology of George Herbert Mead: Selected Writings of an American Pragmatist

P 8 *T. V. Smith:* EDITOR: Philosophers Speak for Themselves: From Thales to Plato

P 9 *T. V. Smith:* EDITOR: Philosophers Speak for Themselves: From Aristotle to Plotinus

P 16 *Karl Löwith:* Meaning in History: The Theological Implications of the Philosophy of History

P 17 *T. V. Smith and Marjorie Grene,* EDITORS: Philosophers Speak for Themselves: From Descartes to Locke

P 18 *T. V. Smith and Marjorie Grene,* EDITORS: Philosophers Speak for Themselves: Berkeley, Hume, and Kant

P 19 *Paul Tillich:* The Protestant Era

P 30 *Rudolph Carnap:* Meaning and Necessity: A Study in Semantics and Modal Logic

P 34 *Marjorie Grene:* Introduction to Existentialism

P 44 *Richard Weaver:* Ideas Have Consequences

P 67 *Yves R. Simon:* Philosophy of Democratic Government

P 81 *Hans Reichenbach:* Experience and Prediction: An Analysis of the Foundations and the Structure of Knowledge

P 92 *Joachim Wach:* Sociology of Religion

P 95 *Archibald G. Baker,* EDITOR: A Short History of Christianity

P 110 *Manley Thompson:* The Pragmatic Philosophy of C. S. Peirce

P 112 *Leo Strauss:* The Political Philosophy of Hobbes: Its Basis and Its Genesis

P 114 *Lewis White Beck:* A Commentary on Kant's Critique of Practical Reason

P 128 *Michael Polanyi:* The Study of Man

P 131 *Perry D. LeFevre:* The Prayers of Kierkegaard

P 137 *Dallin H. Oaks,* EDITOR: The Wall between Church and State

P 141 *Solomon Goldman:* The Ten Commandments

P 142 *Charlse Hartshorne and William L. Reese,* EDITORS: Philosophers Speak of God

P 143 *Karl Jaspers:* The Future of Mankind